India's Policy Milieu

Published by
ACADEMIC FOUNDATION
in association with

ISID

INSTITUTE FOR STUDIES IN INDUSTRIAL DEVELOPMENT (ISID),
New Delhi

ABOUT THE AUTHOR

S.K. Goyal, after obtaining doctoral degree from Delhi School of Economics (1961), taught in Deshbandu College, Kirori Mal College and subsequently at the Indian Institute of Public Administration (IIPA), where he was Professor of Economics and Public Policy. He founded the Corporate Studies Group at IIPA, which was later transformed into the Institute for Studies in Industrial Development (ISID), New Delhi. He steered ISID as its Founder-Director during 1986-2003. He is currently Emeritus Professor and Vice-Chairman of ISID.

His intellectual journey covered a vast area specifically industrial and trade policies, planning, public sector, monopolies, foreign capital and the corporate sector. He directed a number of research projects relating to the functioning of industrial regulations, public sector, Indian big business, multinational corporations and foreign investments. He has many publications to his credit and has pioneered the building of extensive databases on the Indian corporate sector and Indian social science literature and a Press Clippings Archive. He was also associated with a number of important official committees: Study Team on Machinery for Planning at the Central and State Levels (1966-67), Industrial Licensing Policy Inquiry Committee (1967-1969) and the Research Advisory Committee, Planning Commission, Government of India, in the rank of Cabinet Minister (1991).

India's Policy Milieu

Economic Development, Planning and Industry

S.K. Goyal

ACADEMIC FOUNDATION
NEW DELHI

www.academicfoundation.com

First published in 2014
by

ACADEMIC FOUNDATION
4772-73 / 23 Bharat Ram Road, (23 Ansari Road),
Darya Ganj, New Delhi - 110 002 (India).
Phones : 23245001 / 02 / 03 / 04.
Fax : +91-11-23245005.
E-mail : books@academicfoundation.com
www.academicfoundation.com

in association with
Institute for Studies in Industrial Development (ISID), New Delhi.

Disclaimer:
The findings/views/opinions expressed in this book are solely those of the author and do not necessarily reflect the views of the publisher.

Cataloging in Publication Data--DK

Courtesy: D.K. Agencies (P) Ltd. <docinfo@dkagencies.com>

Goyal, S. K.
India's policy milieu : economic development, planning and industry / S.K. Goyal.
p. cm.
ISBN 9789332701274

1. Economic development--India. 2. India--Economic policy--1991- 3. Banks and banking--India. 4. International business enterprises--India. 5. Private companies--India. 6. Small business--India. I. Title.

DDC 338.954 23

Typeset by Italics India, New Delhi.

Printed and bound by The Book Mint, New Delhi.
www.thebookmint.in

Contents

III. Multinational Corporations

IV. Public Sector

V. Journalist Miscellany

List of Tables and Figures

Tables

Figures

Professor S.K. Goyal

An Intellectual Journey

Surinder Kumar Goyal, Emeritus Professor, is the founder of the Institute for Studies in Industrial Development (ISID). This collection of essays, compiled for his 80th birthday celebrations, is intended to draw attention to an intellectual journey that began from studying cooperative farming as a doctoral student at the Delhi School of Economics (DSE) to a broader encounter with industrial and trade policies, planning, public sector, monopolies and foreign capital and the corporate sector. These research interests evolved in a political-economic conjuncture that saw a distinctly leftward shift in India's policy regime.

This was a milieu shaped by the imperatives of planning. Intellectuals like Prof Goyal still believe that the state has an important role to play in the making of an independent nation. That there was a need to insulate it from the pernicious influence of private business interests and the predations of global capital. Such beliefs might appear outdated in the current context in which the state has retreated from the commanding heights and market forces dictate policy. But this is far from the case as two decades of economic reforms since the early 1990s have only reinforced crony or oligarchic capitalism in the country.

The nationalist streak in Prof Goyal—also referred to as SKji or Surinder by his friends—stems from the fact he is the son of a freedom fighter. After being awarded a doctoral degree in 1961 by the University of Delhi, he taught in Deshbandu and Kirori Mal colleges. In 1965, Dr Goyal joined the Indian Institute of Public Administration (IIPA) and was associated with the Study Team on Machinery for Planning at the Central and State Levels, constituted by the Administrative Reforms Commission under the chairmanship of R.R. Morarka (the then chairperson of the Public Accounts Committee of Parliament).

This provided him with a valuable opportunity to visit most states in the country and interact with senior civil servants, Members of Parliament (MPs) and planning officials. His continued association with the Indian Institute of Public Administration (IIPA) also turned out to be invaluable as he could interact with senior civil servants and gain first-hand knowledge of the process of policy formulation. This close interaction with the powers-that-be certainly was responsible for his playing an important role in the formulation of industrial policy of the country, especially the regulatory systems, at an important juncture of the 1960s and 1970s.

During the late 1960s, at the request of the then General Secretary of the Congress Party in Parliament, Prof Goyal along with colleagues also prepared a report on the issue of commercial banking in India. This involvement had a basis earlier when he circulated a paper in 1963 on the operations of banking institutions at a seminar of the staff and research scholars of the DSE. As an expert in banking, he was requested by the General Secretary—who was none other than Chandra Shekhar—to produce a report at very short notice in a month's time. This became the basis for the historic decision by government to nationalise 14 private commercial banks in 1969.

Prof Goyal first met Chandra Shekhar in 1962 after his intervention in Rajya Sabha supporting the private Member Bill seeking nationalisation of private commercial banks. He made a logical presentation in support of the Bill. Prof Goyal was impressed and requested K.V. Raghunatha Reddy to introduce him to Chandra Shekhar. They met in the first floor restaurant of the Parliament building. This was the beginning of a long and fruitful personal association whose bond was a common interest and attitude on economic policies. The report on banks—prepared by Dr Goyal, Prof H.K. Manmohan Singh, Dr V.B. Singh and Dr Sulekh C. Gupta—was released at a press conference. These not-so-well-known intellectual underpinnings of bank nationalisation deserve wider attention.

This story also had lots of drama and suspense. On July 19, 1969, S. Mohan Kumaramangalam, leading Communist leader who was close to the Congress Party, rang up Prof Goyal at lunchtime and asked him to rush to the Industrial Licensing Policy Inquiry Committee (ILPIC) office. His request was to close all doors and take no phone calls. Prof Goyal was asked to pen a brief note giving reasons for bank nationalisation. Kumaramangalam took the note and cautioned him that not a word must be spoken to anyone. At 5.30 PM that day, a news flash conveyed that the note's recommendations had been approved by the cabinet. A new chapter in the economic policy of India had been opened.

Prof Goyal was no stranger to ILPIC. During the late 1960s, the Congress Party was in turmoil. The adoption of the Avadi All India Congress Committee (AICC) resolution on the 'socialistic pattern of society' in January 1955 had set the ball rolling. Though the term socialistic pattern was a vague concept, it was sufficient to inspire and activate a large number of Congressmen in and outside the party to demand state action for socioeconomic change. Chandra Shekhar as the leading Young Turk was one such Congressman who forcefully highlighted the contrasts between what the government had already committed to and how the system operated in reality.

A significant starting point was an empirical study by Prof R.K. Hazari of Bombay University. The general thrust of the study was that a few business houses led by the Birlas enjoyed so much influence in the political and economic structure of the economy. This was also the time when the Morarka-chaired Parliamentary Public Accounts Committee made critical remarks against the house of Birla on a case of favour bestowed by the government to enable them to achieve monopoly status in certain industries and products. The Birlas, who were quite confident of their capacity to influence, had reportedly threatened that Morarka would not be allowed to return to Parliament.

All of this naturally triggered a long drawn parliamentary debate on the influence of big business on the political and administrative system of the country. The uproar against the Birlas resulted in the appointment of ILPIC, with Prof M.S. Thacker, Member, Planning Commission, as Chairman and Kumaramangalam and H.K. Paranjape as members. Prof Thacker resigned shortly thereafter and in his place came Subimal Dutt, India's first foreign secretary. Prof Goyal was appointed honorary economic advisor. A large number of background papers were prepared and a massive database was built around different aspects of industrialisation and operations of public sector financial institutions. A decade later, Prof Goyal started concentrating on the large Indian corporate sector. This culminated in the establishment of the Corporate Studies Group (CSG) at the IIPA. The reports prepared by the CSG drew wide attention in the press, the Parliament as well as academic circles.

Dr Goyal directed a number of research projects relating to the functioning of the public and private sector and guided the building of an extensive computerised database known as Corporate Information System within the CSG. His empirical study on trends in concentration of economic power in India was published as a book titled *Monopoly and Public Policy: Business and Economic Power* (Allied Publishers, 1979). At the request of the United Nations Economic and Social Commission for Asia and the Pacific, he prepared the study 'Impact of Foreign Subsidiaries on India's Balance of Payments.' This study was very widely quoted and discussed, as this was the only empirical study on the functioning of multinationals in India.

There were several other studies prepared by the CSG under Prof Goyal's direction like the *Small-scale Sector and Big Business, Functioning of the Industrial Licensing System* and *Comparative Performance of the Public and Private Sectors in India*. The CSG had indeed helped to trigger a new trend in industrial policy research in India. Based on this experience, and following the recommendations of a committee set up by the Indian Council of Social Science Research (ICSSR) under the chairmanship of C.H. Hanumantha Rao which reviewed the work done under the research programme, ISID was registered as a society in October 1986 under the Societies Registration Act XXI, of 1860, to carry on the activities of CSG, with Prof Goyal as the Founder-Director. ISID came under the fold of ICSSR in the end of 1987-88. Under his guidance, a number of research projects encompassing foreign investments, international trade, corporate sector and public enterprises were conducted at the institute. As a former ISID director put it, "The idea was born in the 1960s, crystallised in the 1970s, took roots in the 1980s, started growing in the 1990s with all the attendant problems, and reached a stage of take-off in the 2000s."

During the 1980s, Indian economic policies were fast losing their national character and international institutions started exerting pressure for suspension of planning process and withdrawal of various regulatory mechanisms. The climax was reached when Ajit Singh, the then Minister for Industrial Development, announced a new industrial policy withdrawing restrictions on foreign private capital and Indian monopoly houses. Chandra Shekhar expressed opposition to these policies. A large amount of data was compiled and evidence assembled and presented at a very widely attended press conference in Delhi. To the leading segments of the media, there was no doubt regarding the identity of the think tank that provided the input for this press conference.

In 1991, the Congress Government adopted what has been described as Structural Adjustment Programme. This was nothing but a version of the Washington Consensus. The new regime started with practically abolishing the regulatory mechanism which was evolved to give a direction to new investments; setting aside important provisions of Monopolies and Restrictive Trade Practices Act (MRTP); and taking the sting out of the Foreign Exchange Regulations Act (FERA). All these policies and actions—delicensing, deregulation and decontrol—sought to liquidate the planning exercise and take the country more towards a market-oriented economy. Chandra Shekhar shared his views with like-minded intellectuals like Prof Goyal and launched a campaign opposing the influence of multilateral bodies on the economic policies of countries like India. The information collected earlier was later published as *Political Economy of India* in 1992.

Simultaneously, Prof Goyal got busy in organising the new research centre, ISID. Prof Moonis Raza was its Founder-Chairman. After his tenure, Chandra Shekhar accepted Dr Goyal's invitation and took the responsibility of providing guidance and patronage to ISID. The 1990s was indeed a trying period for ISID. Chandra Shekhar, however, gave full support to help establish ISID as a centre of excellence. After attaining the age of superannuation, Prof Goyal relinquished ISID Directorship and focussed on his cherished dream of giving ISID its own campus with the most modern infrastructure and research facilities, including a state-of-the-art auditorium. A major achievement of ISID under Prof Goyal's direction was the development of an online index (OLI) of Indian social science journals and the press clippings index (PCI). In his zeal to help the social science community and promote research on India-related issues, he made these databases freely available to scholars the world over, through the institute's website. During 1990-1992, he was the honorary chairman of the Research Advisory Committee of the Planning Commission in the rank of a Cabinet Minister. While at the Commission, the National Informatics Centre (NIC) was under his charge. Under his guidance, NIC made long strides in introducing modern technology to social science institutions in India, especially those affiliated to the ICSSR.

Among the distinguished positions he has held include: Chairman, Indo-Dutch Programme on Alternatives in Development (IDPAD); Advisor, Parliamentary Committee on Railways; Member of the Board of Directors, National Small Industries Corp Ltd. (NSIC); Member, Governing Council, Small Industries Training Institute; and Advisor to the Government of Uttar Pradesh on the restructuring of the sugar industry in the state. Prof Goyal also undertook major international assignments such as being an economic advisor to the Government of Iraq during the early 1970s. An important contribution was the preparation of a strategy document for Iraq's planned development. He also helped the Ministry for Commerce in dealing with the congestion at the Basra Port.

Section I comprises his path-breaking work on the concentration of economic power. This includes articles on the industrial licensing system and its functioning, big business and small-scale industry. Despite the government's avowed commitment towards a socialistic pattern of society, the fact is that the system also facilitated concentration in the Indian economy and the growth of big business in India. The various articles in this section highlight the fact that rules and regulations never had a clear-cut aim of restricting the growth of big business; that the growth of industrial houses has been encouraged under the belief that "really speaking, they alone can deliver the goods!"

Section II highlights the real story behind the nationalisation of banks and will fill a major lacuna in the popular perception of the whys and wherefores of this landmark political decision in 1969. While the politics behind bank nationalisation is well known, not much is known of its economic underpinnings. Prof Goyal's report that he co-authored with other economists had an immediate impact as it became policy shortly after it was submitted—a fate unfortunately not shared by numerous reports that are destined to gather dust.

Prof Goyal's work on multinationals leads Section III. Multinational corporations (MNCs) are invited into the economy by policy makers as they would help solve India's major problems—may it be foreign exchange, inflation, unemployment, interpersonal inequities or regional imbalances. The various articles in this section examine the direct and indirect implications of such policy initiatives. On the foreign exchange front, for instance, the second article deals with the impact of foreign subsidiaries on India's balance of payments. Foreign subsidiaries spent more foreign exchange than they earned from their operations. The net annual impact of the operations of foreign subsidiaries was therefore negative on the balance of payments situation of India.

Given the spirit of the socialistic 1960s, he also devoted a lot of his writings to the public sector that occupied the commanding heights of the Indian economy. This constitutes Section IV of this publication. According to Prof Goyal, the public sector needs to be restructured and reformed so that the sector continues to play an important role in the process of economic development. While loss-making enterprises can be considered for privatisation or disinvestment, he strongly urges a more constructive look at the possibilities of restructuring in individual cases instead of following a distorted policy of disinvestment for only meeting the fiscal deficit.

Section V covers Prof Goyal's journalistic commentary and critiques on the important economic issues of the day. He wrote a regular column in *The National Herald* in the 1960s under the pen name of Economicus and Politicus, and *Young Indian* and the *Daily* in the early 1970s and 1980s. This miscellany of his finest writings concludes with an interesting study that he undertook for the Second Press Commission in which he advocated nationalisation of the big business dominated newspaper groups of the country. Predictably, this study generated a lot of discussion. The Second Press Commission, for its part, wrote to the newspaper establishments seeking their response to what Prof Goyal had written. They either attempted to contradict his findings or kept a discreet silence. This article is included as it forms an integral element of Prof Goyal's vision that state control was desirable as big business has been successful in influencing governments to deviate from declared public policies.

Contemporary readers will find this collection of articles by Prof Goyal—written under a different political-economic context—of continuing relevance. Prof Goyal's intellectual journey has not ended. He continues to strive hard to make ISID a self-sustaining institution so that it can promote informed debate on contemporary economic issues without any fear or favour.

—Team, ISID

Section I

Concentration of Economic Power

1 Government Policy and Concentration in the Indian Economy

In India, during the 1960s, considerable concern had been shown about the question of furtherance of monopolies and concentration in the ownership of wealth and means of production in the hands of a few. The Mahalanobis Committee[1] appointed to review the trends in the economy during the First and Second Plan periods confirmed a widely shared view that "in part at least, the working of our planned economic growth has encouraged this process of concentration by facilitating and aiding the growth of big business in India." The Monopolies Inquiry Commission (MIC) in its majority report while accepting the position that the degree of concentration has increased held a view that the emergence and continuance of big business have helped the process of capital formation in the country. The commission considered the phenomenon as an unavoidable evil. Dissenting member, R.C. Dutt, however, emphasised that one of the factors which has inhibited the growth of professional class of managers and has also resulted in opportunities being denied to unattached persons is the existence and operation of economic power in the hands of a few families.

The furtherance of concentration in the Indian economy has not been disputed. But the allegation that the economic power enjoyed by the dominant families has been used as an instrument of exploitation of the society or that economic power has been used against the common detriment is not always recognised. In early 1967, a study by Dr R.K. Hazari suggested that during the Second and Third Plan periods, a few industrial houses were able to obtain a very large number of the industrial licences. This was particularly true of the Birlas. This house has, for some years, been the second biggest house of the country in terms of the

1. Mahalanobis Committee set up in 1960 to study the "Distribution of Income and Levels of Living" during the First and Second Plans.

magnitude of assets under its control. The study highlighted the outcome of the operation of the licensing system. Hazari's study also indicated that some big houses had indulged in the practice of pre-empting capacities by which new entrants to the industries were kept out and monopolist control retained. Since it was not an official study, the findings of Hazari were disputed by many. However, in view of the importance of the subject, the government appointed a three-man committee to ascertain facts about the operation of the industrial licensing system and other related matters. The essence of the terms of reference of the Industrial Licensing Policy Inquiry Committee (ILPIC) was whether big business houses have received preference from the government and other public institutions and if they have, whether this was due to technical and economic logic (say economies of scale) and in the interest of optimal exploitation of the scare managerial talent and other resources held by big business or the preference to big business houses was due to political, administrative, personal and other influences. Secondly, whether the favours shown to big business have, at least, been justified since the licences granted to them were utilised effectively and the process of industrialisation pushed further. The ILPIC undertook an exhaustive study, and to the surprise of many, it not only established what Hazari's study had shown, but gave a very comprehensive account of the manner in which a few larger industrial houses had operated and exercised power in governmental decision-making.

The findings of the ILPIC show that there has been no clarity in the minds of the government, more so the administrators, whether the growth of big business has to be curbed as a national policy or not. And further, the provisions of the various legislative measures and rules and regulations evolved had never a clear-cut aim of restricting the growth of big business.

In the absence of any clear policy about the place and role of big business, the growth of industrial houses has been encouraged under the belief that 'really speaking, they alone can deliver the goods.' On the one side, the government policy statements since Independence have given the impression that the economy would progressively move towards more and more socialistic content and on the other, increasingly larger concessions have been announced to the Indian and foreign private sector in general and big business in particular. A closer study of the last two decades would show that the public pronouncement in industrial policy and practice have tended to move in opposite directions to each other.

For example, the Indian Constitution does not place the national objective as socialism. If at all, most of the early public documents maintained that India was a mixed economy and would continue to be so. In 1954, the Parliament accepted 'Socialistic Pattern of Society' as the national objective. To give a socialistic(!) orientation to the policies, the Industrial Policy Resolution of 1948 was revised in 1956. Some of the industries exclusively reserved for public sector under the Industrial Policy Resolution of 1948 were thrown open to the private sector. In the late 1950s, the 'socialistic pattern' gave way to 'socialism.' The enhanced dose of socialist element was soon accompanied particularly after the mid-term appraisal of the Second Plan by open invitation to foreign private capital (to meet the foreign exchange crisis) and big business to enter in areas so far reserved exclusively for the public sector. After border conflict with China and Indo-Pakistan war, when the need for planned economic growth was higher than at any other time earlier, the economy was given a plan holiday. It is also a curious coincidence that while concern over furtherance of concentration in the economy was being shown with considerable intensity after 1964, partial delicensing of industries and entry of foreign private capital in fertilisers, so far reserved for public sector expansion, were announced and this too with majority participation. An interesting part of the present day discussion on industrial policy is that on the one side pious resolutions are being announced to restrict furtherance of concentration in the economy and on the other invitation to big business to collaborate with government as majority partners in the core industries has been extended with great fanfare and with little awareness of the implications of such a policy. It is equally interesting that the present government asked for a clear mandate from the people on questions like curbing of concentration of economic power. In a way, the people of India were asked to give their verdict if they were for socialism or for the vested interests and big business. The Indian voters gave their verdict in favour of socialist policies. Curiously, the leadership in government, at all levels, is crying hoarse against monopolies and big business, but a large number of decisions have been taken to allow the larger industrial houses and foreign companies to enhance their stranglehold over the economy.

The above account may appear dramatic but it suffers from the limitation that it ignores many important details and thereby fails to reflect the true intensity of the character of the trends. However, the point to be underlined here is that the type of policies adopted by the government has been such which could not but further the degree of concentration in the economy, though the emphasis in public pronouncements against concentration and private monopolies has been progressively on the increase. This is very clearly reflected in the rate of growth of the two largest industrial houses of the country (Tatas and Birlas).

The assets of the public companies under the Birlas were estimated at about ₹ 51.14 crore in 1951, this figure rose to ₹ 112.92 crore in 1958. The assets of the Birla companies were placed by the MIC at ₹ 292.72 crore in 1964, that is an increase of nearly two and a half times in six years. In the next four years (by the end of 1968). Birla assets rose to the level of ₹ 575.60 crore. The trends show not only the growth of the Birlas in absolute magnitude, but interestingly the marginal growth rate has been higher in the succeeding years. With the granting of licence for Goa Fertiliser Company to the Birlas and other expansions, it is now estimated, in knowledgeable circles, that the assets of the Birla companies had crossed the mark of ₹ 800 crore in 1970-1972. In the case of the Tatas, the growth has been from nearly ₹ 95.0 crore assets in 1951 to nearly ₹ 280 crore in 1958, ₹ 417.72 crore in 1964 and ₹ 505.35 crore in 1966. The Tatas have been cleared to go ahead with their Mithapore Fertiliser Project, expansion of Tata Chemicals and many other licences. The net result of all the new sanctions is bound to lead the Tata assets to more than ₹ 850 crore during the year. These figures are strictly not comparable as the agencies compiling these data differ and each one had defined the houses according to its own criteria and purposes. However, even if one was to make an allowance for bringing the data on a comparable place, the essential point, namely, the increasing tempo of growth of the biggest two business houses would not be affected (see Table 1.1).

The reasons for the widening gap between what was desired and what actually happened are many but the crucial ones appear to be two. One, the lack of proper appreciation of the nature and character of concentration, and consequently, non-identification of the important elements which cause or are constituents concentration in the private hands. And two, the absence of the requisite machinery in the form of administrative set-up with professional and competent staff and the legislative and other provisions to deal with the problem. This note attempts to bring out some characteristics of the Indian larger industrial houses which may help to discuss the implications of the new industrial policy announced in February last year, which in turn may suggest the type of policy changes necessary to restrict further growth of concentration in the economy.

In addition to the 75 houses, there were 60 independent large companies each having assets of more than ₹ 5 crore. The total assets with them were ₹ 891.67 crore. The biggest company was Oil India (a joint enterprise of the government and a foreign company) with assets of ₹ 90.79 crore. Burma Shell Refineries Limited which occupied second position had ₹ 34.25 crore assets, and Imperial Tobacco now known as India Tobacco followed with ₹ 34.20 crore. GKW and Hindustan Lever were another two companies having more than ₹ 30.00 crore assets each. Other important companies (each having assets of more than ₹ 20.00 crore) were Indian Aluminium, Union Carbide and Standard Refining Company. It would be seen that a very large majority of the large independent companies are either subsidiaries of foreign companies or have majority shares, held outside India. In addition to these 60 foreign-controlled companies there were 288 units which operated in India either as foreign subsidiaries or branches each having assets of less than ₹ 5.0 crore. A feature of the large independent companies is that most of them have areas of specialisation, though some have diversified activities too.

In the study of the problem of 'concentration' in the economy may also have a look at the spread of the activity of the houses from the view-point of the number of states in which each one operates and the extent of diversification in their activity. A good indication of these aspects is provided by the ILPIC data on licences issued. One finds that it was only the House of Birlas which had obtained licences in 16 states; Bangur and Soorajmull Nagarmull had their interest in 10 states and Tatas in 9 states only. Out of the 20 larger houses, Scindias had interest in only one state, Killicks in two, Andrew Yule, Bird Heilgers, Kilachand, Mafatlal, Martin Burn, Sarabhai and Walchand in three states each. ACC and Shri Ram obtained licences for eight states, J.K. Singhania for seven, Thapars for six and the Goenkas, ICI and Sahu Jain in five states each. The distribution suggests that the size of some houses was large but their activities were confined to few states only. This would possibly be accompanied by the fact that the houses operating in a few states of the country only had specialised in one industry and the industry was a capital intensive one. For example, Scindias had assets of ₹ 55.98 crore in 1966 but most of it was accounted for by their shipping activity. One a few had nationwide spread. Out of the 53 large houses (ILPIC), but for 5 houses, all other had licences for less than five states. Kanoria (B) had licences in seven states, Dalmia (J) in six and Bajaj, Jaipuria and Macneil Barry and Binny in five states each.

The ILPIC had grouped the licences under 232 product industries. The extent of diversification in industrial activity undertaken by a house can be seen in the number of product industries for which a house obtained licences. Out of the 20 larger houses, the highest number of products licenced was for the Birlas, i.e., 106. The next largest variety of licences was obtained by the Tatas, i.e., 66. This was followed by J.K. Singhania (39), Shri Ram (37) and Soorajmull Nagarmull (35). Among the rest of the houses (comparatively smaller ones), it was the Modi House which had the largest variety of industries with 24 product industries.

When the size of the assets under the control of a house is large, it does give the holder substantial economic power. If the largeness of the house is due to its capital being invested in one state and in one industry only, probably, the house would have product monopoly or be a dominant producer in the industry of its interest. There may be some economic case for even allowing such undertakings (and thereby the house) to grow in size on grounds of economies of scale or for encouraging specialisation. There would, however, be problems of monopoly control and regulation. But the growth of such houses does create problems which are associated with concentration of economic power in a few private hands.

The degree of diversified activity of the houses is also reflected in the number of companies under the control of few larger houses. The total number of companies, under the 20 larger houses was 1,005. Out of these companies, data are available for 815 only. The largest number of companies was that of the Birlas (203). It was followed by Soorajmull Nagarmull (104), Bangur (93), Bird Heilgers (76) and Tatas (70). The smallest number of companies was with ACC (5), ICI (6) and Scindias (8).

From the above account, one thing which emerges strikingly is that the house which has the largest degree of diversification is the House of Birlas. It is also the second largest house. Its activities were spread all over the country. Tatas are also quite prominent in this respect though not always as diversified as some others. Soorajmull Nagarmull and Bangur are comparatively smaller houses but have larger spread and greater diversification.

It may be a general impression that big business would operate through big companies only. However, a distribution of the companies of the 20 larger houses shows that nearly one-third of the companies under their control had less than ₹ 25 lakh assets each. Nearly 60 per cent had assets below ₹ 1 crore. On the one hand, only 6 per cent had assets below ₹ 1 crore. On the other hand, only 6 per cent of the companies had assets more than ₹ 10 crore. In numbers, there were only 28 companies (out of the 816 for which data are available) which had assets of ₹ 15 crore each.

If one takes the two largest houses (Tatas and Birlas), one finds that in the case of the Tatas, barely six companies (each with assets of more than ₹ 15 crore) accounted for 70.8 per cent of their assets. And if we add the next four companies, each with assets between ₹ 10 and ₹ 15 crore, the biggest 10 companies of the Tatas claim nearly four-fifth of the Tata assets. Similarly, the top 10 Birla companies accounted for more than half of their assets. In the case of ACC, only two companies were responsible for nearly 98 per cent of the assets. And in the case of Martin Burn and Scindias, only one of their companies was responsible for their being included under the larger industrial houses.

The six companies of the Tatas (each having assets of more than ₹ 15 crore) were Tata Iron and Steel Company (TISCO) (183.23), Tata Engineering Locomotive Company (TELCO) (78.35), New India Assurance (33.77), Voltas (31.04), Tata Power (29.86) and Indian Tube (21.76). The total assets of these were ₹ 378.01 crore, that is nearly 70 per cent. For, Birlas, the 10 companies were: Hindalco (49.39), Hind Motor (29.80), Orient Paper (28.70), Century (26.16), Grasim (22.99), Texmaco (18.94), Kesoram (18.27), Birla Jute (15.69), Jiyajeerao (15.65) and India Steamship (15.34). Out of the 28 big companies of the 20 larger houses (ILPIC), 16 were of the Tatas and Birlas.

Supposing we confine ourselves to the two top houses to understand the reasons for their phenomenal growth, we find that their growth is explained by their entry and expansion in such industries which according to the industrial policy resolutions of 1948 and 1956 should have been developed in the public sector only. For example, TISCO and TELCO engage themselves in basic and heavy industries which were the preserve of the public sector. In the case of Hindustan Aluminium and Hind Motors, the exception carved out of the area of public sector is well known. The effect of the exemption made in the fertiliser industry on the growth of the larger houses should again be very clear. The Goa Fertiliser Project would add assets of nearly ₹ 100 crore to the Birlas. Similarly, allowing of the Mithapore Fertiliser Project to the Tatas would at once push the Tatas assets by 20 per cent in two to three years. The same is the case with the Shri Ram House and the EID Parry. An equally striking example in this regard is that of the Mafatlal House.

If the new industrial policy allows the larger houses or foreign companies to take up big projects in the core industry, the implications on the rate of growth of the houses should be quite obvious to anyone. On the other hand, if the decision is that no larger house would be allowed to take up any new project which requires investment of more than ₹ 2.5 crore or so, the growth rate of the larger houses could effectively be contained. On the other hand, if the government were to take a decision to takeover all companies having assets of ₹ 10 crore, the degree of concentration could be reduced in a substantial manner and yet the number of companies to be taken over would not be more than 150 or so.

The primary question to be settled is whether the government earnestly believes that growth of concentration in the private sector is to be restricted and curbed or it has to be accepted as an unpleasant reality. To many it may appear to be a political question, though it is equally an economic one. But even accepting this as a purely political question, the answer has to be given by the political leadership. As one reads the public pronouncements from the top leadership and the party in power, one gets an impression that the implied meaning of their language, usages and expressions is clearly for adoption of radical policies to liquidate monopolies and reduce disparities and the existing degree of concentration of ownership and control over national wealth in the hands of private and few hands. In the face of such assertions, what puzzles most is the host of specific decisions being taken which cannot but enhance the degree of concentration in the private sector.

If it is felt by the government that it is necessary to allow furtherance of concentration in the private hands to ensure higher rate of economic growth, it would be only appropriate that an effort is made to educate and convince the people about it. Also the repeated emphasis on 'socialism' must give way to a political language of 'free market economy.' There should be no hesitation, on the part of the Congress Party and the government, to reshape and revise their objectives. Such a position would not be different from what the MIC Report had taken nor the assumptions on which the Planning Commission has been formulating the Five Year Plans so far. It does not serve much purpose if on the one hand there is public condemnation of the big business and on the other all concessions are made to allow them to proceed with their expansion plans. The gap must be bridged.

On the other hand, if it is observed that growth of concentration in a few private hands is not only against the spirit of the Directive Principles of the Constitution but it is pregnant with dangers to the very functioning of the democratic institutions in the country, there is an urgent need to give a new orientation to the overall economic policies of the country. To the present author, it does appear that the most serious threat posed by furtherance of concentration is to the very process of planned economic development in India. The ILPIC Report provides abundance of qualitative and quantitative evidence in this regard. The Planning Commission and many in authority have taken a view that growth of concentration and disparities is inevitable in any process of growth. In support of this thesis, the pattern of disparities as it prevailed in the 19th and early 20th centuries in Europe and the USA has been cited. Those who place so much confidence in the history of the presently developed societies of the West somehow fail to appreciate that the international environment as well as the socioeconomic and political institutions under which Indian economy is now operating have no parallel with situations in which higher growth rate was possible only with the continuation of disparities and furtherance of concentration.

If, however, it is accepted that there is an economic justification and political necessity to reduce the degree of concentration in private hands, it is evident that the government will have to give fresh thought and new orientation to many of its policies and particularly the one relating to licensing. The minimum of the requirements, to contain concentration at the existing level, would be to decide that all projects above a certain size of investment, say ₹ 1 crore, would be only allowed in the public sector. And if the intention is to drastically reduce the existing degree of concentration, it appears, the effective remedy lies in taking over the ownership of all industrial units having assets of more than ₹ 5 crore.

Table 1.1

Showing Estimates of Assets for 20 Industrial Houses during 1958-1968

	Hazari 1958	*MIC 1964*	*ILPIC 1964*	*Datta, B 1967-68*
ACC	-	77.36	89.80	105.84
Andrew Yule	16.60	41.89	46.75	54.12
Bangur	26.54	77.91	104.31	124.88
Bird Heilgers	22.53	60.10	68.62	78.62
Birla	112.87	292.72	457.84	575.60
Inder Singh	4.41	19.40	10.55	11.92
J.K. Singhania	16.80	59.20	66.84	78.75
Kasturbhai Lalbhai	13.06	33.94	51.19	59.21
Khatau	2.82	13.62	40.09	46.85
Kirloskar	3.93	19.12	43.02	61.20
Mafatlal	11.46	45.91	92.70	135.87
Mahindra and Mahindra	6.74	20.12	38.58	51.34
Martin Burn	72.95	149.61	153.06	174.29
Ramakrishna, V	8.19	13.61	18.78	23.95
Sahu Jain	55.11	67.69	58.75	79.68
Seshasayee	4.25	26.69	32.72	40.69
Shri Ram	19.82	54.68	74.13	107.41
Tata	223.41	417.72	505.36	584.63
Thapar	19.60	71.90	98.80	103.20
Walchand	12.63	55.17	81.11	86.24

Source: (A) Hazari R.K. (1967). *The Structure of the Corporate Private Sector: A Study of Concentration, Ownership and Control.* London: Asia Publishing House.

(B) Government of India (1965). *Report of the Monopolies Inquiry Commission 1965* (Chairman: Shri. K.C. Das Gupta). Volume I and II. New Delhi: Ministry of Finance.

(C) Government of India. (1969). *Report of the Industrial Licensing Policy Inquiry Committee (Main Report)* (Chairman: Shri. Subimal Dutt). New Delhi: Ministry of Industrial Development. pp.4-15.

(D) Datta, B. (1970). "Growth of Industrial Houses: A Survey for the Period 1963-64 to 1967-68", *Company News & Notes* VIII (9&10), May 1 & 16.

Table 1.2

Number of Companies in Different Size-Groups during 1966

S.No	Name of the House	More than 15	10-15	5-10	1-5	0.5-1.00	0.25-0.5	0.0-0.25	Net Av.
(1)	(2)	(3)	(4)	(5)	(6)	(7)	(8)	(9)	(10)
1.	Tata	6	4	7	16	6	8	12	11
2.	Birla	10	-	16	37	25	17	81	17
3.	Martin Burn	1	2	1	5	4	6	1	4
4.	Bangur	-	1	7	10	16	16	27	16
5.	Thapar	-	2	5	15	6	8	13	10
6.	Soorajmull Nagarmull	-	1	1	24	9	19	25	25
7.	Mafatlal	-	5	3	4	2	-	6	14
8.	ACC	2	-	-	-	3	-	-	-
9.	Walchand	2	-	3	4	3	3	11	3
10.	Shri Ram	1	1	-	7	1	4	5	17
11.	Bird Heilgers	-	1	2	16	7	6	21	23
12.	J.K. Singhania	-	-	5	8	6	4	20	4
13.	Goenka	-	-	5	12	8	13	14	17
14.	Sarabhai	1	1	1	5	2	3	14	2
15.	Sahu Jain	1	-	3	9	4	-	7	5
16.	Scindia	1	-	-	3	1	1	2	-
17.	Killick	1	1	1	5	2	2	4	1
18.	ICI	1	1	2	1	-	-	1	-
19.	Andrew Yule	-	1	-	13	7	6	3	13
20.	Kilachand (Tulsidas)	1	-	-	5	1	2	7	8
	Total	28	21	62	199	113	118	274	190

Source: Government of India. (1969). *Report of the Industrial Licensing Policy Inquiry Committee (Main Report)* (Chairman: Shri. Subimal Dutt). New Delhi: Ministry of Industrial Development.

Table 1.3

Distribution of Assets in Different Size-Groups of Companies during 1966

(₹ crore)

SNo	Name of the House	Total Assets	Assets of Companies						
			More than 15	10-15	5-10	1-5	0.5-1.00	0.25-0.50	0.0 to 0.25
(1)	(2)	(3)	(4)	(5)	(6)	(7)	(8)	(9)	(10)
1.	Tata	505.36	357.92	51.86	51.88	33.55	4.78	2.99	1.10
2.	Birla	457.84	240.93	-	101.81	83.64	17.14	6.16	7.39
3.	Martin Burn	153.06	103.95	26.20	7.65	10.22	2.94	1.92	0.15
4.	Bangur	104.31	-	10.84	48.66	24.32	11.19	5.99	3.15
5.	Thapar	98.80	-	23.74	39.42	26.08	4.89	3.82	1.21
6.	Soorajmull Nagarmull	95.62	-	14.72	7.18	57.53	6.42	7.19	1.45
7.	Mafatlal	92.70	-	59.22	21.78	9.98	1.37	-	0.29
8.	ACC	89.80	87.65	-	-	-	2.14	-	-
9.	Walchand	81.11	45.94	-	21.74	8.87	2.30	0.96	1.25
10.	Shri Ram	74.13	44.73	10.17	-	17.10	0.53	1.49	0.07
11.	Bird Heilgers	68.62	-	13.49	13.10	34.43	4.89	2.05	0.56
12.	J.K. Singhania	66.84	-	-	38.09	21.22	4.30	1.51	1.65
13.	Goenka	65.34	-	-	30.30	22.21	6.18	4.68	1.87
14.	Sarabhai	56.71	22.45	10.74	5.71	13.44	1.71	1.13	1.51
15.	Sahu Jain	58.75	16.58	-	21.47	16.57	3.28	-	9.77
16.	Scindia	55.98	51.21	-	-	3.55	50.58	0.34	0.29
17.	Killick	51.07	22.23	11.18	5.18	10.15	1.20	0.63	0.46
18.	ICI	50.06	15.22	12.23	18.99	3.97	-	-	1.57
19.	Andrew Yule	46.75	-	11.74	-	27.98	4.53	2.08	0.34
20.	Kilachand (Tulsidas)	37.22	17.93	-	-	16.92	0.88	0.66	0.80
	Total	2310.07	1006.74	256.14	432.96	441.74	81.25	43.01	25.88

Source: Government of India. (1969). *Report of the Industrial Licensing Policy Inquiry Committee (Main Report)* (Chairman: Shri. Subimal Dutt). New Delhi: Ministry of Industrial Development.

2 Concentration of Economic Power[1]

Discussions on the problem of monopolies, concentration and disparities in wealth or control over means of production in an economy are perhaps always and everywhere exciting issues of public importance. This, in any case, has been true of the '1960s' in India. Though there were occasional references to the emergence of monopolies and growth of concentration particularly in the corporate private sector during the '1950s', specific questions on this subject were posed for public inquiry only in 1960 by the Prime Minister Jawaharlal Nehru. The theme of his questions was derived from one of the Directive Principles of State Policy i.e., the State shall direct its policy towards securing "that the operation of the economic system does not result in the concentration of wealth and means of production to the common detriment." The Mahalanobis Committee which was appointed to ascertain the trends and changes in the distribution of incomes and wealth during 1950-1960 observed that the working of the planned economy had "encouraged the process of concentration by facilitating and aiding the growth of big business in India."

The Committee drew a distinction between: (i) concentration in an industry (as represented by share in the output) and (ii) concentration in wealth and means of production or financial control. The latter, according to the Committee was only a means to an end which is concentration of economic power. The Monopolies Inquiry Commission (MIC), however, used the expression "concentration of economic power" to cover both 'industry-wise concentration' and 'country-wise concentration.' The Monopolies and Restrictive Trade Practices (MRTP) Act which has come into force from 1st June this year has not attempted to give any precise definition of the concept but the constituents of 'concentration of economic

---

1. The script of the broadcast in the Home Services, All India Radio, News Services Division, "Spotlight" by Dr S.K. Goyal on June 13, 1970 at 21:15 hours.

power' have been indicated. These are: (i) all undertakings which have total assets, in combination with their inter-connected undertakings, more than ₹ 20 crore, and (ii) all such 'dominant' undertakings which have themselves, or in combination with their interconnected undertakings, assets of more than ₹ 1 crore.

The phrase 'concentration of economic power' has been used to underline: (i) the size of capital under common control, i.e., the degree of concentration in the control over capital, and (ii) the extent of influence that the holders may have over the consumers, their competitors and other institutions in society. The measurement of the size of the capital under common control is possible but the latter is not amenable to statistical quantification. The control over large quantum of capital is certainly one of the essential bases for influence but the degree of influence is not always directly in proportion to the quantum of capital held under control. Many other factors like: (i) the nature of the economic activity undertaken by a group and the existing regulatory mechanism over pricing policy and distribution of the production, (ii) the locational spread and (iii) the equations and contact of the group with political and public institutions are equally important factors in determining the degree of influence and power enjoyed. However, it cannot be questioned that control over large capital resources is a very important and basic factor.

The new legislation would require that all proposals for expansion, undertaking of new activity or merger by those industrial houses whose assets exceed ₹ 20 crore, should be examined by the Monopolies Commission. This, however, does not mean that the Monopolies Commission would not allow expansion of large houses in an arbitrary manner or the size of the large houses would be frozen henceforth. What the Monopolies Commission would examine is whether there was an economic justification for the new proposals of the house and whether further expansion would not be against public interest. A question, very naturally, would be asked as to what is meant by 'public interest.' It is not easy to define precisely but a group can, when faced with a specific case, undoubtedly say if a proposal was in public interest or not.

Under the act, the Commission would also examine the 'scheme of finance' of the new proposals of larger industrial houses. This, in my opinion, is the most important aspect of the legislation. It would be recalled that the Industrial Licensing Policy Inquiry Committee had brought out some of the revealing facts about the growth of larger industrial houses. The Committee had shown how in a very large number of big industrial projects of business houses, most of the finance was provided by public sector financial institutions. Now onwards, one should hope that big business houses wanting to undertake new projects would have to raise their own resources instead of being allowed to grow on the strength of finance from public sector financial institutions. Similarly, one could expect that foreign collaborations on non-essential items of production would not be so easily allowed as has been the case in the past.

In certain quarters, this legislation has not been welcomed. And it is argued that this would curb initiative and become a hurdle in the process of economic growth. I do not happen to entertain any such fears. On the contrary, I feel that some of the provisions of the Monopolies Act are too weak to enable the government to restrict the growth of concentration of economic power. In a way, the Act does not provide the government with the requisite authority to break monopolies and correct some of the existing problems of monopoly and exploitation of the consumers. To place all hopes in one legislation to curb monopolies or to restrict furtherance of concentration in the private hands would be only too naive. Under the Monopolies Act, the monopolies and the growth of big houses can be regulated, but it cannot be stopped.

The real answer to the problems of concentration lies in the entry and expansion of the public sector. Take the instance of oil industry. For long, had been in the hands of a few private foreign companies. The situation was that of a near monopoly. But with the entry of the public sector in the oil industry, the economic power of the foreign oil monopolies has been brought down in a significant manner. Similarly, in the drug industry, the existing power of the few large pharmaceutical companies can only, and effectively, be curbed with the entry of public sector in a big way for production and distribution of basic and essential drugs.

What holds true of individual industries holds equally true of the economy as a whole. The real answer to restrict the growth of monopolies and concentration of economic power in private hands lies in taking up of a bold programme of expansion of the public sector. Secondly, to reduce the existing degree of concentration in the private sector, the government would do better to enact the necessary legislation to convert the loan and other financial assistance into equity—as suggested by the Industrial Licensing Policy Inquiry Committee. While these measures are undertaken, it has to be kept in mind that no single legislation, howsoever comprehensive it may be, can achieve the objective by itself. What is necessary is the evolving of a comprehensive scheme of regulations and their effective coordination.

The political leadership and the government do appear to be conscious of the problem and the need for reducing and restricting the growth of private monopolies and concentration of economic power in private hands. It is too early to predict the extent to which the evil would be curbed. It is, however, satisfying that there is widespread appreciation of the problem and a beginning has been made.

3 The Concept and Measurement of Concentration

Discussions on the problem of monopolies, concentration and disparities in wealth or control over means of production in an economy are perhaps always and everywhere exciting issues of public importance. This has been true of the 1960s in India. Though there were occasional references to the emergence of monopolies and growth of concentration particularly in the corporate private sector during the later years of the 1950s, specific questions in this regard were posed for a public inquiry only in 1960 by Prime Minister Jawaharal Nehru.[1] The theme of his questions was derived from one of the Directive Principles of State Policy i.e., the state shall direct its policy towards securing "that the operation of the economic system does not result in the concentration of wealth and means of production to the common detriment." An expert committee under the chairmanship of Prof. P.C. Mahalanobis was asked to ascertain the trends and changes in the distribution of income and wealth in the economy during the plan decade 1950-1960.[2] The committee could not obtain the requisite data to reach firm conclusions on many of the issues it was required to go into, but it had somewhat better data to observe that the working of the planned economy had "encouraged the process of concentration by facilitating and aiding the growth of big business in India."[3]

---

1. See *Lok Sabha Debates*, August 22, 1960, pp.391-93.
2. Planning Commission, *The Committee on Distribution of Income and Levels of Living: Report*, Part I, February 1964. The Committee is widely known after its Chairman, Prof P.C. Mahalanobis.
3. Ibid.: 53.

The Concept

The committee drew a distinction between: (i) concentration in an industry (as represented by share in the output) and (ii) concentration in wealth and means of production or financial control. The latter, according to the committee, was only a means to an end which is concentration of economic power. Further, it was added that a small group of individuals or groups may not have control over a large percentage share of the national aggregate in each case; but this can be sufficient to "set them so much higher than any other individual or group in the relevant context that it gives them a *disproportionately* large influence and enables them to exercise economic power not measurable statistically by mere ratios of concentration"[4] (emphasis added). The Monopolies Inquiry Commission (MIC), appointed in pursuance of the recommendations of the Mahalanobis Committee, used the expression "concentration of economic power" to cover both "industry-wise concentration" and "country-wise concentration."[5]

Chapter III of The Monopolies and Restrictive Trade Practices Bill, 1967, deals with 'concentration of economic power' but it does not attempt any precise definition of the concept. The constituents where 'concentration of economic power' is considered to be existing are: (i) all undertakings which have total assets, in combination with their interconnected undertakings, as more than 20 crore, and (ii) all such 'dominant' undertakings which have themselves, or in combination with their interconnected undertakings, assets of more than ₹ 1 crore.[6] The bill has referred to the existence of 'concentration of economic power,' both when the concentration was 'industry-wise' as well as 'country-wise' i.e., the interconnected undertakings as represented in business houses as well

---

4. Ibid.: 25-6.

5. *Monopolies Inquiry Commission: Report*, Vol. I & II, 1965, pp.1-2. One Member of the MIC, R.C. Dutt, in his Note of Dissent differed with the majority for including both 'industry-wise and country-wise' types of concentration under the "concept of concentration of economic power". See pp.190-91.

6. *c.f.* Monopolies and Restrictive Trade Practices Bill, 1967, Bill No. XV of 1967 and Report of the Joint Select Committee on the Bill (February, 1969). See Clause 20 of the Bill as amended by the Joint Select Committee.

as individual undertakings enjoying 'dominant' position in the respective industry.[7]

R.K. Hazari, while admitting that economic power is essentially a qualitative concept and not amenable to measurement in precise terms, undertook an exercise to measure the degree of concentration in the Indian corporate private sector on the assumption that the degree of 'concentration of economic power' can be measured in the percentage share in the means of production.[8] Conceptually, he confined the term monopoly in particular markets or industries and referred to monopoly of capital as "concentration of economic power."[9]

There seems to be not much of a dispute about product monopoly. It is fairly well understood. There are, however, practical difficulties regarding the fixing up of a percentage beyond which if a firm commands share in the total output, it should be considered as a dominant undertaking. Also there are problems of defining an undertaking (should one include the output of interconnected undertakings?) and the output (should one take national output or that of organised private sector?) for purposes of determining the place of an undertaking in the industry. The main point is that product monopoly refers to the share in the output and is not always related to the capital, employment or income.

The phrase 'concentration of economic power' has been used to underline: (i) the size of the capital under common control, i.e., the degree of concentration in the control over capital and (ii) the extent of influence that the holders may have over the consumers, their competitors and other institutions in the society. The measurement of the former is possible but the latter is not amenable to statistical quantification. The

7. According to the *MIC Report*, the scope of the area included under 'concentration of economic power' was much wider as the MIC had proposed to inclusion of all groups having combined assets of their interconnected undertakings above ₹ 5 crore as against ₹ 20 crore now provided a 'Dominant Undertaking' having been defined as one which controls (individually or in combination with its interconnected undertakings) more than one-third of the national production of the organised industrial sector. See Clause 2 of the Bill as returned by the Joint Select Committee.

8. Hazari, R.K. (1966). *The Structure of Corporate Private Sector*. Bombay: Asia Publishing House, p.3.

9. Hazari, R.K. (ed.) (1966). *Monopolies and Their Regulations in India*, Papers read at the Indian Economic Conference. Calcutta. Bombay: Popular Prakasan, p.vii.

control over large quantum of capital is certainly one of the essential basis for influences but the degree of influence need not always be directly related to the quantum of capital held under control. Many other factors like: (i) the nature of economic activity, (ii) the locational spread and (iii) the relationship with political and public institutions are important in determination of the influence. The emphasis placed by Mahalanobis on the 'disproportionately large influence' than what is represented in the percentage share of the capital is of significance and a basic one. Hazari, while admitting that economic power is essentially a qualitative concept and not amenable to measurement in precise terms, did in practice employ the expression 'concentration of economic power,' to highlight the existence of significant concentration in the capital of the corporate private sector.

One would suggest that the phrase 'concentration of economic power' should be used carefully and not, as it may be convenient for other objectives in view, to express the degree of concentration in the private capital of the corporate or industrial sectors. The expression would be more appropriately employed in reference to the economy as a whole and not while dealing with a sector or particular market. There would, undoubtedly, be some advantage if more work is undertaken to identify various constituents, and their respective weightage which goes into the creation of economic power. But in that case, the subject matter of inquiry may tend to travel beyond the realm of economics.

Measurement of Concentration

One of the early attempts at measuring the degree of concentration in the corporate private sector in India was made by R.K. Hazari.[10] He reached the conclusion that there was a clear and significant increase in the degree of concentration in the corporate private sector between 1951 and 1958.[11] The conclusion was based on indicators: (i) that the share of the four top business houses (Inner-circle) which stood at 17.91 per cent of the total share-capital of non-government public companies in 1951 had risen to 22.34 per cent and (ii) a similar trend was noticed in the sharing of total

10. Hazari, R.K. (1963). *The Corporate Private Sector*. Bombay: Asia Publishing House.

11. Ibid.: 18.

gross capital stock.[12] The Committee on Distribution of Income and Levels of Living (1964) relied in a considerable manner on Hazari's study while discussing the problem of concentration in the non-governmental corporate sector.[13] The MIC also made an estimate of the degree of concentration in the corporate private sector for the year 1963-64.[14] The methodology employed by the MIC was similar to Hazari, i.e., working out of the percentage share of the houses in the: (i) paid-up capital and (ii) gross capital stock.

The above studies refer to the degree of concentration in the corporate private sector. Hazari's reference period has been 1951-1958, during which the corporate sector was predominantly in the private sector. And a study of the degree of concentration in the corporate private sector tended to be a study of the concentration in the organised sector of the Indian economy as a whole. However, since then the public sector expansion has been rapid, and discussions on the degree of concentration should be in reference to the corporate sector as a whole. It may also be quite pertinent to mention that according to the Industrial Policy Resolution of 1956, one of the ways of reducing concentration of economic power in the hands of a few private individuals was sought to be achieved through rapid expansion of the public sector. The Industrial Policy Resolution of 1956 states: "Accordingly the State will progressively assume a predominant and direct responsibility for setting up new industrial undertakings and for developing transport facilities."[15]

The number of registered companies (public and private) in India declined from 27,403 in 1958 to 27,047 in 1966.[16] The paid-up capital (PUC) of these, however, rose from ₹ 1,515.6 crore in 1958 to ₹ 3,154.4 crore in 1966. Out of the total increase of nearly ₹ 1,638.8 crore of the

---

12. Ibid.
13. *The Committee on Distribution of Income and Levels of Living Report*, Part I, Manager, Government of India Press, 1964, See Chapter IV, pp.25-55.
14. *Monopolies Inquiry Commission: Report*, 1965. Manager, Government of India Press. pp.121-22.
15. *Industrial Policy Resolution, 1956*, para 5.
16. For an overall picture of the corporate sector see *Working Group on Company Law Administration Report* of the Administrative Reforms Commission, June 1958, under the Chairmanship of Shri D.L. Mazumdar (Mimeographed).

PUC, more than half was accounted for by the 'Government Companies'[17] alone. During this period, the number of government companies rose from 104 to 232 and their PUC from ₹ 428.9 to ₹ 1,391.5 crore. The rise in the PUC of the corporate private sector was from ₹ 1,086.7 to ₹ 1,762.9 crore. Taking the PUC as a broad indicator of the trends in the corporate sector it seems, with the emergence and rapid growth of government companies during 1958-66, the relative importance of the corporate private sector declined in a significant manner and to that extent the possibility of the growth of concentration in the private hands, in the corporate sector as a whole, has been lessened.

Sharing of PUC: 1958 and 1966

The two bases employed for measuring the degree of concentration in the corporate private sector have been the percentage share of the top Houses in the (i) PUC and (ii) capital stock. It may be of interest to see the trends in the degree of concentration in the corporate private sector on the same yard stick. The broad pattern of sharing of PUC in 1958 and 1966 is given in Table 3.1.

Table 3.1

Sharing of the PUC in 1958 and 1966

S.No.		*1958 (₹ crore)*	*1966 %*	*1958 %*	*1966*
1.	73 Large Houses*	487.09	815.94	45.00	46.30
2.	PUC 53 Large Houses*	149.80	281.74	13.78	15.98
3.	PUC 20 Larger Houses*	337.29	534.20	31.04	30.30
4.	Large Companies	92.29	209.40	8.49	11.88
5.	Foreign Companies	12.71	42.86	1.17	2.43
6.	Private Corporate Sector	1,086.70	1,762.90	100.00	100.00
7.	Government Companies	428.90	1,391.50	—	—
8.	Corporate Sector	1,515.60	3,154.40	—	—

Note: * Inclusive of the Second Tier; —: Not available.

Source: Government of India. (1969). *Report of the Industrial Licensing Policy Inquiry Committee (Main Report)* (Chairman: Shri. Subimal Dutt). New Delhi: Ministry of Industrial Development.

17. Under The Companies Act, 1956, any company in which not less than 51 per cent of paid-up share capital is held by the central or by any state government or partly by the central government and partly by one or more state governments, is called a 'government company.'

In the corporate private sector as such, the share of 73 industrial houses, as defined and outlined by the Industrial Licensing Policy Inquiry Committee (ILPIC), in the PUC was nearly 45.0 per cent in 1958[18] and 46.3 per cent in 1966 (see Table 3.1). When the 73 houses are sub-grouped under '20 large houses'[19] and '53 large houses,' one finds that the share of the '20 larger houses' in the corporate private sector PUC declined from 31.04 per cent to nearly 30.30 per cent and that of the '53 large houses' (which are relatively smaller in size as judged on the basis of their assets of 1964) increased from 13.78 per cent in 1958 to 15.98 in 1966. The changes in the share of the '73 large houses' in the PUC of the corporate private sector or that of the '20 larger houses,' though marginal, would suggest that there has not been any furthering of the degree of 'concentration' in the corporate private sector during 1958-1966. The enhanced share of 'large independent companies' (each having assets as more than ₹ 5 crore in 1966 and not associated with any of the 73 industrial houses) in the PUC provides further support to the above observation.

The total PUC of the '20 larger houses' increased from ₹ 337.29 crore to ₹ 534.20 crore during 1958 and 1966. The two largest houses (*viz.*, Tata and Birla) jointly accounted for 42.26 per cent of the PUC of the '20 larger houses' in 1958; the percentage fell to 39.56 in 1966 (see Table 3.2). The relative position of the next two largest houses (*viz.*, Martin Burn and Bangur) increased marginally and Thapar's, the next in the descending order of assets, share fell. In this manner, one finds that the relative position of 6th house to the 10th one improved and that of the others got slightly reduced. But for the Mafatlal house, the others (amongst the 20) do not appear to have lost or gained in their ranking to any significant extent, Broadly speaking, a similar picture emerges from the *inter se* comparison of the '53 large houses.'

---

18. The PUC data for 1958 is given in *ILPIC Report*, Appendix III-A(3).

19. "20 larger houses" are the ones that had assets as more than ₹ 35.00 crore during 1964-65 which house composition of the MIC. The MIC had identified 75 business groups but the ILPIC has reduced them to 73 (Macneill and Barry has been merged with Binny and the House of G.D. Kothari has been treated as Second Tier of Birlas). The BIC has also been taken as associated with Soorajmull Nagarmull. It has been shown independent as its control seems to have been taken over from 1961.

Table 3.2

Relative Share of the Houses in PUC during 1958 and 1966

S.No.	House	% Share in PUC of 1958	% Share in PUC 1966	Difference between Col. (3) and (2)
	(1)	(2)	(3)	(4)
1.	Tata	23.78	21.21	-2.57
2.	Birla	18.48	18.35	-0.13
3.	Martin Burn	4.23	4.41	+0.08
4.	Bangur	3.78	4.13	+0.35
5.	Thapar	3.93	3.24	-0.69
6.	Soorajmull Nagarmull	3.94	4.35	+0.41
7.	Mafatlal	2.24	4.28	+2.04
8.	A.C.C.	5.88	5.76	+0.38
9.	Walchand	2.20	3.33	+1.13
10.	Shriram	2.01	2.54	+0.53
11.	Bird Heilgers	2.98	2.90	-0.08
12.	J.K. (Singhania)	2.82	2.63	-0.19
13.	Goenka	3.03	3.08	+0.05
14.	Sarabhai	1.18	1.18	--
15.	Sahujain	4.92	3.08	-0.84
16.	Scindia	3.18	2.33	-0.85
17.	Killick	4.48	3.09*	-1.39
18.	I.C.I.	2.60	2.92	+0.32
19.	Andrew Yule	3.89	2.17	-1.72
20.	Kilachand (Tulsidas)	1.10	1.88	+0.77
	Total	100.00	100.00	--

Source: Table is compiled on the basis of the information given in the *ILPIC Report*, Appendix III.

The changes in the distribution pattern of the PUC amongst the '20 larger houses' during 1958-1966 would also suggest that the degree of concentration in the corporate private sector has not been furthered. If at all there is any conclusion that one may draw, mainly on the basis of the changes in the share of the corporate private sector PUC, it is that during 1958-1966, there has been a reduction in the degree of concentration in private hands as compared to the trends observed for 1951-1958.[20] This is not supported by the facts known otherwise.[21]

20. *c.f. op.cit.* no.8.

21. *c.f.* Dutta, B. (1969). "Growth of Business Houses", *Company News and Notes* VII(I): 1-25.

One may use PUC data as a 'very rough' indication of the existence of concentration in the corporate private sector, but its use as a measure of the degree of concentration has serious limitation—more so while reaching any conclusion about trends in concentration. The changes observed in the pattern of distribution of the PUC do not represent changes in the sharing of the assets. By its very character, PUC represents the subscribed capital at face value. It does not include reserves built up or the depreciation funds which in many cases are equally, if not more, important than the equity capital or the PUC as a whole (inclusive of preference capital). What it may indicate (and this too not always very correctly) is the quantum of subscribed capital. If one was interested in going into the question of the risk capital contributed initially by the promoters of a corporate body, one may study the equity capital and distribution of the equity shares. But, for purposes of study on concentration in the corporate private sector, a better indicator would be the assets or capital stock.

Capital Stock

The second basis for Hazari to reach the conclusion on increasing concentration is the trend observed in the estimated 'gross capital stock' of the 'corporate private sector.' Unlike the actual totals of the PUC, the corresponding aggregation of the capital stock of the corporate private sector is not compiled by any agency.[22] The estimates of capital stock for 1951 and 1958 were derived by 'boosting' the Reserve Bank of India (RBI) data on the assumption that "the ratio of paid-up capital to fixed assets and inventories in various groups (based on the type of business, location, age of companies and size of business) remain more or less the same."[23]

The MIC attempted an exercise for estimating the 'assets'[24] of the corporate private sector for the year 1964. The technique adopted was the

22. Though it could be easily done by the Company Law Board, Ministry of Industrial Development, Company Affairs and Internal Trade if they had.

23. Support to the capital stock ratio is provided by a study by Sastri, N.S.R. and K.A. Antony (1960). 'Capital Formation in the Corporate Business Sectors in India' in V.K.R.V. Rao and others (eds.), *Papers on National Income*, Volume II. Asia Publishing House, p.163, as quoted by Hazari (1966). *The Structure of Corporate Private Sector in India*, p.15.

24. The 'gross capital stock' has been taken as fixed asset plus inventories plus depreciation. 'net capital stock' equals 'net assets' which equals, total liabilities. The MIC and ILPIC data is for 'net assets'.

same as that of Hazari and Antony, i.e., boosting of the PUC figures by the ratio between capital stock and share capital, as observed in the RBI studies.[25] The basic assumption in the estimation of assets of the corporate private sector was that there is a definite and precise relationship between PUC and capital stock.

The objective of the RBI studies on finances of joint stock companies, which have been used for the boosting purposes, has been to evaluate the trends in the finances of the largest companies as to get an idea of the sources and uses of funds in the corporate sector as well as in certain industrial categories.[26] Since the objective of the RBI studies have been to attempt an analysis of the finances of the largest companies, the samples are confined to: (i) only public limited companies and (ii) companies with PUC of more than 5 lakh only. The bias of the RBI sample for larger public limited companies is also reflected in the fact that though in numbers the coverage of the RBI sample was nearly 12 per cent of the total public limited companies in 1958 (1,001 companies cut of the 8,255), the sample accounted for nearly three-fourth of PUC of the public limited non-government companies. The overall capital stock/PUC ratios observed by Hazari for the house companies (inner and outer circles, individually and as complexes) were similar to that of the RBI.[27] Possibly, the constituent companies of the two studies were very similar—which is not very unlikely

25. *op.cit.* no. 14.

26. *c.f. Reserve Bank of India Bulletin*. 1953 and Hazari (1996) *op.cit.*: 303.

27. Hazari's data on companies of the inner and outer circles of the houses showed almost identical relationship with the one observed in RBI studies. In a situation where the capital stock/PUC ratio is the same for the houses as assumed while estimating capital stock for the corporate private sector, the trends in concentration shown in the data on PUC and gross capital stock cannot but be similar. The ratio for 1958 as observed by Hazari are:

S.No	Coverage	Capital Stock (₹ crore)	PUC (₹ crore)	Capital Stock/ PUC Ratio
	(1)	(2)	(3)	(4)
1.	Antony's Estimates for private corporate sector	3,402.00	1,086.00	3.13
2.	Hazari's 20 Group Inner Circle	283.54	895.62	3.16
3.	Hazari's 13 Largest Groups (Inner Circle)	268.70	840.01	3.13

Source: Hazari (1966) *op.cit.*: 38-40.

in the Indian situation, as a good number of the bigger companies would fall in one or the other industrial house. However, even in Hazari's sample, one finds that capital stock/PUC ratio varies from one house to another and for the four top houses, the ratio is higher than that of the 20 houses when taken aggregatively.[28]

The asset/PUC ratio in 1966 for the different constituents, when taken separately, of the corporate private sector seems to vary materially. The ratio is higher in the large sized companies and lower in the smaller ones. Even within the '73 industrial houses' (ILPIC) the assets/PUC ratio is higher for the '20 larger houses' than of the '53 large houses'—each one of which is a comparatively smaller house (see Table 3.3). The comparatively higher ratio in the bigger-sized companies is also indicated if one compares the ratio of the house companies grouped according to their size. But, even otherwise, it is not unrealistic to expect the asset/PUC ratio to be higher in the public limited and bigger-sized companies than the private limited and smaller ones. The reasons are: (i) the eligibility of public limited companies to raise public funds through debentures; (ii) non-availability of finance to private limited companies from some of public sector financial institutions; (iii) continuation of traditional credit-worthiness criteria, mainly based on the assets of the borrower in the banking system; (iv) to some extent, the general confidence with public may show in bigger-sized companies; and (v) the fact that there is considerable 'inter-locking' between the banks and the controlling interests of the large industrial houses.

Since the RBI sample studies have a bias towards bigger public limited companies of the corporate private sector, the assets/PUC ratio of the sample cannot but be on the higher side for the corporate private sector as a whole and the private limited and small-sized companies, in particular. In that case, an estimate of overall assets of the corporate private sector obtained by boosting RBI data would, naturally, be inflated ones. And the use of such estimates for working out of the degree of concentration (as percentage share of the houses) in the corporate private sector would be an underestimation.

---

28. Because of the higher capital stock/PUC ratio for the four top houses, as compared to the one accepted for the corporate private sector as a whole, one finds that the four top houses had greater share in capital stock than in PUC. At the same time because the ratio for the 20 houses was similar to the RBI sample, the share of the 20 in PUC and capital assets is very similar (see Hazari (1966) *op.cit.*: 16).

Table 3.3

Gross Capital Stock/PUC Ratios for 1966

(₹ crore)

S.No.	Group	Assets	PUC Stock	Ratio of Col.(3) to (2)
	(1)	(2)	(3)	(4)
1.	20 Larger Houses	2,381.95	534.20	4.46
2.	53 Large Houses	1,148.42	281.74	4.08
3.	73 Houses	3,530.37	815.94	4.32
4.	RBI 1333 Public Limited Companies for 1965-66	40.63	8.80	4.62

Source: *ILPIC Report*, Vol. II for lines 1-3; and for line 4 *RBI Bulletin*, December 1967, from "Finance of Indian Joint Stock Companies."

One should hope that sooner or later it would be possible to have a total of the assets and break-up of some other basic data about all companies of the corporate sector and there would be no need for scholars to depend upon the rough estimates. The appropriate agency for this is the Company Law Department. But would the balance sheet data on assets be a good indicator of the value of the assets? If the current controversy over the principles of compensation is any indicator, the book value can hardly be taken as representing the correct picture about the assets of the companies.

Summing Up

This note has attempted to underline only five specific points. One, that it is necessary to have a clear distinction between: (i) concentration in output of a product, (ii) concentration in ownership of control over capital and (iii) concentration of economic power. Two, while dealing with the problem of concentration in capital, it would be more appropriate to have an overall view of the public and private sectors jointly. Three, the pattern of sharing of the PUC does not reflect the degree of concentration and it cannot be treated as a basis for study of trends in concentration. Four, the methodology adopted for estimates of the assets of the corporate private sector so far tends to over-estimate the national assets and the use of such estimates underplays the share of the big business. And five, even when the actual totals of the national assets are available from the balance sheets of the corporate bodies, the real degree of concentration would be understated if the due consideration is not paid to the assessment of the market value of the assets of the units under study. The need for more empirical research work and organisation of basic data on the corporate sector, even from this limited view point, is obvious.

4 Nature and Growth of the Indian Corporate Sector*

I

The Indian corporate sector has two main components, namely, government-owned and privately-owned companies. The size of both the components, in terms of both numbers and capital, has grown fast, particularly since the beginning of the 1970s (see Table 4.1). Government companies are mainly in the basic, heavy and capital-intensive industries, whereas the private sector is predominantly in industries which cater to the consumer markets directly. It is due to such a basic difference that while the government sector accounts for nearly two-third of the productive industrial capital, its share in the net value added is less than one-third.[1] And the opposite is true of the private sector. The differing nature of the activities undertaken by the two sectors is also reflected in the pattern of industrial activities of the two sectors. For instance, energy—which is a pre-requisite for processes of economic development—alone accounts for more than 44 per cent of the capital investment of the central government production enterprises, another 15 per cent investment is in steel, 11.4 per cent in chemicals, fertilisers and pharmaceuticals and nearly 8 per cent in minerals and metals.[2]

Being government-owned enterprises, the choice of investment, location, pricing, employment and all other important policies are centrally

---

* This chapter was delivered as the Brij Narain Memorial Lecture at Punjab University, Chandigarh, in January 1987.

Disclaimer: In a discussion on the private sector, one cannot avoid references to individual actors on the corporate scene. The citations and names are brought in not because of any bias or prejudice, but primarily because without this the presentation would appear more a fiction than a reality.

1. Central Statistics Office (CSO) (1981). *Annual Survey of Industries 1980-81*, Vol I. The low value added could also be attributed to the pricing policies of the government as the gross output in value terms is dependent on the prices.
2. Bureau of Public Enterprises (1983-84). *Public Enterprises Survey*, Vol. I: 20.

Table 4.1

Growth of the Indian Corporate Sector (1956-57 to 1990-91)

(PUC in ₹ crore)

Year	Govt. Companies (Public and Private Limited)		Non-Govt. Companies					
			Public Limited		Private Limited		All Companies	
	No.	PUC	No.	PUC	No.	PUC	No.	PUC
(1)	(2)	(3)	(4)	(5)	(6)	(7)	(8)	(9)
1956-57	74	73	8771	696	20512	309	29357	1078
1957-58	91	257	8255	756	19934	294	28280	1307
1958-59	104	429	7608	782	19691	305	27403	1516
1959-60	125	477	7151	814	19621	327	26897	1618
1960-61	142	547	6663	915	19344	356	26149	1819
1961-62	154	630	6399	1093	18422	296	24975	2019
1962-63	160	786	6404	1171	19058	300	25622	2257
1963-64	176	961	6474	1281	19282	361	25932	2603
1964-65	183	1115	6492	1329	19909	336	26584	2780
1965-66	214	1248	6410	1346	20386	355	27010	2949
1966-67	232	1392	6309	1402	20706	361	27247	3155
1967-68	241	1559	6497	1684	20606	430	27344	3674
1968-69	259	1715	6454	1712	21260	433	27973	3860
1969-70	282	1791	6436	1741	22242	447	28960	3979
1970-71	314	2064	6443	1775	23655	462	30412	4301
1971-72	352	2369	6703	2036	25212	536	32267	4941
1972-73	390	2998	6819	2176	27147	575	34356	5749
1973-74	450	4645	7071	2323	29964	663	37485	7631
1974-75	573	4966	7275	2484	32736	750	40584	8200
1975-76	651	6122	7593	2675	35162	822	43406	9619
1976-77	701	7175	7794	2808	37371	897	45866	10880
1977-78	745	8528	8028	3113	39521	957	48294	12598
1978-79	782	8315	8309	3240	42427	1020	51518	12575
1979-80	825	10070	8864	3445	46804	1091	56493	14606
1980-81	851	11443	9388	3550	52475	1152	62714	16145
1981-82	894	13309	10169	3716	61339	1245	72402	18270
1982-83	943	16535	11371	3839	70589	1347	82903	21721
1983-84	973	19511	12523	3996	80768	1455	94264	24962
1984-85	980	22447	14149	4260	92240	1578	107369	28285
1985-86	1020	27088	19837	7139	103522	2368	124379	36595
1986-87	1053	32873	21442	8435	118175	2660	140670	43968
1987-88	1104	37169	22507	9966	134713	2989	158324	50124
1988-89	1134	42572	23749	11773	155445	3358	180328	57704
1989-90	1160	47451	25217	13573	175751	3620	202128	64643
1990-91*	1167	49424	26813	14569	196472	4117	224452	68111

Note: Private and public limited companies are grouped together in case of government companies.

* Provisional.

Source: (i) Ministry of Industrial Development & Company Affairs, (Dept. of Company Affairs), *Annual Report*, 1986-87. (ii) Ministry of Law Justice & Company Affairs, *Directory of Joint Stock Companies in India: 1980*, Vol.1.

decided. These have to be in conformity with the macroeconomic and socioeconomic objectives—which are multiple and sometimes even self-contradictory.[3] The constituents of the private sector do not have multiple objectives to pursue; the purpose of a private business organisation is clear i.e., to operate as a business enterprise—and business means profit and economic advantage and not social service. The primary test of performance of a private enterprise is in terms of the profits it can make.

Private corporate sector, unlike the government sector which comprises of about a little more than 1,000 companies, consists of more than 2 lakh units. An operational division within the sector exists i.e., 'private limited' and 'public limited' ones.[4] Generally speaking, private limited companies are small and closely held; the public limited are large and widely held. While in terms of numbers, the public limited companies are only 12 per cent of the total, more than three-fourth of the total paid-up capital (PUC) of the private corporate sector is accounted for by them.

In 1956-57, the number of 'public limited' private sector companies was 8,771 and in 1984-85, it stood at 26,813. The size of PUC in this period increased from ₹ 696 crore to ₹ 14,569 crore.[5] The sector is marked by the existence of high degree of concentration, i.e., a small number of large-sized companies enjoying a dominant place. In 1980, the small-sized companies, each with less than ₹ 5 lakh PUC, accounted for nearly half of the public limited companies but had less than 2 per cent share of PUC. On the other hand, less than 6 per cent of the large-sized group, each with

---

3. Kidwai, Waris R. (1986). "The Threatening Storm over Public Sector in India", in Raj K. Nigam (ed.), *Towards a Viable and Vibrant Public Sector in India*, Documentation Centre for Corporate and Business Policy Research.

4. (i) Private Limited companies are those in which the number of shareholders is limited to 50 and which are prohibited from inviting public from subscribing to any of their stocks. The right to transfer shares is also restricted. Government companies are those in which not less than 51 per cent of the PUC is held by the central government or by any state government or government companies. See, Ministry of Law, Justice & Company Affairs, Companies Act, 1956 (as modified up to 1.6.1981). Sections 3 and 617.

   (ii) In 1990-91, the number of public limited private sector companies was 26,813, while the size of PUC was ₹ 14,569 crore.

5. Ministry of Industry and Company Affairs (Department of Company Affairs), *Annual Report*, various issues. It can be seen from Table 4.1 that there was a gradual decline in the number of public limited companies in the initial phase, the minimum having been reached in 1966-67 at 6,309.

₹ 1 crore and more of PUC accounted for nearly two-third of the gross PUC. If one combines the last two categories in Table 4.2, the companies with more than ₹ 50 lakh each as PUC are seen to account for a little less than four-fifth of the total PUC of the 'public limited' companies of the private corporate sector. The highly skewed nature of the public limited companies is only too obvious.

Table 4.2

Distribution of Public Limited Companies in the Private Corporate Sector as on March 31, 1980

(PUC in ₹ crore)

PUC Range	*No.*	*PUC*	*Percentage*	
			No.	*PUC*
(1)	*(2)*	*(3)*	*(4)*	*(5)*
Less than 5 lakh	4078	55.0	49.58	2.00
5-10 lakh	979	74.3	11.90	2.70
10-25 lakh	1332	211.9	16.19	7.70
25-50 lakh	724	255.9	8.80	9.30
50-100 lakh	566	349.4	6.88	12.70
1 crore and above	546	1805.0	6.64	65.60
Total	8225	2751.5	100.00	100.00

Note: Information on the aggregate position of the corporate sector normally undergoes substantial changes. The discrepancy between the total number of companies and their PUC as reported in Table 1 and here is due to the updation of the figures in later years.

Source: Based on Lall, Shadi (1981). "The Corporate Sector in India: As on 31-3-1980", *Company News & Notes*, July.

In the recent past, one observes a trend towards furtherance of concentration, especially at the top, in the Indian private corporate sector. The Gini coefficient of concentration increased from 0.56 in 1969-70 to 0.65 in 1981-82 and 0.74 in 1987-88 (also see Table 4.3).[6] Figure 4.1 shows the changes in concentration during 1969-70, 1981-82 and 1987-88 for companies having more than ₹ 50 lakh as PUC. The distribution shown is based on sales turnover.

6. For a method of calculating the coefficient and drawing the concentration curve, see: William I. Greenwal, *Statistics for Economics*, 1963.

Table 4.3

Distribution of Large Private Companies

(₹ crore)

Sales Range (₹ cr.)	1969-70		1981-82		1987-88		Percentage					
							1969-70		1981-82		1987-88	
	No.	Turnover	No.	Turnover	No.	Turnover	No.	Turnover	No.	Turnover	No.	Turnover
	(1)	(2)	(3)	(4)	(5)	(6)	(7)	(8)	(9)	(10)	(11)	(12)
Less than 5	392	855.54	382	750.87	1122	1483.42	56.40	15.45	30.46	2.26	42.15	1.98
5-10	159	1105.49	212	1574.96	359	2641.11	22.88	19.99	16.91	4.74	13.49	3.51
10-25	99	1521.69	332	5452.22	530	8528.11	14.24	27.47	26.48	16.41	19.91	11.35
25-50	34	1062.07	158	5422.89	313	11044.29	4.89	19.17	12.60	16.33	11.76	14.70
50-75	4	252.67	76	4599.35	112	6830.27	0.58	4.56	6.06	13.85	4.21	9.09
75-100	4	343.68	28	2414.23	66	5636.87	0.58	6.20	2.23	7.27	2.48	7.50
100 and above	3	398.12	66	13002.94	160	38982.11	0.43	7.19	5.26	39.14	6.00	51.87
Total	695	5539.26	1254	33217.46	2662	75146.85	100.00	100.00	100.00	100.00	100.00	100.00

Note: Only those companies for which information on sales is provided are taken for analysis.

Source: Based on 'Factsheets on Non-Government Companies with Paid-up Capital of ₹ 50 lakh and above', Research and Statistics Division of the Department of Company Affairs, Government of India.

Figure 4.1

Distribution of Large Private Companies

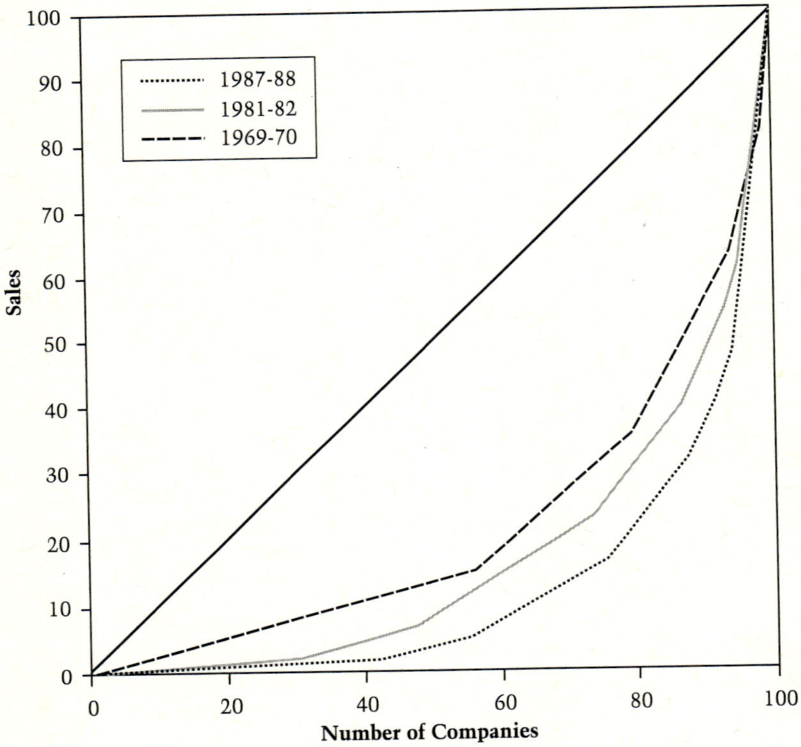

Source: Same as Table 4.3.

The size distribution of companies, however, is not an adequate basis to assess the trends in concentration. To understand the true magnitude and trends in concentration in the private sector, one needs to see the share and pattern of growth of the interconnected companies as a group. The concept of a 'business house' is only too well known to need any elaboration.[7] Table 4.4(a) and 4.4(b) show the growth of the top 20 business

7. Mehta, Ashok (1950). *Who Owns India*. Hazari, R.K. (1966). *The Structure of the Corporate Private Sector—A Study of Concentration, Ownership and Control*. Planning Commission (1964). *Committee on Distribution of Income and Levels of Living* (Mahalanobis Committee). *Monopolies Inquiry Commission: Report* (MIC), 1965; and *Report of the Industrial Licensing Policy Inquiry Committee* (ILPIC), 1969, have discussed the concept. For a discussion on the evolution of the concept, see: Goyal, S.K. (1979). *Monopoly Capital and Public Policy*. Chapter III. Allied Publishers.

houses during 1972-1984, as per the official sources. The overall assets of these 20 'business houses' have multiplied more than five times in the during 1972 to 1984.[8] These rose from less than three thousand crore in 1972 to over fifteen thousand crore of rupees by 1984. A similar picture emerges if one takes the turnover as a base to reflect changes in the market concentration in the Indian private corporate sector.[9]

Table 4.4(a)

Growth in Assets of the Top 20 Houses (1972-1984)

(₹ crore)

	Assets			*Share in Increase (%)*	
House	*1972*	*1980*	*1984*	*1972-1980*	*1980-1984*
(1)	*(2)*	*(3)*	*(4)*	*(5)*	*(6)*
Birla	589.42	1431.99	3359.04	18.48	23.32
Tata	641.93	1538.97	3120.13	19.67	19.13
JK Singhania	121.45	412.72	858.37	6.39	5.39
Mafatlal	183.74	427.54	786.60	5.35	4.35
Thapar	136.16	348.06	699.35	4.65	4.25
Reliance	*	166.33	672.96	3.65	6.13
Modi	58.05	198.82	610.30	3.09	4.98
ACC	134.36	274.51	554.16	3.07	3.38
Bangur	125.26	264.33	508.84	3.05	2.96
Larsen & Toubro	79.03	216.03	480.79	3.00	3.20
Sarabhai	84.44	317.94	462.88	5.12	1.75
Bajaj	63.32	179.26	425.97	2.54	2.99
ICI	135.21	343.01	425.52	4.56	1.00
Mahindra	58.49	186.03	408.17	2.80	2.69
Shriram	120.77	241.00	406.69	2.64	2.01
Walchand	99.47	150.36	405.31	1.12	3.08
Kirloskar	86.46	220.37	397.81	2.94	2.15
ITC	74.65	156.29	393.15	1.79	2.87
TVS Iyengar	50.97	188.64	387.25	3.02	2.40
Hindustan Lever	77.87	219.30	381.81	3.10	1.97
Total	2921.05	7481.50	15744.80	100.00	100.00

Note: The asset figures refer to only those companies which are registered under the Monopolies and Restrictive Trade Practice (MRTP) Act, 1969.

* This House emerged after 1972.

Source: Based on replies to questions in the Parliament.

8. During the same period, the PUC of the private sector increased from ₹ 2,572 crore in 1972 to ₹ 5,451 crore in 1984. This is nearly a little more than doubling of the overall magnitude compared to the fivefold increase in the assets of the top 20 houses. The assets and PUC data are, however, not strictly comparable.

9. The asset figures are less of depreciation and reflect neither the 'gross value' nor the 'market value' of the company assets.

To identify the trends in concentration, one may divide this period into three parts, namely 1972-1980, 1980-1984 and 1984-1990.[10] One would observe that:

(a) The rate of growth in assets of the top 20 business houses in successive period was higher than in the previous period.

Table 4.4(b)

Growth in Assets of the Top 20 Houses (1984-1990)

(₹ crore)

House	*Assets*		*Share in Increase*
	1990	*1984*	*1984-1990*
(1)	*(2)*	*(3)*	*(4)*
Tata	8530.93	3120.13	20.20
Birla	8473.35	3359.04	19.09
Reliance	3600.27	672.96	10.93
Thapar	2177.15	699.35	5.52
JK Singhania	2139.00	858.37	4.78
Larsen & Toubro	1681.52	480.79	4.48
Modi	1399.37	610.30	2.95
Bajaj	1391.06	425.97	3.60
Mafatlal	1343.35	786.60	2.08
SPIC	1273.35	272.00	3.74
Hindustan Lever	1209.46	381.81	3.09
United Breweries	1189.24	262.00	3.46
TVS Iyengar	1177.10	387.25	2.95
ITC	965.13	393.15	2.14
Shri Ram	933.93	406.70	1.97
ACC	902.72	654.16	0.93
Oswal Agro	870.34	*	3.25
Mahindra & Mahindra	773.55	161.00	1.36
Essar	756.49		2.22
Kirloskar	735.51	397.81	1.26
Total	41522.82	14737.562	100.00

Note: * This is a new house.

Source: Same as for Table 4.4(a).

10. As the list of top houses changed substantially overtime, for the 1984-1990 period, a different set of houses based on their ranking in 1990 was taken for this purpose.

(b) During the three periods, the lead has been maintained by the top two houses as one set and the others as another set. The Birla and the Tata houses seem to have been growing as if it was a neck to neck race (see Figure 4.2).

Figure 4.2

Growth of Top Five Monopoly Houses (1972-1990)

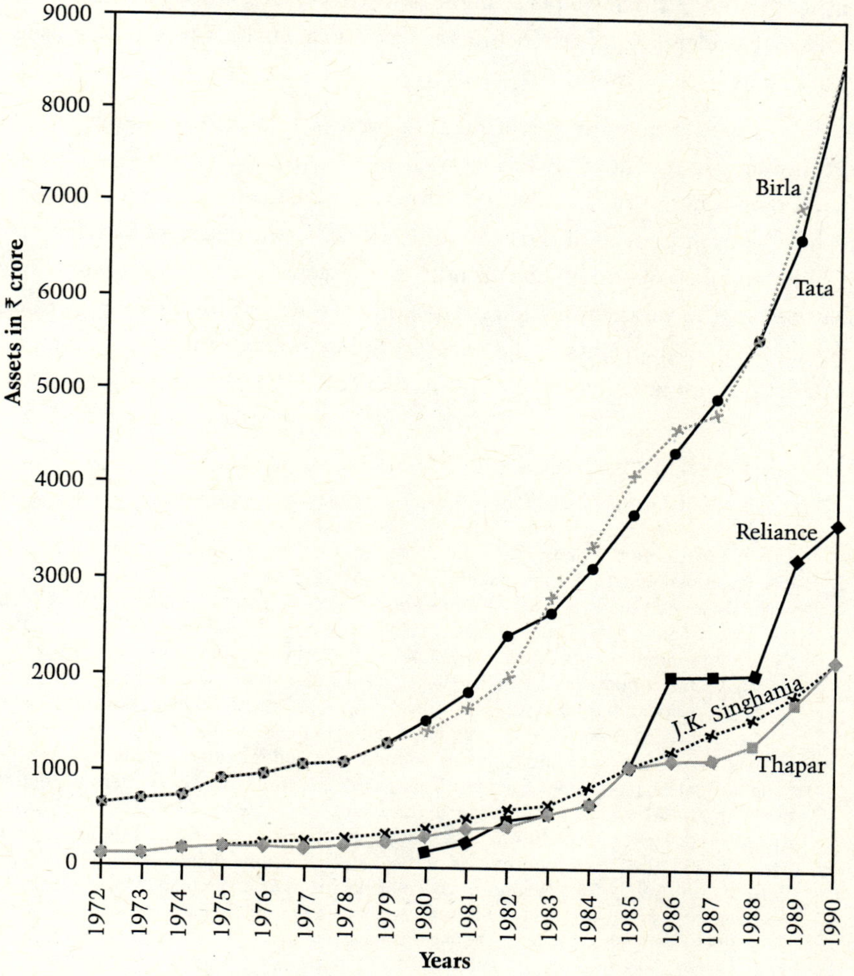

Source: Same as Table 4.4(a) and Table 4.4(b).

(c) While in terms of percentage growth of assets, the relatively smaller houses demonstrate a similar trend, the two top houses had the lion's share and claimed nearly 40 per cent of the overall addition to the assets of the top 20 during 1972-1984 as also during 1984-1990.

The official figures on the magnitude of growth rates in terms of assets are known to be underestimates of the real size or the extent of market dominance of individual houses. This was the main theme of one of our earlier studies.[11] It showed that due to a variety of techno-legal reasons, the extent of underestimation in official estimates on business house assets could be as high as 30-40 per cent.[12]

Is there an economic justification for the high growth experience of the Indian big business? If fast growth in size of an enterprise or a group was a consequence of the adoption of new, sophisticated and more efficient technologies or to avail of the economies of scale, one could well understand the inevitability of some such trends. The acceptance of such unavoidable features in the process of industrialisation would simultaneously demand the adoption of appropriate and effective public policies to meet the menace of emerging monopolies, and curbing tendencies at resorting to restrictive

---

11. Goyal, S.K. (1979). *Monopoly Capital and Public Policy*. Chapter V.

12. It is also interesting that many a time the house lays its claims to a much larger empire than what the Parliament is informed by the government. For instance, in a paid advertisement titled 'Tata Enterprises' placed in *International Herald Tribune*, the Tatas claimed that their assets exceeded $2.8 billion (₹ 2,200 crore approx.) while the government placed the figure at ₹ 1309 crore only for the year 1979 (see the supplement of the paper "Made in India" issued in December 1979). Apart from the underestimation resulting from avoidance of registration under the MRTP Act by big business companies, the official figures suffer from the fact that they do not take into account the value of assets held abroad by these houses. Surprisingly, the official estimates treat the constituents of a single house as parts of different houses or even hold them to be independent entities thus under-estimating the real strength of individual houses (see Chalapati Rao, K.S. (1985). "A Study of Inter-connections under the MRTP Act in the Context of the Asset Limit Hike", *EPW*, July 6). Probably, a matter of serious concern is the government's incomplete knowledge of such investments (see Ranganathan, K.V.K. (1984). "Indian Joint Ventures Abroad", *EPW*, May 19-26). The change in the criteria for inter-connection under the MRTP Act was introduced in 1984, though a welcome one, and has improved the situation regarding registration of large house companies, there are enough cases to show that the criterion are still not adequate to reflect the full extent of economic power as individuals. The trusts controlled by the large industrial families do not find a place in the list of MRTP undertakings, though it is well known that these are used for tax avoidance and also play a role in the control mechanism of the houses. To illustrate, it would suffice to say that none of the companies involved in the Reliance loan scandal are registered under the MRTP Act.

trade practices. Further, it also necessitates measures aimed at consumer protection and safeguards to protect national interest, which private interests invariably have the temptation to violate. These and related aspects of concentration in the private organised sector are not receiving much attention of the social scientists or the policy makers.[13] There is no doubt that the existence, and much worse the strengthening, of such trends has, apart from economic consequences, a few but serious sociopolitical implications.

The logic of industry specialisation to harness economies of scale and adoption of new technologies to cut down costs of production does not appear to be a strong point with most of the big business houses in India. Each large house appears to be wanting to produce as many varieties of goods as possible. The diversity is impressive and specialisation the least significant. To illustrate, the Birlas are in jute, textiles, sanitaryware, cement, steel, plastics, dairy, newspaper industry, shipping, automobiles, electricals, tea and sugar in addition to trading in investments.[14] The Birlas are, of course, now entering in a big way into chemicals and fertilisers.

13. There was a time when the growth of big business and consequent harmful effects on the sociopolitical and economic development of the country were discussed and examined in great detail. It was only such concern which culminated in the enactment of the MRTP Act in 1969. The reports of the Mahalanobis Committee, MIC and Industrial Licensing Policy Inquiry Committee are cases in point. While there have been few important studies by individual scholars, the area did not attract many scholars. A firm foundation to the studies on business houses was laid by R.K. Hazari in his study *The Structure of the Corporate Private Sector*. A special mention may be made of H.K. Paranjape who has been consistently working in the area of monopoly regulation both during his term as member of the MRTP Commission and subsequently too. The Corporate Studies Group of the Indian Institute of Public Administration is trying to institutionalise studies on industrial economics, with a special emphasis on the regulatory policies of the government towards monopoly and concentration.

14. It is interesting to find that more than one Birla company manufactures cement. Besides the two cement companies Mangalam Cement and Mysore Cement, other Birla companies which diversified into cement are: Birla Jute, Century Spinning, Gwalior Rayon, Indian Rayon and Kesoram Industries. Similarly, three companies of the J.K. Singhania House namely: Straw Products, J.K. Synthetics and Raymond Woollen Mills have entered into the cement industry. Indeed one can see a mad rush at diversifying into new profitable areas of the day. This appears to be a characteristic of the Indian big business. It happened with fishing, shipping and more recently with electronics and petrochemicals. In the process, they will be forced to go in for imported technologies because: (i) they would not be having any experience till then in the area and (ii) since more or less all constituents of the big business become aware of the possibilities simultaneously, they would like to show their one-up-manship by going for technology imports.

Similarly, one has only to glance through the list of new products in which even an industrial house like that of the Tatas, which by popular perception is associated with steel, trucks, power generation and other high technology areas, is now having a hold in such low technology areas like hotels, paints, cosmetics, toiletries and garments besides trading in a variety of consumer goods. The Tatas have now gone in for production of tomato ketchup, fruit juices and soft drinks. Examples can be multiplied to bring home the point that growth in concentration of the productive resources in the Indian private corporate sector has not been accompanied by industry specialisation, which could reap economies of scale or could help achieve technological breakthroughs by undertaking worthwhile research and development (R&D) activities. Even in the use of non-sophisticated technologies, the corporate sector in India has largely depended on imported technologies.[15] The spurt in foreign collaboration agreements during the '1980s' is one indication of this trend.

There has to be a continuing examination of the trends to keep ourselves aware of the implications of capital concentration. The plea for special emphasis on this sector also arises from the fact that one of the Directive Principles of State Policy makes it obligatory on the part of the government to direct its policy in such a way that "ownership and control of the material resources of the community are so distributed as best to subserve the common good; and ....that the operation of the economic system does not result in the concentration of wealth and means of production to the common detriment."[16]

After outlining a broad picture of concentration in the private corporate sector, one may address to oneself the question: How does big business manage to grow so fast? Is it that the large companies and big business houses grow on the strength of the internal resources and profits generated by them? If this was the case, there could be one type of justification for rapid growth of the companies. For this one may have a quick look at the profitability of the top 500 companies of the Indian private corporate sector. During the three-year period 1981-82 to 1983-84, of the 500 companies

15. *Report of the Industrial Licensing Policy Inquiry Committee*, 1969, p.130-32.

16. Ministry of Law, Justice and Company Affairs, The Constitution of India (as modified up to August 15, 1983), p.20.

covered in the Reserve Bank of India (RBI) study, 79 companies incurred losses in 1981-82. This number went up to 108 in 1982-83 and further to 138 in 1983-84. In spite of a nominal increase in dividend payments, the average dividend on paid-up capital came down to 12.6 per cent from 13.2 per cent earlier. The number of companies declaring equity dividend of 15 per cent or more came down from 249 in 1981-82 to 238 in 1982-83 and 221 in 1983-84.[17]

The loss-making companies are not the ones which are small and isolated entities. The overwhelming majority of these happen to be associated with one or another big business group.[18] There are undoubtedly a fairly good number of private sector companies which have shown unique performance in growth as well as profitability. In a way, some of these are a marvel to be admired at first sight. While appreciating the high profitability and gross returns to investments to shareholders, one must not avoid asking if the halo around such companies was more a result of financial manipulations and political patronage or is borne out of violations of the regulatory mechanisms of the society. In a similar manner, one needs to examine the factors responsible for the phenomenon of sickness in the Indian industrial sector.[19]

---

17. Reserve Bank of India (1984). "Finances of Large Public Limited Companies, 1983-84", *Reserve Bank of India Bulletin*, November.

18. The sickness in the Indian private sector generally gets hidden over time as either some of the sick companies are absorbed in the public sector or they are amalgamated with other profit making companies, very often belonging to the same house. While the phenomenon of nationalisation of sick units is better known, the practice of mergers is relatively unknown. There are several instances of mergers of sick companies with other companies in the same house. Tata Merlin Gerin amalgamated in Voltas, Bally Jute in Birla Jute, J.K. Steel & Industries in J.K. Synthetics, Cooper Engineering in Walchand Nagar Industries, Alkali & Chemical Corporation in IEL and International Tractor Company in Mahindra & Mahindra are a few cases in point. It is an interesting feature of the larger Indian Corporate Sector that the house of Modis is one of the fastest growing but its overall profits are in the negative; same holds true of the Bangurs and Sarabhais.

19. This is particularly so since a RBI Committee found that in as many as 222 (65%) out of 341 sick units studied management-related problems were present. See: RBI, *Report of the Committee to Examine the Legal and other difficulties faced by Banks and Financial Institutions in Rehabilitation of Sick Industrial Undertakings and Suggest Remedial Measure Including Changes in the Law*, 1984.

    Sick companies, irrespective of their house association, are awarded a variety of fiscal and financial concessions. Given the scope of the present paper, it would not be possible for us to go into the nature or the causes for industrial sickness—this warrants a separate and exclusive treatment—but the fact is that for individual houses

The fact that 'profits or reserves' have not been the main source for expansion of the private corporate sector is also evident from the pattern of funding of industrial projects, as observed during the past four years. The importance of "Reserves and Surpluses" has varied between 0.63 to 10.5 per cent of the total project cost (See Table 4.5). The main sources have been the public sector financial institutions and the share capital (which in turn is again substantially funded by the financial institutions). But in the latter half of the eighties, especially 1988-90, share capital and debentures have been more dominant, while financial institutions have become relatively less important.

In the process and the mechanism of business house construction and rapid expansion, with consequential concentration, four factors in our view have played the main role. These are: (i) participation of financial institutions in equity capital; (ii) intra-house corporate investments; (iii) new joint sector enterprises wherein state-level institutions join with house

---

declaring of a company as a sick one is an economic proposition. To illustrate the point I may give here only two quotes from company annual reports.

(a) In the case of the Tinplate Company of India Limited (a Tata House Company) the company informed its share holders that the financial institutions and Banks have, as part of a programme for revival of the company agreed in principle to grant various package of reliefs, *viz.*, (i) to write-off ₹ 300.00 lakh; (ii) to convert ₹ 200.00 lakh into equity shares at par out of the accumulated interest on Term Loans as on 31.3.1984; (iii) to fund interest on interest-free basis; (iv) to charge concessional rate of interest on the balance accumulated interest; and (v) to defer repayment of Term Loans and funded interest...etc., (emphasis added) (See the Annual report of Tinplate Company of India Ltd. for the year 1984-85).

(b) In case of another company, the *Annual Report* observed:

The amalgamation of the former Ahmedabad Laxmi Cotton Mills Co. Ltd. (LCM) with your company was completed in April 1979. The new unit has been named as 'Ankur Textiles', a division of the Arvind Mills Ltd. .... You will find from the Profit & Loss account that no provision for taxation is made for 1979 as the accumulated loss of LCM has been set off against the profits of your company under Section 72A of the Income-Tax Act, 1961 resulting in tax saving of ₹ 148.90 lakh. (See the Annual Report of Arvind Mills Ltd for the Year 1979).

Not all companies openly admit the financial advantages from changes in fiscal or financial policies. The limited point to be observed is that the overall concessions to sick units may appear to be common for all but if one were to put together the house-wise gain of the concessions announced as a public policy, the main advantage would seem to have been taken by big business companies.

Table 4.5

Financing of the Project Cost of Companies Issuing Capital

(₹ crore)

S.No.	Source of Funding	Total Cost 1989-90	Percentage to Total Cost								
			1981-82	1982-83	1983-84	1984-85	1985-86	1986-87	1987-88	1988-89	1989-90
	(1)	(2)	(3)	(4)	(5)	(6)	(7)	(8)	(9)	(10)	(11)
1.	Reserves & Surplus	52	5.50	10.50	2.80	6.00	1.54	3.04	2.55	2.01	0.63
2.	Capital Market	6963	34.10	46.60	42.90	43.60	44.82	50.60	59.25	52.93	84.14
	(a) Share Capital	4283	18.90	24.70	38.60	35.70	38.76	28.47	47.53	22.80	51.75
	(b) Debentures	2681	15.20	21.90	4.30	7.90	6.06	22.21	11.72	30.14	32.39
3.	Borrowings	1231	59.90	41.40	51.90	48.00	51.79	44.37	37.24	44.08	14.88
	(a) FIs	754	29.50	24.50	34.70	24.70	33.00	28.95	22.92	17.95	9.11
	(b) Banks	158	19.30	7.80	5.00	5.60	5.67	7.53	4.41	4.02	1.91
	(c) UTI/LIC/GIC	25	2.50	2.20	2.10	5.60	1.80	0.96	2.05	0.55	0.30
	(d) State Govts/FI	14	2.60	2.80	4.10	1.70	2.18	1.73	1.41	0.52	0.17
	(e) Others	280	6.00	4.10	6.00	10.30	9.14	5.20	6.46	21.04	3.38
4.	Others	29	0.50	1.50	2.40	2.40	1.86	1.11	0.97	0.98	0.35
	Total	8275	100.00	100.00	100.00	100.00	100.00	100.00	100.00	100.00	100.00

Source: (1) Till 1984-85: P.K. Ahuja, "Capital raised from Public by Non-government, Non-financial Corporate Sector", *Company News and Notes*, September 1986.
(2) 1985-86 to 1989-90: Reserve Bank of India, *Report on Currency and Finance*, Vol. II, Statistical Statements (Various Issues).

companies;[20] and (iv) financial and technical collaborations with transnational corporation (TNCs).[21]

We have examined the shareholding structure of the top companies of the Indian private sector. Invariably, large companies happen to have substantial public sector holdings.[22] Out of the top 289 companies, each with a ₹ 10 crore assets/turnover, we could obtain the distribution schedules for 204 companies only. Out of the 204 companies, only 17 did not appear to have large house association. In the case of 98 companies, the stake of the public sector financial institutions in equity was more than 25 per cent.[23] Taken in terms of house association, the number of companies of the Birlas and the Tatas was the highest; Table 4.6 shows the distribution of the 204 companies according to the extent of risk capital of public sector institutions. In contrast to public sector holdings, the members of

20. It was a conscious and deliberate decision of the government to establish state financial corporation (SFCs) and state industrial development corporations (SIDCs). These were to promote local and new entrepreneurs. In reality, however, the joint sector (in which the SIDCs and central financial institutions hold majority or near majority holdings) has become a system of expansion of large politically influential houses. The risk is public and profits private. For the role played by the financial institutions, see, Ministry of Industrial Development Internal Trade and Company Affairs, Report of the Industrial Licensing Policy Inquiry Committee, 1969 (appendix IV in particular).

21. On top of the above is the process of takeovers, mergers and fairly rapid internationalisation of the Indian big business. The attitudes of the Indian industrialists are no more restrictive. Direct involvement of transnational corporations with Indian private big business is becoming a more important feature than it used to be. The character, mechanism and processes which enable fast expansion of private big business need to be underlined in some more detail.

22. During the controversy over the takeover bids of the ESCORTS and Delhi Cloth Mills (DCM) by Swraj Paul, it was brought out that the real issue was not with regard to whether Swraj Paul had more shares than the Nandas in the ESCORTS or the Shriram family in the DCM. The real voice, in determining as to who should have the management control rested with the public sector financial institutions. See Goyal, S.K. (n.d.). "Private Managements and Take-overs of Public-owned Companies: Some Issues for Debate", *Corporate Studies Group Working Papers*, Volume I.

23. According to the Companies Act, 1956, if more than 50 per cent of the shares of a company are held by another company, the former is treated as a subsidiary of the latter. In determining the association, the Foreign Exchange Regulation Act (FERA) has placed the cut-off point at 40 per cent; under the MRTP Act 1969 for Group of Inter-connected Undertakings, the criterion was one-third of the company equity (which is later modified to one-fourth); the RBI, for its survey of assets and liabilities had taken 25 per cent equity as an adequate basis to classify a company as foreign controlled. The Dunn & Bradstreet's Who Owns Whom classifies a company as an associate on the basis of 10 per cent share holding.

Table 4.6

Distribution of Companies of the Large Private Corporate Sector Houses according to the Share of Public Sector

S.No.	House	Percentage Share of Public Sector					Total
		0-5	5-10	10-25	25-50	50 and above	
	(1)	(2)	(3)	(4)	(5)	(6)	(7)
1.	Birla	1	1	7	6	1	16
2.	Tata	3	-	2	10	-	15
3.	JK Singhania	1	-	1	1	-	3
4.	Mafatlal	1	-	4	2	-	7
5.	Thapar	-	-	2	-	-	2
6.	Modi	-	1	1	3	-	5
7.	ACC	-	-	-	1	-	1
8.	Bangur	-	-	-	7	2	9
9.	Larsen & Toubro	-	-	-	1	-	1
10.	Sarabhai	-	-	-	1	-	1
11.	Bajaj	1	-	2	-	-	3
12.	ICI	1	-	1	2	-	4
13.	Mahindra	1	-	1	2	-	4
14.	Shriram	-	-	-	1	-	1
15.	Walchand	-	-	-	1	-	1
16.	Kirlsokar	1	-	1	3	-	5
17.	ITC	-	-	-	3	-	3
18.	TVS Iyengar	-	-	1	-	-	1
19.	Hindustan Lever	-	1	1	-	-	2
20.	Other Houses	7	4	25	24	6	66
21.	Foreign Controlled Cos.	4	4	18	11	-	37
22.	Other Companies	1	1	5	7	3	17
	Total	22	12	72	86	12	204

Note: This analysis is based on the Share Distribution Schedules obtained from the companies. For purposes of obtaining the public sector share shareholdings of insurance companies, term lending institutions, Unit Trust of India (UTI), nationalised banks, central and state governments and government companies have been clubbed together.

Source: Institute for Studies in Industrial Development (ISID), Delhi.

the boards of directors seem to have a very marginal stake. Inter-corporate investments, however, do seem to have an important place, even though in larger companies, the largest block of shares is still that of the public institutions or is distributed among a large number of small shareholders. Table 4.7 shows the distribution of a sample of companies as per the

Table 4.7

Distribution of Companies according to the Share of Directors and their Relatives

(No. of Companies)

	House	*Percentage of Shares held by Directors and Their Relatives in Company Equity*															
		<1	*1*	*2*	*3*	*4*	*5*	*6*	*7*	*8*	*9*	*10-15*	*15-20*	*20-25*	*>25*	*USP*	*Total*
	(1)	*(2)*	*(3)*	*(4)*	*(5)*	*(6)*	*(7)*	*(8)*	*(9)*	*(10)*	*(11)*	*(12)*	*(13)*	*(14)*	*(15)*	*(16)*	*(17)*
1	Birla	8	3	1	-	-	-	-	-	-	-	-	-	-	-	4	16
2	Tata	6	-	1	-	-	-	-	-	-	-	-	-	1	-	7	15
3	JK Singhania	1	-	-	-	1	-	-	-	1	-	-	-	-	-	-	3
4	Mafatlal	4	1	1	-	-	-	-	-	-	-	-	-	-	-	1	7
5	Thapar	2	-	-	-	-	-	-	-	-	-	-	-	-	-	-	2
6	Modi	-	-	-	-	1	1	-	-	-	-	-	-	-	1	2	5
7	ACC	1	-	-	-	-	-	-	-	-	-	-	-	-	-	-	1
8	Bangur	5	1	-	-	-	-	-	-	-	-	-	-	-	-	3	9
9	Larsen & Toubro	1	-	-	-	-	-	-	-	-	-	-	-	-	-	-	1
10	Sarabhai	1	-	-	-	-	-	-	-	-	-	-	-	-	-	-	1
11	Bajaj	-	-	-	1	-	-	-	-	-	1	-	-	-	-	1	3
12	ICI	1	-	-	-	-	-	-	-	-	-	-	-	-	-	3	4
13	Mahindra	1	-	1	-	-	-	-	-	-	-	-	-	-	-	2	4
14	Shriram	-	1	-	-	-	-	-	-	-	-	-	-	-	-	-	1
15	Walchand	1	-	-	-	-	-	-	-	-	-	-	-	-	-	-	1
16	Kirloskar	1	1	1	-	-	-	-	1	-	-	-	-	-	-	1	5
17	ITC	3	-	-	-	-	-	-	-	-	-	-	-	-	-	-	3
18	TVS Iyengar	-	-	-	-	-	-	-	-	-	-	-	-	-	-	1	1
19	Hindustan Lever	2	-	-	-	-	-	-	-	-	-	-	-	-	-	-	2
20	Other Houses	16	4	4	1	2	1	1	1	5	2	1	3	2	5	6	6
21	Foreign Control	23	1	1	-	-	-	1	-	-	-	-	-	-	-	11	37
22	Other Companies	5	-	1	-	-	-	-	-	-	-	-	-	-	2	9	17
	Total (1-22)	82	12	11	2	4	2	1	2	1	2	5	2	2	6	70	204

Note: For purposes of this tabulation, only those cases where the share-distribution schedules specifically mentioned the share of "Directors and their Relatives (as defined under the Companies Act, 1956)" were taken note of. Also footnote Note 23. USP = unspecified

Source: ISID, New Delhi.

extent of direct interest of the board of directors and their relatives in their respective companies.[24]

While scrutinising the data on the pattern of shareholdings in the large private companies, two main questions stare at the observers. Firstly, if the risk capital of the company managements and the other house companies is not very substantial, would it be logical to expect that the house managements would devote their full energies at maximising the profits of the company? And secondly, if there are substantial inter-corporate investments, what could be the motivation for such holdings? The main consideration could not be in terms of return on investments. There could, however, be other forms of gains. Unfortunately, information on these aspects is not easily available. It remains a grey area wanting further investigation. There are departmental reports but these are kept confidential. For individual scholars, however, there appears to be hardly much scope for inquiry.

Let us take a look at the broad pattern of shareholdings of the largest private sector enterprise in India, namely, the Tata Iron and Steel Company (TISCO). TISCO is under the management of Tatas. The direct interest of the Tata house can be placed at three per cent only in the risk capital of the TISCO[25] (see Figure 4.3). Could one expect the Tata directors to be working exclusively for the best interests of the TISCO in which their share was only 3 per cent, whereas nearly half of the profits would go to the public sector financial institutions and nationalised banks? Alternatively, one may ask: which interest group of shareholders in the TISCO would want the enterprise to have the maximum profits? The direct institutional stake is more than 45 per cent.[26] If one does not question the basic premise that business houses are in business and not in social service, one should

---

24. The information refers to a wide period (1980-1985). During this period, the pro forma prescribed by the stock exchanges was modified and in the modified format, the companies were required to specify the shares held by the board of directors and their relatives. While the earlier format contains the particulars of top 10 shareholders, the modified pro forma gives a full picture of the shareholding structure of the company in terms of different categories of shareholders. This information, thus, could be compiled only for 134 companies.

25. *op.cit* no. 21.

26. It may not be out of place to mention the cases of India Cements, Binny and National Rayon, where the financial institutions and the banks intervened to change the managements of the companies in view of the bad state of affairs prevailing in them.

not expect at the individual company level that profit maximisation would be the main motivation for company managements to stick to the management control of enterprises like the TISCO. In that case, the question would be as to why would a particular house be interested in continuing to hold on to the management? The obvious answer is that the management should be deriving economic and financial advantage in a variety of other forms than merely seeking to earn high dividends on their investments.

Figure 4.3

Shareholding Pattern of Tata Iron and Steel Co Ltd (As on March 31, 1988)

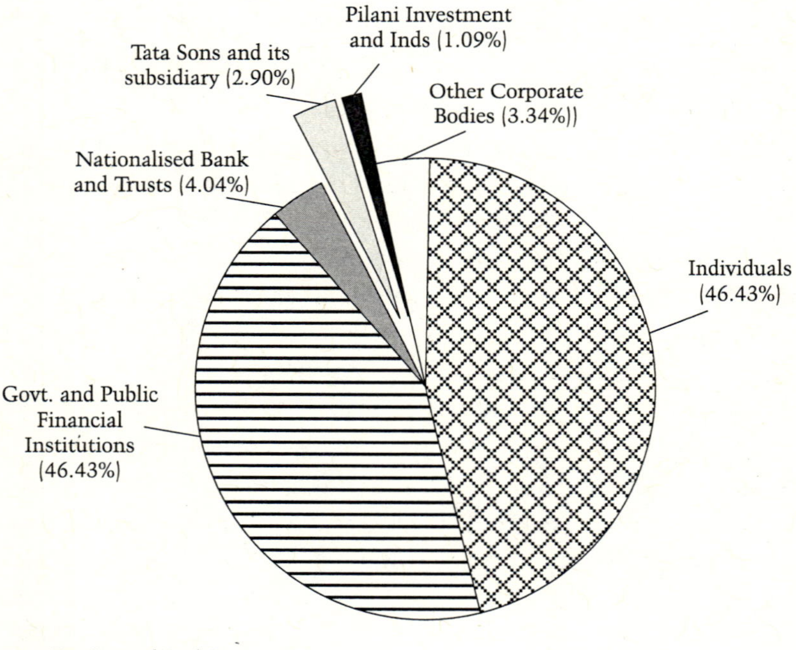

Source: Tata Iron and Steel Company.

The management control carries with it the power to take decisions for the company without having to face inquisitive auditing[27]—in contrast

27. The practice of having the same set of auditing firms for all the house companies is a common practice among the big houses in India. Even then very often one finds in company annual reports cursory statements like 'The auditors remarks are self-explanatory' in lieu of proper explanations by the board of directors in response to the qualifications noted by the auditors.

to public audit or parliamentary accountability that goes with government enterprises. The managements enjoy the authority to purchase raw materials, hire services, fix sales norms, make agreements, enter into collaborations, operate finances and have a vast discretionary power in company's day-to-day operations. The economic powers enjoyed by the management of large private corporations can be well visualised. The power exercised by the management of large corporations may be enormous by itself but the real advantage of such power can be optimised only if the same management has other associate network of companies. The potentiality of transferring resources from one company to another would naturally be a function of the company size and the number and variety of other associate companies.

High level of public sector holdings or substantial inter-corporate investments, when viewed for the house as a whole, do prove helpful in demonstrating that the public sector stake in the private big business houses is indeed much larger than what gets revealed, when each company is taken in isolation of the other. We have been seeking to obtain a macro view of the individual big business houses, as also to trace if there were some clear patterns in the intra-house investments. Such models and exercises could be attempted in terms of vertical industry linkages, inter-locking of company directorships or other key variables. On the basis of the inter-corporate investments, one finds three main types of house structures.

(a) Single-line structure—Wherein each associate company has substantial or main investments held by the apex company. The control mechanism in this set-up is obvious and undisputed. Most of the subsidiaries of foreign companies and closely held small groups would tend to fall in this category.[28]

(b) Joint Structure—In this type of structure there are clearly identifiable two or more centres. This could be an internal phenomenon of a house or it could take place in association with government or any other large enterprise.

---

28. The house of Shaw Wallace is an excellent example in this regard. Practically all the companies are subsidiaries of the parent company, namely, Shaw Wallace & Co. Ltd. The parent had as many as 28 subsidiaries in the year 1985. Another house which nearly falls in this category is that of United Breweries. United Breweries Ltd. the main company of the house had 30 subsidiaries operating in 1985.

(c) Inter-locking structure—Where house companies have a complicated network of inter-corporate investments. The investments are so managed that marginal resources from the apex house body enable the house to control large resources. For instance, company A may invest in company B and B in A by the same magnitude, implying no additional resources mobilisation, whereas the overall size of the house gets inflated. The same effect could be achieved through a chain of investments in a manner that without any additional resource mobilisation or additional input, the apparent stake or the management gets enlarged.[29]

Figures 4.4 and 4.5 show the basic patterns. There is, however, no hard and fast rule that a house must keep to one pattern as its unique

---

29. The practice of the inter-locking of investments had been well documented by Hazari in his study on concentration and ownership in the private corporate sector. See, Hazari, R.K. (1967). *The Structure of the Corporate Private Sector*. He had noted that "several circular chains of equity investments enable many companies to indirectly purchase their own shares" (p.56). The role played by inter-corporate investments was also studied by Vinod Singhania who observed that a significant proportion of inter-corporate investments is controlled by the industrial companies (see Singhania, Vinod K. (1980). *Economic Concentration Though Inter-Corporate Investments*. Himalaya. A few specific examples might make the point clearer. For instance, Kirloskar Brothers Ltd. held 74,994 shares of ₹ 10 each in Kirloskar Electric Co. Ltd. In its turn, Kirloskar Electric Co. held 50,00 shares of ₹ 10 each in Kirloskar Brothers in 1984 (see annual reports of the respective companies for the year 1984).

Interestingly enough, in its annual report for the year 1982-83, TISCO informed its shareholders that it had taken up a part of the shares being offered by Tata Sons of Tata Industries Ltd. According to the company:

Tata Industries Ltd. proposed to enlarge the scope of their activities and were interested in promoting new projects which would be implemented by them jointly with other Tata Companies. With this objective and with a view to enabling other Tata Companies to participate in such new activities. Tata Sons Limited, the holding Company of Tata Industries Ltd decided to offer a part of their holding in Tata Industries Ltd to various companies.

Thus while Tata Sons would get the money from companies in which share of the house interest is very little, Tata Sons would still be able to control Tata Industries through the public companies. In a sense, it would get back at least a part of investment in these publicly owned companies via the sale of Tata Industries shares for further expansion of its activities.

Another case of interest is of the three erstwhile FERA companies which had diluted their foreign equity to avail of the liberal licensing policies. Mcleod Russel, Makum Tea and Namdang Tea companies came to an understanding to issue some shares of each of the companies to the remaining two. It is observed that the net transaction among them would be zero, while this would effectively give the foreign shareholder control on each of the three companies.

entity. In fact, in actual business environment, while there are dominant variants, there can be traces of each pattern present. It appears that the house structures very quickly adopt themselves to demands placed by expansion and family resources. The structures are also considerably influenced by the nature of the regulatory mechanism, the system of concessions, subsidies and preferences and the agility and extent to which the administrative system is able to discover the implications of business practices by structural re-organisation.

The attempt here is not to elaborate on the typology of Indian house structures. The reference to the structures was brought in to show that in terms of risk capital, involvement of public sector financial institutions is in reality much higher than what gets reflected when each company of a house is taken in isolation. The inter-corporate investments get canceled out, but the investment of the financial institutions keeps accumulating. If one were to conduct an intensive inquiry into the distribution of equity shares of the industrial houses, one may discover that the real stake of the managements, families, closely held companies, private trusts, etc., is marginal, whereas they do happen to enjoy command over vast financial and other resources of the society.

The process of rapid expansion of the big houses has been assisted in a meaningful manner by financial and technical collaborations. For obvious reasons, transnational corporations would prefer to join in establishing joint projects with large companies and the houses which command control over large economic resources enjoy high status as also have capabilities to obtain political and administrative patronage. International monopoly capital would only join hands with entrepreneurs who are at least constituents of the national monopoly capital.[30] The size of the TNC-Indian big business venture has to be large; it cannot be small scale. Take the establishment of Tata Engineering Locomotive Company (TELCO). It is a joint venture of the Tatas and the Daimler-Benz; Voltas was formed by Volkart Brothers and the Tatas; and Associated Bearing a joint venture of the Tatas and Atkiebolaget Svenska Kullagerfabriken of Sweden. One needs hardly mention the Tata-Burroughs, Tata-Finlay, Tata-Yodogawa, Tata-Robins-Fraser, etc. In case of Birlas, the Hindustan

30. Goyal, S.K. (n.d.). *Impact of Foreign Subsidiaries on India's Balance of Payments*. A study conducted for the UNCTC-ESCAP. p.22.

Figure 4.4

Single-line Structure

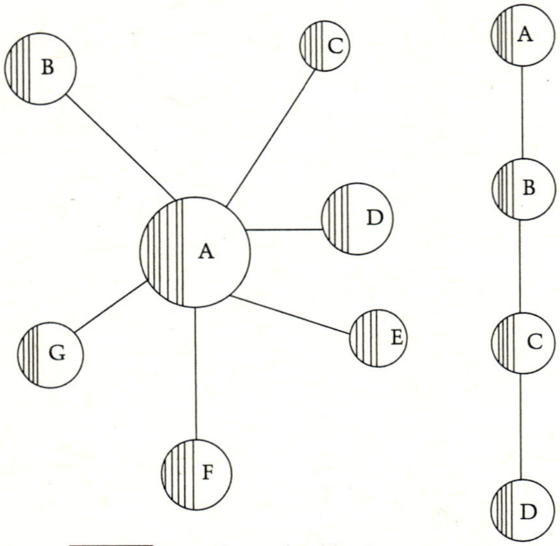

Share of Public Sector

Figure 4.5

Joint Structure

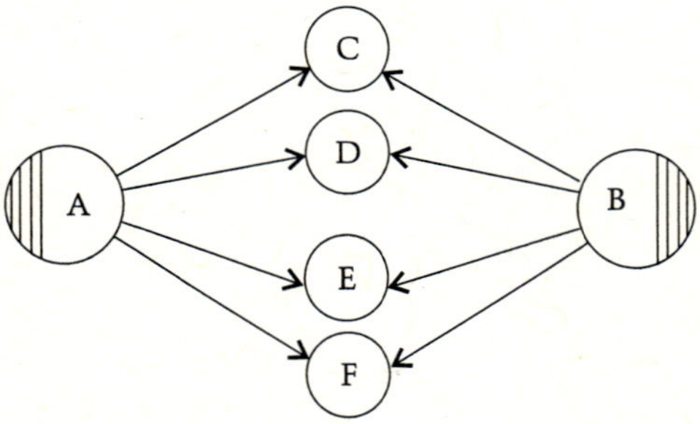

Inter-locking Structure

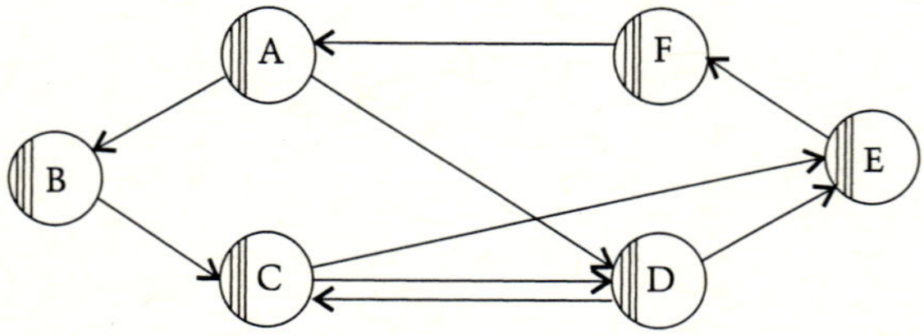

Share of Public Sector

Aluminum came up with financial collaboration of Kaiser Aluminum and Chemical Company of the USA, Zuari Agro Chemicals with Armour Co. of the USA and Century Enka with AKZO of the Netherlands. Birla-Yamaha is one of the recent instances.

Many of the transnationals which had been operating as single companies have now become big houses with multiple associates and subsidiaries. The ICI, Hindustan Lever, ITC, Brooke Bond, GEC and Philips are the well-known instances. Their growth too has been phenomenal.

II

In Part I, an effort was made to sketch out the structural and control aspects of the Indian private corporate sector. These may be treated as background to what follows. It has been shown that during the past couple of decades, there has been a reasonably good growth of the Indian private corporate sector; the growth rate has, however, been faster with the larger companies and a phenomenal one with the top business houses. Secondly, the evidence provided showed that the process of growth in private corporate sector has come about with substantial support of the public sector financial institutions. In an economy where financial institutions including insurance companies and commercial banks happen to be in the government/public sector, the dependence of the private corporations on loans and other banking support is only too obvious to deserve more discussion. Therefore, there was no need to specifically refer to the non-risk financial support. The presentation, by choice, illustrated the extent of risk capital provided by the public sector financial institutions. An attempt was also made to present the mechanism of fast construction (or emergence) of massive conglomerates, generally known as business houses in India. The four clearly identifiable factors responsible for the rapid expansion in the numbers and the size of big business house phenomenon are:

(a) The system of inter-corporate investments.

(b) The wide participation of public sector financial institutions in the risk capital.

(c) The growing inter-locking and business collaborations of transnational corporations and large private companies.

(d) The entry of state-level corporations in establishing 'joint sector' projects in which the obtaining of industrial licences, foreign collaborations, financial and other infrastructural support is organised by the state governments, but the management is left to the private co-promoter/private company which in larger projects happens to be an associate company of one or the other big business houses.

The above four factors have been the major contributors. But, one should in no way discount the role of a variety of economic policies in their true content and implementation than the original intentions and the changed nature of public concerns—irrespective of the reasons which might have been responsible for the new idiom and the socioeconomic environment.

In terms of the profitability criterion, the private corporate sector, as a whole, does not give an impressive account of itself. The phenomenon of sickness is not only confined to one industry, namely, textiles; it is related to mismanagements and a variety of other manipulative practices.[31] It would, however, be a wholly misplaced conclusion to say that there are no success stories of the private entrepreneurs or companies under large house managements having a sound and profitable track record of financial performance. For instance, the rise of the Reliance has been meteoric. It is not uncommon to come across nationwide publicity campaigns showing the annual rate of return on investments as high as 70 per cent or more by some of the big business-controlled companies. There are certainly a few 'blue chips' in the Indian share market.

The fast expanding companies—an interesting aspect of the Indian private sector's high growth—have among them those enterprises that have been at the 'zero level' of tax obligations.[32] Even when there were profits

31. According to a study by the RBI, of the 378 sick units examined, more than half were turned sick either due to mismanagement or management deficiencies or infighting among the persons controlling the units.

32. Reliance Industries Ltd., for instance, has not provided for any corporate tax in its annual accounts during the period 1979-1985, whereas TELCO did the same during 1977-1983. For the subsequent years 1983-84, 1984-85 and 1985-86 tax provided for by TELCO amounted to only 10.86, 14.42 and 7.63 per cent respectively of the respective year's profit before tax (see: *Bombay Stock Exchange Official Directory*, 1986, loose leafs).

thanks to the structure of the Indian fiscal system, there is little obligation to make payments as corporate tax. There are a variety of tax exemptions, incentives, subsidies, concessions and these permit higher returns to shareholders (as dividends and appreciation of value of shares).[33] The Indian capital market being a limited one, the gains of such corporations though appear to be shared by large many in numbers, in reality, the lion's share of the financial gain goes to a small section of the population and what is called the category of "closely held and associate companies, relatives and friends."[34]

If one looks at the fast expanding and high-return-to-shareholder companies, one may find that invariably the impressive business performance is a projection of the 'wizardly' capabilities of a mastermind behind such companies and the capacities of the companies' tax planners rather than the contributions of these corporations in the area of cost reduction, productivity, technological breakthroughs or internal company reforms and more professionalism in management. To maximise the business advantage, one has to identify the technical loopholes in tax laws and adjust the company financial statements in the optimal mix and exercise pressure through lobbying for special concessions and exemptions which would enable them to expand. There can be two view points with

33. A number of incentives are provided if the companies undertake to export, set up manufacturing units in industrially backward areas, participate in rural development programmes or invest in R&D etc. In government, strangely enough, there is no system to quantify the precise loss of revenue to the state due to these concessions and exemptions. For example, assuming a uniform tax rate of 55 per cent on corporate profits, it comes out that the exchequer had forgone nearly ₹ 600 crore during the three-year period 1982-83, 1983-84 and 1984-85 from the top 535 companies alone. Interestingly enough, the largest among these were paying a lower percentage of their profits as corporate tax than smaller companies. The tax provision as a percentage of profit before tax in case of 13 companies with ₹ 25 crore and more of PUC works out to be 18.4, 21.1 and 18.3 per cent for the years 1982-83, 1983-84 and 1984-85 respectively when compared to the average rates of 35.1, 43.6 and 41.2 per cent, respectively for the total (based on the information provided in "Finances of Large Public Limited Companies, 1984-85", *RBI Bulletin*, December 1985). It also needs to be mentioned that in practice the tax figures reported in company annual reports turn out to be much larger when compared with the figures submitted to the tax authorities. The extent of loss to the exchequer would indeed be higher than the above estimate.

34. The phenomenon of insider trading is only too well known to be elaborated here. Those who have the knowledge of the working of the company and those who are going to take decisions for the company can easily pass on the information to relatives or use dummies to get underhand advantage from the market.

regard to high profitability and zero or low tax obligations. One, that these corporate bodies tune their investments and corporate decisions exactly in the manner and style in which the government wants them. These companies might appear to have accepted the norms and priorities of the state and, by doing so, are able to deliver high return on the share holders' investments. If so, the managements of these companies would argue, why should there be an accusing finger raised towards them? And on the other hand, a view could be that policy makers were responsive and considerate to adopt policies, in response to the representations from certain influential private entrepreneurs, or the public sector financial institutions were able to influence the process of decision making in government in a manner that specific fiscal measures got evolved to protect and promote interests of the public sector financial institutions. Whatever may be the reason, there can be no denying of the hard reality that a good number of enterprises grew fast and the public exchequer made a substantial contribution to their growth.

At the macro-level, one will need to take a view on such a phenomenal growth of the few. As a public policy, the objective can never be to assist growth of a few and this too for all times to come. There would have to be re-adjustments. It is also not that a financial wizard can play the same game life long. Economic history of business is full of instances of rise of private giants as also of crashes and nosedives. One does not wish to be a 'kill joy' for individuals who put stakes at the stock exchange; there is, however, a need in India to raise questions in terms of the future and the concerns for a stable process of industrialisation. In an advanced and capitalist society like the USA, there could be a view that as long as there is good reward for investors in the corporations, there was hardly an issue for public concern. If a few companies got liquidated or closed down, it did not matter. While such could be a quick response regarding the experiences of an industrially advanced capitalist country, it cannot also be denied that threat to automobile manufacturers and individual large companies in electronics, even in the recent past, did become a matter of government and public concern in the USA. In a developing country like India, apart from the fact that the large private corporate sector (comprising big business and large-sized companies) has grown primarily at public cost and with a variety of direct and indirect support, the significance of the private large enterprises is such that the future of these cannot be left at the total discretion of private interests.

Projecting one's vision into the future, on the basis of the experience in India and abroad, it does appear to us that there is bound to be a process of disintegration of the family-based private conglomerates.[35] The Indian big business houses are family and individual based—more in terms of control and coordination and less in risk sharing. While the family's hold on individual closely held companies would certainly continue, the conglomerates (business houses) with wide dispersal of shares, large share holdings of public financial institutions and heavy dependence on the inter-corporate investments would have to break down. The disintegration may some time be a result of internal contradictions of the family-based business houses or at other times due to outside policy interventions. This may start happening much earlier than many would expect today. One may be wrong on timings but the process is an inevitable one. For policy makers, the challenge is not in avoiding the discharge of their public obligations, by drawing themselves into a shell. On the contrary, they should be able to foresee the inevitable and start exploring the alternative models in national interest.

In more ways than one, large private enterprises should be as much a matter of concern for the government as the government sector corporations. This is necessary for ensuring a coordinated pattern of investments and asset utilisation in the broad framework of planned socioeconomic development in India. If there is need to acquire and adopt modern scientific technologies in production processes, there is equally, and probably, a greater need to revise the old concepts, managerial and control structures in managements and control mechanisms. For evolving of such an approach, the basic pre-requisite lies in having an objective assessment

35. A number of changes have been happening in the large private sector which have not received much attention. While new Houses like Reliance, Nagarjuna, Mallyas, Jhawars, TCI, Ruia Bros and Piramals are emerging some of the older ones like Martin Burn, Kamanis, Andrew Yule, China, etc., have practically disappeared. Moreover, houses like Wallace, EID Parry and Gillanders Arbuthnot have been absorbed in other houses. Infighting in a few of the industrial families comes into the open and often talked about. The convulsions the Sarabhai House is going through are really sad.

of the realities of the corporate sector to obtain an understanding of the true nature, main characteristics, motivations, the formal and informal control structures and other business practices.

Let us now take a few of the specific policy issues which are currently being debated. There is a view, widely shared by many in the policy-making circles, that the Indian economy has been subjected, for too long a period, to excessive regulations and physical controls. In specific, the system of industrial licensing has proved to be counter productive. Therefore, under what has generally been known as new economic policy, the coverage of the licensing system has been reduced in a substantial manner. The assumption is that with removal of restrictions on new investments, there would be an all round improvement in the economic situation. Investments would pick up and the country would witness a high rate of growth.

The results of such a policy have already started surfacing. There is growth but it is confined to a small section. The furtherance of concentration in the private corporate sector is one inevitable consequence. The plea for enabling the industry to harness economies of scale along with cost reduction through adoption of more efficient technologies was well argued but there does not appear to be any evidence of such a process showing itself in price reduction for consumers—except, however, for computers, televisions, stereos and some varieties of other electronics and elite consumer items in which the prices have been substantially reduced, though this has not been due to the efforts of the Indian manufacturers. The international prices of these goods have crashed, and since import component in these products has been high, this cannot be described as a miracle. In addition to this, liberal imports and reduction in excise and other taxes for such commodities were bound to result in a downward trend in the prices.

We are conscious that there is little need to put forth a fresh defence for industrial licensing system.[36] It may, however, be necessary to bring

36. The author's association with the Industrial Licensing Policy Inquiry Committee (ILPIC) during 1967 and 1969 provided an opportunity to study and learn the operation of the regulatory systems with respect to the Indian corporate sector. Subsequently, the studies at the Corporate Studies Group have confirmed that without hard choices and effective implementation, the system cannot be expected to deliver results.

out one industrial reality not very well known or shared. First, a survey of industrial capacities of the private sector for the year 1979-80 showed that the sector had large under-utilised capacities—both as installed to licensed and production to installed ratios.[37] It would be surprising to note that even the large houses have a number of unutilised licences (see Table 4.8). While there was a very low rate of capacity utilisation in the private industry as a whole, there were some products in which the private industrialists had been engaged in open violations of the official licensing policy. The licensing violations, it so happened, were more by the foreign-controlled companies and companies belonging to big business houses than by the rest of the private corporate sector. An analysis of the licensing violations also showed that the violations were concentrated in such areas which happened to have been ear-marked for development in the cottage and small-scale sectors. Above all, it was also observed that no single case had been brought to book inspite of repeated references to specific cases of violations of the regulatory legislation, in reports of public inquiries, parliamentary debates, press reports and representations from small-scale industry associations.[38] Instead, the government preferred to regularise the unauthorised capacities through capacity re-endorsement schemes.[39]

---

37. Corporate Studies Group, *Functioning of Industrial Licensing System: A Report*. Indian Institute of Public Administration (*mimeo*), 1983.

38. Many of the big business companies and TNCs were not only violating licensing norms with regard to products reserved for the small-scale sector, but also set up small-scale units to take advantage of concessions and facilities meant for the small sector. For an account of the ways in which such benefits were being availed by the large sector, see: Goyal, S.K., K.S. Chalapati Rao and Nagesh Kumar (1984). "Small Scale Sector and Big Business". Indian Institute of Public Administration (*mimeo*).

39. Replies to Parliament Questions in 1983-84 provide details on capacity re-endorsement cases in the drug industry. Of the 37 cases involving bulk drugs, in 25 cases, the reported re-endorsed capacity exceeded the then existing licensed capacity by over 100 per cent. Three companies, Organon India, Wyeth Labs and Searle Indian, were allowed to regularise capacity for bulk drugs which was more than 1000 per cent over the licensed capacity. See: Goyal S.K. (n.d.). "A Preliminary Survey of Excess Industrial Capacities with the Indian Corporate Sector", *Corporate Studies Group Working Papers*, Volume I, for an analysis of the capacity re-endorsement policy introduced in 1980.

Table 4.8

Distribution of Licences held by the Top 20 Industrial Houses according to the Extent of Utilisation (Production to Licensed)

S.No.	Industrial Houses Licences Studied	No. of Licences in Utilisation Range				Total
		Zero (%)	1-25 (%)	25-60 (%)	60-100 (%)	
	(1)	(2)	(3)	(4)	(5)	(6)
1.	Birla	50 (22.7)	38 (17.3)	39 (17.7)	52 (23.6)	220 (100.0)
2.	Tata	57 (28.8)	40 (20.1)	51 (25.8)	31 (15.7)	198 (100.0)
3.	Mafatlal	5 (14.3)	11 (31.4)	8 (22.8)	8 (22.8)	35 (100.0)
4.	J.K. Singhania	7 (20.0)	10 (28.6)	6 (17.1)	7 (20.0)	35 (100.0)
5.	Thapar	9 (20.9)	7 (16.3)	9 (20.9)	11 (25.6)	43 (100.0)
6.	Sarabhai	2 (28.6)	0 (0.0)	1 (14.3)	4 (57.1)	7 (100.0)
7.	Bangur	7 (24.1)	4 (13.8)	10 (34.5)	5 (17.2)	29 (100.0)
8.	ICI	1 (4.2)	4 (16.7)	4 (16.7)	10 (41.7)	24 (100.0)
9.	ACC	4 (40.0)	3 (30.0)	1 (10.0)	2 (20.0)	10 (100.0)
10.	Shri Ram	11 (25.0)	11 (25.0)	3 (6.8)	13 (29.5)	44 (100.0)
11.	Kirloskar	19 (22.6)	36 (42.9)	18 (21.4)	9 (10.7)	84 (100.0)
12.	Hindustan Lever	0 (0.0)	4 (30.8)	0 (0.0)	1 (7.7)	13 (100.0)
13.	Larsen & Toubro	8 (18.6)	16 (37.2)	7 (16.3)	9 (20.9)	43 (100.0)
14.	Modi	3 (13.6)	1 (4.6)	4 (18.2)	10 (45.5)	22 (100.0)
15.	Chowgule	1 (33.3)	1 (33.3)	0 (0.0)	1 (33.3)	3 (100.0)
16.	Bajaj	6 (18.8)	11 (34.4)	2 (6.3)	11 (34.4)	32 (100.0)
17.	Lalbhai	6 (27.3)	3 (13.6)	7 (31.8)	4 (18.2)	22 (100.0)

Note: 1. The Tin Plate Co. of (I) Ltd. which is inter-connected with companies both of Oil India and Tata Houses is included in the House of Tatas. No company belonging to Scindia and Bhiwandiwala Houses is represented in the Survey of Company Annual Reports for the period 1979-80.

2. Figures in brackets are percentages calculated with respect to the house totals.

Source: The Corporate Studies Group, *Functioning of Industrial Licensing System: A Report*, January 1983.

Existence of large unutilised industrial capacities is well recognised by the policy makers. In fact, the criticism, a valid one indeed, has been that due to low capacity utilisation, the Indian industry has been suffering from high production costs. If this was believed to be the case, one would have thought that all out efforts would be made to utilise the already sunk national capital and not to give more freedom to the industrialists for new and additional capacities. The licensing system could not be taken as the villain. There is, if any, a case for a more rigorous implementation of public policies and for making the regulatory mechanisms more effective. The licensing relaxations, a component of the liberalisation package, would in any case have little meaning for those who already hold licences and have unutilised capacities. The real advantage, however, would be reaped by those who would otherwise have been penalised for economic violations by way of entry or expansion of capacities reserved, as a national economic policy, for public sector, or small and cottage industries. Under the situation, delicensing is likely to hurt those who had some protection under the reservation mechanism.

In this regard, it is suggested that physical controls can be substituted by fiscal and monetary policies. This could certainly be an alternative if India had a delivery system that could reach those who were not well versed with the intricacies of law and if the administrative system could be assured to be as responsive for the small as it has been for the influential and the rich. In any case, fiscal and monetary systems function well when information and access to market mechanism is free and unrestricted. The plea for substitution of physical controls by fiscal controls also does not take note of the fact that in an economy, ridden with wide disparities, the reliance on financial instruments has serious limitations.

The policy-making circles in India, generally believed, have been discussing the need for initiation of a process which has come to be known as 'privatisation' of government enterprises. The suggestion is based on the assumption that public sector managements cannot demonstrate dynamism and foresight that make the private business perform. Many of the public enterprises in India have been running under losses, have low capacity utilisation and high production costs due to overstaffing and wastages. These features, it is argued, are inevitable when bureaucratic systems are installed in enterprises which need to be run on business principles. In this regard, we wish to make only these brief observations. The question of financial returns and profits in the Indian public sector has never been very clear. If highest financial returns is to be the motivation, then why call it a public sector? One thought that public sector owed its origin to public concerns, especially in a society ridden with extreme disparities in ownership of wealth and incomes. But quite apart from the purpose and objectives, one does not understand how commercial enterprises operating in a monopoly and near monopoly market structure can remain loss making. Of course, these enterprises would have to be given the freedom to fix prices on the principle of what the market can take. Loss-making public enterprises can overnight be made into high profit-yielding enterprises only if the government was ready to take hard decisions on its own. Privatisation only shifts the burden to take hard decisions.[40] The process of privatisation cannot bring-in efficiency by itself. But quite apart from this, as outlined earlier, is not the Indian large private sector indeed a 'privatised sector' of the Indian economy? It is true that government enterprises have been running under losses. What one should ask is if it is inherent in the very nature of these enterprises that these have to make losses or the public enterprises make losses because the government does not wish to give them the autonomy that company managements enjoy in the private sector.

Another important component of the policies towards liberalisation of the economy has been in the overall approach to liberalised imports and a new thrust on stepping up of exports. There is also the argument for encouraging big business and especially the TNCs to achieve this end. One cannot go into the variety of assumptions that the policy makers have made. We shall only highlight some aspects of the export performance of the large houses and foreign-controlled companies.

The need to raise the level of exports from India has for long been assigned a priority. A variety of fiscal and monetary concessions are available to exporters from India. In addition to the financial advantages, in the recent past, the foreign trade rules have been simplified and regulatory provisions set aside. As a consequence of the efforts made at promotion of Indian exports, it is believed that the country would emerge as an important

---

40. Goyal S.K. (1985). "Privatisation of Public Enterprises: Some Issues for Debate", Paper presented in *IPE-London Business School International Seminar on Public Enterprise Policy in the Eighties*. February 11-14. Hyderabad.

exporter in the world market. Such an expectation does not appear to be well justified. The relative position of india in the world exports has not changed for the better.[41] The export-related issues need to be examined in more detail. At the present moment, we wish to draw attention to the performance of the large private corporate sector. This may be specially relevant as the new thrust towards export promotion places a considerable faith on the capacity of large enterprises to deliver goods. The data for the largest 400 companies of the private sector, for which information is available for 1975-76 and 1983-84, would suggest that:

(a) Between the period 1975-76 and 1983-84, the value of exports by them rose from ₹ 493 crore to ₹ 803 crore i.e., growth rate of nearly 7.85 per cent per annum.

(b) During the same period, the imports of these companies, however, rose from ₹ 358 crore to ₹ 1196 crore, i.e., an annual growth rate of 29.26 per cent.

(c) In view of higher rate of increase in imports as compared to exports, the net foreign exchange outflow due to their trade and other operations was ₹ 462 crore during 1983-84 as against ₹ 93 crore in 1976.

(d) If one takes the value of exports as a percentage of the overall turn-over, one finds that the Indian large private sector is far less export oriented in 1983-84 than in 1975-76 (see Table 4.9).

(e) Transnational corporations operating in India are increasingly looking towards domestic market for expansion.[42]

(f) The pattern of foreign currency utilisation for 1976 and 1984 would reveal the continuation of 'raw materials' as the single most important item of imports.

---

41. In 1960, the country's share in total world export stood at 1.04 per cent. This declined to 0.42 per cent in 1970 and by 1980, it had further dipped to 0.04 per cent (see, Ministry of Commerce (1984). *Report of the Committee on Trade Policies*. Dec., p. 100).

42. Of the 400 companies for which information was available for 1975-76 and 1983-84, 104 were initially registered under the Foreign Exchange Regulation Act, 1973. While in 1975-76 the percentage of exports in sales turnover was 6.03, it had declined to 5.10 in 1983-84.

Table 4.9

Distribution of Companies according to Export Intensity (1976-1984)

(No. of Companies)

S.No	Percentage Range	1975-76	1983-84
	(1)	(2)	(3)
1.	0	108	135
2.	0-2.5	110	144
3.	2.5-5.0	55	43
4.	5.0-10.0	65	47
5.	10.0-15.0	19	10
6.	15.0-25.0	28	15
7.	25.0-40.0	9	2
8.	40.0-50.0	1	3
9.	50.0 and above	5	1
	Total	400	400

Source: Based on an analysis of the foreign exchange utilisation data of companies having PUC of ₹ 1.00 crore or more in 1983-84.

Here the attempt is not to argue that exports should not be promoted. The question being raised is: At what cost and by whom? Does India need to follow the export strategy which does not add to the net earning capabilities on the one hand and leads the economy towards higher concentration on the other? One needs to examine and debate such live issues having long-term implications.

A few policy alternatives with regard to the Indian private corporate sector may be put forth for discussion. The basic assumptions underlying these and which emanated from the above presentation are:

(a) The large private corporate sector has acquired a significant place in the Indian economy.

(b) Because of its size and place in the Indian economic system, any distortions in the sector would have high economic costs.

(c) If one goes by the extent of direct and indirect share in the equity in individual companies as also in the privately managed and controlled house companies, public sector financial institutions taken together are the single largest shareholders. In fact, the macro picture would reveal that the share of the public sector financial institutions is a multiple of the net risk borne by those who happen to enjoy management control.

(d) The old and traditional systems of control and managements need to reform their structures and bring in more rational system of social accountability than what has so far been true.

(e) There is a need for the investment pattern to be governed by national plan priorities than by considerations of the effective market demand.

(f) There is a need to review the very logic, merits and demerits of the traditional family based business house concept.

(g) There could be serious long term implications of the trends which seem to suggest that India was witnessing a rapid growth in concentration of productive wealth in a few private hands; and these trends have been partly due to the very nature of the economic system and partly as a result of the self assigned "on lookers" role by the public bodies; and

(h) That there is a need to have more critical investigations and empirical verification as input for the process of public policy evolution.

In view of the above mentioned assumption, one would put forth the following as policy alternatives:

(a) Let there be a recognition that all large sized corporate entities, irrespective of the fact of today's classification as 'private sector' and 'public sector' be declared as constituents of sector of national importance.

(b) There should be intensive monitoring of these companies with a view to bring in professional managements.

(c) An industry-wise review should be done with regard to size, technology, location and the desired production basket. The plan could examine mergers, or break-ups, as per technology requirements and weed out high cost, un-economic and low technology units.

(d) The nationally important sector companies should be given clearly defined specific objectives on which the performance of the managements would be reviewed periodically.

(e) There should be public norms which provide for incentives and penalties to those involved at different levels in these large-sized corporations.

(f) In view of the national requirements of earning adequate foreign exchange, there should be an export plan for each sector.

These proposals are only by way of outlining of an approach. One cannot expect readymade answers for all the questions which may arise while having a serious view of the new approach.

Annexure A-4.1

Illustrative List of Joint Sector Companies Promoted by State Industrial Development Corporations in Association with the Large Industrial Houses

S.No.	Name of Joint Sector	Name of the Promotor	House Association	State
	(1)	(2)	(3)	(4)
1.	WEBEL Jyoti Power Electronics Ltd.	Jyoti Ltd.	Amin R K	West Bengal
2.	Andhra Petrochemicals Ltd.	Andhra Sugars Ltd.	Andhra Sugars	Andhra Pradesh
3.	Madhya Pradesh Fibres Ltd.	Apeejay-Surrendra Group	Apeejay	Madhya Pradesh
4.	Automotive Castings Ltd.	Ashok Leyland Ltd.	Ashok Leyland/FCC	Tamil Nadu
5.	Maharastra Scooters Ltd.	Bajaj Auto Ltd.	Bajaj	Maharashtra
6.	Girnar Scooters	Bajaj Auto Ltd.	Bajaj	Gujarat
7.	Mysore Petrochemicals Ltd.	Shekavati Invst. Corpn. Ltd.	Bangur	Karnataka
8.	Uptron Shreetronix Ltd.	Amalgamated Devt. Ltd.	Bangur	Uttar Pradesh (1)
9.	West Bengal Pulpwood Devt.	Titagarh Paper Mills Co. Ltd.	Bangur	West Bengal
10.	Bihar Caustics & Chemicals Ltd.	1. Gwalior Rayon Silk Mfg. & Wvg. Co. Ltd. 2. Hindustan Aluminium Corpn. Ltd. 3. Pilani Invt. Corpn. Ltd.	Birla	Bihar
11.	Gujarat Instruments Ltd.	Taylor Instrument Co (I) Ltd.	Birla	Gujarat
12.	Nicco Orissa Ltd.	National Insulated Cable Co.	Birla	Orissa
13.	Tamil Nadu Flourine & Allied Chemicals Ltd.	1. Gwalior Rayon Silk Mfg. & Wvg. Co. Ltd. 2. Hindustan Aluminium Corpn. Ltd. 3. Pilani Invt. Corpn. Ltd.	Birla	Tamil Nadu

contd...

...contd...

S.No.	*Name of Joint Sector*	*Name of the Promotor*	*House Association*	*State*
	(1)	*(2)*	*(3)*	*(4)*
14.	Malabar Building Products Ltd.	Hyderabad Industries Ltd.	Birla	Kerala
15.	West Bengal Alloy Steel Ltd.	Texmaco Ltd.	Birla	West Bengal
16.	Vindhya Telelinks Ltd.	Universal Cables Ltd.	Birla	Madhya Pradesh
17.	Western India Sponge Iron Co.	Gwalior Rayon Silk Mfg. & Wvg. Co. Ltd.	Birla	Maharashtra
18.	Krishna Heavy Chemicals Ltd.	Birla Eastern Ltd.	Birla	Andhra Pradesh
19.	Webel Texmaco Electronics Ltd.	Texmaco Ltd.	Birla	West Bengal (2)
20.	Eastern Organics Ltd.	Hindustan Heavy Chemicals Ltd.	Birla	
21.	General Synthetic Corpn. Ltd.	Birla Eastern Ltd.	Birla	West Bengal
22.	Zenith Fibres Ltd.	Birla Eastern Ltd.	Birla	West Bengal
23.	Neptune Papers Ltd.	1. Sirpur Paper Mills Ltd. 2. CentralIndiaInds. Ltd. 3. Vimal Invts. Ltd.	Birla	West Bengal
24.	Karnataka Pulpwood Ltd.	Gwalior Rayon Silk Mfg. & Wvg. Co. Ltd.	Birla	Karnataka
25.	Indo-Gulf Fertilizers & Chemicals Corpn Ltd.	1. Gwalior Rayon Silk Mfg. & Wvg. Co. Ltd. 2. Hindustan Aluminium Corpn. Ltd. 3. Indian Rayon Corpn. Ltd.	Birla	Uttar Pradesh
26.	Southern Petrochemical Industries Corpn. Ltd.	Chidambaram M A	Chidambaram M A	Tamil Nadu
27.	Southern Agrifurane Inds. Ltd.	Chidambaram M A	Chidambaram M A	Tamil Nadu
28.	Tamil Nadu Petroproducts Ltd.	Southern Petrochemical Inds. Corpn. Ltd	Chidambaram M A	Tamil Nadu

contd...

...contd...

S.No.	Name of Joint Sector	Name of the Promotor	House Association	State
	(1)	(2)	(3)	(4)
29.	Tuticorin Alkali Chmls & Fertilizers Ltd.	Southern Petrochemical Inds. Corpn. Ltd.	Chidambaram M A	Tamil Nadu
30.	Tamil Nadu Pearls Pvt. Ltd.	Southern Petrochemical Inds. Corpn. Ltd.	Chidambaram M A	Tamil Nadu
31.	Mandovi Pellets Ltd.	Chowgule & Co. Ltd.	Chowgule	Goa (3)
32.	Gujarat Heavy Chemicals Ltd.	Golden Tobacco Co. Ltd.	Dalmia J	Gujarat
33.	J & K Cigarettes Ltd.	Golden Tobacco Co. Ltd.	Dalmia J	Jammu & Kashmir
34.	North Eastern Tobacco Co. Ltd.	Golden Trading Co., Bombay	Dalmia J	Assam
35.	Webstar Ltd.	Dunlop India Ltd.	FCC	West Bengal
36.	Premier Morarji Chemicals Co. Ltd.	Premier Enterprises Pvt. Ltd.	Dharamsi Morarji Kerala	
37.	Gujarat Drugs & Chemicals Ltd.	Infar India Ltd.	Dunlop/FCC	Gujarat
38.	Punjab Anand Lamp Inds. Ltd.	N.V. Philips, Netherlands,	FCC/C.L. Anand	Punjab
39.	Indtech Speciality Chemls Ltd.	Indrol Lubricants & Specialities Ltd.	FCC	Karnataka
40.	Noble Explochem Ltd.	Aktiebolaget Bofors, Sweden	FCC	Maharashtra
41.	Orissa Extrusions Ltd.	Indian Aluminium Co. Ltd./ICI	Larson & Toubro	Orissa
42.	Rajasthan XLO Sanwa Midland Ltd.	XLO India Ltd.	FCC/XLO	Rajasthan
43.	Webel Precision Inds. Ltd.	G K W Ltd.	G K W /FCC	West Bengal (2)
44.	Deccan Fibre Glass Ltd.	Phillips Carbon Black Ltd.	Goenka K P	Andhra Pradesh
45.	Webel Video Devices Ltd.	G P Goenka	Goenka K P	West Bengal
46.	Gujarat Carbon Ltd.	Phillips Carbon Black Ltd.	Goenka K P	Gujarat

contd...

...contd...

S.No.	Name of Joint Sector	Name of the Promotor	House Association	State
	(1)	(2)	(3)	(4)
47.	Wiltech India Ltd.	Asian Cables Corpn. Ltd.	Goenka K P	Karnataka
48.	Consolidated Fibres & Chemicals Ltd.	G.P. Goenka	Goenka K P	Tamil Nadu
49.	Phenol Corpn of Gujarat Ltd.	Duncan Brothers & Co. Ltd.	Goenka K P	Gujarat
50.	Haldia Petrochemicals Ltd.	R P Goenka	Goenka K P	West Bengal
51.	India Polyfibres Ltd.	Phillips Carbon Black Ltd.	Goenka K P	Uttar Pradesh
52.	Karnataka Telecables Ltd.	Asian Cables Ltd.	Goenka K P	Karnataka
53.	Upcom Cables Ltd.	Ceat Investment Ltd.	Goenka K P	Uttar Pradesh
54.	Light Metal Inds Ltd.	India Foils Ltd.	Macneil & Magor	West Bengal
55.	Maharashtra Weldaids Ltd.	Indian Oxygen Ltd.	ICI/FCC	Maharashtra
56.	Eastern Explosives & Chml Ltd.	IDL Chemicals Ltd.	ICI/FCC	West Bengal
57.	Gujarat Hotels Ltd.	ITC Ltd.	ITC/FCC	Gujarat
58.	Orissa Synthetics Ltd.	Straw Products Ltd.	JK Singhania	Orissa
59.	Bihar Synthetics Ltd.	JK Synthetics Ltd.	JK Singhania	Bihar
60.	Gujarat Wedge Wire Screens Ltd.	Behubor Investment Ltd.	Jardine Handerson	--
61.	Rajasthan Glyoxal Ltd.	N.K. Jhunjhunwala	Jhunjhunwala	Rajasthan
62.	Gujarat Aromatics Ltd.	1. Raipur Mfg Co. Ltd. 2. Arvind Mills Ltd. 3. Aruna Mills Ltd.	K Bhai Lalbhai	Gujarat
63.	Shree Pipes Ltd.	Girnar Pratisthan Ltd.	Kanoria	Rajasthan
64.	Madhya Pradesh Electricals Ltd.	Shakti Insulated Wires P. Ltd.	Khatau	Madhya Pradesh

contd...

...contd...

S.No.	*Name of Joint Sector*	*Name of the Promotor*	*House Association*	*State*
	(1)	*(2)*	*(3)*	*(4)*
65.	Vanavil Dyes & Chemicals Ltd.	Colour Chem Ltd.	Khatau	Tamil Nadu
66.	Lakshmi Porcelains Ltd.	M D Kanuri	KLN Prasad	Andhra Pradesh
67.	V.P. Switchgears Ltd.	Hindusthan Brown Boveri Ltd.	Larson & Toubro	Uttar Pradesh
68.	National Switchgears Ltd.	Hindusthan Brown Boveri Ltd.	Larson & Toubro	--
69.	Gujarat Prime Movers Ltd.	Hindustan Brown Boveri Ltd.	Larson & Toubro	Gujarat /FCC
70.	Andhra Mechanical & Elec. Inds. Ltd.	IAEC (Bombay) Ltd.	L D Char	Andhra Pradesh
71.	Siroplast Ltd.	Roplas India Ltd.	Mahindra	Maharashtra
72.	Modi Business Systems (Punjab) Ltd.	Modi Group of Industries	Modi	Punjab
73.	Bihar Sponge Iron Ltd.	Modipon Ltd.	Modi	Bihar
74.	Modipic Rubber Ltd.	Modi	--	
75.	Asia Carbon Ltd.	Phillips Carbon Black Ltd.	Goenka K P	Tamil Nadu
76.	Vikrant Tyres Ltd.	Consolidated Coffee Ltd.	Muthiah	Karnataka
77.	Modern Insulators Ltd.	H S Ranka	Modern Group	
78.	Modern Threads (I) Ltd.	H S Ranka	Modern Group	
79.	Punjab Breweries Ltd.	East India Hotels Ltd.	M S Oberai	Punjab
80.	Nagarjuna Paper Mills Ltd.	K V K Raju	Nagarjuna	Andhra Pradesh
81.	Nagarjuna Steels Ltd.	K V K Raju	Nagarjuna	Andhra Pradesh
82.	Nicco Orissa Ltd.	National Insulated Cable Co. Ltd.	NICCO	Orissa
83.	Webel Television Ltd.	NICCO Investment Ltd.	NICCO	West Bengal
84.	Webel Nicco Electronics Ltd.	1. National Insulated Cables Co. Ltd. 2. Nicco Investment Ltd.	Nicco	West Bengal (2)

contd...

...contd...

S.No.	Name of Joint Sector	Name of the Promotor	House Association	State
	(1)	(2)	(3)	(4)
85.	Telelink Nicco Ltd.	National Insulated Cables Co. Ltd.	Nicco	West Bengal
86.	Gujarat Tyres Ltd.	Nirlon Synthetic Fibres & Chmls. Ltd.	Nirlon	Gujarat
87.	Orichem Ltd.	D K Jhunjhunwala & Co. Pvt. Ltd.	Orissa Inds.	Orissa
88.	Punjab Concast Ltd.	Oswal Woollen Mills Ltd.	Oswal	Punjab
89.	Malwa Cotton Spg. Mills Ltd.	Oswal Woollen Mills Ltd.	Oswal	Punjab
90.	Punjab Woolcombers Ltd.	Oswal Woollen Mills Ltd.	Oswal	Punjab
91.	Webel Telecommunications Inds. Ltd.	Peico Electronics & Electricals	Philips/FCC	West Bengal
92.	Raasi Cement Ltd.	N P K Raju	Raasi	Andhra Pradesh
93.	Raasi Synthetics & Chemicals Ltd.	B V Raju	Raasi	Andhra Pradesh
94.	Arkonam Castings & Forgings Ltd.	K C P Ltd.	Ramakrishna V	Tamil Nadu
95.	Raunaq Automotive Components Ltd.	Raunaq Enterprises	Raunaq Singh	Uttar Pradesh
96.	Sigma Paints (Karnataka) Ltd.	Sygma Paints Ltd.	Ruia	Karnataka
97.	Tamparlit Steam Navigation Ltd.	Scindia Steam Navigation Co. Ltd.	Scindia	West Bengal
98.	M P Agro Morarji Fertilizers Ltd.	Dharmsi Morarji Chemical Ltd.	Shahu Jain	Madhya Pradesh (4)
99.	Indian Carbides & Chemicals Ltd.	Asiatic Oxygen Ltd.	Soorajmull N Mull	Orissa
100.	M P Carbides & Chemicals Ltd.	Raigarh Jute & Textile Mills Ltd.	Soorajmull N Mull	Madhya Pradesh
101.	Bihar Air Products Ltd.	1. Asiatic Oxygen Ltd. 2. B P Indl Corpn. Pvt. Ltd. 3. Amstar Invt. Pvt. Ltd.	Soorajmull N Mull	Orissa
102.	Andhra Pradesh Fibres Ltd.	K K Bajoria	Soorajmull N Mull	Andhra Pradesh

contd...

...contd...

S.No.	*Name of Joint Sector*	*Name of the Promotor*	*House Association*	*State*
	(1)	*(2)*	*(3)*	*(4)*
103.	Automobile Corpn of Goa Ltd.	Tata Locomotive & Engg. Co. Ltd.	TATA	Goa
104.	Ipibel Refractories Ltd.	Tata Refractories Ltd.	TATA	Orissa
105.	Ipitata Sponge Iron Ltd.	Tata Iron & Steel Co. Ltd.	TATA	Orissa
106.	Titan Watches Ltd.	Questar Investment Ltd.	TATA	Tamil Nadu
107.	Kumardhubi Metal Casting & Engineering Ltd.	Tata Iron & Steel Co. Ltd.	TATA	Bihar
108.	Almora Manganesite Ltd.	Tata Refractories Ltd.	TATA	Uttar Pradesh
109.	Punjab United Pesticides & Chemicals Ltd.	Excel Industries Ltd.	TATA II/Shroffs	Punjab
110.	Karnataka Oxygen Ltd.	1. Lachhminarain Co. 2. Ambica Textiles	TCI/Bhoruka	Karnataka
111.	Northern Digital Exchanges Ltd.	Ballarpur Industries Ltd.	Thapar	Punjab
112.	Punjab Polyfibres Ltd.	Jagatjit Cotton Textiles Ltd.	Thapar	Punjab
113.	Solid State Devices Ltd.	-- Thapar	--	
114.	Andhra Pradesh Rayons Ltd.	Ballarpur Industries Ltd.	Thapar	Andhra Pradesh
115.	Punjab Display Devices Ltd.	Jagatjit Cotton Textile Mills Ltd.	Thapar	Punjab
116.	Himlon Ltd.	Ballarpur Industries Ltd.	Thapar	Himachal Pradesh
117.	Goa Electricals & Fans Ltd.	Crompton Greaves Ltd.	Thapar	Goa
118.	Lorcom (Protectives) Ltd.	London Rubber Co (I) Ltd.	TTK/FCC	Maharashtra
119.	United Communications Ltd.	United Breweries Ltd.	United Breweries	Orissa (5)
120.	Karnataka Polyster Ltd.	United Breweries Ltd.	United Breweries	Karnataka

contd...

...contd...

S.No.	*Name of Joint Sector*	*Name of the Promotor*	*House Association*	*State*
	(1)	*(2)*	*(3)*	*(4)*
121.	Madhya Pradesh United Chemicals & Pesticides Ltd.	United Builders Constn.(I) Pvt. Ltd.	United Group	Madhya Pradesh
122.	Madhya Pradesh United Polypropylene Ltd.	United Builders Constn.(I) Pvt. Ltd.	United Group	Madhya Pradesh
123.	M P Uni-Magna Tech. Ltd.	United Builders Constn.(I) Pvt. Ltd.	United Group	Madhya Pradesh
124.	Columbia Electronics Ltd.	Deepak Gupta	United Group	Madhya Pradesh

Note: (1) Uttar Pradesh Electronics Corporation Ltd.

(2) West Bengal Electronics Industry Development Corporation Ltd.

(3) Steel Authority of India Ltd.

(4) Madhya Pradesh Agro Industries Corporation Ltd.

(5) Orissa Electronics Development Corporation Ltd.

* Disinvested.

Source: The list is prepared on the basis of the prospectuses available at the Institute for Studies in Industrial Development (ISID), New Delhi, and the list of joint sector companies obtained from the promoting agencies.

5 Organised Sector: Directions of Change

Over the past four decades, the organised sector of the Indian economy has witnessed phenomenal growth. This is reflected in the number and size of paid-up capital (PUC) of entities registered under the Companies Act, 1956 (Table 5.1). From a gross PUC of nearly eleven hundred crore in 1956-57 it had risen to more than 40,000 crore of rupees by 1986-87. The number of registered companies also witnessed a manifold increase and was nearly 1,40,000.

Table 5.1

Growth of the Indian Corporate Sector (1956-57 to 1986-87)

(PUC in ₹ crore)

	Government Cos.		*Non-Govt. Cos*		*Total*		*Share of Govt. Cos. in PUC*
Year	*No.*	*PUC*	*No.*	*PUC*	*No.*	*PUC*	
1956-57	74	73	29283	1005	29357	1078	6.77
1960-61	142	547	26007	1271	26149	1818	30.09
1965-66	214	1248	26796	1878	27010	3126	39.92
1970-71	314	2064	30098	2439	30412	4503	45.84
1975-76	651	6122	42755	3497	43406	9620	63.64
1980-81	851	11443	61863	5914	62714	17357	65.93
1985-86	1202	27087	121139	8596	122341	35683	75.91
1986-87	1053	31124	137133	9383	138186	40507	76.84

Source: Based on Government of India (GoI), Ministry of Industry, Dept. of Company Affairs, *31st Annual Report on the Working & Administration of the Companies Act*, 1956: Year ended March 31, 1987.

The size and fast growth of the corporate sector, however, does not reveal the major qualitative changes experienced by the sector. The first development lies in the emergence of the public sector as an important component of the corporate sector. In terms of PUC, it accounts for more than 75 per cent. The public enterprises are few in number but have among them very large corporations. Also, the public enterprises are generally in a monopoly position. If one includes statutory corporations with public enterprises registered under the *Companies Act, 1956*, one can assert without fear of contradiction that the public sector in India has secured the 'commanding heights.' The state-owned and controlled enterprises have a monopoly in energy, aviation, copper, lead, communications, insurance and an overwhelmingly large share in banking, steel, fertilisers and a number of other areas.

Having reached the 'commanding heights', it is but natural to ask: For whose interest are the 'heights' being operated? Is it the long-term development interests, those who are below the so-called poverty line, the state or the private corporate sector? Should the public sector follow the maxim of 'profit maximisation' as is supposed to be true of private corporations? These questions are as relevant today as they were a couple of decades ago.

The private corporate sector, too, has grown at a reasonably high rate. Within the private sector, however, one observes a few interesting developments. One, the sector has witnessed emergence of a large many big corporations. The number of companies with an annual turnover of ₹ 100 crore was only three in 1969-70, but by 1986-87 the number is estimated to be more than 100. This cannot but result in the growth of concentration within the private sector. It is not appropriate to treat each company as a separate entity. For understanding the phenomenon of growing concentration, one must have a look at the growth pattern of the India's large industrial houses. Table 5.2 shows the assets (at book value) of the top 10 industrial houses. The gross assets of the 10 rose from nearly ₹ 2,000 crore in 1972 to ₹ 17,455 crore by 1986—more than an eight-fold increase in about 13 years.

Two, within the top 10 private family-based business houses, the two the Birlas and the Tatas account for half of the new assets acquired by the 10 (Figure 5.1). The Reliance case is wholly exceptional and its expansion is meteoric. The emergence of Reliance needs a separate treatment. An interesting element in the relative growth rates of the large houses also lies in the fact that the Tatas and Birlas appear to have followed a neck-to-neck race in expansion. If the Tatas led in one year, the Birlas overtake them soon as the race is on (Figure 5.2). The same phenomenon is presented by the J.K., Thapar and Mafatlal houses. If the big houses compete, they would have what they aim at; the rest of the competitors only get in proportion to their own individual and relative strength.

Table 5.2

Growth of Assets of Top 10 Monopoly Houses

(Assets in ₹ crore)

House	1972	1980	1986	Share in Increase (%)		
				1972-1980 excl. Reliance	1980-1986	1980-1986 incl. Reliance
1. Birla	589.42	1431.99	4606.57	27.68	30.76	26.07
2. Tata	641.93	1538.97	4348.94	29.47	27.23	23.08
3. Reliance		166.33	2021.53			15.24
4. J.K. Singhania	121.45	412.72	1229.94	9.57	7.92	6.71
5. Thapar	136.16	348.06	1145.83	6.96	7.73	6.55
6. Mafatlal	183.74	427.54	980.95	8.01	5.36	4.55
7. Modi	58.05	198.82	860.18	4.63	6.41	5.43
8. Larsen & Toubro	79.03	216.03	830.56	4.50	5.95	5.05
9. ACC	134.36	274.51	760.08	4.60	4.70	3.99
10. Bangur	125.26	264.33	670.53	4.57	3.94	3.34
Total (1-10)	2069.40	5279.30	17455.11			
Total (Excl. Reliance)	2069.40	5112.97	15433.58	100.00	100.00	

Source: Based on replies to the Parliament questions.

Three, if one takes the largest private sector companies of India, one finds that an overwhelming part of the assets is held by such private companies in which the majority or the largest block of shareholding was with the public sector. The inter-corporate investments ownership of most big business houses would be clearly seen to be that of public sector and not of those families who control and manage private corporate empires. For instance, the combined share of public financial institutions and of the state and central governments was 42.25 per cent in Tata Iron and Steel Company (TISCO) and 44.84 per cent in Tata Engineering Locomotive Company (TELCO), the largest companies in the private sector in terms of net sales in 1986-87. While the share of Tata Sons in TISCO was placed at less than 2.5 per cent, TISCO was the major private sector shareholder in TELCO. In short, a large part of big business assets is public—when classified as per ownership of risk capital. The truth of this reality would come up in the public glare if the public sector financial institutions were directed to act as if they were private investors. Let them not promote others at their own cost; those corporations should protect

Figure 5.1

Sharing Pattern of New Assets (1980-1986)

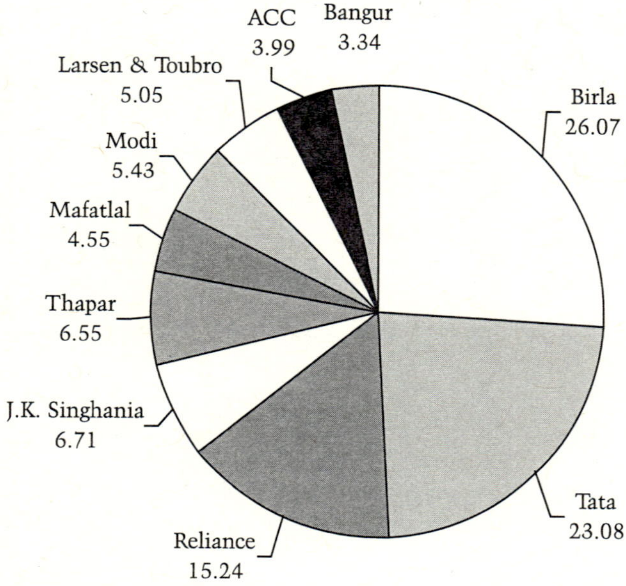

Figure 5.2

Growth of Top Five Monopoly Houses (1972-1987)

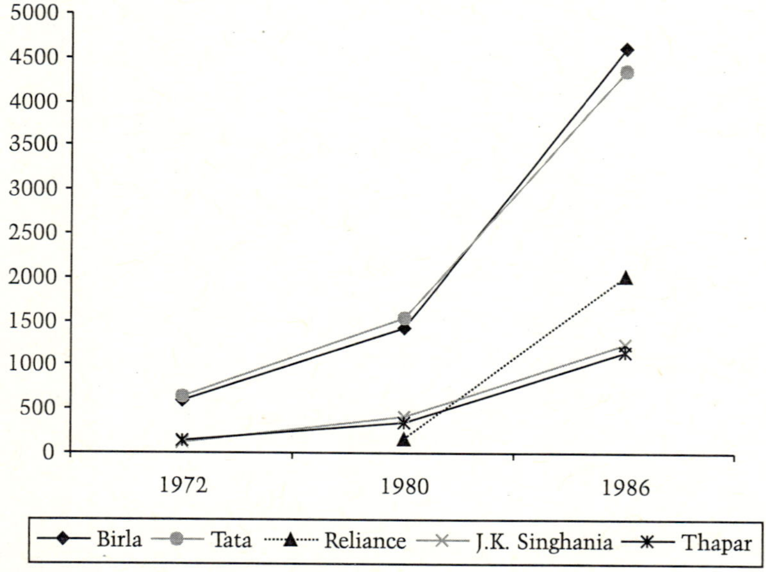

their interests with 'business shrewdness.' The growth and stability of the Indian private monopoly capital, as represented by large houses, is financed, promoted and protected by public sector financial institutions. If it were not to be so, the extent of project funding for large house enterprises by public institutions would not be 80-90 per cent.

Four, unlike the general agreement in policy-making circles during the 1950s, the national private monopoly capital is no more expected to be confined to the 'core sector' industries. Increasingly, the corporations are shedding their 'mono-industry' character. Tatas are no more steel people as indeed Mafatlals are not in textiles alone, ITC are not only in tobacco. Delhi Cloth Mills (DCM) are not only in textiles. Birlas and Goenkas are not only in jute. The character of individual enterprises is becoming more of 'business'—or one may call it mercantilist—rather than their strength lying in any one industry. Private corporations are, therefore, in 'business', and it does not appear a good proposition to remain industry- or location-specific.

Table 5.3

Growing Importance of Financial Collaborations in Indian Industry

(No. of Collaborations)

Year	*Approved Collaborations*		*Share of Financial Collaborations in Total (%)*
	Total	*Financial*	
1977	267	27	10.11
1978	307	44	14.33
1979	267	32	11.99
1980	526	65	12.36
1981	389	56	14.40
1982	588	113	19.22
1983	673	129	19.17
1984	740	148	20.00
1985	1041	256	24.59
1986	958	242	25.26
1987	853	241	28.25
1988	856	276	32.24

Note: Figures for 1988 are extrapolated on the basis of the information available for the first nine months. Out of the 642 collaborations approved during Jan. to Sept. 1988, 207 involved financial participation.

Source: Based on Monthly Newsletter of the India Investment Centre and GoI, Ministry of Science & Technology, Foreign Collaborations, 1985 (A Compilation: National Register of Foreign Collaborations).

Five, the Indian corporate sector is opening up to international technology and capital. This process has reached a new phase with the early

1980s. While the number of technical and financial collaborations does not reveal the magnitude of the 'foreign' element in the Indian industrial sector, the numbers do reveal the magnitude of the 'foreign' element in the Indian industrial sector and other basic trends (see Table 5.3 and Figure 5.3).

Figure 5.3

Increasing Share of Financial Collaborations in Total Approvals (1977-1988)

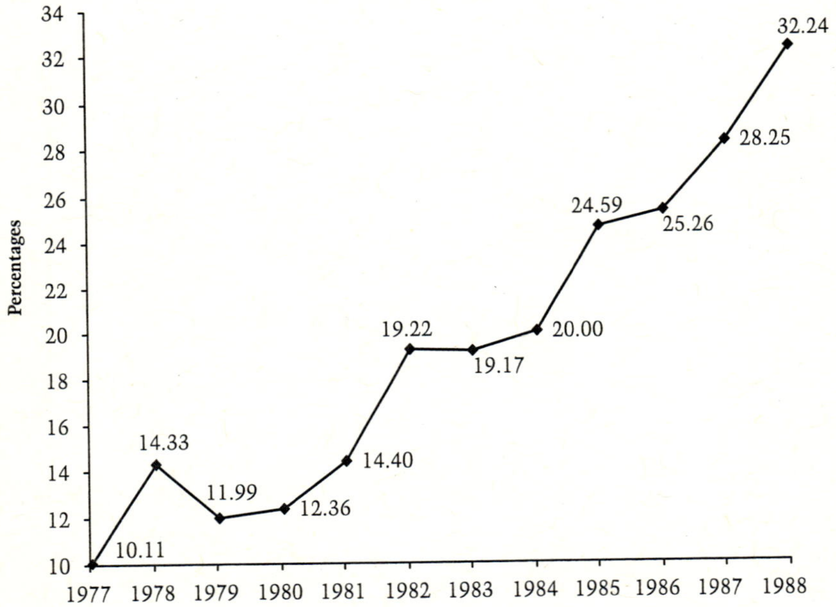

Note: Figures for 1988 are extrapolated on the basis of reported approvals for the period Jan. to Sept. 1988.

Source: Based on Monthly Newsletter of the India Investment Centre and GoI, Ministry of Science & Technology, Foreign Collaborations, 1985 (A Compilation: National Register of Foreign Collaborations).

A significant feature of the 'opening up' process is the prominence with which Indian private monopolies are joining hands with international monopoly capital, the multinational corporations (MNCs) or transnational corporations (TNCs)—whatever one may like to label them as. The new trend in the corporate sector is to have new corporations bearing names of an MNC. The consequence is: Birla-Yamaha, Tata Honeywell, Modi Olivetti, DCM Toyota, etc. (see Table 5.4 for more old and new cases). It is a moot point if Pepsico would have been allowed entry had they not teemed up with the Tatas.

Table 5.4

National and International Capital: Joint Ventures

Beacon **Kone**	Mafatlal **Zinser** Engg
Beacon **Neyrpic**	
Beacon **Rotork Controls**	
Beacon **Tileman**	
Beacon **Weir**	
Essar **Brown Root** (India)	
Essar **Forasol**	
Fuller KCP	
EIMCO KCP	
Escorts **JCB**	
Greaves **Dronsfield**	
Greaves **Foseco**	
Crompton Greaves	
David Brown Greaves	
Drayton Greaves	
Greaves **Midwest Engg**	
Hero **Honda**	
J.K. **Helene Curtis**	
J.K. **Satoh** Agricultural	
Khatau **Junker**	
Kinetic **Honda**	
Kirloskar **Rateau**	
Kirloskar **Cummins**	
Kirloskar **Warner Swassey**	
Kothari **General Foods**	
L & T **Gould**	
Lohia **Starlinger**	
Mahindra **British Telecom**	
Mahindra **Owen**	
Mahindra **Ugine** Steel	
Modi **Telematics**	
Modi **Xerox**	
Modi **Champion**	
Murugappa **Morganite** Ceramic	
Nagarjuna **Singode**	
Nava Bharat **Parker Drilling**	

contd...

...contd...

Nicco **Hambro** Financial
Furmanite Nicco
Nicco **Helifusion**
Shriram **Honda** Power Equip
SRF **Nippondenso**
Swaraj **Mazda**
Tata **Bradbury Wilkinson**
Tata **Klockner** Indl Plants
Tata **Korf** Engg Services
Tata **Timken**
Tata **Robins Fraser**
Tata **Unisys**
Tata **Yodogawa**
Sundaram **Abex**
Sundaram **Clayton**
TVS **Suzuki**
TVS **Whirlpool**
Lucas TVS
(MNC names in bold letters)

More importantly, even the existing MNCs are increasingly seeking the support of the Indian businessmen; the latest in the series being the ICL. ICL had come into an agreement with the Goenkas to run ICIM. Some others falling in this category are: Godfrey Phillips (Modis); Ceat, Bayer, Herdillia Chem (Goenkas); Chloride (Birlas); Cadbury—now Hindustan Cocoa Products—(Mallyas); APV Texmaco (Birlas); Tata MAN (Tatas); etc. Even Philips when it had to enter in a different form (Punjab Anand Lamps Inds) needed a local partner. Similarly, Glaxo—now Glindia—is fast expanding through the joint sector route. If taken along with the large number of joint ventures already existing (Tatas, Birlas, Mahindras, Mafatlals, Thapars have a number of them some of which are included in Table 5.4) and the tendency of the Indian large houses to venture into the developing countries, the distinction between Indian big business and the foreign monopoly capital looks to be hypothetical.

And lastly, the corporate sector of the Indian economy is increasingly seeking to rely on technology imports instead of evolving a plan for national research and development (R&D) or indigenisation. More and more international brand names are being accepted and promoted. There are indications that the lobbying has already begun to revise patents laws.

It is time for debate on the main trends in the organised sector of India. It is equally important that the implications of these developments are worked out and well understood in policy-making circles.

6 New Industrial Licensing Policy

An Empirical Assessment

Under the new licensing policy, as announced by N.D. Tiwari, minister for industries, in the Lok Sabha on April 21, 1982, the government would regularise excess capacities in the scheduled industries established by private sector companies in violation of the Industries (Development and Regulation) Act (IDRA), 1951. The new capacities to be treated as the licenced ones would be on the basis of the highest production level reached during the past five years. The new approved capacities would not only be at the level of actual production, but would be nearly 66 per cent more than the production level already reached. The new policy is justified on the plea of productivity. What are the implications of the new policy? How productive would this concession be?

To understand the real implications of the new policy, one needs to have an objective overview of licences issued and the degree of their utilisation. Table 6.1 shows the level of production as against the size of licenced capacity for 729 companies which are quoted on stock exchanges in India. The data refers to the companies' financial year ending 1979. The overall picture is that out of 2,948 licences held by these companies, in only 186 (6.3 per cent) licences were utilised at a much higher level than the capacity licenced. On the other hand, out of the total, more than 76 per cent of the licences were being utilised by less than 75 per cent of the capacities licenced. In this framework, if the objective of the new policy is to encourage productivity, where should the action have begun? Should the required policy be to reward those who have been persistently violating the licensing provisions by producing far in excess? Or, should the policy be so evolved to assist the 76 per cent to utilise capacities already licenced?

Table 6.1

Showing the Distribution of Licenced Capacities according to the Range of Utilisation

S.No.	*Percentage Utilisation*	*Number of Product Licences*	*Percentage*
1.	0-25	1357	46.0
2.	25-75	905	30.7
	0-75	2262	76.7
3.	75-100	329	11.2
4.	100-125	171	5.8
	75-125	600	17.0
5.	Above 125	186	6.3
	Total	2948	100.0

Source: Based on a survey conducted for the *Report on the Functioning of Industrial Licensing System*, Corporate Studies Group, The Indian Institute of Public Administration, January 1983.

If the objective of productivity improvements was to be achieved, the logical and rational policies would be to enquire as to why the capacity utilisation in the private sector was so poor. It is well known that low capacity utilisation in the public sector is often taken as an index of the inefficiency of the government sector. Executives of public sector enterprises are pulled up and many are sacked for low capacity utilisation, but what is done in the private sector in India is still never discussed openly. If the government's objective is genuinely to raise production and productivity, the decision required would be to cut down licenced capacity to the level of actual production and in lieu of cancellations, issue new licences in these areas to those who would implement these in the minimum possible time. Why should there be a 'ban' list or applicants denied licences when the present licence holders were not able to utilise in full the already licenced capacities? By cancelling or reducing the level of licenced capacities in the light of actual production, the government would be able to end all cases of pre-emption and to reduce the hold of artificial monopolies created and protected by the licensing system. The overall impact of this approach could be the introduction of some rationality in the system.

Apart from knowing the extent of underutilisation, it is equally relevant to ask: who are those licencees who are not utilising their licences fully? Table 6.2 provides an answer. Out of the 2,262 underutilised licences (each being utilised lower than 75 per cent of the licenced capacity), 619 have a zero level of production. Of these, 110 (17.8%) are held by Foreign Exchange Regulation Act (FERA) companies and 229 (37.0%) by companies belonging to Indian monopoly houses. Total neglect of utilisation of licences is more common with the FERA and big business companies than with smaller Indian companies. If one groups all the 2,262 licences, which remain substantially underutilised, one finds, once again, that nearly 55 per cent of the licences are held by those companies which are either constituents of FERA or Indian big business.

Table 6.2

Showing the Licencee Category-wise Distribution of Underutilisation Cases

S.No.	*Licencee Category*	*Range of Utilisation (per cent)*			
		0	*Less than 25*	*25-75*	*Less than 75*
	(1)	*(2)*	*(3)*	*(4)*	*(5)*
1.	Large Houses excluding FCS	229 (37.0)	521 (38.4)	389 (43.0)	910 (40.2)
2.	F.C.C.	110 (17.8)	251 (18.5)	174 (19.2)	425 (18.8)
3.	Others	280 (45.2)	585 (43.1)	342 (37.8)	927 (41.0)
	Total	619 (100.0)	1357 (100.0)	905 (100.0)	2262 (100.0)

Source: Same as Table 6.1.

For FERA or big business companies, the absence of financial resources or technological capabilities could not have been the reason for their poor performance in implementation of the licences held. At the same time, if the poor performance was due to absence of market demand, the remedial policy framework would have to be wholly different. One would need to identify the reasons as to why larger capacities were licenced than demand estimates. After all, creation of industrial capacities does mean utilisation of national resources. One suspects, however, that the lower level of industrial production, as compared to that which is licenced in the private sector, is due more to the restrictive and monopoly practices resorted to by the licencees, than to other justifiable reasons.

There could be one valid reason to explain the lower level of production and that is, shortages of power and industrial raw materials. As a general proposition, one cannot disagree with the plea of shortages, particularly with regard to power. But one has to ask a related question: Is it so that companies which were not fully utilising their industrial licences were unable to do so in case of all the licences held by them? Or, does it happen that the excess and underutilisation phenomena were noticed existing side by side in the same company during the same period? It may be that for a few products, a company produced in excess of licenced capacity, and for many other products, it practised gross underutilisation. An objective answer is provided in Table 6.3. It shows the distribution of 729 Indian companies which hold industrial licences and have production exceeding that licenced, while also holding licences which are not utilised by more than 60 per cent of the authorised capacity.

It would be seen that out of 729 companies, as many as 531 did not indulge in violation of industrial regulation i.e., none of these having produced more than the licenced capacity. These companies did have under-utilisation for the licences held by them. The phenomenon of excess and lower utilisation for the licences held by the same company was observed in 198 cases only. Table 6.3 also shows clearly that there were 9 companies which held 5 and more of underutilised licences, whereas these also had excess production in some of the licences held.

Table 6.3

Showing the Distribution of Companies according to the Number and Excess and Underutilised Licences held by them

Number of licences utilised	*Number of Licences utilised more than 100 per cent*						
	0	*1*	*2*	*3*	*4*	*5*	*Total*
0	114	42	4	2	0	0	162
1	190	24	5	2	1	1	223
2	75	14	3	0	2	2	96
3	43	10	4	4	2	4	67
4	37	4	2	1	1	3	48
5	22	5	1	0	0	3	31
6 and above	50	28	13	7	3	1	102
Total	531	127	32	16	9	14	729

Source: Same as Table 6.1.

Reaching a level of production which is in excess of licenced capacity cannot be without diversion of power and other raw scarce-raw material from the products in which capacity utilisation was low. Many of the scarce raw materials are common for a large many industrial products. A company may decide to produce far in excess of the authorisation by keeping production of the less profitable items at a lower level. Such practices are bound to result in distortions in supply position—excess production for high priced goods and lower production for goods for which higher prices cannot be charged. At the same time, the company would continue to have a valid licence to re-enter the product at a later date. Resort to such practices reduces governmental regulations and attempts at planned development to a farce.

The most significant conclusion emerging from our analysis is that most of the companies which had established capacities for more than six products each were those which happen to be associates of multinationals. This includes, Hindustan Lever, Phillips, Dunlop, Sandoz, Rallis, Siemens, G.K.W., Boehringer Knoll, Glaxo, Union Carbide and GEC. The only Indian companies to fall under this category were Tata Oil (Tata), Gwalior Rayon (Birla), Volta, Travancore Chemicals & Manufacturing Co. Ltd.

The new policy announcement provides that capacities indicated in the earlier industrial licences for such products and those companies which have been producing in excess of the capacities approved would be of no significance. The government would endorse capacities in the light of production level already achieved, the highest during any one of the past five years. The degree of enhanced capacity would be directly related to the extent to which a company had been bold enough in violating the government regulations. Instead of the award of any penalty, the violating companies get reward. To illustrate, Crompton Greaves (a company of Thapars and having 37.5% foreign equity) held a licence for the production of 18,000 sets of metal cased plugs and sockets but its level of production during 1979 was 2,24,297 i.e., nearly 11-fold excess capacity utilisation. As per the new policy, Crompton Greaves would get a licence for 2,98,943 units and would indeed be able to produce more than 3.73 lakh units as against the present licence of only 18,000 units. More serious the violation, higher the reward.

Where do excess capacities exist? For a pointed discussion, it would be more relevant to list cases in which the violation of the IDRA has been more serious i.e., the products in which production level reached during 1979 was higher by 100 per cent and more. Table 6.4 shows the distribution of 62 such cases. It would be seen that 33 out of the 62 cases belong to foreign-controlled companies which are well-known multinationals of the western capitalist bloc. Indian big business and multinational corporations (MNCs) jointly were responsible for 55 cases out of the total of 62 cases of serious violations. Who would benefit the most from the liberalisation policy should be only too obvious. It is only a handful of companies—but these happen to be important and influential.

The new policy also announces the enlargement of the list of industries under Appendix I to the Industrial Policy Government Decision of February 2, 1973. This opens up, according to the new policy only five areas for FERA and Indian big business [Monopolies and Restrictive Trade Practices (MRTP) companies]. A more detailed examination reveals that the new areas are not only the five admitted, but the liberalisation is far more extensive. Annexure A-6.1 shows the changes now introduced as against what was contained earlier. There is, probably, much more in the list than what meets the eye at first look. For instance, by bringing in the 'components' in the case of newly added items, a good deal of scope has been extended in the areas which should have been reserved for development in the small-scale sector.

Table 6.4

Showing the Grouping of Violators of Licenced Capacities

(Number of 100 per cent or more violation cases)

Range of Excess Capacity Utilisation as Percent of Licenced Capacity	*Cases belonging to*			
	Foreign-controlled companies (MNCs)	*Large Houses*	*Others*	*Total*
100-200	19	12	6	37
200-300	5	3	0	8
300-400	2	2	1	5
400-500	2	1	0	3
500 and above	5	4	0	9
Total	33	22	7	62

Source: Same as Table 6.1.

Further, there is no explanation why the new industries have become core industries. Was this a result of any undisclosed objective enquiry or study, or is the list being enlarged to accommodate different pressure groups? It is equally relevant to ask if such substantial changes had to be made, why this proposal could not be discussed by the Parliament or other expert groups, before these industries are elevated to core industries. If nothing else, one should be able to see the core character in the Five Year Plans. Why did this question remain untouched in the Planning Commission perspective?

Another aspect of the new policy concessions is that all large houses and MNCs will also be permitted to set up units outside the Appendix I list of the products if the units are predominantly export oriented i.e., 60 per cent export in respect of items not reserved and 75 per cent for items reserved for the small-scale sector. While granting this concession, no limit has been placed on the new investments of the MNCs or Indian big business. It is obvious that 25 per cent production of a large unit like the Bata, Colgate, Palmolive, Phillips or GEC would be enough to ensure the closure of thousands of small-scale units. The MRTP Commission had shown how Phillips while exporting indulged in transfer pricing. Now combined with the advantage of local market entry such units would flourish fast and make a mockery of the policy of reservations. In any case, it is well known that in operation, the IDRA is being openly flouted by many of the large, influential and foreign companies. For instance, out of 62 cases of gross violation, 8 happen to be in products which are reserved for the small-scale sector. Britannia Industries holds a licence to produce only 3,600 tonnes of biscuits etc., but its actual production during 1979 stood at 34,907 tonnes i.e., excess by 869 per cent. Similarly, in the case of soap, a product reserved for the small-scale sector, the Hindustan Lever held a licence for production of 70,108 tonnes, but the actual production was 162,278 tonnes i.e., 131 per cent excess utilisation. J.L. Morrison held a licence for production of 31.250 kg of medicated toothpaste, but actual production was 67,196 kg i.e., excess production by 115 per cent. (see Table 6.5, and Annexure A-6.2 for a list of all such cases).

Table 6.5

Showing Classification of Cases of Gross Violation of Licenced Capacities

(Number of cases with 100 per cent or more violation)

Range of Violation	*Items Reserved for Small-scale*	*Items Covered under Special Regulation*	*Others*	*Total*
100-200	7	7	23	37
200-300	-	1	7	8
300-400	-	-	5	5
400-500	-	1	2	3
500 and more	1	3	5	-9
Total	8	12	42	62

Source: Same as Table 6.1.

Of the 62 cases of gross violations, there were 12 cases covering products which are under special regulations. In this list also the most prominent one is: HMM Ltd. (FERA company) produced 743 tonnes of ghee and butter against the licenced capacity of 255 tonnes. Hindustan Lever, APV Engineering, Glaxo and Bayer were companies (all foreign controlled) which appear to have flouted the regulatory norms of the government. (See a list in Annexure A-6.3. A list of another 42 cases is given in Annexure A-6.4.)

While the above are only a few case of violations which have been reported for many years, this does not take note of the fact that many companies, particularly those belonging to MNCs, do not even hold any valid licences for production of items which are reserved for the small-scale sector. For instance, Colgate Palmolive in its 1979 annual report has reported production of 19 lakh dozens of tooth brushes and shaving brushes for which they do not hold any licence. The company, in fact, asserts that it does not require any licence. Similarly, Britannia Industries, an MNC, does not show any licenced capacity but has been engaged in the production of more than 40,000 tonnes of bread. Reckitt and Coleman (*1980 Annual Report*) claims that no licensing is applicable to them for production of food products, detergent preparations and polishes and compositions. In its annual report for 1979, Bata only mentions that applications for endorsement of productive (installed) capacities have been made and they are pending under consideration by the government. A large number of such cases of open and blatant violations could be cited. What has the government done either by way of punishment for the violating companies or in the interest of protecting the small-scale units?

The facts bring out that the new licensing policy would indeed benefit only a small number of Companies. The single most important groups would be the foreign-controlled companies and a few of the Indian big business companies which have shown little regard for economic regulations. Secondly, the extent of the rewards of the liberalisation would depend upon the boldness demonstrated during the five years in producing commodities in excess of that authorised. Thirdly, there is virtually no enforcement of reservations for the small-scale sectors. There have been violations in the past and these continue without any punitive action. Now there would be an open entry by large companies into areas reserved, and once production capacities get built—under the plea of exports—the output would be dumped, very conveniently, in the home market. Export obligations, during the past, have proved of no constraint. This was brought out by Tandon Committee as also by many other government inquiries. On one or the other plea, export obligations are waived.

One may ask: how is this new licensing policy, in any way, conforming to the spirit and letter of the 1956 Industrial Policy Resolution? Will such liberalisation help India achieve self-reliance—if indeed, it is intended to do so? And after all this, what doubts can remain about the conditionality of the International Monetary Fund (IMF) loan?

Annexure A-6.1

Showing Additional Items and Elaboration of the Existing Items in 'Appendix I'

Industry	Newly Added Items
1. Metallurgical Industries	Automotive castings, SG iron castings, aluminium foils, sponge iron and pelletisation.
2. Prime Movers (other than Electrical Generators)	Alternate energy systems like solar, wind, etc., and equipments thereof, gas/hydro/steam turbines from 20 mw to 60 mw.
3. Electrical Equipment	Power and distribution transformers, power relays, HT-switchgear, synchronous condensers, industrial furnaces, component wires for manufacture of lead-in-wires, hydro/steam/gas generators from 20 mw to 60 mw.
4. Transportation	Mechanised sailing vessels up to 10,000 DWT including fishing trawlers, public transport vehicles including, automotive commercial three-wheeler jeep type vehicles, industrial locomotives, personal transport vehicles: (i) passenger cars; (ii) automotive two-wheelers and three-wheelers. Regarding two-wheelers, only expansion of existing units, subject to an export obligation of 25% on additional capacity; specialised automotive components, such as pistons and piston rings, fuel injection equipment; auto-electricals, such as starter motors, generators, spark plugs, rear axle assembly, brake and clutch assembly, tyre/tube valves, wheels for automobiles and bimetal bearings.
5. Industrial Machinery	Specialised equipment for industrial machinery: (i) high performance and high fidelity industrial valves as may be specified by the Ministry of Industry, (ii) centralised lubrication systems; (iii) gears, gear boxes and couplings; (iv) rolls for paper mills, rolls for rolling mills; (v) pollution control equipment; (vi) process equipment for utilisation of recycling of wastes.
6. Machine Tools	Controls and accessories for machine tools, cross land tooling, engineering production aids such as cutting and forming tools, patterns and dies and mining tools.
7. Earth Moving Machinery	Construction machinery and components thereof.
8. Industrial Instruments	Electromedical Instruments and laboratory equipment.
9. Chemicals and Petro-chemicals	(i) Catalysts and catalyst supports; (ii) photographic chemicals; (iii) rubber chemicals; (iv) polyols; (v) isochyanates, urethanes, etc.; (vi) speciality chemicals for enhanced oil recovery; (vii) heating fluids; (viii) coal tar distillation and products therefrom; (ix) tonnage plants for the manufacture of industrial games; (x) high altitude breathing oxygen/medical oxygen; (xi) Nitrous oxide; (xii) refrigerant gases like liquid nitrogen, carbon dioxide, etc., in large volumes; (xiii) argon and other rare gases; (xiv) alkali/acid resisting cement compound; (xv) leather chemicals and auxiliaries.

contd...

...contd...

Industry	*Newly Added Items*
10. Paper and Pulp Including paper products	Industrial laminates
11. Automobile Tyres and Tubes	Automobile tyre tube valves, rubberised heavy duty industrial beltings of all types, rubberished conveyor beltings, rubber reinforced and lined fire fighting hose pipes.
12. Plate Glass	Float glass, toughened glass insulators, glass fishres of all types.
13. Ceramics	Ceramic fibres.
14. Cement Products	Gypsum boards, wall boards and the like; high technology reproduction and multiplication equipment.
15. Printing machinery	(i) Web-feb high-speed offset rotary printing machines having output of 30,000 or more impressions per hour; (ii) photo composing/type setting machines; (iii) multi-colour sheet-fed offset printing machines of sizes 18" x 25" and above; (iv) High-speed Rotogravura printing machines having output of 30,000 or more impressions per hour.
16. Carbon and carbon products	(i) Graphite electrodes and anodes; (ii) impressive graphite blocks and sheets.
17.	Pretensioned high-pressure RCC pipes.
18.	Rubber machinery.

Note: SG: spheroidal graphite; HT: high tension; RCC: reinforced cement concrete

Source: *Report on the Functioning of Industrial Licensing System*, Corporate Studies Group, The Indian Institute of Public Administration, January 1983.

Annexure A-6.2

Showing the List of Big Business and Foreign-Controlled Companies Producing Items Reserved for Small scale

S.No.	Name of the Company	Product	Unit	Licenced Capacity	Actual Production	Percentage of Excess Capacity Utilisation	House Associations
1.	Kesoram Inds & Cotton Mills	Sodium Sulphide	Tonnes	79	140	100.0	Birla
2.	Tata Oil Mills	Soaps	Tonnes	40787	95045	133.0	Tata
3.	Oudh Sugar Mills	Soaps	Tonnes	1800	4955	175.3	Birla
4.	Guest Keen Williams	Safety Pins	000 Nos.	224640	538052	139.5	FCC/GKW
5.	Hindustan Lever	Soaps	Tonnes	70108	162278	131.5	FCC/ Hindustan Lever
6.	JL Morrison	Medicated Toothpaste	kgs	31250	67196	115.0	FCC
7.	Britannia Inds.	Biscuit and High-Protein Food	Tonnes	3600	34907	869.6	FCC
8.	Barium Chemicals	Barium Carbonate	Tonnes	600	1323	121.0	Others

Source: *Report on the Functioning of Industrial Licensing System*, Corporate Studies Group, The Indian Institute of Public Administration, January 1983.

Annexure A-6.3

List of Products Produced by Big Business and Foreign-Controlled Companies covered by Special Regulations

S.No.	Name of the Company	Product	Unit	Licenced Capacity	Actual Production	Percentage of Excess Capacity Utilisation	House Associations
1.	Pfizer	Protein Hydrolysate	Tonnes	110	289.5	163.2	FCC
2.	APV Engineering	Fruit Juice De-aereators Pasteurisers	Nos.	3	8	166.7	FCC
3.	Glaxo Labs.	Foods	Tonnes	4120	8673	110.5	FCC
4.	HMM	Ghee and Butter	Tonnes	255	743	191.4	FCC
5.	Hindustan Lever	Milk Powders incl. Baby Food	Tonnes	874	1967	125.1	FCC/ Hindustan Lever
6.	Hindustan Lever	Processed Triglyce-rides/Hydrogenated oils/Vanaspati	Tonnes	44624	101347	127.1	FCC/ Hindustan Lever
7.	Glaxo Labs.	Solids and Powders incl. Ointments and Malt	Tonnes	184	654	255.4	FCC
8.	Bayer (I)	Pesticides/Powders	Tonnes	1882	28139	1395.2	FCC
9.	Bayer (I)	Tablets/Capsules	000 Nos.	48150	283552	488.9	FCC
10.	New Swadeshi Sugar	Spirit	Litres	22700	2413518	10532.2	Birla
11.	Oudh Sugar Mills	Spirit	kls	11500	92980	707.1	Birla
12.	Brindavan Alloys	Rolled Products	Tonnes	5000	10209	104.2	Others

Source: *Report on the Functioning of Industrial Licensing System*, Corporate Studies Group, The Indian Institute of Public Administration, January 1983.

Annexure A-6.4

Showing the List of Big Business and Foreign-Controlled Companies having Excess Capacities in Other Products

S.No.	Name of the Company	Product	Unit	Licenced Capacity	Actual Production	Percentage of Excess Capacity Utilisation	House Associations
1.	Assam Carbon Products	Electrolytic Copper and LF Powder	kgs	30000.0	64396.0	114.7	FCC
2.	Siemens (I)	Rectifier Cubicles and Misc. Equips.	Nos.	64.5	140.0	115.4	FCC/Khatau
3.	Bharat Alums and Chmls.	Oleum	MT	3600.0	7790.0	116.4	Others
4.	Simco Meters	MDI Meters	000 Nos.	10.0	22.0	120.0	Seshasayee
5.	Wood Polymers	Plastic Laminates: Decorative and Indl.	Tonnes	980.0	2157.7	120.2	Others
6.	APV Engg. Co.	Milk Receiving and Storage Tanks	Nos.	12	27	125.0	FCC
7.	Best & Crompton	Transformer Connections	Metres	500	1181	136.2	FCC
8.	Bayer (I)	Pharmaceuticals: Basic Production	kgs	24730	58507	136.6	FCC
9.	Uniloids	Metronidazole	Tonnes	10.0	24.1	140.8	Others
10.	Boehinger-Knoll	Liquids for External Use	kgs	2600	6713	185.2	FCC/Rallis
11.	Cynamid (I)	Antibiotics: Tetracycline	MT	10	26.7	167.0	FCC/Lalbhai
12.	Larsen & Toubro	Press Tools, Jigs, Moulds, etc.	₹ Lakh	100	268	168.0	Larsen & Toubro

contd...

...contd...

S.No.	*Name of the Company*	*Product*	*Unit*	*Licenced Capacity*	*Actual Production*	*Percentage of Excess Capacity Utilisation*	*House Associations*
13.	Glaxo Labs.	Tablets and Capsules	Mn.	576	1585	175.3	FCC
14.	Mohan Meakins	Glass Bottles	Tonnes	7500	20727	176.4	Mohan Meakin
15.	Kirloskar Bros.	Hermatically sealed compressor units	Nos.	16600	38582	132.4	Kirloskar
16.	Glaxo Labs.	Liquids, Orals, Parenterals	kls	1207	2810	132.8	FCC
17.	Glaxo Labs.	Chemicals	Tonnes	491	1150	134.2	FCC
18.	Sandoz (I)	Formulation: Tablets	Mn. Nos.	189	525	177.8	FCC
19.	Elacon Engg.	Specialised Conveying Equip., Stacker	MT	500	1402	180.4	Elecon
20.	Dhrangendhra Chem.	Ammonium Bicarbonate	MT	1300	3707	185.2	S.P. Jain
21.	Electric Const. & Eqpt. Co.	Poly Phase Meters	Nos.	54000	157704	192.6	Birla
22.	Indian Plastics	Urea and Melamine Formaldehyde Moulding Powder	MT	200	599	199.5	Birla
23.	Sandoz (I)	Capsules	Mn. Nos.	22	69	213.6	FCC
24.	Searle (I)	Injections	No. of Ampules	50,000	160815	221.6	FCC/Rallis
25.	Electric Constn. & Eqpt.Co.	Single Phase Meters	Nos.	180,000	623105	246.2	Birla
26.	Hindustan Lever	Synthetic Detergents	Tonnes	18666	67815	263.3	FCC/Hindustan Lever
27.	Premier Cable Co.	PVC Cables	kms	1824	9745	334.3	Others
28.	May & Baker (I) Ltd.	Tablets	Millions	148	829	360.1	FCC
29.	Caprihans (I) Ltd.	Phenol Resin Varnishes	MT	180	1029	471.7	DU

contd...

...contd...

S.No.	*Name of the Company*	*Product*	*Unit*	*Licenced Capacity*	*Actual Production*	*Percentage of Excess Capacity Utilisation*	*House Associations*
30.	Caprihans (I) Ltd.	Melamine Formaldehyde Resins	MT	60	453	655.0	DU
31.	Mettur Chemicals and Indl. Corpn. Ltd.	Bromine	Tonnes	360	4192	1064.4	Seshasayee
32.	Crompton Greaves Ltd.	Metal cased plugs and Sockets	Sets	18000	224207	1145.6	FCC/Thaper
33.	May & Baker (I) Ltd.	Injectables	kls	17	260	1429.4	FCC
34.	May & Baker (I) Ltd.	Liquids	kls	88	1510	1615.9	FCC
35.	Gwalior Rayon	Viscose Staple Fibre	MT	22000	84013	281.9	Birla
36.	Pfizer Ltd.	Oxytetracycline/Tetracycline and its Formulations	Tonnes	14	53.96	285.4	FCC
37.	Voltas Ltd.	Spares for Forklift/ Handlift/Pallet Trucks	₹ Lakh	5.00	20.18	303.6	Tata
38.	Metal Box (I) Ltd.	R.S. Closures	'000 Nos.	84000	342269	307.5	FCC/Metal
39.	Shriram Refrigeration Co.	Water Coolers	Nos.	800	3262	307.8	Shri Ram
40.	Sandoz (I) Ltd.	Liquid	kls	263	1340	409.5	FCC
41.	Caprihans (I) ltd.	Rigid and Flexible PVC sheets	MT	1320	4631	250.8	DU
42.	Travancore Chemicals & Mfgs. Co. Ltd.	Copper Oxychloride 50% WDP	Tonnes	300	749	149.7	Others

Source: Report on the Functioning of Industrial Licensing System, Corporate Studies Group, The Indian Institute of Public Administration, January 1983.

7 Functioning of Industrial Licensing System[1]

The industrial licensing system (ILS) is, on the one hand, restrictive and, on the other, a permissive mechanism. This system, when accompanied by appropriate promotional policies and direct interventions by the state, can play an important role in bringing about ordered industrial development. The Indian ILS owes its legal basis to the Industries (Development and Regulation) Act (IDRA), 1951, a statute that was conceived prior to the initiation of the process of planned national development and is modelled on a similar enactment of the United Kingdom.[2] It is often believed that the ILS has been heavily relied upon for regulating industrial investments to curb duplication and creation of excessive capacities (in addition to restricting entry of certain categories of investors in specified industries). The establishment of such excess capacities involves excessive capitalisation in industry and a diversion of scarce national resources to non-priority areas. The results of this study have to be seen against this overall national framework. They should help also to assess the degree of effectiveness of the ILS in regulating national industrial development. The survey results of industrial capacities in the large private sector are contrary to some of the widely held beliefs and assumptions of Indian policy-makers.

The degree of success of all regulatory mechanisms is considerably dependent upon the reporting system and the efficiency of the monitoring system to take note of lapses and promptly to initiate necessary remedial action, including measures against those who have indulged in evasion or avoidance of the regulatory public policies. If it so happens that information is officially asked for but is neither compiled nor analysed, those who are

1. This article has been taken from the *Report on the Functioning of Industrial Licensing System, 1983*.

2. Goyal, S.K. (1975). "Industrial Regulation: A Trend Report", in *A Survey of Research in Public Administration*, Volume 2. New Delhi: Indian Council of Social Science Research.

required to submit information can easily indulge in violations of law and policy without fear of any punitive action or even detection. This study provides a review of the reporting practices of the private corporate sector with a special focus on the functioning of the ILS. By its very nature, the review is illustrative. The instances cited are many and the purpose is to highlight the need for a comprehensive monitoring system so that large industrial investments do not remain unregulated and devoid of a social and developmental perspective.

Some of the major conclusions emerging from the survey are the following. After the issuance of industrial licences, there seems to be no machinery to ensure that licences do get implemented. Licensees are often able to keep the licences unimplemented for years together without facing the prospect of revocation. It is because of this that in nearly 7 per cent of the licences studied, the licensees had not taken adequate steps to install productive capacities. In a little more than 20 per cent of the cases, the capacities had been utilised by less than 75 per cent of the authorisation. In about 20 per cent of the cases, the capacities installed were in excess of the licenced ones. Out of these in case of 11 per cent (344 licences), the licensees installed capacities in excess of their licenced capacities by more than 25 per cent. The fact that there is no obligation to implement the licences, together with the widespread phenomenon of excessive installation would suggest that the level of licenced capacities need not bear a direct relationship to the level of industrial capacities installed even by the large organised private corporate sector of the country. If planners have to go by the official statistics with regard to capacities, policies and programmes would inevitably be formulated on the basis of wrong assumptions and expectations and projections based on unreliable data.

A comparison of the actual level of production reported by the licensees with the capacities licenced reveals that in over 20 per cent of the total cases, no production had taken place. In another 25 per cent cases, production was less than 25 per cent of the licenced capacity. In all, in a little more than two-third of the cases, the licences were being utilised only to the extent of 60 per cent of the capacities. However, in over 11 per cent of the cases, production exceeded the capacities licenced. Some of the licensees have been producing at levels exceeding twice the capacities licenced. In total 64 cases of this kind are identified in this study. In a country where the need to raise productivity and achieve better utilisation of the invested capital is so well recognised, it normally would appear to be a welcome proposition if some enterprises could achieve a higher level of production than what they were authorised to produce. One could take a position that higher production should be appreciated rather than frowned upon by the taking of a narrow legal view. There would certainly be a good cause for this view, provided the items produced by these companies were not in violation of other economic policies. The 64 cases have been examined from the viewpoint of the products they pertain to. In most of the cases, the products were of low priority or were reserved for the small-scale sector or one of the 'specially regulated industries.' The entry of large industry in products earmarked for production in the small-scale sector cannot but be against the very spirit of the declared policies of the government.

Just as the installed capacities do not always correspond to the licenced capacities, the production levels reported by the large corporate sector do not fully relate to the capacities installed. In nearly two-third of the cases, production was less than 60 per cent of the installed capacity. Only one-fourth of the licences are being utilised fully, i.e., at levels of more than 75 per cent of the installed capacities.

The Indian public sector has often been criticised for poor efficiency. But if one compares the performance of the two sectors in terms of capacity utilisation, one finds that the performance of public sector was far better than that of the large private sector. Out of the total of 131 central government public enterprises, 47 per cent of the units had a capacity utilisation rate of more than 75 per cent. The proportion of licences falling in the same category was only 24.5 per cent in the case of the large private corporate sector.

These industrial capacities could not have been created without a corresponding claim on the scarce national resources in general and company financial resources in particular. The existence of unutilised capacities to so great extent means that society is being deprived of economies of scale while consumers are being deprived of economies of scale while consumers are being denied possibilities of lower costs. The consequences of the high level of depreciation permitted at present on plant and machinery, combined with gross underutilisation of capacities, can bring about growth only at a high cost. Such companies might survive on the basis of a captive Indian market but would not be able to face even mild international competition.

The poor utilisation of the industrial capacities was not peculiar to any single category of entrepreneurs in the private sector. The assumption that monopoly house companies and companies associated with transnational corporations (TNCs), having vast financial and managerial capabilities, a well established marketing network and other advantages, would have a better record of capacity utilisation does not appear to have significant supporting evidence. The performance of the companies belonging to the two largest houses of the country, namely, Tatas and Birlas, is also not found to be any better. For instance, 75 per cent of the licences held by the Tata companies covered in the Survey and 58 per cent of those held by the Birla House companies studied were not being utilised even to the extent of 60 per cent.

Large and excessive investments have already been made in most parts of the Indian industrial sector. One consequence of lower utilisation would be a high capital output ratio for the economy as a whole. The phenomenon of over capitalisation could either be due to or in spite of the existence of the ILS. If the large private sector has been authorised to make investments which are far in excess of the absorption capacity and needs of the economic system, the fault would obviously lie with the rationale and system of planning that fixes the outer limits within which the ILS should operate. There is a need for an objective assessment of the process by which industry-wise plan targets are determined. On the other hand, if the private sector has made large investments without caring to respect the ILS, there is an obvious need to improve the follow-up and monitoring system. Additionally, it is equally important to devise ways and means to ensure that the industrial capabilities do not remain unutilised for considerations of monopoly profits and other restrictive practices.

To the extent that the ILS permits and protects the licensees from new entrants in the scheduled industries, the state has a moral responsibility to control production, distribution, pricing and the quality of the industrial products.

It is an interesting feature of the operation of the ILS that while in a large number of products of the scheduled industries, the utilisation of industrial capacities is extremely poor, the very licensees responsible for this often produce far in excess of the authorised capacities in respect of some other products. This suggests that there could have been considerable diversion of resources and raw materials obtained in the name of one licence to the production of items being produced under another licence. It would also shed doubt on claims often made that particular licences were not implemented on account of bottlenecks like lack of power and so on. Among the undertakings which held multiple licences and had been utilising their installed capacities at a low level for some licences while undertaking production far above their authorisations in respect of certain other products, the most important single group of companies was that of TNCs.

The violations of the ILS, in terms of the undertaking of production beyond the licenced capacity often in non-priority sectors, are confined to 102 out of 769 companies of the Survey. If these companies are grouped according to the ownership and control characteristics, the most prominent category of companies, responsible for this kind of violations of the IDRA, turns out to be that of the TNCs.

One observes an unmistakable trend of gradual reduction in the scope and coverage of the ILS over the years. This is a consequence of successive upward revisions in the exemption limit from licensing and exemption of certain industries from its scope. Frequent amendments in the procedures of ILS have made the issue more complex. Furthermore, the ILS leans heavily on the provisions of the Monopolies and Restrictive Trade Practices (MRTP) Act, 1969, and the Foreign Exchange Regulation Act (FERA), 1973, for its administration. It has been observed that these acts have their own limitations in terms of their coverage. To that extent, the scope of the ILS also gets limited.

The reporting of data and information on industrial capacities by private managements is certified neither by any technical agency nor by the auditors. The declaration is issued only by the managements themselves.

This practice leaves a large scope for the company managements to present facts in a manner convenient to them instead of revealing the true picture.

Inter-industry differences in the pattern of utilisation of industrial capacities revealed that the level of utilisation of licences, in terms of actual production, was worse in the case of capital goods sectors (like industrial machinery, metal products and basic metals), than in the case of consumer goods industries like alcoholic beverages, tobacco, textiles, paper, ceramics and intermediates like rubber products, chemicals, cement, etc. In terms of utilisation of installed capacities too, the performance in respect of alcoholic beverages, tobacco, textiles, paper and non-metallic mineral products was better than in regard to the others.

A detailed study of a specially regulated industry *viz.*, alcoholic beverages revealed that the ILS was wholly ignored by most of the important companies in this industry. While the industry was on the banned list for many years, the companies have gone ahead with their expansion plans. The larger producers of alcoholic drinks have been able to avoid regulation under a variety of pleas. The gap between the declared policies and the actual practice is so large that one is led to wonder if there was indeed any regulatory system in this country or whether the existence of the ILS was merely a matter of fiction.

Violations of the ILS have been frequent and many specific cases have been brought to government notice by committees like the Industrial Licensing Policy Inquiry Committee (ILPIC) and the Hathi Committee. But no one has ever been penalised for the violations. The government is reported to be helpless in dealing with such cases as the violations have been detected after more than one year and thus penal action has been time barred. One wonders if this plea can be justified even after three decades of the functioning of the ILS which provided ample time to remedy any lacunae in the concerned laws.

The review of annual reports revealed that a good number of large-sized companies claim 'non-applicability' of the provisions of ILS either for all or for some items of their manufacture. These companies included MRTP house companies and TNCs. Interestingly enough, a few companies which claimed 'non-applicability' of the licensing system to themselves, happened to be the market leaders in these very items. It is also often found that in respect of the same product, one company indicates its licenced capacity while another claims non-applicability of the licensing provisions in respect of that very product. In certain cases, even while a company reported licenced capacity for a product, its subsidiary claimed 'non-applicability' of the ILS for the same product.

A number of companies claim to have established manufacturing capacities prior to the enactment of the IDRA. Thus they take the position that instead of an industrial licence, they held registration certificates (under Section 10 of the act) which did not specify any productive capacities. The provision of specification of productive capacities on registration certificates was introduced only in 1974 i.e., after the licensing system had already functioned for nearly 24 years. Apparently, the companies concerned had till then been enjoying the freedom to expand and determine their own capacity without showing any regard to the ILS. The companies which were thus virtually unconstrained by the licensing regulations included some of the dominant undertakings registered under the MRTP Act and those belonging to transnational corporations. These companies are in continuous legal battle with the government and have been contending that the capacities they claim to have installed should be treated as their licenced capacities. One cannot be sure of the legal implications but it is obvious that such practices cut at the very root of all efforts to ensure regulated planned development.

A number of companies of the private sector report their licenced capacity in terms which, if permitted by the authorities, would suggest that the ILS was deliberately being deployed to promote and protect private monopolies of the few. For instance, if a company reports that its licenced capacity was the 'entire country's demand,' 'unlimited' or 'unspecified,' it would imply that the authorities had allowed it to exercise monopolistic power in the Indian economy. We had, however, no means to verify if the government had indeed issued licences with such authorisations. That is to say we were unable to determine whether the manner in which the companies concerned presented this information had, in fact, been sanctioned by the government.

A host of companies report capacity/production statistics in such an ambiguous manner that it makes a mockery of the ILS. The drugs and pharmaceutical industry provides a typical example. A large number of important companies in this industry report capacity and production in terms of the forms of packings (like 'tablets,' 'liquids,' 'ointments,' 'capsules' and so on) which has no relationship with the content or product manufactured. For one company, the entire range of 'drugs and pharmaceuticals' formed one category for purposes of licenced capacities and production. This practice has to be viewed with reference to the Companies Act requirements under which the capacity and production data have to be given for each licence held by the company. Such aggregations make it possible for the company concerned to hide the composition of the actual production. This might also enable a company to concentrate on the production of some items while not producing others at all. Furthermore, each industrial licence is location specific and a number of licences have been granted for rapid development of the backward areas. Reporting of production in general and aggregate terms makes it possible for a company, holding more than one licence in respect of the same item for various regions, to concentrate production of the entire licenced capacity at one location while producing nothing at the rest. Some companies give information and data on capacity licenced and production in different units of measurement. This makes it impossible to assess the extent of utilisation of the installed capacities.

Another ambiguity of the ILS is caused by the fact that reference to capacities are made in terms of differing number of shifts. The shift basis was replaced in 1963 by the 'maximum, utilisation' criterion. In 1972, it was directed that licensees operating in a few specified industries should get their licenced capacities endorsed on maximum utilisation basis. Despite increasing the scope of this policy in 1975 to cover all industries, a number of companies continue to report their licenced capacities on shift basis.

One gets an impression that the government is unable to implement the ILS, as many important companies are offering stiff resistance to the acceptance of government directives. This is true at least with regard to the question of a standardised basis for determining licenced capacities. The same problem exists with regard to reserved items, not to speak of the conditions like, export obligations and so on which are often attached to the industrial licences. There are many other loopholes in the ILS, especially in the taking of any legal and punitive action against defaulters. Interestingly, the Estimates Committee (1980-81) was informed by the Ministry of Industry that the government had no power to deal with companies which claimed that production higher than authorised capacity arises as a result of greater efficiency in the use of installed capacity. Apparently, there is no machinery even for checking on such claims. If one leaves aside past history, can the government now claim that it has acquired the necessary power to be effective in this matter? Is it the Parliament which has held back the enactment of the necessary legislation? Or is it the absence of a will to curb violations of the regulations in the first place?

Has the ILS been an effective instrument in the pursuit of regulated industrial development? The empirical evidence leads one to doubt whether the ILS has been able to restrict or curb over capitalisation in the organised large private sector. If the licences had been granted with care and the desired scrutiny, the economy would not have been loaded with such levels of excess capacities. The general thrust of industrial policy in the last one decade, however, has been that the government apparently prefers to avoid all possibility of any objection or criticism from the private sector in general and the more influential industrialists in particular. Successive ministers of industry have, on one occasion after another, taken pride in showing how fast industrial licences can be issued to promote industrial development. It is a wholly mistaken notion, that granting of industrial licences freely can promote industrial development. In fact, planned development does not imply higher investments alone. The achievement of higher level of investments is also sought by societies which make no pretense of being planned economies. The distinguishing mark of a planned society is in the 'pattern of investments.' In a planned society, the objectives of the ILS are very closely related to the pattern of plan outlays and the identification of and support for priority industries. These must naturally be accompanied by a strong and effective mechanism to curb the diversion of capital and other resources for the creation of excessive capacities in low-priority areas.

The fact that the organised large private sector in India has acquired industrial capacities that remain grossly underutilised is a consequence of the liberal licensing policies pursued in the past. If the government policies tend to move towards further liberalisation of the ILS and other regulations, the Indian economy cannot expect to achieve the social and economic objectives that the country is committed to pursue in a planned system. In fact, it is questionable whether the Indian industrial sector can avoid the crisis in which it finds itself, merely through a dismantling of the ILS, or by adopting more liberal policies. The need for discussing the alternative policies and programmes that may be available to meet the challenges is only too obvious.

8 Small-scale Sector and Big Business[1]

The need for protection of the small-scale sector from direct competition posed by large manufacturing units and imports has been recognised for a long time. During the Second Five Year Plan, the significance of the small-scale sector was emphasised in order to ensure that the consumer goods sector does not draw upon scarce resources needed for the fast expansion of the heavy industry sector. While the demand for protection and promotion of the small-scale sector was largely from the view point of social justice, the Second Five Year Plan strategy introduced additional weight to the plea in favour of the sector by providing a plan rationale and macroeconomic logic for the sector. In the later years, the sector has acquired its own identity with the emergence of a good number of influential constituents as also the sector having become an easy escape route for a variety of business objectives. The official policies regarding the sector have been undergoing considerable changes and they appear to have been made more under persuasion or pressure from a few rather than as a consequence of any well worked out plan or logical framework. There has been a considerable degree of irrational action, contradictory policy alterations and measures which could not but defeat the very purpose of the promotional policies for the small-scale sector.

This study has examined three aspects of the policy towards small-scale sector *viz.*, (i) criteria for a small-scale unit, (ii) ownership and control of the corporate units, and (iii) reservation of industries for exclusive development in the sector. The review of policy changes and the amendments to the criteria of a small-scale unit helps in assessing the degree of vagueness involved in defining the target groups which require

---

1. This article has been taken from the report "Small Scale Sector and Big Business" co-authored by S.K. Goyal, K.S. Chalapati Rao and Nagesh Kumar, Corporate Studies Group, IIPA, February 1984.

support of the state. The study of ownership and control structure reveals if the assistance and support provided by the government to the small-scale sector has served the intended objectives of the policy makers. The section on policy of reservation of industries brings out the limitations and related implications of the policy and problems faced in the process of implementation. The following are some of the observations which need to be underlined:

1. The small-scale sector has been treated as an omnibus to achieve a number of divergent objectives. As a result, the programmes and policies for the small-scale sector do not have an identifiable population with certain agreed characteristics.

2. The structure of state assistance to the small-scale sector has become so complex that to take even a partial advantage of the assistance one has to depend on expert advice. In a situation where an overwhelming number of small-scale units are in the unorganised sector, it is only the well informed, organised and urban-based entrepreneurs who can mainly avail of the state patronage and facilities.

3. The direct and indirect forms of the state assistance accorded to the small-scale sector in India amount to a significant support to the sector. It would entail a substantial financial cost to the exchequer, though precise estimates are different to make.

4. Each type of assistance and protection measures attracts a different group of entrepreneurs. To a majority of the small entrepreneurs, the availability of cheap finance, procurement of raw materials and preferential treatment in purchases by the state are likely to be reasonably attractive. On the other hand, for a comparatively larger unit, exemptions from regulatory provisions may be more attractive. While for new and technically qualified persons, a more meaningful form of assistance could be in market guidance, provision of sheds in industrial estates and an opportunity to share common infrastructural facilities.

5. The criteria for small-scale units have been revised, repeatedly. In the process the 'investment' limit has been raised from ₹ 5 lakh to ₹ 20 lakh. Also, under the current definition while calculating

the size of investment, the items to be included have been reduced to only one, namely, plant and machinery. The criterion is linked only to the money value of investment in plant and machinery with no reference to the size of labour force, location of the unit, size of turnover, the nature of production basket, characteristics of the owner or the organisational form.

6. The official approach that 'original price paid by the owner' should be taken as the basis for deciding the size of investment in plant and machinery has a number of operational problems. This is particularly so in the case of older units, the units which buy second-hand equipment from associates and in the case of imported machinery. The approach also does not take note of the genuine provision for depreciation.

7. The optimal size of investment in plant and machinery of an enterprise is determined by the nature of industry, technology employed and location of the unit. Capital-output ratios differ substantially from one industry to another. Thus with the same level of investment in plant and machinery, there can be grossly varying levels of economic operations in the sector. The criteria for small-scale units, therefore, need to take into account these factors.

8. The distribution of small-scale units in India is a highly skewed one. Very few units are in the higher ranges of investment. Therefore, any upward revisions in the investment limit would be of immediate and direct relevance to larger constituents. The revisions have permitted entry of many bigger units who were not formerly eligible for the state support under the programme. This must have promoted an unequal competition in the sector with adverse affect on the former constituents and smaller units.

9. It appears necessary to enquire into the pattern of assistance sharing in the small-scale sector and how the upward revisions in the investment criteria have altered the direction and flow of the benefits.

10. The small-scale sector of today is not confined to proprietary and partnership firms. For various reasons, joint stock companies have come to occupy an important place in the sector. In numbers, the companies may be few but their share in the various forms of state assistance (loans, subsidies, etc.) is likely to be a significant one.

11. If one goes by the size of operations and affluence, a number of companies qualifying for official patronage as small-scale units hardly differ from the large-scale sector companies.

12. If some of the small-scale units grow beyond the permissible limit, there should be a mechanism for automatic deregistration. In the absence of a strict enforcement of deregistration, many undertakings continue to avail of the privileges meant for the small sector.

13. Even while recognising the fact that the "small industries development programme has been introduced by the government for the benefit of a class of people who really deserve and require such assistance," the ownership aspect remained unemphasised in the definition until 1980. As a result, a number of units belonging to the national monopoly houses and transnational corporations (TNCs) could directly operate in the small-scale sector.

14. According to the current official policy, the subsidiaries of Indian or foreign companies and those that are controlled by other undertakings cannot claim themselves to be constituents of the small-scale sector. While there is no difficulty in identifying the subsidiary relationship, the 'control' cannot be easily ascertained. Control over management can be exercised with much less share in equity than required for being a subsidiary. The official policy, however, does not define control. Further, since an overwhelming number of companies in the small-scale sector are private limited ones, which are generally characterised by restrictive clauses, one needs to examine and assess the nature of control and the true beneficiaries through a proper probe.

15. Major policy changes announced by the government may not be followed up by requisite measures to operationalise the changes.

For instance, while the change in the definition of a small-scale unit incorporating the ownership aspect was announced in 1980, it was surprising to know that it was only in 1983 that instructions were issued to "derecognise those registered small-scale units which are subsidiaries or are controlled or owned by large or medium scale units." How far these decisions get actually implemented can only be known after a fresh evaluation.

16. Another interesting phenomenon observed is that a number of companies, though registered under the Monopolistic and Restrictive Trade Practices (MRTP) Act, continue to lay claim to their beings part of the small-scale sector. These cases have a special significance because they were debarred from taking advantage of the exemption from industrial licensing as small-scale units as far back as in 1973. The existence of such cases is an indication of the ineffectiveness of the administrative system on the one hand and absence of inter-departmental coordination on the other.

17. There are no restrictions on large companies in matter of taking over the existing small-scale units. We find that many a taken-over unit continued to be in the small scale sector even after becoming 'divisions' or 'subsidiaries' of large-scale companies. The absence of any restrictions on take over might lead to a situation where large-scale companies could resort to taking over existing small-scale units to increase their share in the 'industries reserved for small scale sector' or to enter these areas afresh, thereby defeating policy objectives.

18. For more than a decade, it has been the declared policy of the government that companies in which more than 40 per cent of the equity was held abroad cannot take advantage of licensing exemption as small-scale units. With the enactment of FERA, 1973, all such companies would have diluted the foreign equity in them to 40 per cent. Hence technically speaking, no foreign company would be in the small-scale sector. But in reality a small-scale company with upto 40 per cent foreign equity may still be under effective foreign control. It is indeed the case with a number

of affiliates of transnational corporations operating as small-scale units.

19. The nature of relationship between ancillaries and their principals in a complex one. It appears that a number of ancillary units are indeed promoted by persons closely connected with large umbrella units. The contracts for supply of materials and components and other business dealings between ancillary units and the large parent units tend to leave little scope for an ancillary unit to be operating as an independent small-scale unit. There is need for a proper probe into the phenomenon of ancillary development.

20. There appear to be no common technological, production or market characteristics among the groups of items reserved for exclusive development in the small-scale sector. The operationalisation of the reservation policy has been ridden with *adhocism* and frequent changes in the list of reserved items without apparent justification.

21. The number of items in the reserved list and the expansion of the list does not necessarily reflect an enlarged area reserved for the small-scale sector. To a large extent, the longer list of the reserved items is a result of 'spelling out' details of the product groups already reserved.

22. In the recent past a number of items have been dereserved. The reasons for the dereservations are explained only in statements like "the above list (of reserved items) is being reviewed periodically to ensure that production in the small scale sector is economic and of acceptable quality."

23. The practice of partial dereservation (through changes in nomenclature) has reduced the area of protection in many cases. The revisions in products like confectionery, fibreglass reinforced plastic (FRP) products and automobile radiators suggest the exercise of influence and presence of strong lobbying pressure in the system.

24. Allowing production of reserved items by the large-scale manufacturers for captive consumption defeats the very purpose of the reservation policy. Such a policy is bound to affect the

small-scale units engaged in the manufacture of such items adversely.

25. The reservation policy is pursued through the operation of the industrial licensing system. The inability of the government to implement the licensing system effectively is well known. The major problem in implementing the reservation policy is with respect to the existing large-scale/large house manufacturers of reserved items. Under the present policy, the capacities of the large sector are supposed to be frozen, though there can be exemptions for purposes of exports. Since the reserved areas provide a sheltered market for the existing large-scale manufacturers, as no new large-scale manufacturer can officially enter the reserved areas and the small-scale manufacturers cannot provide any worthwhile competition, it is quite common to observe violations of the capacity norms by the large-scale manufacturers in terms of producing far in excess of the authorisations. Not even a single case is reported to have been penalised for violation. This fact by itself is an indication of the impunity with which monopoly houses and transnational corporations can operate in the reserved areas.

26. A number of corporate entities claim non-applicability of the licensing provisions for the reserved items. It could be because while the items have been reserved for the small sector the same were not put on the IDRA Schedule. Garment industry provides an example where large house companies have for long been claiming non-applicability of the licensing obligations. Obviously, there can be 'no excess production' in these cases as there is no 'licensed capacity.'

27. A number of companies claim that since their manufacturing undertakings were established prior to the enactment of the IDRA or before its provisions were made applicable to them, the licensing system was not applicable to them. Such companies often engage the government in prolonged disputes in matters of capacity fixation while continuing to produce goods without adequate authorisation. This process is also existing conspicuously for some of the items reserved for the small-scale sector.

Transnational Corporations like Bata, Colgate and Britannia are cases in point.

28. While reporting details of the products manufactured, it is quite common to find that companies perform this obligation in such a vague manner that no meaningful conclusions about the adherence to the licensing provisions can be drawn by any agency. The practice of multiple products being entered in the licences has added additional complications. The existing vagueness can only help the process of violations by the large-scale sector. The changes in nomenclature that are increasingly taking place now will only complicate the issue further. The need to fix capacities in precise terms and units, particularly in the case of reserved items, is only too obvious.

29. The export obligations attached to industrial licences are not always complied with. Such obligations are very often imposed in the case of products reserved for the small sector. According to the present policy, the single transport contract (STC) is expected to purchase the unexported production of such manufacturers. The STC, however, has not found it possible to take over and export such production. And consequently, the large-scale sector is able to enter directly in the home market. This has become another way of defeating the reservation policy.

30. Large houses can enter the reserved areas by employing a variety of practices. Niky-Tasha gas stoves and cooking ranges, PHILIPS hearing aids and LEO toys illustrate a few methods employed by the large-scale sector for entering the reserved areas.

31. The policy of allowing additional industrial capacity to large-scale manufacturers of reserved items, if they undertake to market equal quantities produced by the small-scale units, will undoubtedly harm the interests of the small-scale units in the long run. The large-scale manufacturers may eventually be able to squeeze out the small-scale units whose production they may now agree to market under their own brand names.

32. Marketing arrangements by large companies with small-scale manufacturers are becoming more and more prominent. While

> this may solve to some extent the marketing problems of the small units, it can also be a means for large units to avoid licensing provisions and excise duties and to avail of a host of other advantages at the cost of the exchequer, the small manufacturers, the consumers and the workers. The implications of this are not being fully grasped by the policy makers. There is an urgent need of a comprehensive review of this practice.

This study indicates the distortions which have crept into the small-scale sector programmes during the process of implementation. While there has been a frequent criticism about the registration of bogus small-scale units to avail of the various forms of state patronage, the fact that large industrial houses and TNCs have been, directly and indirectly, operating in the small-scale sector is less known and much lesser discussed. Besides providing fiscal concessions and financial accommodation, the membership of the officially recognised small-scale sector has helped many a big business company to avoid a variety of regulatory obligations. It needs no elaboration that the presence of big business companies in the small-scale sector is detrimental to the interests of smaller constituents of the sector. The operation of the reservation policy has not proved to be much of an advantage to the small sector. The distortions are significant and only too clear. But quite apart from this, there have been a variety of new trends in the Indian corporate sector, in general, and the small-scale sector, in particular. One such important development is the fast expanding phenomenon of sub-contracting. The long-term implications of these trends are, we afraid, not being appreciated by the policy makers, and indeed not even by the associations of the small sector.

The need to introduce clarity in the objectives of the small sector programmes is only too obvious. There is also a need to question a large number of assumptions on which policy packages for the sector have been evolved. The loopholes and other limitations of the administrative system can, of course, only be taken care of if there was a continuing system for monitoring and coordination of the small-scale sector programmes. Once the objective conditions now prevailing in the sector have been understood, the task of evolving alternative strategies would become possible.

Section II

Bank Nationalisation

9 Bank Nationalisation[1]

Nationalisation of 14 private commercial banks has been realised. And with this, the control of public sector commercial banks has increased from nearly 27 per cent to nearly 87 per cent of total bank deposits. It may reach 90 per cent if one takes into account the subsidiary character of some private commercial banks. But then what?

There were many reasons which provided support to the demand for nationalisation. The most important, it appears to me, was the economic one. It is unfortunate that since the demand for nationalisation was pressed for by political parties, it was completely labelled as a political demand. And by describing it as a pure and simple political move, an impression is sought to be created that the act of nationalisation was devoid of any economic rationality. Here, perhaps, two things are confused: the rationality of the act and its timing and developments in the political scene preceding the ordinance on nationalisation. On the need for nationalisation, the only point made is that the same 'objective' could be achieved under the scheme of 'social control.' It is fortunate that no one disputes the objectives. As long as there was unanimity over the purpose, one could argue that the choice between 'social control' and 'nationalisation' could be treated as a matter of administrative prudence. And naturally the choice had to be made by the government—which in a democratic setup is bound to be under one or the other political party. But the real point is that the purpose of social control was certainly not the same as it is for nationalisation. These are two distinctly different measures.

The objectives as spelled out under the 'social control' measures were extremely limited. In fact, to describe those measures as 'social control' was a misnomer. This needs to be seen with reference to the basic objectives. The demand for takeover of banks was related to one of the

1. As broadcast in the home service, All India Radio, News Services Division, "Spotlight" (21:15 hrs), New Delhi on August 14, 1969.

Directive Principles of the Indian Constitution *viz.*, "In economic sphere, the State is to direct its policy, in a manner as to secure the distribution of ownership and control of material resources of the community to sub-serve the common good and ensure that the operation of the economic system does not result in the concentration of wealth and means of production." Any measures undertaken in pursuance of this directive would be expected to mention the curbing of concentration as its primary objective. But, surprisingly enough, there was no such direct or indirect reference. The scope of the 'social control' measures was limited to certain formal changes in the management boards and enhanced administrative powers of the Reserve Bank of India (RBI). The purpose of mentioning this here is to emphasise that it is not correct to say that 'social control' measures had the same objective as are sought to be achieved through nationalisation. Therefore, it was not a matter of choice for one administrative set-up over another. If at all there was any choice, it was between: (i) recognising the need to curb concentration and (ii) in the acceptance of the evil of concentration in the economy in the belief that it was a pre-requisite for rapid economic growth.

The question is largely an economic one *viz.*, whether in a developing economy like Indian, concentration of wealth and economic power helps to achieve higher rate of economic growth or its existence, and more so the accentuation, restricts the process of planned development. As a general hypothesis, one has to face the question. Are inequalities a pre-requisite to higher growth rate? This is a question of applied economics in the present day Indian setting. We have to examine the relevant facts to come to a conclusion. The experience of the past 18 years of planning offers a lot of evidence required to come to a judgement on this question. Viewed from this angle, the *Report of the Industrial Licensing Policy Inquiry Committee* should serve an excellent base for informed discussion.

One cannot go into various details of the report in a short talk like this. However, the principal conclusion of the inquiry is that a few larger industrial houses were able to influence government decision-making at various levels, in very important matters, in their favour while others were deprived of their rightful opportunities. Similarly, financial resources, set aside for encouragement of new entrepreneurs in priority industries, were mainly obtained by the few larger houses for projects which did not always have a relationship to Plan priorities.

In brief, it means that economic power has been in operation, and in this process, the degree of concentration in the economy has increased. Important decisions were influenced by consideration of the few powerful interests at the cost of the public at large and the plan priorities in particular. The strength of such influence has not been fully recognised in the Indian discussions on planning and developmental efforts. My submission is that planning exercises undertaken in the absence of a proper assessment of the pattern of ownership and the character and personality of the Indian industrialists were bound to have a limited impact.

In our efforts at planning we have not paid much attention to this aspect of our economic structure. In fact, if I may say so, there are many who have a general belief that not only the existence, but even the furtherance of inequalities may be desirable to achieve higher rate of economic growth. This belief, however, true it might have been in the 19th Century, does not hold good today in a developing country like India. What is to be realised is that all measures which reduce concentration and bring about better distribution of resources would help to achieve a broad-based, stable and higher rate of economic growth.

The extent to which nationalisation of banks would restrict concentration in the economy, one can venture to say, it would promote economic growth and not retard it. Viewed in this manner, bank nationalisation is an institutional change in the economic organisation of the country. With the nationalisation of banks, the close connections between the few industrialists and banks have been severed. The public sector managements, one hopes, would not be under the influences of big business, and the management would be able to take decisions which were directly related to plan priorities and other national objectives. It needs hardly an effort to establish that the extent to which credit was used to adhere to plan priorities the rate of economic growth would be higher. However, to reach this objective, the Planning Commission and various economic ministries would have to be more precise and clear on their objectives. For instance, the first requisite would be to prepare a detailed credit plan as also fix *inter-se* priorities for the industrial sector. It is only with the preparation of such a framework that nationalised banks would be able to play an effective role in the process of planned economic development. Undoubtedly, if such exercises are undertaken, some important changes in the size and pattern of investments visualised in the Draft Fourth Five Year Plan would be inevitable. This also means a shift in the relative role of the private and public sectors. If the nationalised banks are able to mobilise savings in the rural and agricultural sectors, it should be possible to undertake some of the priority projects earlier and thereby step up the overall rate of investment in the economy. The combined effect of larger investments according to plan priorities can undoubtedly ensure higher rate of economic growth than what would have been possible otherwise. But all this depends on how intelligently we make use of these newly acquired institutions and how clearly we are able to spell out our objectives and policies. Much more work will need to be done in this direction.

10 Banking Institutions and Indian Economy

A Critical Review[1]

Structure and Trends

In recent years, India's national economy has developed certain serious economic maladies. In the first instance, the economy has become heavily dependent on foreign aid. The proportion of foreign aid in the Plan Development Programme has been continuously rising since the First Five Year Plan. Since the prospects of the availability of foreign aid in the last two or three years have become very uncertain and rather dim, there has been a slack in the levels of economic activity and employment in the country.

Secondly, there has been the paradox of inflationary recession having come in the economy and tending to become all-pervasive. The chief characteristic of recession is that, while on the one hand there are large unutilised industrial capacities in the economic system, the supply of raw materials and other components for production of final goods is extremely deficient. The decline of agricultural production explains only a part of this phenomenon, while another part will have to be ascribed to the general shortages in the economy which have been generated as a result of the growing intersectoral imbalances caused by the functioning of financial institutions and the economic system in a particular manner.

The most curious aspect of the present situation is that the price level of industrial and agricultural goods continues to be very high despite slack demand. Obviously, the financial system of the country seems to have acquired such characteristics that it is able to sustain a prolonged holding of goods in

1. This report was co-authored by H.K. Manmohan Singh. V.B. Singh, S.C. Gupta and S.K. Goyal and submitted on October 1967.

the economy without leading to the adjustments of the price level with the existing state of demand and supply.

The role of bank credit is obviously an important factor to be examined in so far as it helps to create the present situation as well as maintain it for a long period.

In addition, due to various political and economic reasons, both national and international, the perspective of long-term development of the economy is tending to get blurred. The commitment to long-term programmes of plan development has tended to become weak in recent years and greater attention is being given to measures of policy which seek to attain economic stability rather than economic growth. In this context too, it has become necessary to examine the role the banking system of the country has played so far in promoting the long-term growth of the economy as well as in creating conditions in which further growth of industry and agriculture has been halted in recent years.

With this background in our mind, we have examined the structure and functioning of our banking system and drawn necessary conclusions regarding its reorganisation, which in our opinion are vital for accelerating further growth of the economy and the achievement of broader social objectives.

The magnitude of bank deposits in 1965 was only 15 per cent of national income (at current prices). The corresponding figure for 1951 was 9 per cent. In money terms, bank deposits have grown on an average at the rate of nearly 16 per cent i.e., from ₹ 908.47 crore in 1951 to ₹ 3073.36 crore in 1965.

This fact indicates two things. One that bank deposits in India represent a significant part of the nation's disposable resources. And secondly, the growth of bank deposits has been nearly five times the rate of growth of national income. With each successive year of planning in India, the banks have been accumulating larger and larger financial resources of the society. On the assumption that the past trends would continue, it can be safely projected that banks would very soon acquire command over the bulk of the nation's financial resources.

Declining Number of Banks

The banking institutions in India can be broadly grouped under two categories *viz.*, (i) scheduled and (ii) non-scheduled. Since 1951, there has been a significant decline in the number of these institutions. From a total of 566 banks (of both categories) in 1951, the number had come down to only 109 in 1965. The reduction in the number of non-scheduled banks has been phenomenal—from 473 to mere 33, and the scheduled banks from 92 in 1951 to 76 in 1965. As is only natural, with reduction in numbers on the one side and growth in banking deposits on the other, it has led to larger concentration within the banking sector.

Scheduled and Non-scheduled Banks

Out of the total bank deposits of ₹ 3183.20 crore in 1965, the non-scheduled banks, which numbered 33, held deposits worth ₹ 24.15 crore only. Similarly, the significance of non-scheduled banking has been very little in terms of advances and other operations. Past experience provides support to the idea that small financial institutions have little place in a developing society. These do not enjoy confidence of the public in general; nor do these institutions have the resources to organise such facilities which can be easily provided by the large-sized national financial institutions. Therefore, for the purpose of our discussion, the non-scheduled banks have very little significance.

The scheduled banks are 76 and these can be grouped under: (i) the public sector and (ii) the private sector. The former comprises of the State Bank of India (SBI) and seven of its subsidiaries.[2] Out of the remaining 68 scheduled banks, 15 banks are of foreign origin and the rest are private sector Indian banks.

Foreign Banks

The total number of scheduled bank offices, at the end of 1965, were 6,133 only. Table 10.1 gives details of the state-wise bank offices.

2. The subsidiaries to SBI are: (i) the State Bank of Bikaner & Jaipur; (ii) the State Bank of Hyderabad; (iii) the State Bank of Indore; (iv) the State Bank of Mysore; (v) the State Bank of Patiala; (vi) the State Bank of Saurashtra; and (vii) the State Bank of Travancore.

Table 10.1

Showing State-wise Break-up of Bank Offices in India

S. No.	States	No. of Offices in Each State				% of Offices in Each State		
		SBI and Sub.	OISB	FB	Total	SBI and Sub.	OISB	Foreign Banks
	1	2	3	4	5	6	7	8
1.	Andhra Pradesh	205	217	2	424	10.7	5.6	2.2
2.	Assam	34	24	1	59	1.8	0.6	1.1
3.	Bihar	93	120	-	213	4.8	3.1	-
4.	Gujarat	155	329	1	485	8.1	8.4	1.1
5.	Jammu & Kashmir	2	12	1	15	0.1	0.3	1.1
6.	Kerala	126	257	4	387	6.6	6.6	4.3
7.	Madhya Pradesh	134	104	-	238	7.0	2.7	-
8.	Madras	161	679	10	850	8.4	17.4	10.9
9.	Maharashtra	199	587	23	809	10.4	15.1	25.0
10.	Mysore	137	429	1	567	7.1	11.0	1.1
11.	Nagaland	2	-	-	2	0.1	-	-
12.	Orissa	49	20	-	69	2.6	0.5	-
13.	Punjab	143	232	4	379	7.4	6.0	4.3
14.	Rajasthan	125	119	-	244	6.5	3.1	-
15.	Uttar Pradesh	213	325	2	540	11.0	8.3	2.2
16.	West Bengal	94	229	25	354	4.9	5.9	27.2
17.	Union Territories	48	209	18	275	2.5	5.4	19.5
18.	Total	1920	3892	92	5904	100.0	100.0	100.0

Note: SBI: State Bank of India and Subsidiaries.
OISB: Other Indian Scheduled Commercial Banks.
FB: Foreign Banks.

Source: Reserve Bank of India (RBI), *Statistical Tables Relating to Banks in India, 1966*.

It would be seen that out of the 92 offices of the foreign banks, 75 offices were located in four states of the country, i.e., Maharashtra, 23; West Bengal, 25; Delhi, 17; and Madras, 10. Punjab and Kerala had 4 offices each. States like Bihar, Madhya Pradesh and Orissa did not have even a single branch of foreign banks. It is, therefore, obvious that the foreign banks have generally confined themselves to centres of international trade. Also it is by no coincidence that the majority of the foreign bank offices have been at the seaports of the country, except Delhi, for obvious reasons.

Concentration of Banking Operations: State-wise

In the case of Indian scheduled commercial banks, it can be seen that bank offices are concentrated in a few states only. For instance, a large number of offices are located in five states, *viz.*, Maharashtra, Madras, Gujarat, Mysore and West Bengal. The five states' combined total of bank offices was 3,065 out of the total of 5,812. States like Jammu & Kashmir (J&K), Bihar, Orissa and Madhya Pradesh had a significantly smaller share in the national total. However, two states, namely Kerala and Mysore, are exceptions. Otherwise, the bank offices have been mainly located in the comparatively well-off states of the country.

Another way of studying the special distribution of banking activity is to have a look at the distribution of bank offices according to the population of urban centres. The following table shows the number of offices in centres of varying population (see Table 10.2 showing distribution of bank offices according to population centres)

From this, it is evident that the banking activity has been mainly confined to urban centres. For instance, nearly two-third of the bank offices are located in centres having population of more than 1 lakh. On the other hand, only 15 per cent of bank offices are located in towns with population of 10,000 and lesser.

In Tables 10.1 and 10.2, if one compares the degree of spatial concentration of banking activity, as represented by the offices, one notices that the degree of dispersion is comparatively higher in the case of the SBI and its subsidiaries. Comparatively, SBI offices are more evenly distributed than those of private commercial banks. Similarly, a large percentage of the SBI offices are located in smaller towns as compared to the private banks. Nearly one-fifth of the private banks are in big cities, whereas the corresponding percentage for the SBI is only 5.6. There is clear indication that the SBI offices are opened in such areas where the private banks hesitate. It could happen only because the SBI had followed a different policy as regards the opening of offices, from that of the other banks.

Table 10.2

Showing Distribution of Bank Offices according to Population of the Locations

S. No.	Population Range	Number of Offices as on December 31, 1965						
		Foreign Banks	SBI and Sub.	Other Indian Scheduled Banks	Total	% of Col. 2	% of Col. 3	% of Col. 4
	1	2	3	4	5	6	7	8
1.	Unclassified	-	74	42	116	3.8	1.0	2.0
2.	Less than 5,000	-	104	117	221	5.4	3.0	3.8
3.	5,000 to 10,000	1	289	258	548	15.0	6.6	9.4
4.	10,000 to 25,000	1	620	625	1246	32.3	16.0	21.4
5.	25,000 to 50,000	3	315	510	828	16.4	13.1	14.2
6.	50,000 to 1 lakh	-	161	486	647	8.4	12.5	11.1
7.	1 lakh to 5 lakh	11	192	849	1052	10.0	21.8	18.1
8.	5 lakh to 10 lakh	5	58	230	293	3.0	5.9	5.5
9.	10 lakh and above	71	107	775	953	5.6	19.9	16.4
10.	Total	92	1920	3892	5812	100.0	100.0	100.0

Source: Reserve Bank of India (RBI), *Statistical Tables Relating to Banks in India*, 1966.

However, the overall picture of banking in India is that of uneven distribution. It becomes further clear from the state-wise break up of banking offices, deposits and bank credit in relation to population. From the following table, it would be seen that the most highly developed states, from banking viewpoint, are Madras, Mysore, Kerala and Gujarat. The worst in order are: Orissa, J&K, Bihar and Assam. In the first category of state, a bank office exists for every 50,000 persons, whereas in the worst an office is for more than 2 lakh persons (see Table 10.3 showing distribution of bank offices, deposits and bank credit in different states, 1965).

Per capita Deposits in States

From column 3 of Table 10.3 it is also clear that per capita deposits are the highest in these states which have larger number of offices. For instance, the four states (after excluding two states, namely, West Bengal and Maharashtra where the higher per capita deposits can be explained because of the high quantum of demand deposits of the industrial and business enterprises) with the higher per capita deposits are those which had larger banking offices.

Table 10.3

Showing Distribution of Bank Offices, Deposits and Bank Credit in Different States (1966)

S.No.	States	000 Persons per Office	Per capita Deposits	Per capita Bank Credits	Credit Deposit Ratio
	1	2	3	4	5
1.	Andhra Pradesh	90	30.0	17.5	58.0
2.	Assam	227	22.7	9.1	40.0
3.	Bihar	234	19.3	6.9	36.0
4.	Gujarat	47	103.7	57.7	56.0
5.	Jammu & Kashmir	246	43.7	3.4	78.0
6.	Kerala	48	51.1	31.0	61.0
7.	Madhya Pradesh	148	21.9	14.9	68.0
8.	Madras	41	57.5	60.8	106.0
9.	Maharashtra	53	184.8	152.1	82.0
10.	Mysore	45	57.4	39.5	69.0
11.	Nagaland	-	-	-	-
12.	Orissa	273	9.3	4.6	50.0
13.	Punjab	59	78.9	33.6	43.0
14.	Rajasthan	91	23.2	12.1	52.0
15.	Uttar Pradesh	145	28.8	12.7	44.0
16.	West Bengal	112	115.8	123.1	106.0
17.	All India Average	80	64.2	44.6	67.0

Source: RBI, *Statistical Tables Relating to Banks in India*, December, 1966.

Looked from the per capita bank credit angle, it would be seen that except for the four states (namely, Maharashtra, West Bengal, Madras and Gujarat), the per capita credit in 12 states was lower than the national per capita average of ₹ 44.6. In Maharashtra, the per capita credit was ₹ 152.1; West Bengal ₹ 123.1; Madras ₹ 60.8 and in Gujarat ₹ 57.7. On the other hand, the per capita bank credit was as low as ₹ 3.4 in J&K; ₹ 4.6 in Orissa; ₹ 6.9 in Bihar and ₹ 9.1 in Assam. In the rest of the states, the figure varied from ₹ 12.0 to nearly ₹ 40.0.

Credit-Deposit Ratio

It is of interest to see the credit-deposit ratio in states. It is only in the case of two states, West Bengal and Madras, that the ratio is more than 100 showing that the bank credit is 6 per cent more than the deposits. In the case of the rest of the states, the ratio is less than 100. In five states, the ratio is less than 50 with J&K having the ratio as low as 7.8.

Bank Investments

It needs to be mentioned here that credit-deposit ratio does not represent the true picture. It is so because out of the total deposits, investments accounted for nearly 935.16 crore in 1965. Nearly four-fifth of the bank investments were held in the form of securities of central and state governments. Investments, other than in government securities, were of the order of ₹ 159.97.

Table 10.4

Showing Pattern of Investments of the Scheduled Bank (March 1965)

S.No.	*Source of Investment*	*Amount*	*Percentage*
	1	*2*	*3*
1.	Government Securities	755.12	80.7
	(a) Central	562.69	60.2
	(b) States	191.20	20.4
	(c) Others	1.23	0.1
2.	Domestic Investments	159.97	17.1
	(a) Trustee Securities	114.53	12.2
	(b) Shares of Joint Stock Companies	25.04	2.7
	(c) Real Estate	10.21	1.1
3.	Foreign Investments	20.7	2.1
4.	Total	935.16	100.0

Source: RBI, *Statistical Tables Relating to Banks in India*, December 1966.

From this, it would be seen that investments account for nearly 30.7 per cent of the total deposits. Therefore, credit-deposit ratio should take into account the spatial investment pattern as well. In the absence of more details on state-wise bank investments, for the purpose of understanding real credit policies, one may deplete the deposits of each state, on an average, by the percentage of investments to deposits. For instance, one can take it that each state has to share its bank deposits with the central and state governments by a certain ratio. For the year 1965, one may spread the bank investments of ₹ 935.16 crore equally over all states.

Movement of Resources

Table 10.5 shows state-wise bank deposits and credit as on March 31, 1965. Column 3 gives the adjusted deposits as is shown in columns 4 and 5. From these columns, it emerges that out of the 16 states of the country, only 3 states are such which draw more bank credit than their deposits. It can be seen that through the institution of banking, nearly 345 crore of rupees are channelised for purposes of business and industrial activity

Table 10.5

Showing Variation in Bank Deposits and Credit (State-wise)

S.No.	*States*	*Deposit (in Crore)*	*Credit (in Crore)*	*Deposits after Accounting for Investment (in Crore)*	*Excess Deposits*	*Excess Credit*
	1	*2*	*3*	*4*	*5*	
1.	Andhra Pradesh	114.3	66.8	79.2	+12.4	-
2.	Assam	30.4	12.2	21.0	+8.8	-
3.	Bihar	-96.6	34.6	66.9	+32.3	-
4.	Gujarat	235.3	130.9	163.1	+32.2	-
5.	Jammu & Kashmir	16.1	1.3	11.1	+9.8	-
6.	Kerala	94.3	57.2	65.3	+8.1	-
7.	Madhya Pradesh	77.3	52.6	53.6	+1.0	-
8.	Madras	202.4	214.0	140.3	-	73.7
9.	Maharashtra	795.5	655.0	551.3	-	103.7
10.	Mysore	146.3	100.6	101.5	+0.9	-
11.	Nagaland	-	-	-	-	-
12.	Orissa	17.6	8.7	12.2	+3.5	-
13.	Punjab	175.7	74.1	121.8	+47.7	-
14.	Rajasthan	51.3	26.9	35.6	+8.8	-
15.	Uttar Pradesh	225.9	99.3	156.5	+57.2	-
16.	West Bengal	453.0	481.4	313.9	-	167.5
17.	All India	3049.2	2116.4	2116.4	+344.9	344.9

Source: RBI, *Statistical Tables Relating to Banks in India*, December, 1966.

from the other states and made available to West Bengal, Maharashtra and Madras. The situation can also be described as one in which the commercial banking institutions act as instruments of mobilising saving from the other states of the country for supporting investments and other economic activity in the three states which are already well developed.

Viewed from another angle, the banks act as instruments to ensure flow of financial resources from underdeveloped areas to the industrially advanced ones. If one looks at the pattern of advances and deposits, according to the centres of population, one finds relatively much higher concentration of advances in cities. The advance-deposits ratio for large cities works out to be as high as 91.3, whereas the ratio is 39.2 in the case of small centres.

Another factor which needs to be kept in mind is that the nature of deposits also varies from centre to centre. However, broadly speaking, fixed and saving deposits form higher percentage of the deposits in smaller centres whereas in larger cities (as is also true of industrially developed states), the deposits are more of the nature of demand deposits. Viewed in this light, the flow of funds from underdeveloped states may appear to be even more significant. Similarly, it would be seen that banks help to mobilise saving from smaller population centres to larger ones.[3]

From the above account, it may be said that banking institutions in India have not been uniformly developed in all states. Also there is evidence that bank offices have been mainly operating in thickly populated centres. In this regard, a better spatial dispersion of the SBI is well recognised than of the other commercial banks. The disparities in the level of growth of banking are indicated by number of offices, and the magnitudes of bank deposits and credit. Another interesting feature of the Indian banks operation is their impact on the flow of financial surpluses from different states to only three states of the country. As can be expected from the above pattern of the growth of banking in this country, evidence to the fact exists that banks act as instruments of mobilising savings from smaller centres for providing credit in the urban and industrial centres of the country.

3. For an analysis of the deposits and advances in cities and smaller centres, See: Kanvinde, D.J. (1967). "Some Trends in Indian Banking", *State Bank of India, Monthly Review* 6: 234-46.

Paid-up Capital and Deposits Ratios

Another important feature of the Indian banking system is the extremely low ratio between the paid-up capital (PUC) and bank deposits. Initially, banks were established with very little PUC and the situation continues to be so. For instance, the PUC of most banks has been around one to two crore. The total PUC of all the Indian scheduled banks (numbering 61) stood at ₹ 44.36 crore only. However, because of the continued persuasion on the RBI, the banks have built up some reserves. The total equity capital of the scheduled banks was ₹ 61.78 crore in 1951 and it rose to ₹ 93.25 crore in 1965. The rise in the amount has been mainly due to the building up of reserves. The rise in PUC and reserves has been by about 50 per cent only, whereas the bank deposits have grown by nearly 238 per cent. As a result, the ratio of PUC and reserves to deposits has gone down from 9.7 per cent in 1951 to 3.4 per cent in 1955.

The PUC to deposit ratio for the overall banking sector is low in itself, but if one looks at the ratio in the individual banking companies, one would notice that the same is extremely low in the case of the bigger banks of the country. How important this ratio is needs to be underlined because it is the PUC the ownership of which determines controlling authority over the banks. Table 10.6 shows PUC to deposits ratio of the important banks in the country.

Table 10.6

Showing Paid-up Capital and Deposits Ratio in the Indian Banks (1965)

S.No.	*Name of the Bank*	*Paid-up Capital and Reserves (Cr)*	*Deposits (Cr)*	*Ratio (Col. 2/3)*
	1	*2*	*3*	*4*
1.	Bank of Baroda	2.0	185.91	1.07
2.	Bank of India	4.0	235.72	1.69
3.	Central Bank of India	4.7	306.04	1.53
4.	Punjab National Bank	2.0	232.96	0.86
5.	United Commercial Bank	2.8	141.15	1.98
6.	Five Banks (1 to 5)	15.5	1101.78	1.48
7.	State Bank of India (and its Subsidiaries)	10.63	881.47	1.20
8.	All Scheduled Banks	44.4	2814.66	1.57

Source: RBI, *Statistical Tables Relating to Banks in India*, December, 1966.

Ownership of Bank Shares

The quantum of PUC or its relationship with deposits is not in itself of much significance as the implications of the pattern of ownership of bank shares which form the PUC. Take the case of the Central Bank of India. The PUC is ₹ 4.70 crore. According to the information provided in the balance sheet of the bank, the bank had 12.6 lakh shares held by 24,800 shareholders. Nearly 92 per cent of the shareholders held less than 100 shares each. Another 5 per cent held shares between 100 and 200 each and 2 per cent held shares between 200 and 500. It was only one per cent of the shareholders who held more than 500 shares, individually. From another point of view, 49 per cent of the shares were held by 3 per cent of shareholders and 36 per cent shares were owned by one per cent of shareholders.

The pattern of ownership is widely dispersed. If one were to have details regarding the spatial distribution of bank shareowners, one would find that a large part of the shares are held by small isolated individuals scattered throughout the country. On the other hand, a fraction of the shareholders own a big block of shares. The wide dispersion of shareholders helps to strengthen the control of a small section of the shareholders in the banks. In a company in which all shareholders could be present at its general meetings, the group which wishes to carry majority would require 51 per cent votes. But if the shareholders are scattered all over the country a particular interest group can enjoy control over the company with even much lesser votes. Because of the wide distance and lack of interest by an average shareholder, control over banks is exercised by a small group. Even keeping the numbers aside, one needs an investment of ₹ 1 crore only to obtain control over a bank with PUC of ₹ 2 crore. It is through this mechanism that control over each banking institution has come to rest with a group of persons or a few families.

It is in this regard that the Governor, RBI, said:

> One of the structural features of Indian banking is this concentration of power which, in some cases, is enormous in relation to the capital actually employed. From time to time we come across cases in which a family or group has a controlling interest in a bank and it has become a major task of inspection to prevent the exercise of this interest in undesirable ways.

Ownership and Control of Banks

On account of the scattered nature of shareholdings of private commercial banks as well as the limited amount of PUC in relation to the total deposits, it is necessary to examine the ownership and control of private commercial banks in India. Here, it is necessary to distinguish between the persons who own shares in banking companies and those who put their deposits in banks. As we have seen, the ratio of PUC of the total number of deposits is extremely low. Consequently, the depositors have much higher stakes in the successful operations of private commercial banks, financially speaking, than the owners of share capital. Nevertheless, it is found, as already indicated above, that the ownership and control of the total finances of the banking system rests with very small number of persons who are able to determine the patterns of allocation and investment of bank finance according to their own individual interest and convenience.

With the present system of private ownership of banks, the security enjoyed by the depositors is considerably weakened since it rests on the ability and competence of those who control the allocation and investment of bank finances. But from the point of view of social justice and of encouragement of the confidence of depositors in the banking system, it is necessary that they should be ensured a complete security for their deposits with the banks which can be done only if the banking system was to be nationalised and the ownership of banks was to rest in the government. This is because the first claim on the resources of a bank in case of its failure would be that of depositors and not of the owners of share capital, and this would be best ensured by a nationalised banking system.

While under any law the private banking institutions can go bankrupt, there is nothing like a phenomenon called government going bankrupt. Hence the interests of the depositors cannot be admittedly secured beyond any doubt, whereas in case of private banking, insecurity can never be ruled out.

If ownership alone is to be the criterion, it stands to reason to state that the depositors whose deposits are infinitely far greater in proportion to the total PUC should be considered the legitimate owners of the banks rather than the market shareholders, and an ordinary depositor, in fact, exercises greater control over government and governmental activities than he can ever do in the case of private bank.

Thus even from the point of view of exercise and control in the case of nationalised institution, the depositor will not be an invisible owner but an active participant in the exercise of control.

Ownership of Deposits

The total number of bank accounts stood at 1.02 crore in 1965. Out of this, fixed deposit accounts were nearly 19 lakh and the saving deposits nearly 67 lakh. The number of current accounts is around 16 lakh. Table 10.7 provides break-up of the accounts and deposits.

Table 10.7

Showing Distribution of Accounts and Deposits

S.No.	*Category*	*Accounts*	*Deposits (Cr)*	*Accounts %*	*Deposits %*
1.	Demand Deposits	16,32,000	835.7	15.9	30.8
2.	Savings Deposits	67,28,000	581.7	65.7	21.4
3.	Fixed Deposits	18,74,000	1,296.5	18.3	47.7
4.	Total	1,02,34,000	2,713.9	100.0	100.0

Source: Same as Table 10.6.

It would be seen that nearly 31 per cent of the deposits are demand deposits held by nearly 16 per cent of the accounts. The savings accounts form nearly two-third of the total bank accounts.

For the purpose of the study of the ownership pattern of the bank deposit in clientele can be grouped under three broad heads: (i) personal and partnerships; (ii) government, public sector and cooperatives; and (iii) corporate sector (see Table 10.8).

Out of the total demand deposits of ₹ 835.7 crore, nearly 24 per cent belonged to the corporate sector. In the case of savings accounts, the entire deposits of ₹ 581.7 crore belonged to personal accounts. Similarly, about three-fourth of the fixed deposits were that of personal and partnership accounts. If one looks at the savings and fixed deposits collectively, one would see that out of the total deposits, less than 8 per cent of the deposits (amount) belonged to the corporate sector. For the purpose of our discussion, one can combine the ownership category of personal and partnerships with the government and cooperatives. The ownership pattern of bank deposits indicates that practically nine-tenth of the bank deposits belong to a large number of small depositors or government institutions and cooperatives.

Table 10.8

Showing Ownership Pattern of Demand, Savings and Fixed Deposits under Three Categories

S. No.	Category	Personal and Partnership		Govt. and Cooperative		Corporate Sector	
		000 Accts.	Cr. Amount	000 Accts.	Cr. Amount	000 Accts.	Cr. Amount
1		2	3	4	5	6	7
1.	Demand Deposits	1,529	468.9	41	185.7	63	181.1
2.	Savings Deposits	6,728	581.7	-	-	-	-
3.	Fixed Deposits	1,855	929.9	10	218.0	9	148.5
4.	Total	10,112	1,980.5	51	403.7	72	329.6

Source: Same as Table 10.7.

Industry and Banks

However, the control over banks is enjoyed by the corporate sector only. This is evident from three sets of statistics. One, the close relationship between the corporate sector and the bank directors; two, the nature of credit policies as pursued by banking institutions; and three, the extent to which the directors of the banking companies have taken loans from the banks.

Inter-locking

To study the extent of inter-locking between leading banks and other companies, a study was conducted in the Company Law Department by Shri R.K. Nigam. According to the survey of directorships of the 20 leading banking companies, a total of 188 persons served as directors on the boards of these 20 banks. The 188 bank directors held 1,452 directorships of other companies also. The total number of companies under these directors is 1,100. This excludes non-profit making organisations (see Table 10.9).

Table 10.9

Structure of Demand, Savings and Time Deposits

S. No.	Deposits	Limited Companies		Govt., Quasi-Govt. and Coops		Personal and Partnerships	
		Accts. in 000	Amounts in crore	Accts. in 000	Amounts in crore	Accts. in 000	Amounts in crore
	1	2	3	4	5	6	7
I.	**Demand Deposits**						
	(i) Industry	18	64.6	1	38.4	64	25.3
	(ii) Trading	30	46.1	1	7.8	588	158.2
	(iii) Financial	8	54.9	-	2.6	-	2.3
	(iv) Others	9	15.5	39	136.9	877	282.1
	Total (I)	63	181.1	41	185.7	1529	468.9
II.	**Savings Deposits**						
III.	**Time Deposits**						
	(i) Industry	3	73.8	1	31.8	3	9.7
	(ii) Trading	3	38.6	-	12.2	56	36.6
	(iii) Financial	1	6.7	-	5.9	-	0.4
	(iv) Others	2	29.4	9	168.1	1796	883.2
	Total (III)	9	148.5	10	218.0	1855	929.9
	Grand Total	72	329.6	51	403.7	10,112	1,980.5

Source: RBI, *Statistical Tables Relating to Banks in India*, December, 1966.

A detailed study of the directorships held by the directors of the five leading banks reveals that through common directors, these five banks are connected with 33 insurance companies, 6 financial companies and 25 investment trusts. Further, these banks were connected to 584 manufacturing and other companies and 26 trading companies and 15 associations not for profit (see Table 10.10).

The close relationship between the private corporate sector and the banking institutions was also underlined by the Mahalanobis Committee Report. It had specially noted that: "The dominance of industrial directors on the boards of the commercial banks is seen to be much greater in the case of the first eight banks, in whose case they numbered 59 out of 77 or nearly 77 per cent of the total."

Table 10.10

Showing Distribution of Directorships Held by the Directors of the Leading Five Banks

S.No.	Name of the Bank	Number of Directors	Number of Directorships held	Directorships held in					
				Insurance	Financial Companies	Investment Trusts	Manufacturing and Other Cos.	Trading Companies	Associations not for profit
	1	2	3	4	5	6	7	8	9
1.	Bank of India	11	174	10	1	8	146	9	-
2.	Central Bank of India	10	108	4	1	3	94	4	2
3.	Bank of Baroda	12	196	9	-	9	162	7	11
4.	United Commercial Bank	13	144	6	2	4	127	3	2
5.	Punjab National Bank	9	65	4	2	1	55	3	-
	Total	55	689	33	6	25	584	26	15

Source: Nigam, R.K. (1963). *Company News and Notes*, October, 1, pp. 62-74.

Financial Accommodation to Directors

A very natural corollary of the close relationship between banks and industrial enterprises is the advantage that these industrialists enjoy for the purpose of credit accommodation to their own concerns. Due to obvious reasons, a bank director is in a better position to obtain credit from his bank. The debt due to the bank directors or their companies was nearly ₹ 55.8 crore in 1954. But the amount had risen to ₹ 290.0 crore by 1965. The debt due reflects only the amount due at the end of the year. The bank loans given to the directors and their companies in the same year stood at ₹ 317.4 crore.

The figures given above should only be taken as broad indications of financial accommodation that the bank directors obtain directly from their own banks. But the advantages enjoyed by the bank directors and the ease with which they can secure bank credit are not reflected in these figures. There is no doubt that the director of a bank commands status and reputation and thereby his association helps the companies to secure easy credit practically from any banking institution. Moreover, the phenomena of 'back scratching' and its implications cannot be assessed through these figures.

Back Scratching

Supposing 'X' is the director of 'A' bank and 'Y' that of 'B' bank. With mutual understanding, bank 'B' can lend loans to 'X' and in return 'Y' can obtain similar financial accommodation from 'A'. In this way both banks have not lent to their own directors, and yet bank credit has been made available to both the bank directors. This phenomena is a well known one in the financial circles. It would be no surprise if the total bank credit advanced, directly or indirectly, to bank directors works out to be around ₹ 600 crore to ₹ 700 crore. Thus out of the aggregate bank credit, a few industrial houses would be claiming a large chunk.

The figures of bank credit to their directors also suffer from another serious limitation. According to the Bank Companies Act, no bank director can hold directorship of another bank and there is also a limit beyond which no individual can hold company directorships. These legal provisions are very easily set aside if one has his wife alive, and the situation is most convenient if one is lucky enough to have a large number of children or relations. In India, therefore, it poses no problem to keep oneself within the legal limits and yet operationally continue as one would if there were no legal restrictions.

Thus the quantum of bank loans, shown against the directors and their companies in the above statements, is only the direct and a clear one—for which returns have been filed to the RBI. But the extent of 'back scratching' can only be known through a study of the manner in which the bank credit in India has been shared by individuals, the banking magnets and the few big industrial and business houses to which the directors belong.

Lion's Share in Bank Loans

An indication of the gross underestimation of bank loans to directors and their companies is revealed by a compilation of the data regarding bank loans and advances for the year 1966. The total bank credit for this year stood at nearly ₹ 2432 crore. This amount was shared by nearly 9 lakh accounts. A break-up of the bank loans and advances for this year indicates that out of this ₹ 1,800 crore were lent to nearly four thousand accounts only. It has also been brought out that in June 1966, 572 borrowers in the entire banking system were extended nearly ₹ 1,400 crore out of the bank credit of nearly ₹ 1,800 crore given for industrial and commercial purposes to the big borrowers. This means that nearly two-third of the total bank credit was obtained under less than 600 accounts in the country which formed a fraction of the total borrowers.

If the 500-600 accounts were to be identified by industrial and business houses, one would find that the number of borrowers are in fact only four or five and also those only who enjoy control over the largest banks of the country. Thus the figure of ₹ 292 crore as debt due from the bank directors and their companies reflects less than one-fourth of the financial consideration that has been actually shown to the banks.[4]

Another indicator of the phenomena of 'back scratching' is evident from the extent of mutual accommodation of big houses while appointing directors

4. The Minister for Planning Shri Asoka Mehta while delivering convocation Address at Saugar on 4th February 1996 said: "Broadly speaking about 650 accounts in this country constitute roughly two-thirds of the total advances of the banking system."

over the bank management boards. Even a cursory glance at the composition of the boards of directors of the five largest banks would show that the bank managements are closely interlinked with one another through different members of the same family holding directorships in three or four, out of the five, largest banks. For instance, four members of one family held a bank directorship each in the Punjab National Bank, the United Commercial Bank, the Bank of India and the Bank of Baroda. Similarly, the Birlas held directorships on two banks, *viz.*, the Bank of Baroda and the United Commercial Bank. Apart from the interlinks through family members, the close links within the banking sector have often been seen through the non-family group-members also. Another interesting feature of the bank directorships is that there are very few changes in the composition of the bank directors overtime. In a rare case where a bank director did not continue for another term, it is not abnormal that the same individual was accommodated in one of the other banks or some other companies.[5] The hold of a family on a bank is unfortunate and it creates problem of its own, but when a group of families control all the major banks jointly, very serious implications are bound to follow.

Bank Credit for Industry and Commerce

Thirdly, the close links between industry and banking institutions are also indicated in the pattern of bank advances. For instance, out of the bank credit of ₹ 2097.7 crore for the year 1965, an amount of ₹ 1287.3 crore was extended for industrial purposes and another ₹ 536.8 crore for commerce. In other words, nearly 87 per cent of the bank credit was utilised for purposes of industry and commerce. Since 1950, the beginning of the Indian planning era and the time from when onward the banking business in India started growing at a fast rate, the pattern of bank loans has changed in such a manner that larger and larger share of the total bank credit is being directed to support industrial and commercial activities. For instance, in the year 1953 (September), the total loans for industrial purposes stood at ₹ 182.39 crore only against the sum of ₹ 1,287.3 crore in 1965. This is an increase of 6 to 7 times, whereas the total bank advances had increased by a little over 4 times only. As a result, one notices that

5. This becomes unavoidable as no one can hold directorships in two banks, and also holding of very large member of directorships of companies does not find favour with government.

industrial loans which comprised nearly 36.4 of the bank credit in 1953 accounted for 61.5 per cent in 1965. The trend in bank loans extended for agricultural purposes was absolutely to the contrary. In 1953 (September), agricultural loans stood at ₹ 19.01 crore, whereas the amount was ₹ 3.9 crore only for the year 1965. Not only the amount of absolute loan for agriculture had come down to one-fourth of what it was in 1953, but more significant is the fact that the share of the agricultural loans in total bank credit declined from 3.8 per cent to its nearly one-twentieth, i.e., 0.2 per cent only.

Table 10.11

Showing Debts due by Companies or Firms in which Directors of the Bank are Interested

(₹ in crore)

Year	*All Banks*	*Scheduled Banks*	*SBI*	*Other Indian Banks*	*Foreign Banks*	*Non-Scheduled Banks*	*Five Banks*
1	*2*	*3*	*4*	*5*	*6*	*7*	*8*
1954	-	55.83	18.31	31.83	5.69	-	-
1955	52.35	51.19	15.13	31.04	6.80	1.16	-
1956	66.50	65.63	20.85	36.76	8.02	6.87	-
1957	103.14	102.41	39.44	54.20	8.95	0.73	-
1958	109.57	108.99	51.03	50.57	7.39	0.59	-
1959	110.13	109.52	43.79	56.60	9.67	0.61	-
1960	142.13	141.96	63.17	68.11	10.70	0.15	-
1961	156.30	155.92	67.81	72.92	14.19	0.38	51.96
1962	183.68	183.47	72.81	96.81	13.85	0.21	73.90
1964	228.57	228.35	29.43	111.89	13.39	0.22	-
1965	290.90	290.87	126.36	135.07	13.89	0.90	-

Source: RBI, *Statistics Tables Relating to Banks in India*, 1955-1965.

Bank Credit and Plan Priorities

From the above account, it is obvious that the bank credit in India is being increasingly directed for industrial and commercial activities in the country, and out of the industrial loans a lion's share is claimed by a few industrial houses. Further, the tendency of increasing dominance of few houses in bank credit is on the increase. One can safely make a generalisation that the banks have become instruments of mobilising community savings for the growth of a few big industrial houses. We will deal with this aspect a little later but the point to be emphasised here is that normally one would expect that the pattern of bank loans would reflect the Plan priorities not only in its distribution to individual sectors but more so in conformity with the Plan priority industries and other social considerations. One is not sure if it was so. On the contrary, it appears that bank credit has been used for a number of such industries which had the least priority under the Plans and only those few who have, due to some historical reasons, come to enjoy control over the banking institutions.

It needs to be said that the financing of industries in general and that of big industrial units is not the same thing as of the 'big industrial houses.' Within the broad category of loans for 'industrial purposes,' it is often observed that not only the resources are directed to non-priority industries but also to industries which are surely contrary to the broad social objectives—other than 'concentration of economic power.' Therefore, while considering the fact that bank loans are increasingly used for industrial purposes, one must distinguish between the desirable and the undesirable industries.

Concentration in Consumer Goods Industries

Since we have said above that there can be certain industries which may run contrary to the overall national and social objectives, we may explain this a little further with reference to the consumer goods industries. It is well known that there has been a clear but recent tendency in the industrial consumer goods production to have large-scale production units.

On the one hand, concentration of production in consumer goods industries leads to discourage the growth of small-scale industries, and on the other, it reduces opportunities of employment since large-scale production is more mechanised. Very obviously such concentration in production and industrialisation runs contrary to the social objective of ensuring maximum employment opportunities in the economy. The process is not complete here. More relevant question to be asked is whether the price charged from the consumer is higher than what could be for a similar product of small-scale enterprises and in view of the advantages of economies of scale, which are available to large-scale production units and what happens to the difference between the price paid by the consumer and the actual cost of production of a big industrial unit. If the pricing policy of these units was a deliberate one and was used for the purpose of mopping away surpluses in the economy, or for ploughing back the surplus resources raised in this manner, there could be some justification for such concentration in production of consumer goods. But unfortunately, surpluses obtained by this type of concentration of production in consumer goods industries do not get invested for expansion or establishment of other essential or priority industries. A very little of this price differential is ploughed back. It happens so because large enterprises have to maintain huge sales organisations. As a result, the administrative and supervisory cost of distribution of these products involves 30-40 per cent of gross sales. In the case of small enterprises, the sales costs are very limited. Thus, what is gained by way of economies of large-scale production is lost in supporting a huge administrative and distributive system by the big industrial units.

From our preceding discussion, it is evident that the private commercial banking system in our country suffers from serious structural maladies. These have thwarted a purposeful use of bank credit in the Indian economy along desired lines. On the contrary, banks have led to the creation of conditions in which economic results that are contrary to our planning priorities have followed.

Moreover, it has been reported that a recent official document on social control over banking contains a detailed study of India's banking system in which the following conclusions have been reached by the author:

(a) The private commercial banks have failed to attract deposits of the rural masses in spite of the fact that the rural depositor is more than willing to take to banking habits once he comes into contact with the organised banking sector.

(b) The private commercial banks have mainly acted to drain away deposits from rural and semi-urban centres by means of fixing a low rate of interest on such disbursements.

(c) Private commercial banks have contributed an extremely small proportion of bank credit to small industry and agriculture despite the fact that 40 per cent of India's industrial production comes from small industry and 45 per cent of total national income from agriculture.

(d) There is no basis in the arguments usually given by the private banks for their failure to help small-scale industry and agriculture.

(e) The new entrepreneurs whose main capital is their technical and managerial skill have been denied bank credit facilities almost completely.

(f) The use of bank credit is exclusive and highly concentrated which have led to many undesirable social consequences and conferred the benefits of public savings upon only a few persons and industrialists. Private commercial banks, by their credit policies, have added, abetted and supported social desirable activities.

(g) The support and attitudes of commercial banks in favour of certain industrial houses have vitally added to their capacity and influence to raise internal capital and secure foreign collaboration. (This has been clearly pointed out in the report of Dr Hazari.)

(h) The private commercial banks have not been guided in their credit policies and practices by any positive social objectives, and the major commercial banks have been highly selective and exclusive in their credit policies.

Since the above conclusions are admittedly true, we do not wish to burden this document by presenting an analysis which would lead to the same conclusions. Hence we have deliberately avoided including a discussion of this aspect and take the above conclusions for granted for our purpose.

Plan Objectives

The basic objective of planning in India is to unleash a process of development which will raise standards of living, help to create new economic opportunities for the vast masses of the country and lead towards the establishment of a 'socialist society.' The planning problem is basically that of utilising more effectively the potential resources available to the community. However, the economic system of a country at a given time is the product of its broader social environment, socioeconomic institutional arrangements, values of the people and operational goods of the state. The objective of plan efforts in India has been to bring about the necessary changes in the functioning of the economic system by introducing the required institutional and other reforms. It is in this context that one has to consider the question of management and control of the banking set-up which is undoubtedly a strategic institution in any economy. How can the achievement of national objectives be facilitated by introducing a change in the control and management of banking institutions? This is a question which can be more fruitfully discussed only when the national objectives have been identified in a precise manner. With this purpose in mind, an effort has been made in the following pages to identify the major objectives before the Indian economy and explain some of the recent trends in these.

Economic Growth

Very few objectives are amenable to as many interpretations as the expression 'economic growth.' It can be measured in many ways, and each has its own purpose. Generally, however, economic growth is equated with the growth rate of national income. But the rate of growth, whether it is measured in terms of national income or in terms of *per capita* income, is not an objective in itself. All attempts at improvement of growth rates are mere means of achieving the basic objective of ameliorating the living conditions of the Indian population. Even at the cost of a little deviation from our main discussion, it would be necessary to underline that a mere talk about the achievement of higher rate of national income growth has no meaning unless it was ensured that the benefits of growth are shared by the largest numbers of people.

Therefore, it is essential that the process of economic growth is also accompanied with efforts at reduction of disparities in incomes and wealth levels. Viewed from this angle, the yardstick of economic growth is not only the growth rate of national or per capita income, but also the extent of improvements in the average living standards of the large sections of the population. It follows from this that economic growth in a country like India must necessarily be accompanied by a reduction of disparities in levels of income and wealth—or at least to ensure that these do not get aggravated.

Income Disparities

The government's policies at reducing disparities in income levels are expected to be two pronged. Firstly, to follow such fiscal monetary and regulatory policies which would not allow the gap in income levels to widen, and secondly, to undertake upon itself the direct responsibility to provide basic amenities to the weaker sections of the community. This would have involved the pursuance of a well worked out incomes and wage policy. However, we have yet to evolve such a policy. Consequently, along with the evolving of appropriate policies to correct imbalances, it is equally, and perhaps more, important to pay attention to reform the economic system and establish such institutional arrangements which would allow the fullest utilisation of the community's resources as would ensure against the exploitation by a few of the many.

For instance, the progress of land reforms has not been uniform in the states. One must admit that the programme has made significant changes in the countryside. But the progress of these efforts would have been more impressive if only due attention was given to the understanding of the purposes for which land were being suggested. Moreover, while pursuing reforms in the countryside, a logical step was to evolve the corresponding policies for urban property. In the present situation, one can rightly ask "why should reform be confined to the agricultural sector alone? Why should there be a ceiling on land holdings when in the urban centres there was no ceiling on holding of property or number of houses? This has been mentioned to point out that the approach to incomes and wage policy has to be applied throughout and not confined to a part of the economy.

How far the disparities in incomes had worsened during the first decade of planning in India was brought out by the Mahalanobis Committee Report. Speaking about the urban and industrial sector, it was categoric that the inequalities had grown. The reasons given were:

(a) The operation of the economic system with its criteria of creditworthiness and security of lending and investment tends to support the large established enterprise against the small and struggling entrepreneur. The large companies and bigger enterprises have an easier access to the capital market as banks, life insurance companies and trusts; besides individuals have a preference for investing in shares of large companies.

(b) The government's policy during the Plan period has been responsible for the growth of the private sector and in the process especially of big companies. In addition to affording a protected market and necessary overhead facilities and maintaining a budget policy with a middle inflationary bias favourable to industry, the government has been permitting the growth of private industry by extensive tax incentives.

(c) One of the factors accounting for an increase in economic power of the large groups in recent years has been the larger flow of foreign investment and technical know how through joint ventures.

Concentration of economic power is not objected to on non-economic considerations alone. To some extent, and in certain cases, concentration may be justified on functional grounds but the report observes, "concentration of economic power in the private sector is more than what could be justified on functional grounds."

These observations have to be seen in the context of the Directive Principles of the Indian Constitution, one of which reads, "In the economic sphere the State is to direct its policy in a manner as to secure the distribution of ownership and control of material resources of the community to sub-serve the common good and ensure that the operation of economic system does not result in the concentration of wealth and means of production."

In brief, the objective of economic growth is not an end in itself. The basic purpose of growth in national income and per capita incomes is the improvement of living standards of the masses. Thus if there was growth in the economy accompanied by widening of the gulf between the few and the large many, this cannot be considered as economic growth. Moreover, one is not sure if there can be sustained growth in any economy if the disparities do not get reduced. Even from the purely economic angle, disparities are least conducive to a continuous sustained growth of any economy. As economy which has concentration of economic power is also the one which is most liable to severe fluctuations, depressions, recessions and booms. Thus, it is imperative to realise that economic growth which does not reduce disparities is neither socially desirable nor economically sound development in the long run—leave apart the political implications of such developments.

Balanced Growth: Intersectoral

Another objective in the process of planning is that of ensuring balanced growth in the economy. The concept of balanced growth can be interpreted in three ways. One, it may be interpreted to mean a balance between the rates of growth of different sectors of the economy. It does not, however, mean equal rate of growth of all sectors. For instance, for obtaining a 5 per cent rate of overall growth, a few sectors may grow at the rate of 10-15 per cent whereas in certain others the growth may be around 3-4 per cent only. The essential meaning of a balanced growth would be to ensure that the intersectoral balances are not disturbed since excess or lower production in one sector leads to a number of bottlenecks which would stand in the way of a smooth and sustained rate of economic growth. To ensure this, the government would have to use taxation, credit and other regulatory measures to support or discourage production in a matter that the supplies of various inputs are available in the required quantum. This is a function which cannot be left to the operations of the market forces. In some measure, one is afraid that our past experience has not been a very happy one in this respect. At many a point of time, shortages have created bottlenecks for production. Especially a number of plan priority industries which should have been developed had lagged behind, whereas in a number of non-plan industries, the growth has been phenomenal.

Inter-regional

Balanced growth can also be referred to the ensuring of reductions in the inter-regional disparities over space. However, the situation that is obtained in the country today presents a picture of considerable disparities in levels of growth—from one state to another (see Table 10.12). To some extent, the inter-state disparities are corrected by central investments but unfortunately the private sector growth has tended to negate the trends towards spatial balances.

One can measure the level of economic activity in states in many ways. But no single indicator would reveal the real inter-state disparities. A broad indicator of the states level of development is provided in state-wise per capita income estimates (see column 2 of Table 10.12). However, a more important indicator of the differences in levels of growth of the states would be in the study of the share of each state in the national productive capital in factory establishments. It would be seen that two states, namely, West Bengal and Maharashtra claimed nearly two-fifth of the national productive capital in the private sector. Rajasthan was the least industrialised having only one per cent share in this capital (see column 3 of the Table 10.12). To some extent, the existence of varying shares in productive capital may be explained by the differences in state potentials. But, surely enough one cannot argue that the existing distribution of national productive capital in the private sector reflects nothing but spatial differences in potentials. For instance, from all accounts, it seems clear that states like Mysore, Kerala, Andhra Pradesh and others do have considerable scope for the establishment of industries. This has also been indicated by the techno-economic surveys of the states. The real reason for development of only a few states lies in the manner in which the Indian economic system operates and is also to some extent due to historical and political factors. It would be noticed that the two states which claim two-fifth of the national productive capital in factory establishments are the states which were initially developed as centres of commerce and trade. And due to a variety of reasons, growth of industries has followed the same spatial pattern as that of commerce and trade. One would not, however, argue that there have been deliberate attempts at developing only the states of Maharashtra and West Bengal, whereas no efforts were made towards industrialisation by the other states.

In our opinion, the main reason for this unbalanced growth of regions in the country has been the functioning of our economic system which contributes towards the growth of such areas which are already better developed against those which are poorer. A similar pattern of distribution was noticed regarding the growth of banking institutions. Our study has indicated how the operations of the banking system in India have led to movement of nearly ₹ 390 crore from the poorer states to three states, namely, Maharashtra, West Bengal and Madras. Since banking set-up is an

Table 10.12

Showing Indicators of Economic Activity in States in India

S. No.	States	Per capita income (₹) (1961-62)	% Share in the Nations Productive Capital in Factory Establishments 1963	% of Central Investment 1965-66	% of Total Villages Electrified 1965-66	Length of Roads per 100 km 1965-66	Per capita Bank Deposits (₹) 1965
	1	2	3	4	5	6	7
1.	Andhra Pradesh	287.0	5	4.5	20	17	30.0
2.	Assam	333.3	2	2.6	1	4	22.7
3.	Bihar	220.7	13	16.0	6	14	19.3
4.	Gujarat	393.4	8	3.0	9	13	103.7
5.	Jammu & Kashmir	289.0	-	-	10	4	43.7
6.	Kerala	314.9	2	2.3	39	43	51.1
7.	Madhya Pradesh	285.3	9	20.5	2	10	21.9
8.	Madras	334.1	7	7.0	7	38	57.5
9.	Maharashtra	468.5	20	3.7	11	15	184.8
10.	Mysore	304.7	3	1.4	15	28	57.4
11.	Nagaland	-	-	-	-	-	-
12.	Orissa	276.2	7	16.5	1	9	9.3
13.	Punjab	451.3	3	1.1	25	17	78.9
14.	Rajasthan	267.4	1	0.5	4	8	23.2
15.	Uttar Pradesh	297.3	5	6.4	9	14	28.8
16.	West Bengal	464.6	20	14.5	5	30	115.8
17.	All States	334.5	100	100.0	10	17	64.2

Source: Col. 2: National Council of Applied Economic Research.
Col. 3: *Annual Survey of Industries*.
Col. 4: Planning Commission.
Col. 5: Planning Commission.
Col. 6: Planning Commission.
Col. 7: RBI.

important and potent part of the economic system, it is no surprise that the operation of the overall economic system has helped the growth of certain states at a faster rate than the others. While the strategic institutions are allowed to operate as they do now, there can be little hope for inter-regional balances or for attempts at reductions in the inter-state levels of economic activity and growth rates (see Table 10.12).

To some extent, central public sector plan investments can attempt to correct such inter-regional imbalances. However, in the initial stages of economic development, the location of central plan projects has to be more on considerations of immediate economic advantages than other social objectives. Therefore, the central outlay can be used for this purpose in a limited manner only. We would not even for a moment suggest that the plan investments should not be used as an instrument for ensuring greater inter-state balances, wherever it can be done it should be only too welcome. On the other hand, it is a well-known fact that a large many medium-scale industrial units and 'foot loose' industries can be established in places which do not have minerals or other basic materials but have abundance of surplus labour supply—which is an important resource. The point to be emphasised is that left to the existing economic system as such there can be little hope of development for the depressed areas. It is so because the level of underdevelopment is in itself a great handicap for the poorer states. Therefore, it has to be recognised that a number of institutional reforms are a basic prerequisite to the attainment of spatial balances in the country.

Self-reliance and Foreign Exchange

Another objective before the Indian economy is the conservation and enhancement of foreign exchange resources—both by judicious use of the foreign exchange for purposes of development of strategic and basic industries and also by making every effort at stepping up of exports. The purpose of being careful in the use of foreign exchange is to ensure that the Indian economy reaches a state, as early as possible, from where onwards its normal growth would not remain heavily dependent upon the assistance of the outside world. We are conscious that many a time the interpretation of the objective of 'self-reliance' is stretched too far. Some have entertained ideas that self-reliance would mean being self-sufficient in all matters—social, economic and political. For them, the concept of self-reliance is another form of isolation from the rest of the world. But the purpose, which we have in mind, is a limited one we do not visualise that India can be or it need to be self-sufficient in all respects. We visualise that India's overall trade transactions would get enlarged and India would become an important country from its exports viewpoint as also it would continue to import goods from abroad.

Exports

But the relevant question would be: Why with all the developments in industrial sector has not India become an exporter until now? The answer to this lies in three factors, *viz.*, (i) failure of the Indian industrialists to compete in the world market because of their high cost of production, (ii) lack of attempts on the part of the Indian exporters to win confidence of the foreign countries by maintenance of better uniform standards of their products and (iii) absence of any economic pressures and challenges which would force the Indian industrialists to go in search of markets abroad. The three factors are not independent of each other. The basic reason for these has been the existence of seller's market for too long a period accompanied by a variety of subsidies and the pursuance of fiscal and regulatory policies which have discouraged imports and created conditions of an extremely sheltered market for the local industrialists. This question is again closely related to the manner in which the newly established industries were provided conditions for the emergence of monopolies. Many a time licence was given to an industry because it was expected that it would boost up Indian exports. But once the licence was granted, imports of machines and raw material allowed and collaborations arranged, these very industrialists came forward with the plea that the Indian products cannot be exported because they cannot compete in the world market. And, therefore, industries which were established with the clear understanding that the bulk of their product would be exported divert their produce to the home market—which is only too ready to absorb anything that is available and where no other foreign competitors would be allowed to threaten the monopoly privileges of the so called 'national' enterprise.

As far as the lack of efforts at maintaining standards of quality of the industrial products is concerned, this is a hypothetical question in a 'sellers market.' Very rightly, as long as there was excess demand to what can be met by the local producers, the immediate problem of any rational producer would be to maximise profits by reducing his immediate costs and in this, he is only too easily tempted to do his job in a half-baked manner as also charging the highest price that he can. Where does come the question of consumer satisfaction? Or for that matter, where was the threat to his sales? And under these conditions, it would be only an idealist or an unintelligent person who would harp on maintenance of quality or reasonable prices.

Thus, the question of Indian producers having failed to evolve their standards of quality is only of academic value. The reality of life is too hard to be fully appreciated, and that is in a monopoly situation the consumer satisfaction or attempts to reduce costs of production remains an unreal question. Similarly, one may ask: Why should the Indian industrialists go abroad for securing new markets when they have the exclusive rights of sales, to their full capacity production, within the economy?

Imports Substitution

On the other hand one has to ask: 'Why India imports so many goods both consumer goods and producer goods?' One can understand the need to import such commodities which are not produced in sufficient quantity within the country. For instance, foodgrain imports may be justified for short periods. But why have we continued food imports? It is not for us to discuss the question of food here, and therefore, much against the temptation to do so, we would raise another specific question i.e., 'Why do the consumers as well as the producers—the big as well as the small—prefer imported commodities, from any luxury item like lipsticks to imported cars and machines?' Leaving aside the import of machines which are not produced within the country why should even an average man consider imported products as superior to the home-made ones. Have we as Indians lost all the national pride? The answer to this is not in lack of sentiments but in the lack of faith in the quality of goods produced by the Indian industries. This again brings us to the question of the lack of efforts by the Indian industrialists at maintaining certain uniform standards.

In this respect, the responsibility has to be shared equally by the government as well as by the industrialists. The government's failure has been in not enforcing—more so where the monopolies exist—the minimum standards for their products. For example, how much deterioration had taken place in a commodity like automobiles—which is used by the most vocal and influential strata of the Indian society—is too well known. We hope the committee appointed to go into the causes responsible for worsening of the quality of cars would indicate how far the existence of monopolies, and inability of the government to control them, along with the prevalence of sellers market, has been responsible for this deterioration. The basic point in referring to this to underline is that no amount of moral persuasions can prove of any use unless the government took active and continuing interest to impose conditions of quality maintenance and consumer satisfaction. For doing this, the government has the obligation to the society, since a large amount of foreign exchange resources were made available to such units by denying the average citizen the rights to import goods from outside. The allotment of foreign exchange to industrial concerns had become possible only when someone else was denied its use. Thus the grant of a licence is not only a social sanction but is also accompanied with a privilege and economic benefit for availing the scarce resources of the society. This sanction was provided by the government, and in return, it was an obligation to ensure that the sanction was not used against the broader interests of the society.

A very closely connected question with the low-efficiency of the industrial sector in India has been the fact that the so-called industrial entrepreneurs have not made any efforts to achieve specialisation in one type of activity. On the contrary, each big industrial house has attempted to enter as many industries as it was capable of. For instance, Dr R.K. Hazari had pointed out in his Interim Report that the Birlas had entered practically all types of industrial enterprises which included textiles, aluminium, electrical goods, chemicals, cement, a man-made fibre and yarn, heavy engineering, timber products, news print, sugar, vanaspati and so on. Very obviously one industrial house could not have developed specialisation—within such a short period—in all such industries. The diffusion itself is a contraindication that it is impossible to develop expertise on such a huge scale. And yet the fact remains that the government did grant licences to the Birlas. The real reason for this lies in their capacity to muster a substantial financial support to all proposals irrespective of the merits. The finance, however, it would be readily agreed have not been out of the savings or profits of these big industrial houses. Basically, the finance become available because each one of the big houses in India controls one or two large banking institutions.

In brief, one would say that the objectives of achieving self-reliance are very closely dependent upon the way the industries are managed and the manner in which these are regulated to become conscious of the necessity of reducing their cost structure as also in maintaining—leave apart improving—the standards of quality to win confidence of the foreign and

Indian buyers. It is only then that India can hope to step up her exports and earn foreign exchange which in turn would allow us to accelerate the pace of our movement towards industrialisation and self-sufficiency.

Summing up, one would say that the three national and plan objective before the nation are: (i) to ensure steady, continuous rate of improvement in the living standards of the large many; (ii) to achieve and ensure that economic growth is not accompanied by widening of disparities—inter-state and intra-personal; and (iii) to ensure that the growth of the economy is on such lines which would enable India to reach a stage, as early as possible, from where onwards its growth would not remain heavily dependent upon foreign assistance.

These three objectives are complementary to one another. The realisation would obviously depend upon the pursuits of such policies which would help to reorganise the present economic structure and develop it along lines which would ensure the fulfilment of these objectives.

Evidently, the financial system of the country, specially the private commercial banking system, had to be devoted a great deal of attention from the point of view of realising the above objectives. However, we have seen that while the country has already completed three Five Year Plans, there has been no provision for any type of credit planning in the Indian economy. The Indian plans, while laying down various targets for development programmes, have not simultaneously realised the need for allocations of appropriate bank finance for different projects, in the public and private sectors. Since the government financing of development projects has been confined only to the resources of the state with no efforts at the regulation of bank credit in plan directions, it has often happened that private commercial banks have financed industrial projects which have enjoyed either a low priority in the plans or are outside the plans. Moreover, in extent to which such projects have been financed has been out of all proportion to the needs of the economy or the patterns of demand for these industrial products, which have already emerged in the economic system. In this way, the commercial bank finance has tended to be working against the plan priorities and helping to create imbalances in the growth of the economy from time to time. These aspects of the working of the private commercial banking system have already been documented in a number of government publications and the First Five Year Plan.

Of course, it is well known that the banks have financed largely those projects for which licences have been given essentially because the private industrialists have been able to claim the availability of bank finance for financing their projects. Thus licensing of industries and their financing with bank credit have both been 'enterprised' in a vicious circle which have to give help to deflect the course of India's plan development from its expected national priorities, and it is high time that we take necessary steps to break this vicious circle lest it may lead to the end of planned development of the economy.

Resource Mobilisation

The basic truth regarding underdevelopment of countries is the absence of adequate productive capital—physical and human. And therefore, all efforts at planning are in essence directed towards the creation of the capital of both types. It is only when the human and physical capital is developed in a harmonious and systematic manner that a country can ensure a rapid sustained and balanced rate of growth. In this effort, a country may depend upon foreign capital or mainly rely upon its own capacity to mobilise resources. There is no given rule about the manner of building up national capital. For instance, the American development in its early phases was greatly facilitated by the import of human and other capital from the European countries, and the most recent example is that of Israel where foreign capital played a very significant role. On the other hand countries like USSR and China have mainly depended upon their own resources.

How fast an economy can grow is determined by the rate at which the productive capital is built up. And the rate of capital built up is determined by two factors, *viz.*, the rate of internal savings and the magnitude and nature of foreign assistance. Whatever may be the extent of foreign assistance, the entire cost of growth in any case cannot be borne by the outside world. The two factors are not substitutes for one another. In any case, it is necessary to raise corresponding internal physical and financial resources despite all foreign assistance. The situation is simply this: the more efforts a nation is prepared to put in, more countries can be found willing to help. A country which is not prepared to put in its own efforts at development can hardly expect other nations to foot the entire bill of development. In fact, one can even go to the extent of saying that the rate of savings in a community would determine its overall rate of investments and that in turn will determine the rate of economic growth. Therefore, the stepping up of the savings rates is of crucial significance for the growth of a country.

The rate of savings in a country depends upon the extent to which the country is prepared to, willingly or unwillingly, reduce its aggregate consumption. A higher rate of savings would enable higher investments and thereby additional incomes in the subsequent years. Again, the additional incomes generated may be largely saved or go to improve the level of consumption. But greater the willingness on the part of an economy to 'tighten the belt' higher would be the rate of capital accumulation. This is what one calls as the sacrifice of the society for its own growth. Normally the term 'savings' indicates voluntary savings of the individuals. But in the context of national savings, one has to take account of the voluntary savings of the individuals and other private agencies as also the compulsory savings affected through tax mobilisation for investment and the surpluses of the public enterprises which have been ploughed back for creating additional capital. Under the voluntary saving, one may include savings in the form of bank deposits, personal cash hoardings, purchase of shares of the corporate sector and other investments and loans made to the public and private agencies. While compulsory savings would be that part of the public sector and government expenditure which is diverted for productive purposes.

Compulsory Savings

The extent of compulsory savings is very much dependent upon the extent to which governmental agencies can pursue policies of resource mobilisation by: (i) enhancing the rates of taxation, (ii) widening the coverage of taxable population or (iii) following such pricing policies in the public enterprises which would yield the requisite surpluses. It need to be recognised at the very beginning in a democratic set-up like ours imposition of fresh taxes, etc., is not as easy as it could be in a society under some other political system. There are limits within which the government efforts have to be confined. Moreover, the taxation structure cannot be used with as much of intensity as it can be in a developed economy to raise resources. For instance, too high taxation measures can lead to some uneconomic efforts e.g., discouragement to new enterprise and incentives. However, it does not mean that underdeveloped countries always exhaust all revenue collections. For instance, in India it would be only a fool hardy scholar who would argue that the taxable capacity of all sections of the economy has been fully harnessed.

It is, however, true that in underdeveloped economies, there are limits beyond which direct taxation cannot be introduced without discouraging the level of investments in the private sector. At the same time, if more reliance was placed on indirect taxes, the problem comes that of excessive economic sacrifice imposed upon the poorer sections of the community. Thus in an underdeveloped economy, the use of direct and indirect taxes has its own limitations. This would, therefore, require a very careful and judicious view, on the part of the government, regarding the emphasis that it may place on other sources of revenue.

In the field of compulsory savings, we would like to make a special mention of the role of public sector enterprises. Fortunately enough it is by now well recognised that the public sector has a special place in the underdeveloped economies. Specially the public sector enterprises are a necessity in such field where private enterprise does not enter because the magnitude of investments involved is very high, the gestation period is large or the expectations of return on investments are not directly remunerative as against the amounts of investment. Therefore, in such areas, the role of public sector enterprises is well appreciated even by the most conservative economists. It is agreed that the public enterprises have a special place in furthering the overall rate of economic growth of a country by providing the economic and social overheads and thereby facilitating the growth of many large private enterprises. For this purpose, the public enterprises have to directly enter into the productive system of the economies. It is in this regard that the public enterprises in India have come to occupy a significant role in the development of the country. Thus, the importance of public sector in the development process is not disputed. For example, in the post World War II period, the French economy took over a large part of the national capital under ownership and control.

The controversy arises around the question whether or not the public enterprises should follow similar policies in their functioning as does the private sector. One view is that public sector enterprises should function on no-profit no-loss basis. It is suggested that the attempt should be to help the growth of the private sector by providing the necessary requisite infrastructure for helping them to overcome such difficulties which individually no private enterprise can meet. In this concept, we would like to make it clear that the role of the public enterprises should not be viewed as mere promoters of the private sector. In a developing economy, the public sector enterprises have a very direct role other than what is generally to be the case, in resources mobilisation and the direction of development. In the Indian economy, the public enterprises should certainly be used as an instrument of resource mobilisation and for providing a sense of direction in the planned process of growth.

There is a difference between the profits of a private enterprise and a public sector enterprise. The distinction is that the surpluses of the public sector enterprises become available to the government and the public agencies and decisions on the use of such resources are directly governed by social and economic considerations of the economy as a whole. The profits of the private enterprises are mainly directed and regulated in a manner which depends on an individuals' opinion about a profitable investment. In a developing society like ours, the surpluses of the public sector should in fact be viewed as compulsory savings of society which would go for further the build up of the national capital—and the capital build-up on the lines which would be in accordance with the plan priorities and overall social objectives.

Voluntary Savings

Voluntary savings in a society take various forms. The important organised forms are: (i) deposits with commercial banking institutions, (ii) life insurance policies, (iii) general insurance, (iv) post office savings deposits, (v) government bonds and certificates, (vi) deposits with cooperatives and, (vii) cash hoardings.

The relative importance of each one of these is broadly indicated in Table 10.13. The table has been compiled to indicate a very broad comparison of the different forms of savings in the community. The data are not strictly comparable as these relate to different periods of time as also the types of the data referred to are not identical.

Table 10.13

Showing a Broad Comparison of the Forms of Voluntary Savings

S.No.	*Agency*	*Remarks*	*₹ Crore*
	1	*2*	*3*
1.	Commercial Banks	Deposits (1965)	3,049.0
2.	Life Insurance Corporation	Investments (1964 March)	763.5
3.	General Insurance	Assets (1963)	90.2
4.	Post Office	Deposits (1965)	555.6
5.	Government Banks and Certificates	Outstanding (1965-66)	449.8
6.	Cooperative Societies	Deposits of Individuals (1964-65)	303.0

Source: Same as Table 10.11.

Out of the above-mentioned organised financial institutions, the commercial banks are the most important ones. Also, except for the banks, the other institutions cannot be considered as primarily and wholly the financial agencies. The resources collected by agencies like post offices and life insurance corporation are incidental to their other operations. Therefore, while discussing voluntary savings, one has to place special reliance on banking institutions. It is so because the banks are organised with the basic purpose of mobilising financial resources and for providing credit to the economic functionaries of a society.

Banking Institutions

The magnitude of resource mobilisation by banking institutions is related to the capacity of these institutions to reach numbers and to their success and efficiency in looking after their clientele. For instance, if the banking offices were confirmed to a few centres of the country only, very naturally, the capacity of the banks to mobilise deposits from the public would remain limited to that extent. And if the network of banking offices was extended to all parts of the country and most of the population could reach one or the other bank office conveniently, the deposits would be of a larger order. Similarly, if the banking institutions functioned efficiently and made rigorous efforts to provide satisfaction to the savers—irrespective of the fact how big were the deposits of a saver—the banks could still improve their effectiveness in deposit collections. In a developing economy, banking institutions have a special role in making people 'bank minded.' For a large majority of those who can save, opening of an account in a bank would be a new experience. And therefore utmost care would need be taken in seeing to it that the experience is not so unfortunate that an average saver would decide to never visit a bank office again. If a visit to a bank office could be made a pleasant experience, the banks would become still better institutions of deposit mobilisation.

This aspect needs to be underlined since very often it is not realised that in underdeveloped economies, the savers are not as enlightened as to always bother to look into the economies of returns of their savings. Their values and decisions are dependent upon, at least equally, on considerations other than the interest rates. And one of the important factors is the security of definite and the personalised service and the consideration they would receive from the bank staff. The importance of enhancing savings may not be fully appreciated by an ordinary man. For this, one can only say that if the banks can draw out financial surpluses from the community—by way of the deposits—to that extent the buying power in the community gets contracted. And by that magnitude, there is a reduction in the aggregate consumption with a corresponding release of physical resources which can be diverted towards the creation of additional national capital. Similarly, by practising selected credit policies, the banks can influence the consumption pattern in the society. The banks are important agencies for ensuring greater savings to help economic development.

The capacity and will to save on the part of the savers is not in itself sufficient to ensure deposits. What is equally important is the existence of an institutional framework which makes it convenient to save. One has no measure to assess the level of willingness but it would not be too wrong to presume that everyone, whether rich or poor, would have a desire to save. The degree of will power would, however, vary from one individual to another. In a country which recognises private property and rights to inheritance, an average man would undoubtedly like to save. But the real problem is that of impressing upon the savers that the function of saving was also a national obligation and each person must save by habit and in an organised manner.

The task of making 'savings' conscious is only possible if there was an institutional framework which would undertake this task vigorously and continuously. And further to this, the set-up must ensure the necessary physical and organisational conveniences to the savers. It is in this context that one has to evaluate the capacity of the existing financial structure as instruments of enhancing and further mobilisation of savings.

Our study has pointed out that commercial banking in India has remained concentrated in urban centres and also in the comparatively advanced states of the country. It would not be correct to form an impression that banking offices are evenly spread over space within the urban centres or in the comparatively better-off states. A study of the spatial distribution of banking offices in these cities would indicate that a very large number of offices were located in the two cities of Bombay and Calcutta, whereas the smaller towns and rural areas were as badly neglected as in any other state. Furthermore, a look at the distribution of bank offices in these cities would indicate that more bank offices are located in such areas of the two cities which are trade centres or are inhabited by richer sections of the urban population. Very rarely bank offices are located in areas where the poorer sections of the community live.

From the view point of savings potential, it would be appropriate to mention the general belief that the poorer sections in the Indian society have very little savings capacity is completely misplaced. In fact the savings with the lower-income groups in the urban centres—which will equal the middle-income groups of the rural population—are of a significant order. While the middle-income groups enter into a race for consumption of 'prestige goods' and become victims of the 'demonstration effect' and have lesser willingness to save, the lower-income groups are still conservative and do affect savings. Considering the numbers involved, even small saving when aggregated would come to a fairly significant order. There is no doubt that dealing with very small amounts and with large numbers of comparatively lesser educated depositors would involve higher costs of administration of these bank offices. The same is true about rural areas. But the benefits of such savings are many times more than the costs of deposit collections. But this approach can only be followed by such institutions which have the proper perspective of their role and are even prepared to bear short-term promotional losses in the overall and long-term interests of the society.

Rural Banking

For a long time, the official view regarding the provision of banking facilities to the rural areas has been that extension of banking facilities to the rural sector should be earmarked for the cooperatives and urban banking should be largely left for the commercial banks. While nationalising the Imperial Bank of India (IBI), it also argued that the private commercial banks cannot reach the villages because opening of branches in the rural areas was not a profitable proposition. It was, therefore, suggested that with the nationalisation of the IBI, the SBI would have special responsibility to provide banking facilities in smaller towns and villages. Thus, the official attitude seems to have been that the SBI and the cooperatives would specialise in rural banking, and the private commercial banks would confine their activities to the urban centres.

The implication of this division of areas between the public sector banking (SBI) and the cooperatives *vis-à-vis* the private commercial banks is that the non-profitable banking should be the main responsibility of the public sector institutions, whereas the profitable ones should be earmarked for private banking institutions. It is recognised that since rural banking is not a profitable business (and that is why private banks do not attempt this), therefore, the cooperatives and the SBI have to be adequately subsidised for such bank offices which run under loss and were opened with the intention of covering rural areas. For this, the RBI meets the deficit of a branch opened by the SBI.

Such an approach would be all right if it was clearly understood that the cooperatives and the public sector banks were not to be judged on the same criteria as the other commercial banking institutions. The public sector banking institutions may, therefore, be judged on different standards than the private ones. But unfortunately it is argued that private banks do not want to go to rural areas because it was not profitable and therefore the public sector (SBI) should undertake the responsibility of entering into the losing business. In the same breath, it is also expected that the SBI should show at least the same profits as other private banks. This really means that the non-profitable propositions are meant for the public sector and the profitable ones for the private sector. And then we turn back to judge the efficiency on private profit criteria. No logic could be strange than this.

Cooperative Societies

As for the role of cooperatives in rural banking is concerned, it is high time that we understood what the cooperatives can do and what these cannot. We must understand the structural handicaps of the cooperative credit system in an economy like ours. It is only after a proper appreciation of the capacity of the cooperatives that one can decide as to how far the cooperatives can offer a solution to the problem of providing banking facilities in the rural areas.

It should, however, be made clear that we do not doubt the importance and the role that cooperatives play in ameliorating the economic and social conditions of the rural areas in general and the farmers in particular. Basically, the cooperatives movement is a sound one and has many a merit. For instance, agricultural, marketing, service, industrial and consumers' cooperatives are of great significance in a developing society like ours. However, the need for opening of bank offices in rural areas is not purely the provision of credit to agriculture. It is more than this. In this respect, we need to understand some of the structural and other inherent limitations of the cooperative credit societies. Also one has to take due note of the present defects in the cooperative movement. No doubt some of the defects in the cooperative credit movement can be set right with appropriate reforms. But, the inherent limitations of this movement for purposes of extending banking facilities to rural areas can hardly be met by such actions. At the same time, we visualise that opening of branches of the organised banking institutions in rural areas would help to strengthen the cooperative credit movement in the countryside. The existence of organised banking is not a substitute or a rival development to cooperative credit societies. On the other hand, in our view, organised banking is a complementary and a pre-requisite for effective functioning of the cooperative credit institutions.

In principle, credit cooperative societies need not necessarily be dependent upon the governmental finance alone. The objective of establishing cooperatives in India, as also anywhere else in the world, is to bring the various economic functionaries together for mutual help. For instance, credit societies, it was expected, would receive deposits from those of their members who had surplus resources, and in turn, these resources would be lent to those who need financial assistance. In this manner, the cooperatives could eliminate the money lenders who discharged this function of receiving deposits and lending credit to the farmers. In this manner, the cooperatives could provide a system of mutual help and eliminate the exploitation of the private moneylenders. The cooperatives, viewed from this angle, are an institutional reform where intermediaries are attempted to be eliminated. This is the spirit of cooperative movement. In the initial stages, the government and other public institutions could provide financial assistance to the cooperatives if the requirements of the members of the cooperatives were more than what the cooperatives could raise from their own members. But unfortunately, in India cooperative credit movement has come to a stay as heavily dependent upon the governmental finance. It is evident from the fact that out of a total working capital of the cooperative credit institutions of ₹ 2,101.44 crore in 1963-64, nearly ₹ 500 crore was the share capital and resources. The deposits from its members and other stood at ₹ 303.40 crore only. The rest was provided by the RBI, by the government and other public institutions. Since the credit cooperative societies have not succeeded in resource mobilisation from their members or otherwise, these have remained instruments of one way flow of finance—from the government to the members of these cooperatives. Thus the credit cooperatives are in practice only credit distributing agencies. No doubt this is an important function in itself. But this certainly is not banking for rural areas.

The cooperative movement has been heavily subsidised by way of cheap and easy credit by the RBI. Because of this, most of the cooperatives were organised by those only who wanted to avail of the governmental financial assistance. Right from the beginning, the objective of organising cooperative credit societies was to avail facilities rather than to become a forum for local farmers and other 'ruralites' for mutual help. Secondly, cooperative societies, being each independent of the other, have to function in isolation and therefore these societies cannot offer the normal banking facilities which an organised bank can. Due to this handicap, very naturally the depositors prefer to maintain their surplus either with the moneylenders or hoard the amounts in cash with them than handing over the same to a local cooperative credit society which cannot allow similar and easy withdrawal facilities as a private moneylender can. Of course, provision of other banking facilities like transfer of funds from one place to another and safe deposit facilities is out of question. Therefore, the depositors are not encouraged to use the cooperative credit societies as institutions where they can deposit their surplus financial resources. Also, because of the advantages offered and the considerable subsidy element, the membership of the cooperatives (which is true about all types of cooperatives) is taken to be closed for others and is confined to a small section of the population of a village. A number of studies conducted by the RBI and other scholars on the working of the cooperative credit societies indicate that majority of the cooperatives can hardly be described as genuine cooperative societies. These are either group organisations or family organisations. A study of the central cooperative banks would also indicate that the control and management of the cooperative finance is generally in the hands of a family or a group of persons and the functioning of the cooperative banks is not much at variance from any other private financial institution.

Even as credit distributing agencies, the cooperatives have not made the desired impact. The main reason for this has been the unwillingness on the part of the cooperatives to depart from the creditworthiness criteria for extending financial accommodation. As a result of this, cooperative credit has been availed by those only who could even otherwise raise capital of their own if they chose to do so. A study of the cooperative credit distribution would indicate that a large share of total credit has gone to a fraction of the population comprising of big landlords and so on. This to some is unavoidable in a society whose membership comprises of a heterogeneous group with a few dominating the decisions and functioning of the society. There cannot be any meaningful cooperation between the unequals. The situation can, however, be better dealt with by such organised agencies which are independent of local and vested interest and would function on considerations of merit, not always, and only based on the conventional criteria of creditworthiness of a borrower.

Another structural defect of the cooperatives, mainly dealing with farmers, is that a good part of the financial resources remain idle during the year. For instance, credit needs of the farmers are the most in the sowing seasons and the pre-harvest periods. The loan recoveries are made after the harvest. Since there is time gap between the sowing and harvesting seasons, during the middle periods the finances of the cooperatives cannot but be idle. However, the requirements of the agricultural trade and processing industries are the most in the post-harvest period. But because of the absence of any institutional mutual arrangements, the idle resources of the cooperatives do not become available for the latter purposes. This cannot be helped if the cooperatives remain in isolation of the organised banking structure.

The net result of the division of responsibility between private commercial banks and the RBI in financing of industry and trade on the one hand and agriculture on the other respectively has been a fragmentation of India's financial system into two water-tight compartments. The private commercial banking system operates in unplanned isolation from the needs of the rural sector, while the cooperative banking system finances agriculture without any coordination with the needs of the industrial and urban sectors. The inevitable economic consequence is that there is misallocation of financial resources between the two sectors. This comes about because the funds earmarked for the rural sector remain idle for a major part of the year, while the idle funds of the private commercial system during the lean period cannot be utilised for short-term financing of the agricultural operations. Inevitably, too much finance is thus tied up merely because the financial system is fragmented into these two broad divisions.

If the private banking system was to be nationalised, it would be possible for the government to integrate the financial system of the country into one complete whole. This would help to save idle resources of both the financing sectors as well as help to coordinate and integrate their financing operations into a system of planned development. Moreover, the skilled personnel of the cooperative financial sector as well as of the private commercial banks can be integrated with one another in order to provide a much large cadre of trained personnel in banking operations of the country.

Such integration of two major financing sectors in the country would also help to curb the flow of financial resources into the unorganised money market which plays havoc with the economy in the present situation of acute scarcities and shortages. Once the two financing sectors, that is the private commercial banks and the cooperative sector, are integrated, they would constitute a major source of attraction for all voluntary savings of the community in so far as they would reach out to all the areas of the country from the highest to the lowest range of society, and provide the best security for the deposits of all savers, big or small.

Moreover, in the presence of such a unified financial system, the unorganised money market would lose much of its attraction and concealed power to engage any financing operations which will be beyond the purview of the organised financial system. Let us not imagine that the unorganised money market in the country operates entirely outside the banking system. There are strategic points of linkage, between the unorganised money market and the banking system. These linkages would come to full view once the banking system is fully unified under state control, and it will be easy to keep a watch and regulate the activities of the unorganised money market far more effectively than has been possible hitherto.

Rural Savings Potential

Sometimes one also hears that there was very little surplus resource potential in the rural sector which could be tapped by banks. But the facts do not bear testimony of such a belief. For instance, the amount of deposits which post offices have increased during the last 15 years significantly. We are conscious that the post office bank savings are not a substitute for banking. This is only an indicator of the potential resources which can be mobilised from the lower-income strata and the rural communities. In the year 1950-51, the total post office saving bank deposits stood at ₹ 187.28 crore, whereas in 1965-66, the figure touched ₹ 641.2 crore. The receipts for the year were ₹ 173 in 1956-57 and the corresponding receipts of the post office saving bank deposits were ₹ 366.27 crore. Similarly, the rate at which small savings have grown as indicated by the number of saving bank accounts with the commercial banks and also the share of small savings in total bank deposits is an indicator that the small amounts are not really small if only these could be tapped properly.

Earlier, it has been seen that the intensity of banking varies from state to state. In some states, there is a bank office for more than 2.5 lakh population, whereas in a few others, a bank office exists for less than half lakh of population. The magnitude of *per capita* bank deposits also varies from one state to another. The highest per capita deposit being nearly ₹ 185 and the lowest was ₹ 9. This variation could be explained to some extent in the differences in per capita incomes in states. But essentially the lower per-capita deposits are because of the absence of banking facilities. This is evident from Table 10.3. It would be seen that there was a very high degree of co-relationship between the degree of concentration of banking facilities and the per capita bank deposits. Those states which have a bank for 40,000-50,000 people are the states where per capita bank deposits are the largest. We do no believe that what hold true about the states where banking facilities have been extended would not hold true about the states where banking is absent. The non-development of banking in the states has undoubtedly meant lesser deposits mobilisation for the community. And if the national objectives are to enhance savings, it is necessary that the banking institutions were more evenly distributed than what these are today.

The savings potential of the rural sector can be appreciated only if one takes into account the level of inequalities in the agricultural sector. Howsoever unfortunate it may be, but one has to recognise the existence of considerable disparities in land holdings—which is the source of incomes—in the rural sector. One can broadly group the agriculturists under two broad categories *viz.*, the ones which would have agricultural produce for the market after meeting their own requirements and those who are just on subsistence level. In numbers, the former category is much smaller but the agricultural land with them constitutes a very large part. There are, however, variations from state to state. The agricultural classes which produce for the market have been at a considerable advantage because of the recent rise in prices of foodgrain. This has raised the incomes of the land-owning classes in a substantial manner. However, the costs of inputs have remained comparatively lower. The net result of this is the enviable prosperity of the land-owning classes of the rural sector. Where would additional incomes thus generated go? One does not wish to argue that all the extra income would be received in the banks, but surely enough a significant part of it can be mobilised if only there was a proper institutional framework. Otherwise one is afraid that ready cash has always the temptation of slipping out of the hands for non-essential purposes.

In brief, one could say that the lever for growth is the rate of savings an economy can achieve. And the rate of savings in turn is dependent upon the taxation measures and the nature of pricing policies that the public sector enterprises pursue. The view that public sector should not attempt at taking advantage of the market forces for resources mobilisation is wholly misconceived. The public sector profits should be viewed as not only desirable but as necessity. But apart from the compulsory savings, the role of voluntary savings is of crucial importance in an underdeveloped economy. The private banking institutions which operate on profit considerations cannot take up the responsibility of building up a financial and institutional set-up to cover the rural and urban areas or reach all sections of the community. As far as the rural banking is concerned, the cooperatives alone do not provide the answer. Extension of organised banking for rural areas is a necessary complimentary development to the cooperative movement. Apart from this, the function of resource mobilisation can be only undertaken by organised banking institutions.

Social Objectives and Commercial Banking

Resource mobilisation is one aspect of the banking operations. It has been seen, however, that the growth of the banking institutions has remained confined to the urban centres as also to the new industrially better advanced states of the country. Not only there is concentration of banking offices over space, but also the intensity of the banking offices is so distributed that the banks have not made any efforts to reach large majority of the population. As a result its capacity to muster surplus financial resources with the community has remained a limited one. Specially, the present banking system has neglected the poorer sections of the community as also the rural sector.

Profit Motive of Private Banks

The main reason for this unbalanced growth of banking in the country has been the manner and the criteria of the private sector which determines the operations and the direction of development of these agencies. Because of the smaller amounts, larger number of persons to be dealt with and scattered nature of the villages, the administrative costs of managing banking offices in the rural areas are considerably higher than that of the bank offices which are located in urban centres where the clientele is generally educated, have better incomes and there exist a number of other facilities like better and easy communication. Therefore, opening of bank offices in the rural areas is not a profitable proposition in the immediate sense. This obviously is a limitation of the entire banking system when it is operated in the private sector which seeks to confine its operations in such areas which would yield handsome profits. Therefore, it is no surprise that the bank developments in India have remained confined to urban centres only, and yet the fact remains that in the overall interest of economic development and for achievement of other social objectives, it was necessary to extend banking facilities evenly both spatial and from the viewpoint of intensity of coverage in the urban centres.

Banking as Public Utility Services

Sometimes it has been suggested that this uneven growth of banking in the country can be improved and set right if only the private banks were enlightened on the necessity of providing banking facilities to the rural areas and were to be under moral pressures by the RBI and government. For this, it is further suggested that the private commercial banks should be helped, even subsidised, to develop research departments and development wings whose main task would be to locate potential areas where a bank could open its new offices. One wonders if moral pressures can be used to persuade the private sector banking companies to accept *non-profitable* business of extending banking offices in the rural areas. Reliance on such a belief is not only too idealist but also misconceived. As long as the banks are under the control and management of private sector, no amount of persuasion can, and would be, effective to follow policies which are against their own economic interests.

On the other hand, to expect that in the absence of the private banking institutions being ready to open bank offices in the rural areas, the public sector banking should undertake this job which is extremely illogical because this would imply that the profitable areas of banking may left to be harnessed by the private bankers, whereas the public enterprises should run the non-profitable and losing banking business. A more rational view would be that the profits from the banks were not viewed as a very important criteria but the banking institutions were essentially considered as *public* utility services. There perhaps one could even argue that a principle of no-profit-no-loss may be adopted to compensate the deficit incurred by the banks by opening branches in the rural areas from the profits they may earn by banking operations in the urban centres. This obviously would mean the negation of the rights of the private sector to take advantage of their investments in the banking institutions—because no one would like to make investments unless these did offer some scope for direct returns.

Therefore, banking in an underdeveloped economy which attempts at a continuous balanced rate of growth has to be considered as an institution of resource mobilisation. The criteria of their success should be measured in their capacity to increase deposits and consolidate scattered surplus financial resources in the community, thereby to release demand pressures than to assess their functioning on a very conservative and out-dated criteria of profits.

Creditworthiness

Sometimes one hears an argument that private banks are often in a position to judge the creditworthiness of a small man—who is known to the manager of the bank—is likely to be perhaps a little more flexible than a financial institution which has a set of rules and regulations, handed down by someone from the top, and in relation to which if he showed any flexibility, the manager may often be accused of corruption, favouritism and so on. This element of knowing the local man was a very important factor in the development of private banking in countries like the United Kingdom.

But how did private banks develop in these countries inspite of the tendency of the banks to prefer to stay in the urban centres? Historically, one would find that in the period of industrial revolution in Great Britain, there was a system of 'country banks' which were unit banks and did not form a part of branch banking system. Therefore, first of all, the small private banks were subject to directives from above either from the state-owned or the private-owned enterprises, and secondly 'country banks' were allowed to issue currency notes that they had an incentive to work in rural areas. But the right to issue the notes was withdrawn from the commercial banks after Britain had reached a stage of take-off. The main advantage with these banks was that the lenders could exercise their judgement regarding the characters of their borrowers and watch their varying fortunes, on day-to-day basis even if the borrowers could not offer good security. In other worlds, the whole problem of dealing with the small man, who may have some potential or entrepreneurial ability, was overcome with the help of unit banks which were small and enjoyed confidence of the local people.

But the present-day banking is not mere unit banking. From the operational view point, it hardly makes any difference whether banking was in the private sector or in the public sector because in branch banking, the managers or the bankers can never claim to know the local people so intimately as it was possible for 'country bank.' The question of public versus private sector banking comes up only if one considers the basic conflict between the private and the public sector. The banking activity, by its nature, involves a conflict between the small man, the illiterate man, the man who does not have the banking habit and the big man who has banking habit and who has control over the commercial banks. Therefore, the question of nationalisation of banks is really a question of resolving the conflict between the big and the small. What is the social objective? Is it to strengthen the hands of the few who are big or is it to help the common man?

More Controls: Futile

One hears quite often an argument that the apparent conflict between the big and the small can be resolved by regulatory and credit control measures. It is suggested that the RBI has sufficient powers or it can be given more powers to exercise better supervision if the trends in the private banking were not in accordance with the overall social objectives of the country. It has also suggested that some sort of a credit council could lay down broad policies for the private banks. In this manner, a great faith is shown in the effectiveness of regulatory and other controls. This is a rather amusing situation because such an argument is advanced by those very persons of the private sector who have the least faith or belief in administrative controls—may these be concerned with any aspect of personal life or otherwise. The persons who show great exuberance regarding the effectiveness of controls, regulatory measures and moral pressures of the government and the RBI are in fact those persons who do not believe, ideologically speaking, that governmental control can ever prove effective.

However, it would be of interest to see what is meant by regulatory control and other improvements which have been suggested to direct the functioning of private banking institutions so that these functions are in accordance with social objectives. The two instruments in the hands of the RBI for regulating the functioning of the private banks are: (i) periodic reporting of the banking operations and (ii) periodic inspections.

How far the existing controls are superficial is only too obvious to need any fresh emphasis. The successive failure of banks like Palai Bank and Travancore National Bank in the recent past is only too fresh to remind us that the RBI or any other similar institution cannot supervise the functioning of thousands of bank offices in the country. Moreover, the RBI can at best have once in a year or twice inspect the record of commercial banks, and very obviously, such an inspection would amount to a post-mortem of what has already been done. If the RBI did not approve the operations of a bank, it remains in doubt whether it should take any punitive action or impose any fines on the banks because such an action would jeopardise the confidence of depositors in the concerned bank in particular and banking institutions in general. Therefore, the limitations of the RBI should ensure that banks pursued the Directives it issues from time to time which is an extremely difficult task, and the net result is that the RBI has failed to achieve the objective for which it was given a number of statutory sanctions.

It will be worthwhile mentioning here that in a country like the United States, no bank can extend loans to any single concern which are more than 10 per cent of the PUC and reserves of the concerned bank. In other words, in the United States, there are severe limits for extending credit in large bulk to an individual concern.

Credit Drain: A Hindrance to Growth

On the other hand, the PUC of all the scheduled banks in India is around 44 crore but the directors of the bank have been shown financial accommodation to the extent of more than ₹ 300 crore. Further as we have mentioned earlier, a small fraction of the total borrowers in the country have claimed nearly two-third of total bank credit. Very obviously when the one/third of the bank credit is spared for a handful of industrialists, the rest of the economy cannot but remain starved of the bank credit and to the extent, the non-availability of credit does not allow the establishment of new enterprises. There is a positive hindrance to the growth of the economy. As noted earlier, a fraction of total borrowers have claimed nearly four-fifth of total bank advances. This needs no further argument to show that presently the banks are being utilised by a small group of industrialists to obtain financial resources for the growth of their own industrial houses. Leave apart any progressive and socialistic concept, let the situation, as it prevails in the country today, be judged on the most conservative policies of those countries who believe in complete capitalism.

Apart from the function of resource mobilisation, the role of the banks in an underdeveloped economy is also to be viewed in terms of credit policies that banks pursue. The close relationship between banking and industries on the one side and banking and commerce on the other side is only too well known to require special emphasis. What role we expect the credit institutions to play in India? Earlier on in this report, we have spelled out the three basic social objectives namely: (i) achievement of sustained economic growth, (ii) a balanced development, and (iii) self-sufficiency.

The Role of Banks

The role of the banks has to be viewed in this context. The broad social objectives of the Indian society are spelled out in concrete terms in our Five Year Plan documents. Each Five Year Plan has a strategy of development. For instance, during the First Plan, greater emphasis was placed on the development of agriculture and irrigation facilities, whereas during the Second Plan, greater emphasis was placed on the development of heavy and basic industries. Thus a Plan document indicates the broad intersectoral priorities which need to be pursued for a balanced growth of the economy. One would normally expect that bank credit is directed in such a manner as to help better implementation of plan priorities. For instance, the banks should give due consideration to the development of agriculture. But we would not like to stretch this point too far because extension of credit to agriculture needs not to be entirely financed through private commercial banking institutions.

One can understand that the main objective of the private commercial banking institutions is to mobilise resources for the growth of the private sector. Not that one would completely agree with this argument but to keep the area of dispute narrow, let us proceed on the understanding that the main function of the commercial banks was to finance the private industrial sector. If that was so, it would be expected that the bank credit was used for the growth of such industries which were given priorities under the Plans. The rationale for giving an industry a priority in a Plan is derived from the overall national plan strategy. For instance, when we think of the establishment of basic industries, the emphasis on these is placed because in the latter years, it would be possible to grow at a faster rate than if in the initial stages the nation places lesser emphasis on the basic capacity. When the Plans indicate a priority for agriculture, it is necessary to understand that it also means a priority to such industries the output of which would be directed to support the growth of agriculture at a faster rate. For instance, when we place emphasis on agricultural development, industrial sector has the responsibility to provide inputs like fertilisers, pesticides and agricultural implements. Therefore, the nature of industries which are helped with bank credit can be such which would make the implementation of the Plan priorities easier and more effective. Thus even when the banks were used to finance industrial activity, one could find that agriculture could be specifically helped in accordance with the plan priorities without bank credit being made available directly to the agricultural sector.

Banks and Industrial Priorities

Similarly, bank credit is a very important instrument of influencing investment decisions and locations of the industrial projects. As mentioned before, nearly two-fifth of productive capital in factory establishments in the country is located in only two states of the country. Certainly, if bank credit was used as an instrument of ensuring better spatial balance in development, banks could have helped in the achievement of the broader social objectives. Also, by the use of differential rates of lending, the banks can be used to help the growth of such industries which have a priority in the Plans and discourage those which are non-priority industries.

Many a time it has not been fully appreciated that the growth of non-Plan industries becomes a great handicap to the process of development. For instance, one often wonders how and wherefrom did the private industries obtain superior quality steel for the mass production of stainless steel utensils. There would be hardly a house which does not have a few stainless steel utensils. Similarly, it is surprising that a large number of household consumer goods of the western type have flooded the Indian markets when these were positively not under any Plan priority. Take the case of air-conditioners and refrigerators which require imported parts and therefore a considerable amount of foreign exchange must have been wasted on the production of such goods. Another case in point is that of the synthetic fibre. We have mentioned these only to underline that the credit mechanism could have been very effectively utilised for discouraging the growth of such industries. The growth of such industries not only wastes foreign exchange and divert other internal raw material but such industries are also instruments of diversion of individual savings. In the same context, one would like to refer to the development of certain industries, which were mentioned earlier, the development of which is certainly against all social objectives.

The bank credit can not only help rational decision making in the field of investments but also be used to regulate the level of activity in the industrial sector. Proper policies of lending credit for meeting working capital could ensure that those industries receive preference where greater production was otherwise desirable. On the other hand, by following proper policies demand for durable use consumer goods like automobiles could be significantly influenced through banking instruments.

The Role of Banks in Trade

The credit institutions, therefore, can play a very important role to regulate and direct the activities of the private sector in the field of industries. Very similar to the objective of regulating industries through credit mechanism, one can show that the bank credit can play a strategic role in determining the pattern of commercial activities in the country. By discouraging speculation in such products which are in shortage, the banks can manoeuvre the price level as also encourage trade where it was desirable to encourage stocks. In this context, one may refer that the food problem is one of the constant problems with us which needs to be squarely dealt with. For this, it is very necessary that large stocks are built up during the periods when we have bumper foodgrain crops. Very often one hears that after 5-10 million tonnes of foodgrain have to be stored, it would be very difficult to find the corresponding financial resources. One does not know why the banking institutions cannot be squarely tapped for ensuring the requisite financial resources for building up of foodgrain stocks. In this manner, banking institutions can play a vital role in holding the price line and regulating the private sector trade and commercial operations.

The banking institutions can also play a very important role in ensuring that credit was made available to such entrepreneurs only who have the necessary competence, expertise and capacity to undertake new industries. For instance, just like the World Bank, the banks could insist upon receiving project reports and satisfying themselves regarding the feasibility of investment proposals before granting loans. In this manner, the banks could help those who would prove efficient and thereby keep the cost of production lower by helping an industrial house which starts a large number of industrial units each different from the other. This fact is mainly responsible for lower efficiency and high cost of production in the industrial sector of our economy.

One need not rule out the possibility of banks being used as institutions which would ensure that industries pursue certain pricing policies and were managed in the manner in which it was not against the overall interests of the social objectives of the society. In the same manner, banking institutions could keep a watch on the operations of the industrial units which were established for the purposes of export promotion or import substitution. The banks could also use their position to ensure better follow-up of the licences which were granted by government. Similarly the financial institutions, when properly operated, would ensure that under and over-invoicing was not resorted by the private sector, commercial and industrial institutions.

Backing to Investment

Sometimes it has been argued that investment decisions are not influenced by the easy availability of bank credit. Bank credit is made available to only such industries which have been granted the necessary licences by government. Therefore, it is argued that banks are the least responsible for encouraging or discouraging plan priority industries. The same argument is put forward regarding concentration of industries and growth of economic power in the hands of a few industrial houses. The argument is an attempt to show the innocence of the banking institutions in matters of helping trends towards concentration of economic power in the country. But this would not stand to reasoning if one was to show that bank credit, though known as short-term credit, can be, and has been, long-term credit as invariably bank credit is rolled over many years. Secondly, the question would arise whether an application which is not supported by a bank guarantee for provision of the necessary financial resources, would ever receive consideration from the government or any committee responsible for granting of licences. It is only with the help of bank credit and easy availability of financial resources that few industrial houses have been in a position to obtain licences because they only could afford to ensure the required financial resources for the establishment of new industrial units.

Foreign Collaboration

Not only this, the bank guarantees have also ensured easy foreign collaborations on instalments where the home entrepreneurs are not required to undertake very large investments. Why it is that an ordinary man cannot get a licence whereas a big industrial house like Birlas can have many licences? The basic reason is that the Birla house has financial resources drawn from commercial banks and an ordinary man can never hope to obtain bank loans to the required magnitude. Thirdly, in the Indian industrial structure, intercompany investments are not unknown. A company which has its own resources to meet its working capital can easily invest its working capital into another country if the bank was ready to provide the necessary working capital. In this and in many other manners, the bank credit can be used for investment purposes.

Credit Concentration

Before we come to the question of nationalisation of banks, we would like to indicate the implications of bank advances being used by a few industrial houses. It is a well accepted fact that nearly one per cent of the total borrowers of the country received nearly ₹ 1,800 crore during the year 1966 from the commercial banks. The rate of interest per annum for scheduled bank advances has varied from 6-10 per cent per annum. The market rate, however, has been between 15-16 per cent. Therefore, ₹ 1,800 crore have been lent to nearly one per cent of the borrowers at a rate which is two-third of the market rate. Firstly, there is a favoured treatment to these industrial houses because these have been given so much of financial accommodation and secondly the rate of interest charged has been around 8-9 per cent. This really means that during the year 1966, these handful of borrowers had obtained an advantage of ₹ 114 crore because of their close communications with banks. In other words, this is the amount of subsidy which the big business houses received at the cost of depositors and average man in the country. The amount of special advantage which they have enjoyed during one year would be more than three times the total PUC of all the scheduled banks of the country. This is really shocking situation where one pleads of compensation to the banks when every year they draw 600 per cent direct returns on their investments in the share capital of the banks.

Case for Nationalisation

The question of bank nationalisation has to be considered in the light of the above account of the operations of the private banks in the country. Firstly, the present banking system has an inherent limitation in its operations and it cannot provide the necessary banking facilities to rural and the lower-income strata of the population. Secondly, the banks have been used for the growth of only a few industrial houses who happened to enjoy control over the banking institutions. Thirdly, the easy credit availability to a few industrial houses has led to the growth of monopolies and helped the process of concentration of economic power in the society. Fourthly, a large number of entrepreneurial ability remains underemployed because the requisite financial resources are denied for their legitimate growth. There is discrimination against those who happen to be competent but unable to satisfy the conservative criteria of credit worthiness. Lastly, the banking institutions, as these are, have helped, because of structural reasons, in the growth of only a few states and have siphoned away large amounts of resources from the poorer states to the comparatively better industrialised states of the country.

No amount of moral persuasion or minor changes here or there can achieve the social objectives which have been spelled out earlier in this report. Further the past experience has shown that regulations and other controls by the RBI cannot prove effective. The basic difference is that of fundamental conflict between the interests of the few and the interests of the many. Under these conditions, there can hardly be any justification for leaving the banking sector in the hands of the few industrial houses. What is necessary is the nationalisation of all commercial banks in the country. Partial nationalisation would neither serve any purpose nor would help to correct the imbalances which have creeped into the working of our economy. We would, however, come to broad policies which must be pursued if the functioning of the nationalised banking has to be more purposive and in the desired directions.

Claims of Bankers Association Unfounded

In the recent past, the Indian Banks' Association and the private banks, individually, have been active in creating an impression that nationalisation of banks would be an economic disaster. The Indian Bankers' Association's statement of July 10, 1967, goes to the extent of saying:

> ... The banks which are the trustees of more than Rs. 3500 crore of deposits from 1.25 depositors mostly representing hard earned savings of small people of moderate means and which are responsible for nearly 100 crore of capital funds belonging to a large body of equally small shareholders cannot meekly submit to pressures that may create a financial panic in the country and jeopardise her economic future. I therefore, wish to send a note of caution that if political or legislative pressures precipitate the issues and force hasty and drastic changes upon banks, *the country may have to pay heavily for it.*

When the attitude of the Bankers Association is that of the issuing warnings to the government, one does not know if one can discuss the question of bank nationalisation with a cool and calm mind. However, one is surprised at the extraordinary interest which the Association has started showing not only through the press but also otherwise on the question of bank nationalisation. Many claims are made which cannot stand the scrutiny of examination. For instance, the Association claims that banks are owned by small shareholders. We have shown how the bank shares of the Central Bank of India are controlled by a small fraction of investors. To repeat, we may mention that from the information published by the Central Bank of India in its Annual Report, it is made out that nearly half of the bank shares were held by 3 per cent of the shareholders. The knowledgeable circles, however, believe that the Central Bank of India is perhaps not a representative bank for the study of the distribution of shares. In most of the banks, controlling shares are held by one or two business houses. This is indicated in the very little change that takes place in the board of directors of these banks as also is obvious from the controlling shares held by a group of persons. Thus the plea of small shareholders does not have much meaning after the controlling shares are held by a small number of persons. In any case, the largeness of shareholders has little meaning if the control and the management of the banks were by big industrial houses.

Political Pressurising

One is surprised that the Bankers Association should issue a warning to the 'political or legislative' agencies of the country. What are the political agencies in the country? Very obviously the sovereign body of the Indian nation is the 'Lok Sabha.' Thus the Bankers Association has directed its warning to the Parliament that "the country may have to pay heavily for it." One does not know what is implied by such a statement. Surely this is not the language of reason or rationality.

The private banks have been inserting huge advertisements in the national press during the last few months. At the face of it, one wonders the provocation for such huge expenditure, out of public resources. If the banks were running so efficiently and so justly, there was no question of any danger to their functioning whether these were nationalised or these remain in the hands of the private sector. It is admitted that banking is a service. If it were so, as it is so, why should the big industrial houses and those who today control the banks get so agitated? Very obviously, one has a reason to doubt if present propaganda and tirade of the private banks is not an attempt to conceal something which is much more anti-social and questionable than what has come to be known to the Parliament and the intelligentsia.

Scare on Depositors: A Myth

Let us take one by one the fears which have been expressed regarding the nationalisation of banks. Firstly, it is argued that nationalisation of banks would result in psychological reaction and as a result, the number of depositors with the banks would get declined. Would this be so the basis for such a fear which appears to be that the nationalised banks would not enjoy the same degree of confidence from savers as is enjoyed by private commercial banks. This argument and 'psychological reaction' were argued when the Imperial Bank of India was to be taken over by the SBI. What has happened to the deposits of the SBI during the last 12 years? Has the SBI lost confidence of savers? This would be indicated by the facts which we can easily cite. Between the period of 1955 and 1965, the deposits of the scheduled banks had risen from ₹ 1,071.73 crore to ₹ 2,814.66 crore in 1965. This obviously is an increase by less than three times. The deposits with the SBI for the year 1955 stood at ₹ 219.80 crore whereas this stood at ₹ 676.92 crore in 1965. This is more than three times that deposits held in 1955. This would indicate that the argument of adverse 'psychological reaction' is only too baseless to require any further discussion.

But more than citing the SBI, one would like to ask as to what is the basis of confidence that people have in banking institutions. This needs to be made clear that confidence in the institutional set-up, whether it is banking or otherwise, is derived from the laws of the nation and the social order. If there was a crisis in the basic structure of an economy, the banking institutions have no separate juridical existence. Referring to the fact that the banking institutions have to deal with the finances which have been created by the RBI and the government, if people's faith in the currency of a country does not exist, or if there is lawlessness in the economy, would the banking institutions provide confidence to the economy? Faith in banking, whether in the private or in the public sector, is provided by an ordered society run according to the rule of law and not through the operations of few industrial houses. In fact, time and again the government has to introduce legislative measures to ensure that the confidence of the people was built up in private banking institutions are only too well-known to be referred to indicate that the source of confidence which the private banks enjoy lies with the government and Parliament and not with the few capitalists and self-styled representatives of the people. It is only a few years back that the government has introduced insurance for small deposits with the banks which ensures that small depositors are not made to suffer if a private commercial bank failed. Thus the argument of adverse 'psychological reaction' is only worsening the faith and the fear for nationalisation so that small section of the population could continue to exploit the community savings for their personal benefits.

It has also been argued that with the nationalisation of banks, bank deposits would get reduced. One may ask which is the section of the depositors who would not like to have deposits with banking institutions? Very obviously, the section which maintains current accounts in the banking institutions, comprising of the business and the corporate sector, cannot but help to maintain accounts with the banks because it was an operational necessity for their working. Also it is only through the current accounts that they can obtain credit from the banking institutions. Thus in our discussion regarding the deposits, one must keep the current deposits outside the discussion. In the rest of the deposits, as has been shown earlier, a large part of deposits come from small savers. This section of depositors is very directly dependent upon the number of banking offices which are located in the economy. It is very obvious that nationalised banking sector would pursue a vigorous policy to cover the rural areas and the small savers in the urban centres, thereby the quantum of deposits as well as the number of deposits would considerably be enlarged. The same could be said regarding the fixed depositors. One does not see which section is referred to when it was argued that certain type of depositors may withdraw their savings from the nationalised banks.

Credit Needs not Affected by Nationalisation

The main argument put forth by private banks is that with nationalisation, the private sector would be adversely affected and it would not be able to obtain credit from nationalised banking institutions. Nothing could be more unreal and superficial than this argument. Though SBI is not a model enterprise, yet it needs to be mentioned that it is the SBI which has shown accommodation to the private sector in a big manner. Even the

Industrial Credit and Investment Corporation of India Ltd. (ICICI) and International Finance Corporation (IFC) as well as the LIC (Life Insurance Corporation) are the financial institutions which have been specifically created by the government to provide finance to the private sector. There is no reason to believe that private sector would not obtain financial accommodation from the nationalised banking institutions. However, one must say that such a fear would be genuine on the part of those who enjoy a privileged position in matters of bank credit not because they have entered priority industries but because of their influence and control over the policies of the private banking institutions. Very certainly, as nationalised banking sector would not be able to allow a favoured treatment to a few only, the degree of discrimination against small borrowers would get reduced. Thus the real danger in the nationalisation of banks is not to the industry as such but to a few monopolists and industrial houses who have been receiving an extremely favourable treatment from the private banks which they own or control.

A general charge against the functioning of the private sector is that the policies of the public sector are influenced by political considerations. Without going into the argument further, one may only state that all that is 'political' is not what is generally made out. There is a difference between the political and personal influence entering into the functioning of public enterprises. In the case of the functioning of the private banking institutions today, the influences 'personal' and vested are largely by the large industrial houses. If the banks were in the public sector, the policies and the management may be under the pressures of parliament and government. Since the parliament and the government are the institutions of society, the influence of tht parliament cannot be considered as derogatory to the overall interests of society. Thus, even for a moment if one takes the political influence will replace the personal influences, the situation may not be against social interests and national objectives. By contrast, the structure of private banking today is such that it functions against broader national objectives, as mentioned earlier in this report.

Managerial Talent

Another fear expressed has been that nationalised banks would not be able to secure the managerial talent required for conducting day-to-day functions of banking institutions. One does not know if such a question needs to be posed by those who claim to have better understanding of banking and private institutions, regarding the question of finding managerial talent immediately after the nationalisation of banks. With the nationalisation of banks very certainly, the present administrative and managerial staff would remain in employment of nationalised banks. The only change will take place in the board of directors, and in this regard, thanks to the close relationship between the industry and the banking, there is no fear of the bank directors going out of job and facing a situation of unemployment if they did not continue on the bank boards. Most of the bank directors hold directorship in industrial companies. Thus the real displacement in personnel would be negligible and no crises would appear after the nationalisation and taking over of the private banking institutions. However, care will have to be taken that special efforts are made to train many more managers and other banking talent which could pursue a vigorous policy of expansion in the rural sectors of the economy. Also the banking institutions would have to develop their own expertise instead of depending upon the normal civil servants, before or after retirement to hold the senior most positions in the nationalised banking sector.

Financial Cost

The total PUC and the reserve of the Indian scheduled banks were around ₹ 69.00 crore in 1965. Even if the government chose to takeover the entire PUC, which really is not necessary, the cost of compensation would not be significant if one compares the additional deposits of nearly ₹ 2,000 crore which would be accompanied by the act of nationalisation. If the differential rate (the market rate and the rate of bank credit) was 6 per cent, the whole amount of compensation could be made within a period of one year alone. Moreover, the question of compensation or financial cost is a very minor point in the discussion of bank nationalisation. The financial cost has to be related with the other advantages which the economy would obtain, and since nationalisation of banks has a structural role to play in the economy, the financial cost should be the least important consideration in deciding about the question of nationalisation. However, it is not a very significant financial cost because compensation would be liquidated by the profits within a period of 5-6 years.

Foreign Investment

In certain quarters, a fear has been expressed that with the nationalisation of banks our foreign trade would be adversely affected. This again is a fear which would not be justified if one conducts an investigation into the nature of imports and export of the country. As far as exports are concerned, there should be no reason to believe that our exports would decline, and on the import side if the imports of non-essential commodities got to be reduced, which unfortunately is a remote possibility, it should be most welcome. One can however, see some justification in the argument that private foreign capital may not be coming as easily as it would otherwise. This seems to be the fear. One must state even at the cost of being repetitive that such fears have been expressed all throughout and these are nothing new for students of economics in the country only to cite a few. At the time of the initiation of the planning process, it was widely publicised that the growth of the public sector and adoption of planning would take us nearer to the communist world and with our closer contacts with the socialist countries, the private capital would feel shy of entering the Indian economy. Once again, at the time of the announcement of the Industrial Policy Resolution, these fears were exaggerated. After the resolution of the All India Congress Committee on democratic socialism, it was openly doubted whether any private industrialist would like to invest in this country and the cost of its entering into the Indian economy has not been a light one.

Therefore, it should be made clear that such fears are a stock argument for any rational decision which does not suit a few industrial houses or goes against the ideological convictions of those who have neither faith in their own social order nor have the right of being Indians. How does it matter for a private investor whether the bank was in the private or in the public sector? It was of least importance for his investments and for his profits. As long as he can obtain fairly good degree of returns to his investment, he would enter into collaborations and invest directly in the country. The private capital will not come on sentimental reasoning but would be attracted by the economic prospect that we can offer.

Monopoly and Competition

Another argument put forth by private bankers and vested interests is that with the nationalisation of banks, there would be no competition in the banking sector. As a result, the personalised service to depositors would disappear. It is further argued that nationalisation would bring in monopoly of government in the banking sector. Before posing this question, one should ask whether in India today banking is not in the hands of a few industrial houses? Is it not theirs a virtual monopoly in the private banking sector? This is further indicated by the fact that all the scheduled bank representatives have come under a common banner 'Indian Bankers Association' to defend the so-called interests of the 'community.' The banks have been today functioning as a monopoly. This point has been amply discussed earlier, and the statistical data clearly indicate that there was a virtual monopoly in the banking sector of the economy. It needs to be mentioned here that a monopoly in the private sector is very much different from the monopoly under the public sector. A public sector monopoly is answerable to the people in general and to parliament in particular, whereas private monopolies are neither responsible nor answerable to any one else than their own selves. Thus even if there was monopoly of the government in the banking sector, it would not be deleterious to social interests as the present monopolistic conditions. However, we would not like to give an impression that the nationalised banking institutions need be negligent regarding providing such services which would attract more depositors and give a sense of personalised attention. Special efforts will have to be made that the nationalised banks pursue such policies. We are dealing with some of the questions later on in this report. By way of indication, the broad outlines of nationalised banking will have to be managed and administered.

Conclusions and Recommendations

In the foregoing parts of this report, we have dealt with many aspects of the present-day structure of the private banking system and its functional maladies. From our analysis, we arrive at the following conclusions:

(a) The private control of commercial banks in a planned economy is an anachronism which has been an obstacle to the achievement of plan objectives in India.

(b) Private banks have failed to mobilise the savings of the community, specially of the rural sector, small towns and the lower-income groups.

(c) The ownership and control of private banks is concentrated in a few hands which militates against the constitutional Directive that the operation of the economic system should not lead to concentration of economic power and widen disparities of income and wealth.

(d) The private commercial banks have mainly been instrumental in draining away the deposits from rural and semi-urban areas to large centres of industry and trade, but have not led to balanced regional development of the economy by means of their credit policies.

(e) The private commercial banks have failed to contribute to the development of the vital priority sectors of the Indian economy, namely, the small-scale and medium industries sector and agriculture.

(f) The private commercial banks have failed to promote and encourage the new entrepreneurs, whose main capital is their technical and managerial skill, to set up industries with the help of bank accommodation.

(g) The private banks have promoted exclusive use of large deposits by a small group of industrial houses, which has directly helped in the concentration of economic power in their hands.

(h) The private commercial banks have abetted and supported socially undesirable activities like hoarding and speculation by violating the rules and regulations laid down by the RBI from time to time.

(i) The private commercial banks have failed to be guided by the positive social objectives laid down in the Five Year Plans.

(j) The private commercial banks have resorted to policies and practices by means of which the supply of bank credit has been unduly increased in certain crucial periods and diverted bank credit into channels which were contrary to the laid-down priorities in the plans.

(k) Easy and cheap availability of credit for a few industrial houses has encouraged the growth of monopolies and in conditions of the 'sellers market' in the country, the monopolists have not paid any attention to the Plan objectives of achieving 'self-reliance' in matters of foreign assistance.

(l) The operations of the private banking institutions have been the basic cause of the lop-sided development of the Indian industrial sector.

On the other hand, in our opinion, the merits of nationalisation of the banking structure would be as follows:

(a) The nationalised banking institutions would be in a position to pursue vigorous and continuous expansion programmes of covering the rural, the small towns and other lower-income groups in the society for ensuring greater resource mobilisation for the economic development of the country.

(b) The nationalised banking would ensure that the credit policies were such which supported plan priority industries and discouraged the trends of investment which were not in conformity with the overall objectives of economic development.

(c) Apart from ensuring better economic growth through better implementation of Plans, it would also be possible to pay special attention to the achievement of the objective of balanced inter-sectoral and inter-regional growth in the economy.

(d) The nationalisation of private banking would snap the control over the community's resources, which exist in the hands of a few industrial houses of the country. Thereby, it would be possible to reduce concentration of economic power which has its own serious implications in the efficient conduct of the economy.

(e) The nationalised banking structure would enable the society to coordinate policies of the various credit institutions in the country in a manner which was necessary for the exploitation of the entrepreneurial and other skills available in the country. In the existing economic system, the RBI cannot exercise effective controls for regulating private banking institutions.

(f) The nationalisation of the banking institutions would bring about more stability in the functioning of the credit institutions and thereby inspire more confidence from the depositors.

(g) Because of the snapping of direct contacts between the few industrial houses and the banking institutions, the discriminations against a large many would come to an end. This will introduce more healthy competition between the entrepreneurs than in the present situation where competition is sought to be between two unequals—big with all the resources at their command and the small denied of any such assistance.

Therefore, we are of the opinion that any attempt which seeks merely to impose greater controls on commercial banks, without interfering with the patterns of ownership and control in few hands, will not achieve any significant results. The last two decades of the planning period in India have clearly shown that despite comprehensive regulatory control of the RBI, it has not been possible to regulate and control the activities of the private commercial banks in accordance with the national interests and also the priorities of planned development. The past experience is sufficient to dispel any further hopes regarding the possibility of the present banking system being regulated through controls.

We are also of the opinion that in the present stage of our economic development, partial nationalisation of banks will not meet the needs of the times. It will create many more difficulties than it will solve because the challenges of the present conditions are such which cannot be met without the complete takeover of the banking system.

Further, while emphasising the need for the nationalisation of the banking system, we would like to make a few suggestions regarding the actual implementation of the policy of nationalisation of banks. These are the following ones.

Credit Policy Guidelines: Working Group

Leaving aside the sins of omission and commission by the banking system, the basic defects in the working of the credit institutions today in terms of planned development arise because no real policy guidelines have been laid down by the Planning Commission, the Finance Ministry or the

RBI which closely interconnect plan requirements with the grant of bank credit. The RBI no doubt attempts from time to time to guide the channels of bank credit, but its guidance is much more related to the current economic situation and difficulties than to the requirements of the Five Year Plans. The fact that there is no such clear guidance given—the outlines of such a policy are not even worked out in operational terms by the Planning Commission and the Ministry of Finance—is indicated by the act that the two most important credit institutions in the country which are already in the public sector, the LIC and the SBI, do not have any policy directions regarding investment and credit which can be said to be in any way closely related to the requirements of development planning as worked out in the Five Year Plans. One of the immediate and crucial tasks, therefore, is to work out what exactly should be the credit policy to be pursued by the financial institutions for the successful implementation of the development plans and for the attainment of the objectives of current economic policy and how should it be laid down by the Planning Commission and the Ministry of Finance. It is also necessary that appropriate instruments to ensure that this policy is carried out in a decentralised way by the banking organisations and their branches should be worked out. The experience of wartime Britain and the planned economies, especially in more recent years, and also that of France, should be studied in this context. One of the essential things to be done immediately would be to set up a competent working party to prepare for the government outlines of this policy so that the strategy of credit planning can be worked out at the earliest.

Management after Nationalisation

The management of nationalised banks will pose quite a few questions and it will not be possible to meet the challenges by the usual methods of management that have been unfortunately prevalent in the Indian public sector. The bureaucratic domination of public enterprise management and the use of completely unsuitable governmental methods have been the bane of our public enterprises. It is essential that once the government decides to nationalise banks, clear decisions would have to be taken that a break with the past tradition of bureaucratic and inefficient management will be made at the same time. The intention to do this has of course always been there. When the Imperial Bank was nationalised, the then finance minister had indicated that while social and economic objectives would be kept before it by the nationalised bank, its management would largely operate on business principles. With this purpose, he even excluded the nationalised bank from the purview of audit by the Comptroller and Auditor General. While this was certainly useful, it has not led to the kind of business-like management of the SBI that one would wish for.

Competitive Structure of Nationalised Bank to be Maintained

We may also suggest that the nationalised banks need not all to be merged together as was done in the case of the LIC. While a few small banks which are found to be uneconomical may be merged in some way or the other to form more economical and efficient units, the units that are well organised and economical have to continue to function independently. There is nothing wrong with the different nationalised banks competing with each other and it may even be useful to allow more competition than the Indian Banks' Association has usually permitted for the private commercial banks in the past. Such competition would ensure that there was incentive for better service to customers and this may even help in attracting more and more deposits to the banking system. This is an important consideration and we have discussed it earlier in this report.

The maintenance of the nationalised banks as independent units would mean that while the boards of directors of the banks would have to change immediately on nationalisation, the management including the bulk of the top management cadre would continue to be the same. Already the pay structure of employees in different banks has been rationalised through the system of bank employees' awards and the categorisation of banks for that purpose. The problems that were faced by the LIC regarding bringing in one pool employees of different life insurance companies would not therefore create any problem for the nationalised banks.

Boards of Directors

The selection of the nationalised banks' boards of directors would be of crucial importance. The tradition of appointing different level bureaucrats on an *ex officio* basis should not be followed in making appointments to these boards. It is true that there is a tradition against appointing persons who are not under government control because of the fear that, if they behave irresponsibly, the government would come into trouble. The underlying assumption of distrust of the non-official citizen is something that needs to be given up as early as possible. This is obviously a heritage from British rule imbibed by the civil service and learnt from them, perhaps not quite consciously, by the political leadership. There are a number of sources for recruitment to the new boards of nationalised banks. For example, experienced officials of the RBI and the SBI, well-known professional experts of existing banks who are not wedded to anti-social and anti-public sector doctrines, professional experts from industry and from the academic world, and labour leaders who have some experience of industry should contribute from two-third to three-fourth of the board members. It is, however, necessary to underline that the directors must be those who have a broader social perspective and have a commitment to the social objectives and are known for their faith in public sector and the philosophy of planning in India.

Employee Cooperation

Unfortunately, the trade unions in India have not always taken a constructive attitude regarding the efficient operations of public sector enterprises, and it would be difficult to expect an overnight change in their attitudes, but it would be useful if an attempt is made right from the beginning to cultivate the bank employees' unions and take them into confidence regarding the post-nationalisation organisation of the banks. While no representatives of the bank employees' unions as such need to be appointed on the board, the appointment of some prominent trade union leaders on the boards of nationalised banks, and an attempt by the new managements and by government to establish an effective system of communication and consultation would help to create a climate where cooperation of employees and their organisation for the efficient functioning of nationalised banks may become available.

Prevent Overcentralisation

One further word of caution is necessary about the management of nationalised banks. Because of parliamentary accountability and the traditional nature of governmental functioning, nationalisation and public ownership especially in India has invariably meant overcentralisation in decision making. This would be suicidal in nationalised banking. A certain part of credit decisions must be left to the local agents of banks, and if a feeling is created that the agents have to refer matters all the time to higher authorities, we may not only create public opinion against nationalisation but also make the functioning of trade and small industry difficult. Within the board policies laid down by the board of directors and subject to the normal supervision, it should be possible to permit local agents to take decisions regarding grant of credit. This would be treated as obvious—but not in the context of the functioning of the Indian public sector.

It may also be necessary to appoint a working group of accountants, specifically to examine past transactions of banks with a view to finding out how far the private ownership of banks was used to further not only the interest of certain business groups but also to evade public policy and RBI directives. Such an investigation may also lead to the unearthing of black money and may generally provide a healthy influence for correcting many ills that pervade the Indian economy today.

Credit Policies and Coordination

A word must be said regarding the need for evolving a set of credit policies which would enable the nationalised banks to pursue the social objectives which are placed before the nation. We have already said that a policy group should be immediately appointed to work out the necessary guidelines for the nationalised banking. There is, of course, no doubt that the impact of the policies would be periodically reviewed to ensure the necessary modifications in the credit and management policies of the nationalised banking institutions. There would also be need to coordinate the functioning of the other financial institutions like the cooperatives, Life Insurance, General Insurance, Unit Trust, Industrial Credit and Investment Corporation of India and the Industrial Finance Corporation. This is extremely necessary to avoid conflicting and wasteful policies by the various financial institutions.

Annual Credit Reviews

Considering the importance and the strategic role of the banking system in the structure of Indian economy, it is necessary to have a comprehensive annual review of the functioning of the various credit institutions in the country and their impact on the furtherance of plan objectives. Until now very little effort has been made in this direction. But one can understand that when banking institutions are not under the direct control of the public sector, such a coordination or even a review is next to impossible. We consider the data on the working of the banking system which are an extremely useful indicator of the level and direction of the economic activities in the society. This information should prove of great advantage to the government and Parliament in evolving effective, timely and more rational policies in the field of planning.

Epilogue

In the foregoing parts of the report, we have dealt with the various aspects of banking in the Indian economy. It is clear that the central control and management of the banking institutions cannot be left in the private sector if plan objectives have to be achieved. However, our conclusions are purely based on economic and social considerations. The case for nationalisation of banks could, however, be also made from the viewpoint of constitutional and parliamentary angles.

The Indian Constitution has enjoined the government-specific responsibility of taking all such measures which would ensure that the operation of the economic system does not lead to concentration of economic power in the country to the common detriment. In this context, we consider nationalisation of the private commercial banking which is only one of the economic reforms of the economic structure which was long overdue to curb tendencies towards concentration of economic power and emergence of monopolies in the productive system of our society.

It is also necessary to take note of the demand often made that in the Indian economy at present, considerations for increased production should precede those of social justice and distribution. It is argued that once production rises and capital is accumulated in a few hands, it would not be difficult to takeover the large private business and industrial organisations into governmental hands, and which is made out of the point, particularly relating to the private commercial banks that the alternative of nationalisation was always open to the government.

In this context, we would like to cite Prof. D.R. Gadgil, the present Deputy Chairman of the Planning Commission, who made the observations in the following manner:

> That increasing inequality or the heavy and continued concentration of the ownership of the means of production in the hands of a few private capitalists is the only way in which you can speed up production, is far from being universal experience in recent times. It is also very doubtful whether you can continue to concentrate economic and other power in society in the hands of small groups and yet later expect that they will quietly allow you to take it away or even that a state apparatus dominated by such interests will want to reverse current policy.

When the foregoing economic analyses impel us to come to only one conclusion that in the given context of Indian economy, meant to progress towards socialism, nationalisation of banks is an inevitable step. However, we should not be understood thereby to mean that either nationalisation of key industries or that of the financial institutions would automatically lead to socialism. It must be pointed out that nationalisation of key industries and financial institutions had been resorted to by several capitalist countries in the world for the purpose of strengthening and stabilising the institution of capitalism. In this context, we would like to quote late Pandit Jawaharlal Nehru, who made the following observations in the context of the Karachi Resolution of 1931:

> In the Karachi Resolution it took a step, a very important step in a socialist direction by advocating nationalisation of key industries and services and various other measures to lessen the burden on the poor and increase it on the rich. This was not socialism at all and a capitalist state could easily accept almost everything contained in the resolution.

Care is, therefore, to be taken that nationalisation of banking system does not become merely a measure to strengthen the economic power of monopolies and big business in the Indian economy. On the other hand, the nationalised banking system should become an instrument to put an end to anti-social tendency of the growth of a few at the cost of many in the country. It is only then that it would be possible for the Indian economy to achieve rapid economic growth.

Under the chairmanship of Pandit Nehru, the National Planning Committee set up by the Indian National Congress had recommended regarding the key industries as follows:

> All these industries being key industries, their ownership or control should, in accordance with the previous decisions of the National Planning Committee, rest with the State.

This policy had found expression in the Industrial Policy Resolutions of the Government of India (GoI) in 1948 and 1956. Hence it is beyond any doubt that even long before India became Independent, it was decided that the key industries should be under public ownership. It should be realised that 'finance' is more basic than even the basic industries, as it is the very basis of any economic development. In any type of planning, 'finance' acts as a lubricant to the wheels of development and determines the economic more directly than any other institution. Hence there is no rationale behind the argument that only key industries must be in the public sector and not the banking industry.

Appendix A-10.1

Congress Party in Parliament

Chandra Shekhar
Secretary

24-25 Parliament House
New Delhi
12th August, 1967

My dear Dr. Goyal:

You must be aware that for the last few months the question of Bank Nationalization is receiving attention of the Indian people in general and that of the policy making sections in particular. Undoubtedly, the question is essentially an economic one though it has direct implications for the social and political aspects of the Indian life as well.

A number of members of our Party in Parliament and outside have expressed their desire to me to get this problem of bank nationalization examined by a group of competent economists who may be in a position to offer their constructive suggestions with an overall perspective of the Indian society and its objective. I have no doubt the question will be also reviewed by the official agencies. And yet the value of an independent group of persons can never be over-emphasized.

It is with this idea that I thought I could approach you for help. I remember nearly four years back you had circulated a paper on the operations of banking institutions which was discussed in a seminar of the staff and research scholars of Delhi School of Economics. Since you have been a scholar of banking alongwith your other interests in the field of planning, I thought you may be kind enough to spare some time for preparing a report for us. I would, however, like to leave it to you to associate two or three other fellow economists who could deal with the question of banking in the light of the demands of the planning process and in that the rural sector in specific. If the report can be a comprehensive document it would provide the necessary perspective for taking a decision on a vital question of the Indian economy.

I hope you would be kind enough to prepare your report by the end of September, 1967. This is a very short notice but I can only hope that you would understand the importance of such a study to allow an enlightened and early discussion on this question.

With regards,

Yours sincerely,
Sd/-
(CHANDRA SHEKHAR)

Dr. S.K. Goyal
IIPA, New Delhi.

Appendix A-10.2

Congress Party in Parliament

Chandra Shekhar — 24, Parliament House
Secretary — New Delhi

Dear Kamarajji,

A few months ago, I had requested some of my economist friends to examine the question of bank nationalisation objectively and dispassionately and prepare a report. They have accordingly made a detailed study of the subject and compiled a report, a copy of which I herewith submit to you.

This study reveals the following among other important conclusions:

(a) The bank deposits have increased from Rs. 908 crores in 1951 to Rs. 3073 crores in 1965 and to Rs. 3500 crores at present. This means an average increase of about 16%. That is the reason why the banks have started having a commanding position over the nation's economy in general and financial resources in particular.

(b) In 1951, there were 566 banks (both scheduled and non-scheduled). In 1965 this number came down to 109. The reduction in the non-scheduled banks has been phenomenal, from 473 to mere 33 and scheduled banks from 92 to 76.

(c) There are 61 Indian scheduled banks today. Through these banks no less than about Rs. 350 crores are mobilised from poorer and backward states and diverted to highly developed states like Maharashtra, West Bengal and Madras, Rajasthan, for example, gets only a mere 1 % of the bank credit. In the 2 states, namely West Bengal and Madras, the banks have given more credit than the deposits they have received there.

(d) The total paid-up capital of all the Indian scheduled banks (numbering 61) is Rs. 44.36 crores only. This has increased by building up reserve by about 50 per cent. The deposits on the other hand, have increased by nearly 240 per cent. As a result, the ratio of paid-up capital and reserve to deposits, has gone down from 9.7 per cent in 1951 to 3.4 % in 1965.

(e) 49% of the shares of the Central Bank were held by 3% shareholders and 36% shares were owned by 1 % of the shareholders.

In this connection the Governor of the Reserve Bank once said:-

"One of the structural features of Indian banking is this concentration of power which, in some cases, is enormous in relation to the capital actually employed. From time to time we come across cases in which a family or group has a controlling interest in a bank and it has become a major task of inspection to prevent the exercise of this interest in undesirable ways".

(f) According to the survey of directorships of 20 leading banking companies a total of 188 persons served as directors on the boards of 20 leading banks. These 188 bank directors held 1452 directorships of other companies also. The total number of companies under these directors is 1100.

(g) Similarly, a detailed study of the directorships held by directors of 5 leading banks reveals that through common directors, these 5 banks are connected with 33 insurance companies, 6 financial companies, 25 investment trusts, 584 manufacturing and other companies and 26 trading companies and 15 non-profit making associations.

(h) Debt due to the bank directors or their companies was nearly Rs. 56 crores in December 1954 but this amount rose to Rs. 291 crores in December 1965. The bank loans given to the directors and their companies in the same year stood at Rs. 317.4 crores.

If allowance is made for indirect loans and advances to the bank directors and their concerns this figure is expected to go somewhere between 600 and 700 crore.

(i) The total advances made by the banks in 1966 were Rs. 2,432 crores to about 9 lakhs accounts. Out of these, Rs. 1800 crores were lent to about 4,000 accounts only. It has also been brought out that in 1967, 572 borrowers were extended nearly Rs. 1400 crores out of the bank credit of Rs. 1800 crores even for industrial and commercial purposes.

If five to six hundred accounts were to be identified with industrial and business houses, one may find that number of borrowers were in fact only 4 or 5.

(j) In September 1953, agricultural loans stood at Rs. 19 crores whereas the same was only Rs. 3.9 crores in the year 1965. Not only the amount of absolute loans to agriculture has come down to 1/4th of what it was in 1953, but the more significant point is that the share of the agricultural loans in total bank credit declined from 3.8 per cent to its nearly 1/20th i.e. 0.2 per cent only.

(k) The bank credit has not been utilised for financing the projects according to the Plan priorities but has been invested in low priority projects or even in those which were outside the Plan.

(l) The powers of control in the hands of the Reserve bank for regulating the functions of the private banks are ineffective because the Reserve Bank has to be very cautious in exercising them lest the confidence of the public in banking in general and the concerned bank in particular, may be undermined.

(m) Even in USA, there is a ceiling for paying loans to a single concern. No bank can extend loans to any concern which is more than 10 per cent of the paid-up capital and reserve of the bank concerned.

The banks give credit to the directors and their associates at rates of interest much lower than those prevalent in the market. This benefit alone amounts to more than 100 crore per year. This means that besides the dividend they get on their shares they get a much more substantial benefit through this concession in interest rates.

(n) The deposits with the State Bank of India which were Rs. 220 crores in 1955 increased to Rs. 677 crores in 1965, that is, more than 3 times. This results the argument that after nationalisation the public deposits will fall.

(o) The private commercial banks have failed to be guided by the positive and social objectives laid down in the Five Year Plans.

(p) Easy and cheap availability of credit for a few industrial houses has encouraged the growth of monopolies and concentration of economic power.

(q) Pandit Jawaharlal Nehru made the following observation in the context of the Karachi resolution in 1931:

"In the Karachi Resolution it took a step, a very important step in a socialist direction by advocating nationalisation of key industries and services and various other measures to lessen the burden on the poor and increase it on the rich. This was not socialism at all and a capitalist sate could easily accept almost everything contained in the resolution".

If you wish to nationalise key industries, you must first nationalise banks. This is inevitable.

I hope that above points would help the deliberations on this important issue at all levels. I am sending a copy each of this Report to Indira Ji and Morarji Bhai.

With personal regards,

Yours sincerely,
Sd/-
(CHANDRA SHEKHAR)

Shri K Kamaraj
President, AICC
7 Jantar Mantar Road, New Delhi - 1

11

Banking Commission Report

Who will ask the Relevant Questions? I cannot say![1]

The Banking Commission, under the chairmanship of R.G. Saraiya was appointed by Morarji Bhai Desai in early 1969. The commission was thought of for giving effect to measures for social control over banks. Morarji Bhai did not believe in disturbing the basic framework of the banking system based on private management and control. It was but natural that he framed its terms of reference according to what he conceived of the role of a banking commission to further his viewpoint as represented in the legislation for social control over banks (1968). It was not unexpected that he would choose members of the commission who did believe in continuation of banks under private management.

Within six months of the constitution of the Banking Commission, the 14 major Indian private commercial banks were nationalised. Morarji Bhai resigned from the office of the Deputy Prime Minister and Finance Minister of India. With nationalisation of the 14 banks, nearly 90 per cent of bank resources came under the direct control of the government.

In brief, a context in which the Banking Commission was appointed underwent a basic change by July 1969. With the change in the context, it was necessary (provided the Banking Commission was to be used as an instrument of reform and making the system more efficient) to modify the terms of reference and to effect changes in the membership of the commission. But, the government did neither modify any of the terms of reference nor did it add any new member. It must be said to the credit of the commission that it did ask the government if it would like to give them new directives. But the government refused to give any fresh directive. Those who look forward to reading this bulky report should not

1. This article appeared in the *Young Indian* in 1972.

be surprised if the report of the commission gives an impression of a lack of perspective.

At one point, the report suggests that the commission was not able to find much logic in the decision to take over only Indian commercial banks and exclude the equally large foreign banks from the coverage of the act of nationalisation. On page 375, the commission observes:

> The criterion used in selecting these banks was the simple one of the size of deposits at the time of nationalization. Yet, those foreign banks which satisfied the criterion were left out. Nor has there been any suggestion so far that any of the remaining Indian banks in the- private sector will be nationalized on these criteria. While the size of the deposits as a criterion for nationalization has a merit of simplicity, unless applied in a consistent manner it is likely to be regarded as a somewhat arbitrary one.

One was happy to read that the commission was posing a right question. On the same logic a question needs to be posed if the government would take over those banks which reach the level of ₹ 50 crore deposits? It is obvious that the banks having less than ₹ 50 crore would one day cross the limit if they grew at the normal rate. But if it is an accepted policy (to take over a bank which has more than ₹ 50 crore deposits), how can one expect the new private banks to make any efforts at deposit mobilisation? One expected some discussion on this aspect of the banking system. One would have, in fact, congratulated the commission for asking bold and logical questions. But, unfortunately, it is not that one does not get this opportunity but one gets a surprising and self-contradictory recommendation. On page 393, the commission observes that:

> The existing Indian commercial banks in the private sector which show good performance should be allowed to continue.

One would have appreciated the commission if it had taken the stand that let us not talk of the past but ensure that the existing private banks should not be disturbed even when the deposits get beyond ₹ 50 crore. It would have, of course, been more logical if the commission had advised that for parity and consistency, all banks should be taken over without any further delay. Similarly, the commission should have recommended that the foreign banks should not be treated differently from the Indian banks. This would have been the only logical projection of the approach the commission put forth on page 375. But, the commission chose to recommend "as regards the foreign banks, they may be allowed to continue as at present."

Two Faces

Why did the commission take one view while discussing the past decision of nationalisation of the 14 major banks and another while making recommendations? Should one seek the answer in the fact that the Banking Commission was constituted by Morarji Bhai and its membership was restricted to those who had no faith in the nationalisation of banks?

The banks were nationalised nearly 2.5 years back. During this period, bank deposits, especially with the nationalised banks, have grown at a higher rate than the foreign or private banks. The deposits increased by nearly 20 per cent during the last year. The numbers of bank offices have also increased in a phenomenal manner due to the direct instructions issued to the public sector banking institutions. It is somewhat surprising that the commission has avoided giving any due credit to the act of nationalisation. A reading of the chapter on the development of banking does not even give the impression that nationalisation has made any effect. Why has the commission avoided even a review of the working of the banks since nationalisation? Is it that they felt ill at ease? Or the commission could not digest the very fact of nationalisation?

The Banking Commission should have gone into the basis of nationalisation and asked if the necessary follow-ups have been pursued by the government. If not, why not? For example, one of the basic objectives of bank nationalisation was to ensure that bank credit was strictly channelised in conformity with the national plan priorities and in accordance with the plan programmes. It needed to be pointed out that a national credit plan should have been drawn simultaneously with the national Five Year Plans. The National Credit Council which was appointed under the scheme for 'social control over banks' has ceased to function. Why has not government thought of institutionalising the relationship between the banking system and the Planning Commission? The commission could have even asked why even now the top executives of the private commercial banks continue to be in position when the banks were nationalised so long back. Why haven't the bank boards of directors been appointed on a regular basis yet?

Obvious Reasons

It so happens that when the banks were nationalised, there was no white paper issued giving details of the consideration that went into the process of decision making. Yet, it is not true that the reasons were not known. One wonders if the Banking Commission could not put the nationalised banking sector in a correct perspective. This would have been a solid contribution by the commission. It could, possibly point out that instead of having a well-planned programme for credit planning, the approach to banking still continues to be determined on vague generalisations like 'help the enterprise' and 'encourage priority industries.' No one doubts the correctness of the decision to have wider dispersal of credit nor does one question the need to give preference to priority industries. But, what are the priority industries? Priority industries are now being defined differently by different agencies in the government. The Planning Commission puts forward a set of priorities. The ministry for industrial development has another set of priorities, and the ministry for foreign trade puts forth its own set of priorities. Which one of the sets of priorities should provide the guidelines for credit? One is yet to be clear about it.

Old Notions Continue

The old notion that more bank credit should be made available to agriculture continues to be insisted upon unmindful of the fact that when one argued for more loan to agriculture, there was an implied meaning that the loan beneficiaries of bank credit should be small and medium farmers and not rich landlords who want to borrow for purposes of purchasing tractors and harvesters. Could not a high powered body like the Banking Commission enquire if the agricultural loans have mainly gone in large amounts to help accentuate interpersonal disparities in the rural India? What percentage of the new credit has gone to help those who needed the credit most for improving their lot? Is it not time to question the very basis of the classification under the broad head of agriculture? One fails to understand how is it that a loan given for a fertiliser factory is non-agricultural and a loan meant for purchasing of a tube-well pumping sets is an agricultural one.

Some Questions

Questions need to be asked how best to use credit more effectively for making the planned process of growth a meaningful one. These are the questions which one expected that the commission (if constituted after nationalisation of banks) would have attempted to answer. But it was not to be so. As the Banking Commission Report is essentially out of focus and lacks the requisite perspective, who then can raise the relevant questions? Can one expect the miserable opposition parties to raise these issues in the Parliament? Or, will the government appoint an experts committee on a continuing basis to give answers to these questions? Or, will these things just drag on?

Section III

Multinational Corporations

12 Multinational Corporations in India

The Need for a Framework[1]

The paper consists of three sections. Section I presents a brief review of the nature of concern being shown with regard to the operations of the multinational corporations (MNCs) in the global context. Section II outlines some of the broad features of foreign investments and MNCs in India. It also attempts to provide a broad strategy for research on MNCs. The last section examines the effectiveness of the Foreign Exchange Regulation Act (FERA) in relation to the objectives it was expected to serve. This paper is based on the empirical results of a study undertaken by the author.

I

The operations of MNCs have evoked considerable interest, particularly during the last few years, amongst social scientists, policy makers and international agencies.[2] While the rapid growth of MNCs in the world economy is seen more of a threat to underdeveloped countries, the concern for control and regulation of MNCs and their global operations has been voiced more intensely in developed societies. Scholars and policy makers in developing countries (a typical case being that of India) are, however, now trying to catch up with their counterparts in developed countries.[3] In 1972, the UN Economic and Social Council appointed a

1. This is the first working paper of the Corporate Studies Group brought out in 1978. An earlier version of this paper was read as a key note address at the Indian Economic Conference, December 24, 1978, Bombay, by the author.
2. For a discussion on the definition, the nature, the impact and tensions, and a tentative programme of action with regard to MNCs, see: *U.N. Multinational Corporations in World Development*, 1973, New York, and *UN Transnational corporations in World Development: A ReExamination*, 1978, New York.
3. Ibid.

group of eminent persons to study the role of MNCs and their impact on the process of development, especially that of the developing countries.[4] The group submitted its report in 1974. In pursuance of the group's recommendations, the Commission on transnational corporations (TNCs) and the 'Centre on TNCs'[5] were established in the UN network as agencies to investigate and render advice to the UN Economic and Social Council and member governments. A few regional offices of the UN Centre on Transnational Corporations (UNCTC) have already been established, the one for the Economic and Social Commission for Asia and Pacific (ESCAP) region being located at Bangkok. The regional offices of UNCTC have a programme to impart skills at negotiations with TNCs, build up comprehensive information systems and prepare case studies.[6] Other organs of the UN, like UN Conference on Trade and Development (UNCTAD), International Labour Organization (ILO), Food and Agriculture Organization (FAO), UN Educational, Scientific and Cultural Organization (UNESCO) and UN Industrial Development Organization (UNIDO), are promoting studies with regard to the operations of TNCs in their respective areas of specialisation. The Independent Commission on Development and International Issues under the Chairmanship of Willy Brandt, with its secretariat at Geneva, is also undertaking more studies on the role of TNCs and other related issues. A good number of academic institutions and research centres in the developed countries are developing long-term programmes to study one or the other aspects of TNCs. For instance, Transnational Institution (TNI) (Centre for Research on Multinational Corporations; SOMO) at Amsterdam and ECIMC at Brussels (a centre funded by a Swiss TNC) are institutions exclusively devoted to study the role of largest giant corporations of the world from the labour, consumer

---

4. The group comprised 20 members. The terms of reference of the group were: "to study the role of multinational corporations and their impact on the process of development, specially that of the developing countries, and also their implications for international relations, to formulate conclusions which may possibly be used by Governments in making their sovereign decisions regarding national policy in this respect, and to submit recommendations for appropriate international action." The resolution further requested the Secretary-General to submit the report of the Group, "together with his own comments and recommendations, to the Economic and social Council at its fifty-seventh session." UN, *The Impact of Multinational Corporations on Development and on International Relations*. 1974, New York.

5. The two expressions TNCs and NCs in this paper are to be treated as the same.

6. For information on the organisation and the objectives of the UNCTC, see: *The CTC Reporter* 1(1), December 1976. New York: UN.

and management viewpoints. Harvard University has published its second revised volume on source material on TNCs. A number of individual researchers in US and European countries are engaged in preparing case studies to highlight problems of transfer of technology or labour relations.

Wide Scope for Research

Western scholars, particularly from the 'TNC home' countries, are generally seen to be critical of MNCs and their writings are well informed. There are, of course, many who see the MNCs as the only hope of the underdeveloped world. The range of information collected and commented upon by scholars from the developed world is large. The areas proposed to be covered are wide ranging e.g., problems of transfer of technology, transfer pricing and resort to Monopolies and Restrictive Trade Practices (MRTP), impact on balance of payments (for host and home countries), promotion of 'research and development' and adaptation of processes to local needs, generation of employment, existence of the wide disparities due to top heavy new class of managers and professionals, introduction of western life styles, growth of indigenous entrepreneurship, cultivation of 'brand' culture, quality consciousness, tie-ups with private national monopoly capital, direct and indirect involvement in influencing public policies and TNCs adaptation to local sociopolitical environment and involvement in building up of infrastructural facilities for the backward societies. In this category would also fall some of the politically inspired publications dealing with the TNCs in countries of Latin America and Africa where ruling elites and governments promote and protect the interests of foreign monopolies rather than the genuine interests of the local population.

Research Host Countries

In contrast to this, with a few exceptions, studies conducted in developing countries officially or at the individual level are invariably at the general level and do not go beyond vague generalisations. The empirical base of studies on the underdeveloped countries continues to be disappointing. Indian economists, generally speaking, have not shown adequate degree of interest in undertaking studies on the private corporate sector, in general, and the foreign sector, in particular. Policy makers in a number of developing countries either continue to operate in a framework that was evolved in the colonial era (which is the historical past of the majority of the developing nations) or pursue policies based on many a vague, unrealistic and misplaced assumptions. Some of the crucial policy formulations with regard to foreign capital, therefore, are nothing short of well-cultivated myths.

MNC Home Countries

The concern shown by western scholars on the operations of TNCs is probably born out of many reasons. However, primarily their concern is a reaction, based on their day-to-day personal experiences and frustrations with the fast extending arms of the 'giant corporations,' whose control mechanism is expanding and tightening fast. Some of them seem to visualise that much sooner than the requisite consciousness arises, the citizen of the free world may lose their economic, social and political choices and be forced to surrender human dignity to the impersonal institutions of TNCs. Hence, the view, that giant corporations are leading the world to a point of crisis. Expressions of revolt against the prospects of being pushed towards a socioeconomic system dominated by private corporation philosophy may be feeble but are certainly distinct.

New Economic Order

Policy makers in MNC 'home' countries have not always viewed with concern the growing interest and direct investments by their MNCs in the underdeveloped world; nor is this true of international agencies. In fact, the 'home' countries alongwith international agencies established under the aegis of the UN, provide support to entry of MNCs in the underdeveloped countries—more by way of direct participation by MNCs than to the limited agreements—for outright sale of technical know how or training. The economic resolutions at the international forums, not surprisingly, though increasingly, emphasise the need for transfer of capital to the third world countries. The developed nations are not hesitant to confess that they are far below the expected level of transfer of 0.75 per cent of their gross national products (GNPs) to the less developed nations. Part of their failure to fulfill their obligations is attributed to the rigidities of host countries to allow entry of foreign capital. The 'capital' it is assumed cannot be separated from 'technology.' The call for transfer of capital is unmistakably accompanied with the plea for reducing hurdles and liquidating sanctions which stand in the way of more exchange of goods (i.e., free trade). Strangely enough, concern against 'protectionism' is now being voiced by some of the developing countries, who would need protection from the direct competition from MNCs. There is emphasis on moving towards a new world order which contemplates that the different parts of the world should be organically interlinked in such a manner that would help knit the developed and the underdeveloped countries together for an everlasting peaceful and harmonious growth of humanity. The operational implications of the proposed New International Economic Order—to which India has most enthusiastically lent her support—are yet to be well understood by developing countries. Primarily, one has to ask the question: to which side would the net balance of advantages tilt, if there is free international exchange, when there exist wide disparities between the economic political strength of the constituents involved? This aspect needs a separate discussion. However, it is worth considering if as a first step, developing nations can start becoming aware of the fact that what they need for development is not so much capital but modern technology in selected areas. Secondly, the primary task before them is to organise themselves for the transformation of their socioeconomic and political structure and institutions than to divert their limited resources and energies towards trying somehow to achieve a fast growth in GNP in the immediate future. And thirdly, there was the need for underdeveloped countries to come together for enhanced mutual cooperation and for evolving mechanisms under which negotiations with the MNCs (and the developed countries) can be for technologies and not for capital, and for agreements which are not based on 'firms' or 'enterprises' but for the country as a whole or for a group of developing countries together. Duplication of efforts and costs can be avoided, if there was a more meaningful cooperation amongst the developing countries as a block instead of the general acceptance of the plea for a new order promoting 'one to one' exchange—irrespective of the comparative strength of the individual participation.

MNCs and Code of Conduct

The concern with MNCs' operations has led to emphasis on the need to evolve a code of conduct for MNCs. The assumption is that

MNCs can be made to abstain from indulging in certain type of practices which would be described as undesirable. The important code being discussed is that MNCs should not involve themselves with the political systems of host countries and observe self-imposed neutrality. Similarly, it is being contemplated that MNCs should not resort to MRTP. It is, however, not being questioned that by the very fact of the underdeveloped countries allowing private direct participation in economic activity, the host countries are opting for an economic system under which 'market mechanism' is allowed to determine the pattern of new investments. Given the assumption that MNCs are to be allowed to have direct investments with softer controls and lesser regulations, it is only logical to expect that private national capital would not be discriminated against, if not awarded preferential treatment. In brief, while the efforts at evolving a code of conduct appear quite reasonable, the fact remains that the entire discussion is in a framework of a free-market economy—the politics of which is certainly not neutral. In India, we know only too well that local entrepreneurs, during the colonial era, were extremely hostile to foreign capital. However, within few years of India's independence, the indigenous private capital became the champion of the cause of foreign companies and MNCs. The Indian industrial houses which had provided support to the struggle for freedom of the country were seen pleading for joint ventures with foreign companies. The Indian private companies have been using all means to influence public policies. It would be no exaggeration to say that Indian corporate sector, particularly the bigger constituents, did participate in the political life of the country and provided financial and other material support to individuals and certain political parties. The Indian corporations have not remained neutral to the political system, nor would indeed they be expected to remain so, in their own interest. The code of conduct for good behaviour may be evolved for the MNCs, but it can certainly not be for local capital who would be increasingly an active partner with MNCs. The essential point, therefore, is that the basic thrust of the entire discussion on MNCs regulation (in the western societies or at the level of UN agencies) is within the framework of free-market mechanism and the need for expanding the role of direct private investments in the developing world. Viewed in this perspective, no code of conduct can be neutral to politics of a country. A related and basic question in this regard is the extent to which expansion of the private capital would be in conformity with the national objectives of developing countries. Most developing countries aim at widening the base and strengthening efforts at planned developments of their societies. For this, invariably, the countries are required to mobilise larger resources and direct these towards areas which though socially more desirable do not always find adequate justification or priority on the logic of 'free-market mechanism.'

Aid and MNCs

The entry and promotion of MNCs need to be seen along with the 'aid' policies of developed and 'home' countries. None would dispute that the quantum and phasing of 'aid' by the donor countries has to be an integral part of the economic and political philosophy and within their own framework of foreign policy. No 'aid' is neutral nor can it be without direct and indirect strings. This is well illustrated by the form in which a part of the PL-480 funds were utilised to encourage such companies which had financial and technical collaborations with US-based firms. In fact, one of the major factors leading to entry of many MNCs from the US on the Indian scene has been the easy and cheap finance to Indo-US joint ventures. A glance at the list of beneficiaries could be rewarding.

II

How have MNCs been viewed in India? At the policy level, there is no distinction between an enterprise that is an MNC or one which is a small entity with parents abroad. At the first stage, the policy regarding MNCs is the same as for foreign private capital in India. However, large foreign companies and dominant firms (in a product) are covered by the Monopolies and Restrictive Trade Practices Commission (MRTPC) as indeed is true for even the wholly owned Indian corporate sector. The specific policies regarding foreign companies in India can be said to be the ones under the FERA, 1973. We shall examine the provisions of FERA in Section III.

Foreign Capital: Classification

Foreign private capital in India can be broadly classified under the following categories:

(a) Companies which are registered abroad but have place of business in India (i.e., branches of foreign companies).

(b) Companies having more than 51 per cent of equity held abroad (foreign subsidiaries).

(c) Companies where the foreign equity is between 40-50 per cent.

(d) Companies with less than 50 per cent equity but under foreign 'effective control' (to be judged from operational and historical background).

(e) Companies with substantial (more than 10%) equity held by a foreign company, which is also having technical collaboration; and

(f) Companies having collaboration agreements with 'licensee' status and having terms which place certain restrictions.

The above classification is for the corporate entities. There do, however, exist other forms of foreign enterprises having places of business in India. We understand, however, that the magnitude of the activity of the non-corporate foreign private capital is not very substantial.

Foreign Company Branches

Branches of foreign companies in India constitute the direct form of investment in India. The number of branches has varied from year to year. The number was: 541 during 1972; 540 during 1971; and 481 during 1976. The number of foreign branches, as such, does not provide any idea of the magnitude and nature of their operations. There are four reasons for this: one, a number of foreign branches have already closed down their business in India or become Indian companies or been dormant for many years. Due to limitations of the information system and the regulatory mechanism, these continue to be reported as branches operating in India during a year. Two, a good proportion of foreign branches are liaison offices, agency offices of shipping and air lines or consultancy concerns not having any manufacturing activity in the country. In such cases, there are no separate accounts for economic activity in India as the accounts of these companies are maintained for their global operations only. Three, the branches also include banking or service companies which cannot be equated with manufacturing or industrial undertakings. And lastly, the list of foreign branches also includes religious and charitable establishments.

For the year 1972, according to the Company Law Department (Government of India; GoI) sources, there were 541 foreign branches operating in India. Of these, only 79 had assets of ₹ 1 crore and above in India; a bulk of them (283 branches), individually, had assets of less than ₹ 1 crore. The total assets of the 362 branches were placed at ₹ 1,001.23 crore.[7] The big 79 (each with more than ₹ 1 crore assets) accounted for ₹ 951.56 crore and the total assets under the control of the 283 (each with less than ₹ 1 crore) were only ₹ 49.67 crore. A similar picture is obtained if one examines the pattern of assets held by foreign branches for the year 1974 or 1976. The only difference is that the magnitude of assets held by large-sized foreign branches (each with assets of ₹ 1 crore and above) was ₹ 1,379.66 crore and their number increased to 104 by 1976.

The distribution of foreign branches, according to the assets under their control, showed high level of concentration. It was true for 1972, 1974 and 1976. The largest foreign branches during 1976 being: Burmah Shell (₹ 70.27 crore), Calcutta Electric (₹ 66.05 crore), E.I.D. Parry (₹ 45.85 crore), Caltex (India) Ltd. (₹ 36.92 crore) and Indian Leaf Tobacco Development Company (₹ 29.04 crore).[8]

The assets under control of the branches of foreign companies need also to be seen alongwith the sales turnover under them. The largest turnover was for Burmah Shell Oil Storage and Distributing Company (₹ 515.00 crore) and Caltex (India) Ltd. (₹ 144.23 crore). Both of the branches are now absorbed in the public sector. The next largest companies were: E.I.D. Parry (sales: ₹ 77.52 crore); Assam Oil Company (sales: ₹ 76.46 crore); and Indian Leaf Tobacco Development Company (sales: ₹ 42.78 crore). The essential point to be noticed is that there were foreign branches which controlled a very large turnover, and these accounted for a high percentage of the economic activity under the branches.

With the taking over of oil companies, the assets under direct foreign control through branches has declined. Also, with the adoption of FERA most of the foreign branches (bulk of whom were in tea plantations) are

7. The estimate of assets is based on the latest available accounts for some branches. The estimate for the year 1972 is, therefore, the nearest approximation.

8. Burmah Shell and Caltex have been taken over in the public sector, E.I.D. Parry converted into an Indian company and India Leaf Tobacco Company has merged with the ITC (a company of the British American Tobacco—a world giant in tobacco).

getting registered as Indian companies with partial sharing of equity by the Indian public. Very soon the only foreign branches operating in India would be in non-manufacturing and non-trading sectors or as agency offices for their parent companies.

Foreign Subsidiaries

The next important form of foreign capital in India is constituted by Indian companies registered under the Companies Act, 1956, and having majority equity held abroad. The number of foreign subsidiaries has been on the decline. In the year 1976, the number was placed at 171 by the Company Law Department. However, the number of foreign subsidiaries stood at 243 in 1966. While the number of foreign subsidiaries declined by 29.63 per cent between 1966 and 1976, the assets under their control increased from ₹ 896.77 crore in 1966 to ₹ 1626.16 crore in 1976, i.e., by nearly 81.34 per cent.

As a result of the enactment of FERA, a majority of the subsidiaries are on way to the so-called 'Indianisation' process. Once the equity held abroad is reduced to less than 51 per cent, the foreign subsidiary companies will no more remain foreign in character (as under the Companies Act, 1956). Some of the important foreign subsidiaries have already become 'Indianised.' The significant ones being ITC with a turnover of ₹ 325.00 crore in 1975; Vazir Sultan Tobacco (₹ 89.68 crore), Godfrey Philips (₹ 57.61 crore), Hoechst Dyes and Chemicals (₹ 45.68 crore) and Macneill Barry (₹ 30.69 crore). During 1969-1976, 108 foreign subsidiaries were dropped out of this category and 36 were added as new registrations. A number of new registrations were the ones which operated as foreign company branches earlier.

We [at the Indian Institute of Public Administration (IIPA)] are attempting to collect some information on all foreign subsidiaries operating in India. The final results of the study [sponsored by the Indian Council of Social Science Research (ICSSR)] would, in all probability, be published in another few months. On the basis of the tentative results, it can be said that the net assets under the control of foreign subsidiaries have been growing at a fast rate. In 1976, the net assets of 171 foreign subsidiaries stood at nearly ₹ 1626.77 crore as against a total of ₹ 896.77 crore for 243 subsidiaries in 1966. The gross income (sales *plus* other income) of the foreign subsidiaries was estimated to be a little more than ₹ 2500 crore during 1976.

A closer look at the foreign subsidiaries reveals, as in the case of foreign branches, a high degree of concentration of assets and sales in the hands of a few large foreign subsidiaries. For instance, out of the estimated gross income of ₹ 2500 crore for the 171 foreign companies, the top five accounted for ₹ 725.90 crore, i.e., a little less than 30 per cent. Each one of the five companies had more than ₹ 100 crore as gross income. The five were: Hindustan Lever, Dunlop, Brooke Bond, Union Carbide and Indian Explosives. Foreign subsidiaries having gross income of ₹ 50-100 crore were only 11 and accounted for ₹ 858.17 crore, i.e., another 34.2 per cent of gross sales and other income of the foreign subsidiaries. It would suffice to say that while the number of foreign subsidiaries (during 1976) was 171, the bulk of the sales and assets were in the hands of a small number, i.e., less than 50 subsidiaries accounted for nearly 90 per cent of the gross income of all the foreign subsidiaries.

How many of these foreign companies can be treated as multinationals? The answer depends on the definition. If one accepts that a multinational would be a company which operates in more than two countries and has large assets/sales to qualify as one of the giants (may be one of the top 100 companies) in its 'home' country, one could be quiet safe in making a generalisation that foreign capital in India is essentially an issue of multinational corporations.

Foreign Capital and its Interlinkages

The Indian corporate legislation treats each foreign company as an independent entity. The MRTPC establishes affiliations on the basis of interconnections existing in India. The official approach to foreign companies is determined on the basis of the Indian assets or share in the Indian market. This approach does not appear a realistic one. For instance, to consider Lintas (a foreign branch, with Unilever as parent company) separate from Hindustan Lever (another subsidiary of Unilever) would in no case be justified. So also would be the case with the Imperial Tobacco Company (ITC) and Vazir Sultan; India Foils and T.I. group of companies, GEC and Marconi International, and Siemens-Philips and Polydor. The examples can be multiplied. The point to be underlined is that if the MRTPC attempts to treat Indian companies, which are closely interlinked, as an 'industrial house', why should the same not be done for foreign companies on the basis of their international affiliations and interconections?

Foreign Control through Minority Equity

The foreign branches and subsidiaries are clearly cases of foreign-controlled undertakings. But it is well known that for exercising control over a company, it is not necessary to have majority equity shares. The management control can be effectively exercised with as little as 10 per cent shares. This is particularly so when the equity shares are very widely dispersed and no other single individual or group holds substantial equity. For the Indian corporate sector, this point is well established and does not warrant much discussion. One should imagine that all such companies, which have recently been asked to dilute foreign equity holdings to a maximum of 40 per cent, would continue to be under the effective management and control of the foreign entities. Under the Companies Act *de facto*, foreign companies can still be treated as foreign and not Indian because the foreign equity has been brought down to less than 51 per cent.

An important area of influence, control and place of MNCs in India also lies in Indian companies which depend on supply of technical know-how from them and have licensee status with the giant world corporations. This being particularly so when the foreign collaborating corporations also happen to hold substantial (more than 10%) equity holdings in Indian companies. It needs to be underlined that the influence of an MNC on an Indian company would be larger, in all probability, if some of the associate companies of the Indian collaborating undertaking were also dependent for technical know-how on the same multinational group of companies. For instance, if a number of companies of 'X' industrial house were in collaboration with one MNC, individual companies of the 'X' house could be expected to have coordination with the directly held companies of the same MNC in India. This may appear to be only an academic assumption. However, why not make an attempt to study this phenomenon on the Indian scene?

To assess the place and role of MNCs in the Indian economy, one needs to approach the Indian scene from the MNCs' end. For instance, the first step should be to have a complete list of foreign companies which are present in India in different forms—inclusive of 0-100 per cent equity participation. After this, one should group the foreign companies together on the basis of their international links, affiliations and business associations. This may help us to clearly identify the multinational groups working in India. In this process, we may also discover that some of the MNCs in India operate from a number of countries under different names and are controlled from places located outside their home countries. The next stage would be in collecting certain basic information on companies in which MNC groups have influence through equity, collaborations or other means. The coverage could be extended for examining the effectiveness or otherwise of many an Indian legislative provision.

III

There is a widely shared public impression in India and abroad that the FERA, 1973, is an important and effective instrument of control and regulation of foreign-controlled companies having business activities in the country. Under FERA provisions: (i) all branches of foreign companies in India are required to get themselves registered as Indian companies under the Companies Act, 1956, and (ii) the foreign subsidiaries are required to reduce foreign holdings in equity in a substantial manner. The dilution of foreign equity is to be affected within a specified time. The administrative guidelines provide that undertakings which are:

(a) Engaged in manufacturing activities falling under the list of priority industries.

(b) Predominantly manufacturing for exports.

(c) Utilising sophisticated technologies.

(d) In trade but have developed skills or facilities (distribution network, etc.) not indigenously available.

(e) Tea plantations.

(f) Branches of foreign companies (engaged unspecified activities) should not have more than 74 per cent of the equity in the hands of foreigners. The rest of the foreign branches, Indian subsidiaries of foreign companies and companies having 40-50 per cent of equity holdings under foreign ownership have to dilute the foreign interest to a maximum of 40 per cent.

The objectives of the equity dilution strategy, as contemplated under FERA, could be: (i) to ensure that with majority equity with Indians, control over companies could, in case of need, be taken over in Indian hands through the simple process of majority voting and (ii) to ensure that foreign companies are not allowed to be a continuing drain on the foreign exchange resources of the Indian economy.

Let us examine as to what extent the dilution strategy could help the country in achieving the above objectives. Can Indian shareholders takeover the control of a company through majority voting? The answer is in the negative because the GoI has approved contracts which do not allow the majority shareholders the same rights as would be true in the case of ordinary Indian companies. To illustrate our point, the Article 187 of the Colgate-Palmolive (India) Limited is reproduced below:

(1) Union Colgate ceasing for any reason whatsoever to hold at least 40% of the total, issued and paidup equity share capital of the Company or upon Colgate terminating a separate Agreement dated the 28th day of September 1978 entered into by and between Colgate of the Part and the Company of the Other Part by a notice in pursuance of any of the provisions therein contained, the Company shall within 60 days from the date of receipt of this notice (a) discontinue the use of the words 'Colgate' and 'Palmolive' as part of its corporate name, trade name or trading style, (b) discontinue the use of the corporate logos of Colgate and (c) take all such steps as may be necessary for the purpose of changing its corporate name, trade name, or trading style as aforesaid. Any new corporate name, trade name or trading style or logos, which the Company may adopt shall not consists of any name, word, letter, expression, logo, symbol or device in any language, script or alphabet similar in sound or appearance to the words 'ColgatePalmolive' or either of them or the corporate logos of Colgate. All the members of the Company shall be deemed to have undertaken to exercise their rights as members and specifically their voting rights in such a manner as would enable the Company to comply with or implement the provisions of this Article and the aforesaid Agreement and shall be deemed to have become members of the Company on this basis;

(2) In case the Company is wound up and its business and/or movable or immovable property and rights are transferred to any person, company

or other body corporate by sale or otherwise, it shall be one of the conditions of the transfer that the words 'Colgate' and 'Palmolive' or either of them and the corporate logos of Colgate shall not be used in any manner by the transferee or transferees without the prior consent in writing of Colgate; and

(3) In case Colgate shall sell or otherwise transfer its shares in the Company or in case for any reason whatsoever (including force majeure) Colgate shall not be in a position to exercise its rights as shareholders, Colgate shall have the right to require the Company, by a registered letter, to discontinue forthwith the use of the trade marks 'Colgate' and 'Palmolive' on all Products.

It is obvious that with the above type of terms already approved by the government, there cannot be any change in the management. If the company has to continue as such, it must remain under the direct control of the former parent company.

With dilution of foreign equity, it is logical to expect that the amount of foreign exchange remittances, on dividend account, would be smaller. The implied assumption in enacting the FERA, the first specific legislation in India to control foreign companies, is that foreign-controlled companies make high profits and one of the major items responsible for foreign exchange drain was in dividend transfers. We made an attempt to examine this assumption on the basis of empirical evidence.

The objective of our study was to identify the pattern of foreign exchange utilisation by the foreign subsidiaries, on a census basis for the year 1976. However, due to certain difficulties, we could cover only 136 foreign subsidiaries out of 171. Out of the 171 foreign subsidiaries, 108 were public limited ones; the study covered 99. In terms of assets, the coverage for public limited companies was nearly 99 per cent. Out of the 63 private limited foreign subsidiaries, we could collect data on 37 companies only. The asset coverage for private limited foreign subsidiaries was a little over 80 per cent. In aggregate, though our survey covered only 136 subsidiaries out of the 171, the asset coverage is nearly 97 per cent. For the present, the results of our study would not be materially changed if one could cover all the 171 foreign subsidiaries. Partly, to compensate the limitations, we included 19 companies which are subsidiaries to the foreign subsidiaries.

Table 12.1 shows the pattern of foreign exchange utilisation by 155 foreign subsidiaries during 1976. The total foreign exchange utilised by the foreign subsidiaries during 1976 was ₹ 220.43 crore. Out of this, the dividend payments accounted for ₹ 10.7 crore, i.e., less than 5 per cent of the total. The most important item responsible for foreign exchange burden was 'imported raw materials.'

If the objective of the FERA was to effectively regulate the transfer of foreign exchange, the equity dilution approach cannot provide the real answer. The impact of the FERA would remain to be only marginal. The real item to be controlled and regulated would be the import of raw materials.

Table 12.1

Showing Pattern of Foreign Exchange Utilisation by Foreign Subsidiaries during 1976

Sl. No.	*Head*	*Amount (₹ Crore)*	*%*
1.	Capital Goods	6.64	3.02
2.	Raw Materials	188.93	85.71
3.	Spares and components	4.71	2.14
4.	Interest	1.36	0.62
5.	Dividends	10.70	4.85
6.	Know-how	1.96	0.89
7.	Royalty	0.80	0.36
8.	Travelling Expenses	0.25	0.11
9.	Commission	1.73	0.78
10.	Other	3.35	1.52
11.	Total	220.43	100.00

Source: Compiled from company annual reports and balance sheets containing details on foreign exchange earnings and utilisation by individual foreign subsidiaries.

We may also mention that an important feature of the 'raw material utilised' by the foreign subsidiaries was that a substantial part of it was imported by the foreign subsidiaries directly on cost, insurance and freight (CIF) basis. The direct imports by the foreign subsidiaries were of the magnitude of ₹ 162.98 crore; out of this, raw materials accounted for ₹ 144.10 crore. Were these imports from the parent companies? Were the prices paid higher than international prices? These and many more are questions which need to be answered on the basis of facts.

In conclusion, it may be said that there was need to undertake empirical studies in the area of foreign capital and the multinationals so that many of the assumptions made and policies formulated, for regulation and control of the foreign capital, can be made more realistic. We need to establish with adequate evidence whether foreign capital in India as a whole and in different sectors has helped us move towards a more self-reliant economy. What are the specific reasons for high growth, rates of the foreign companies? Do foreign companies bring foreign capital? If so, at what price? There are a host of questions regarding the impact and role of foreign companies, particularly the MNCs, on employment, balance of payments, import substitution, transfer of technology and other national objectives. These need inquiry. One hopes that studies in this area would have the necessary impact in making the Indian regulatory mechanism and other policies more realistic and effective.

13 The Impact of Foreign Subsidiaries on India's Balance of Payments[1]

Introduction

This study is an attempt to assess empirically the direct impact of economic activities undertaken by Indian subsidiaries of foreign companies on India's balance of payments in 1975-76.[2] Such an assessment has become possible as a result of a recent amendment of the Indian Companies Act, 1956, which makes it obligatory on the part of all corporate entities to furnish information on foreign exchange earnings and expenditure for the year, in their annual reports/balance sheets. It would indeed have been ideal if there could be time series data on foreign subsidiaries, dating back to the year of entry of foreign subsidiaries into the Indian economy. This is not possible for various reasons. It could, however, be done under special authority of the government or by foreign companies themselves on the basis of their own internal financial records. Private sector companies in India, particularly the ones which are foreign subsidiaries and had gained initial entry into the Indian economy as sale outlets of parent companies, cannot be expected to voluntarily share information, other than what is required as a legal obligation, on any sensitive aspect of their operations. One does, however, hope that the present exercise which is confined to 1975-76 would be repeated for each successive year.

---

1. A study prepared for the Joint Centre on Transnational Corporations-Economic and Social Commission for Asia and the Pacific (CTC-ESCAP) unit, Bangkok, in 1979.
2. The main reason for selecting 1975-76 for this study is the availability of the maximum number of the balance sheets containing details on foreign exchange earnings and utilisation by individual foreign subsidiaries.

Import Substitution?

Second, it needs to be mentioned that this study assesses only the direct impact of foreign subsidiaries in India. Economic activities of foreign subsidiaries in India must have saved foreign exchange for the country by undertaking such production that falls under import substitution efforts. But, it is extremely difficult to identify the extent of real foreign exchange savings since foreign subsidiaries, invariably, have production programmes based on imports from their parent companies. Many an item which may pass as 'local manufactures', signifying a high degree of import substitution, may indeed be nothing but the result of simple assembly and packing activities. The real net foreign exchange savings, under import substitution programmes, need to be more critically examined. In the case of India, to assess the real savings has become all the more difficult because supplies of raw material imports, when obtained through other agencies, are generally treated as if the raw materials were of indigenous origin. It may be recalled that as a result of the Indian government policy of progressive takeover of import trade, a number of raw materials are now covered under 'canalised items,' the imports of which can only be made by the State Trading Corporation—a government enterprise. Because of administrative reasons, imported raw materials supplied by the State Trading Corporation are treated as 'indigenous materials.' No breakup of such supplies is published by the companies.

Third, the value of foreign exchange earned by a company in a year, as per the Indian Companies Act, 1956 (amended), does not relate to exports of company products only. The foreign exchange 'earned' by a company can include value of goods which might have been produced by others. The data, therefore, refers to direct exports/imports by companies. Due to these reasons, it is not possible to estimate the net burden imposed by foreign subsidiaries on India's balance of payments. We have, therefore, limited our analysis to the direct impact as revealed from company balance sheets for 1975-76.

Fourth, it is quite natural for a reader to ask when empirical analysis is confined to only one year, whether the 'net impact' as revealed in the results of that year would be a realistic estimate or not since this would not take note of the initial capital inflow in the form of plant and equipment or cash.

Further, the year covered might be the one during which the companies were expanding their industrial potential and therefore had high level of imports while the export potential was yet to materialise. Alternatively, the year may be the one during which payments abroad were held back for one or the other reason. The basic point in such observations is if the empirical results obtained for one year could be considered representative enough to reflect a close proximity to reality. The present study is based on a census survey of foreign subsidiaries operating in India during the year. If the study was based on a sample, such observations would have been quite relevant. We may also mention that apart from the fact that 1975-76 was a normal year for the Indian economy each one of the foreign subsidiaries has been in operation in India for a long period. Not even a single foreign subsidiary had entered the Indian scene during the five previous years. In fact, most of the foreign subsidiaries came to India during the pre-Independence era.

The primary thrust of the study is to empirically examine the oft-repeated assertion that operation of foreign subsidiaries, particularly the transnational corporations (TNCs), helps host countries in earning much needed foreign exchange. And further, the study attempts to bring out the actual pattern of foreign exchange utilisation by foreign subsidiaries. This analysis is relevant in the face of an equally widespread view that foreign companies remit high profits abroad as dividend payments. It is under such a belief that one finds attempts by host countries to place restrictions on the declaration of high dividends by foreign companies or steps being taken to reduce the percentage of equity shares held abroad. The Government of India (GoI), in order to conserve foreign exchange and reduce the high level of dividend remittances amended the Foreign Exchange Regulation Act (FERA) in 1973. This study provides a basis to examine the appropriateness of recent legislation and the likely effectiveness of measures to achieve the primary objectives which motivated the enactment in India.

Comparative Performance

A very useful line of investigation on the basis of the data on exports and imports could, very rightly, be in examining the comparative performance of Indian and foreign companies, operating in the same industry and between units of similar size and other major characteristics.

A recent study by Subramanian and Pillai[3] has attempted such a comparison for three industries, namely, engineering goods, pharmaceuticals and dyestuffs and intermediate industries. Their general conclusion is that TNCs and companies with high levels of foreign collaborations do not contribute to development of Indian exports. Subramanian and Pillai observe that "trade impact and foreign collaboration are inversely related"[4] and "value added index is found increasing with the decreasing of foreign association/foreign control."[5]

There is a need for more intensive research on comparative performance to critically assess the validity of a variety of myths which are shared by some international institutions and many western scholars in addition to a host of policymakers in developing countries. Published records of private corporate sector allow only a limited analysis. For instance, Indian companies are under no legal obligation to give a break-up of their annual foreign exchange earnings/utilisation nor is the product-wise break-up of exports made public. Also, a fact of the Indian corporate sector is that one cannot identify many firms which were mono-product or mono-industry. The recent trend is towards more and more diversified activities by companies. Excessive reliance on 'export performance' data of companies with diversified activities can be a risky one. For instance, to treat Imperial Tobacco Company (now known as ITC and an associate of British American Tobacco) only as a tobacco and cigarette manufacturing company would be quite misleading since, of late, ITC has made a bold entry into hotel, fishing, cold storage, printing and other industries too. In view of these facts, one has an impression that increasingly it would become difficult to examine comparative performance of different groups of companies in an industry or for a product. A better picture of comparative performance could probably be obtained on project cost data or in assessing the comparative level of imported components in end-products. These exercises could be taken up by cost accountants.

---

3. Subramanian, K.K. and P. Mohanan Pillai (1979). *Multinationals and Indian Exports*, (Mimeo) and later published by Allied Publishers, New Delhi.

4. Ibid.: 58.

5. Ibid.: 113.

Another reason for not drawing intercompany comparisons in this study is that if large Indian units have to be compared with large foreign companies in the same industry, one would find it difficult to identify a reasonable number of instances for the purpose. Most of the Indian large companies have very close links (both in terms of equity and technical collaborations) with foreign companies.[6] There is no 'pure' Indian or pure foreign variety of companies. Their mixed character is becoming more of a corporate rule in India rather than an exception. The assessment of comparative performance of foreign and Indian companies would be also difficult, as the GoI since Independence has followed a policy (deviations from the policy being a separate issue) under which foreign companies are not allowed to undertake industrial activity wherein indigenous companies have already acquired the know-how and necessary expertise. Indian and foreign companies are supposed to be non-competitive and therefore non-comparable. What one should, however, attempt is to examine generally the performance of the foreign subsidiaries in relation to policy assumptions of the regulatory system. The present study, therefore, does restrict itself to the limited objectives as stated above:

(a) to assessing the direct net impact of foreign subsidiaries on India's balance of payments and

(b) to discover the relative significance of profits and other heads under which foreign exchange is utilised by foreign subsidiaries.

The second section presents the empirical results of the study on exports, foreign exchange utilisation and net foreign exchange burden placed by foreign subsidiaries on the Indian economy during 1975-76.

The Results

The capital structure of 133 foreign subsidiaries and 189 foreign-controlled companies (inclusive of 133 subsidiaries) is presented in Table 13.1. The paid-up capital (PUC) of 133 foreign subsidiaries stood at ₹ 3,114 million during 1975-76. The PUC of a company sometimes also

6. Goyal, S.K. (1979). *Monopoly Capital and Public Policy*. Delhi: Allied.

includes preference share capital.[7] However, equity share capital is the one which is the base for determining control of a company. The value of the equity capital, it may be mentioned, is only a technical liability of the company towards its shareholders. This does not represent the market value of shares. The 'Reserves and Surpluses', though shown separately, are, for all practical purposes, a part of PUC. The existence of a large 'Reserves' is an indicator of the high profitability and net-worth of the company. The 'Reserves' in due course of time get absorbed in the share capital against issue of bonus shares. The narrow equity base makes it possible for managements to declare higher dividends, which in turn helps to build corporate image.

Table 13.1

Showing Capital Structure of the 133 Foreign Subsidiaries and 189 Foreign-controlled Companies (1975-76)

(₹ Million)

Sl. No.	*Head*	*133 Subsidiaries*	*189 Subsidiaries and Foreign Controlled*
	1	*2*	*3*
1.	Paid-up Capital	3,114.2 (41.25)	3,968.7 (43.16)
2.	Reserves and Surplus	4,435.3 (58.74)	5,226.2 (56.84)
3.	Total (1 + 2)	7,549.5 (100.00)	9.194.9 (100.00)
4.	Fixed Assets	4,778.1 (39.66)	6,606.7 (39.27)
5.	Investments	86.2 (0.72)	168.5 (1.00)
6.	Current Assets	7,152.6 (59.37)	9,978.5 (59.31)
7.	Misc.	29.9 (0.25)	69.8 (0.41)
8.	Total Net Assets (4+5+6+7)	12,046.9 (100.00)	16,823.5 (100.00)

Note: Figures in brackets indicate percentages.

Source: Compiled from company annual reports on foreign exchange earnings and utilisation by individual foreign subsidiaries.

7. In the case of the foreign subsidiaries, this plays a marginal role.

Paid-up Capital

PUC is the book value of shares at a point of time; it is not an indicator of actual capital contributed by shareholders. The initial share capital of Indian foreign subsidiaries, it has been observed, was built in part against supply of machinery, technical know-how and considerations other than cash. The price of machinery supplied, against which shares were allotted, was fixed by the supplier (the holding company) and it was formally accepted by the subsidiary in India. The extent of precise over pricing in such transactions cannot be known, though it is obvious that the system of issuing equity shares, for consideration other than cash, provides a built-in mechanism to the foreign company to abuse its dominant position.[8] Secondly, the value of PUC, as reported for 1975-76, includes the value of bonus shares, issued in the past. Generally speaking, the older a company is, higher would be the 'bonus' part in the value of PUC. The 'bonus' shares could also be forming a higher percentage if the company enjoys a high profit rate.[9] Thirdly, of late it has been seen that while converting organisational forms (for instance, from a foreign branch to an Indian company, or from a private to a public company), the foreign companies expand the PUC base through a re-assessment of assets held at the time of change. The foreign subsidiaries also build up their reserves by sale of their equity shares to the Indian public at a premium. In substance, therefore, the value of total PUC of foreign subsidiaries in 1975-76 does not wholly represent the initial contribution or direct transfer of financial capital by foreign parents to their Indian subsidiaries. A large part of the controlling capital is out of the profits earned in India.

Table 13.2 presents distribution of 133 foreign subsidiaries according to the size group of the PUC. Seven of the foreign subsidiaries had PUC

---

8. The government has no method of verifying if the prices charged were higher than international prices. Suppliers fix prices according to their bargaining strength. In some cases, when the government asked for cost calculations, the supplier took the plea that their prices are fixed on the basis of a very wide variety of factors, many of which were not quantifiable.

9. For instance, the Hindustan Lever Ltd., a subsidiary of the Unilever and having the largest turnover amongst the foreign subsidiaries in India, had a total PUC of ₹ 168.5 million during 1976. Out of this, 80.93 per cent was because of bonus shares and another 12.10 per cent was explained by non-cash allotment of shares, i.e., the contribution of the Unilever, in cash, was less than 8 per cent. In case of the Bata India, the bonus shares accounted for more than 75 per cent. Similar is the story of other large size foreign-controlled companies.

of less than ₹ 10,000 each. Out of the seven, except for one, all the others were trustee or small trading companies. The number of subsidiaries, each having PUC of ₹ 10 million and more, was 54 and these accounted for 93.14 per cent of total PUC. An interesting part of the relationship between PUC and Reserves is that in a few cases, the magnitude of the latter was a multiple of equity capital. The striking examples of this are: Colgate Palmolive with ₹ 0.15 million as PUC and the Reserves being ₹ 1968 million (more than 135 times); Cadbury with ₹ 1.30 million as PUC and the Reserves ₹ 45.67 million; Aviquipo with only ₹ 1,000 as PUC and the Reserves being ₹ 530 thousand; and the Ingersele having ₹ 13.96 million as the Reserves as against ₹ 1 million only of the PUC.

Table 13.2

Showing Distribution of 133 Foreign Subsidiaries according to Size of Paid-up Capital (1975-76)

Sl. No.	*Range*	*Number*	*Paid-up Capital (₹ Thousands)*	*%*
	1	*2*	*3*	*4*
1.	Less than	10	7	13
2.	10-1000	32	19,356	0.62
3.	1,000-2,500	7	11,350	0.36
4.	2,500-5,000	16	66,050	2.12
5.	5,000-7,500	7	47,372	1.52
6.	7,500-10,000	8	69,530	2.23
7.	10,000 and above	56	29,00,502	93.14
	Total	133	31,14,173	100.00

Source: Same as Table 13.1.

Net Assets

The 133 foreign subsidiaries had net assets of ₹ 12,046.85 million during 1975-76; nearly 90 per cent of the assets were under public limited companies. The size of assets under individual foreign subsidiaries varied widely. The smallest one having nominal assets of ₹ 300 only and the largest subsidiary held assets of more than ₹ 1,000 million. Table 13.3 presents the size-wise distribution of 133 foreign subsidiaries for 1975-76. It would be seen that nearly three-fourth of the total assets of subsidiaries

Table 13.3

Showing Distribution of Companies according to Size Group of Assets (1975-76)

Sl. No.	Size Group (₹ Million)	Nos.	Assets (₹ Million)	%	Nos.	Assets (₹ Million)	%	Nos.	Assets (₹ Million)	%
	1	2	3	4	5	6	7	8	9	10
1.	1-10	25	71.98	0.60	16	32.64	2.27	9	39.34	0.37
2.	10-25	17	281.54	2.34	3	52.10	3.63	14	229.44	2.16
3.	25-50	27	1,017.67	8.45	4	181.57	12.64	23	836.10	7.88
4.	50-100	27	1,498.38	12.44	7	484.81	33.74	20	1,013.57	9.55
5.	100 above	32	9,177.28	76.18	2	685.85	47.73	30	8,491.43	80.03
6.	Nominal	5	-	-	5	-	-	0	-	-
7.	Not Available	38	-	-	27	-	-	11	-	-
	Total	171	12,046.85	100.00	64	1,436.97	100.00	107	10,609.88	100.00

Source: Research and Statistics Division, Department of Company Affairs, Ministry of Law, Justice and Company Affairs, Government of India, New Delhi.

were held by 32 subsidiaries, each with assets of more than ₹ 100 million; the top 60 subsidiaries claimed nearly 90 per cent of total assets. High degree of asset concentration, among the subsidiaries, is very obvious.

Of the total assets of the 133 foreign subsidiaries, nearly 40 per cent of the net assets were in the form of fixed assets, during 1975-76 (see Table 13.1). One important limitation of the value of 'fixed assets,' as given in the annual company balance sheets, is that it does not represent the real value of the fixed assets at a point of time, particularly in India where the government allows a liberal depreciation allowance to the corporate sector.[10] The current assets of the 133 foreign subsidiaries were of the order of ₹ 7,152.6 million and for the 189 foreign-controlled companies, these stood at ₹ 9,978 million. Of the total assets, the current assets accounted for nearly 60 per cent. Other assets (the investments, government securities held, etc.) were negligible.

The total turnover (sales plus other income) of the 133 foreign subsidiaries was ₹ 25,195.6 million; and for the 189 foreign-controlled companies, it stood at ₹ 33,900.4 million, for the year 1975-76. The distribution of 133 foreign subsidiaries, according to the magnitude of turnover, shows a high level of turnover concentration. It is very similar to the pattern of the asset-wise distribution of the foreign subsidiaries (Table 13.3). During the year under the present survey, out of 133 subsidiaries, the top five, each having a turnover of more than ₹ 1,000 million, accounted for ₹ 7,257.6 million (i.e., more than 25% of the total turnover of the foreign subsidiaries). On the other extreme, there were seven of the subsidiaries with negligible turnover. Table 13.4 shows the distribution of 133 subsidiaries, according to turnover size groups. The five top companies, on turnover criterion, were Hindustan Lever, Dunlop, Brooke Bond, Union Carbide and Indian Explosives. The main source of income (turnover) of foreign subsidiaries was from sale of their products. Other income by way of commission and other services rendered was insignificant.

10. For a detailed commentary on the value of assets, as revealed in the corporate annual balance sheets in India, see: Goyal, S.K. (1979). "Trends in Concentration in India (Business and Economic Power)", New Delhi: Indian Institute of Public Administration. May 1979. Chapter IV (*Mimeo*).

Table 13.4

Size-wise Distribution of Foreign Subsidiaries in India according to Turnover (1975-76)

Sl. No.	*Size of Turnover (₹ Million)*	*No. of Companies*	*Turnover (₹ Million)*	*% to Total*
	1	*2*	*3*	*4*
1.	Nil	7	-	-
2.	Upto 10 Million	5	01.6	0.01
3.	10-50	46	966.9	3.84
4.	50-100	26	1,875.0	7.44
5.	100-500	32	6,949.3	27.58
6.	500-1,000	12	8,145.0	32.33
7.	1,000 and above	5	7,257.8	28.81
	Total	133	25,195.6	100.00

Source: Same as Table 13.1.

Export Promotion

Foreign exchange is a scarce commodity for most developing economies. Availability of adequate foreign exchange is considered a crucial pre-requisite for the establishment of modern industries, particularly during earlier phases of development, when a good part of the new industrial machinery and technology has to be imported from industrially advanced countries. Nearly all underdeveloped countries attempt to regulate foreign exchange utilisation. Restrictions on the use of foreign exchange are frequently accompanied by public programmes to step up exports to earn enhanced foreign exchange resources. In India, the need for promotion of exports was realised during the late '1940s' when it opted to undertake planned economic development. To promote exports, the government offers a variety of incentives to export-oriented industries. Broadly speaking, fiscal incentives include tax exemptions, rebate on export production or import content of exports and lower taxes on profits from exports. Financial incentives include cash assistance, import replenishment licences, easy and cheap credit for exports and provision of necessary foreign currency for sales promotion abroad. The third set of measures include the creation of export promotion bodies and establishment of specialised institutions to study and disseminate information to individual exporters on the nature of the export potential in different countries of the world.[11]

Restrictions of Foreign Exchange Utilisation

In attempts to conserve foreign exchange resources of the country, a number of curbs have been placed to discourage non-priority imports. Stringent restrictions on foreign travel, education abroad in areas where facilities exist within the country and high duties on import of foreign goods by passengers are a part of the measures to conserve exchange resources. FERA was enacted to plug some loopholes which were suspected to impose a drain on resources. A part of it is intended to restrict the profit remitting capacity of foreign companies operating in India as branches and subsidiaries. Under FERA, foreign subsidiaries and branches have been placed under an obligation to reduce the percentage of equity held by their parent companies. This, it was believed, would substantially reduce the annual net burden on exchange resources that gets remitted by way of profits by foreign-controlled companies. The guidelines announced, under FERA, indicate that foreign equity holdings, in any individual company, should not exceed 40 per cent. However, exceptions to the rule are made for such companies which are predominantly export-oriented or bring to India a highly sophisticated technology which is not available indigenously. In the case of companies which have claimed to be predominantly export oriented, the government has allowed them to retain 74 per cent foreign equity instead of the 40 per cent prescribed for the rest.

Export Obligations

In India, all new and large industrial investments are regulated under the Industrial Development and Regulation Act (IDRA), 1952. The new investment may be for establishment of a new undertaking or this may be visualised for expanding the existing industrial capacities. If a company happens to be a product monopoly or a large company (with assets of ₹ 200 million), the new investment has also to be scrutinised by the Monopolies and Restrictive Trade Practices Commission (MRTPC).

11. For a brief resume of the export incentives, see: Ramakrishna, S. (1974). "Incentives to Export-oriented Industries in India", *Seminar on Export Promotion: Papers*, New Delhi: Indian Investment Centre.

During the examination of proposals for grant of industrial licences, special consideration is given to applicants who undertake to accept a compulsory obligation to export a substantial part of their additional production. Generally speaking, all industrial licences issued under the IDRA, even prior to the anti-monopoly legislation, included an export condition. In the light of the importance assigned to ensure a substantial increase in exports for the last three decades, it is necessary to examine the export performance of the Indian economy in general and the foreign subsidiaries in particular.

Foreign Exchange Earnings by the Subsidiaries

The total foreign exchange earned by foreign subsidiaries during 1975-76 was ₹ 1,204.3 million only. Out of the 133 foreign subsidiaries, 29 did not earn any foreign exchange either through exports or on any other account. If one takes the earnings of the group of 189 foreign-controlled companies, the total foreign exchange earnings during the year amounted to ₹ 1,776.8 millions. The distribution of the 133 foreign subsidiaries, according to the size of foreign exchange earned, is given in Table 13.5. Of the total exports, more than one-third was accounted for by only two subsidiaries, namely, the Brooke Bond (₹ 290.6 million) and the Hindustan Lever (₹ 134.3 million).

Table 13.5

Size-wise Distribution of Foreign Subsidiaries in India according to Total Exports (1976)

Sl. No.	*Size of Exports (₹ lakhs)*	*No. of Companies*	*Total Exports (₹ Million)*	*% of Total*
	1	*2*	*3*	*4*
1.	1,000 and above	2	425.0	35.3
2.	500-1,000	4	272.1	22.6
3.	250-500	4	126.6	10.5
4.	100-250	11	178.7	14.8
5.	50-100	14	95.5	7.9
6.	10-50	36	92.8	7.7
7.	Below 10 lakhs	33	13.5	1.1
8.	Nil	29	-	-
	Total	133	1,204.2	100.0

Source: Same as Table 13.1.

In view of export obligations placed on industrial licences and expectations of the government from foreign subsidiaries, one should examine the total quantum of the exports, not only in terms of absolute levels, but also as a proportion of total turnover of foreign subsidiaries. The total exports (inclusive of commission) of the 133 foreign subsidiaries for the year when compared to the total turnover of the 133 subsidiaries (the total turnover being ₹ 25,195.6 million) show that the exports formed only 4.78 per cent only. The performance of 189 foreign-controlled companies was 5.05 per cent, marginally better than 133 foreign subsidiaries (see: Table 13.6). It may be mentioned here that obligations, imposed under the IDRA, 1952, are in majority of cases, for undertaking exports as more than 10 per cent of production. For instance, in the case of Philips India Ltd., its overall exports performance during 1970-1973 was less than 3 per cent, whereas it was expected to export 1,020 per cent of its production. The export obligations are, however, more of assurances than of legal bindings.

Table 13.6

Showing Exports in Relation to Turnover (1975-76)

(₹ Million)

Sl. No.	*Head*	*133 Foreign Subsidiaries*	*189 Foreign Controlled*
	1	*2*	*3*
1.	Total Turnover	25,195.60	33,900.40
2.	Exports	1,204.30	1,712.30
3.	Exports to Turnover (Percentage)	4.78	5.05

Source: Same as Table 13.1.

Nature of Exports

The aggregate performance of foreign-controlled companies as shown in Table 13.6 does not reveal the true character of export efforts made by the foreign companies. The export performance of individual companies varies very significantly. It is seen that only a few companies explain more than half of the total export earnings of the subsidiaries. The most important one being only one tea company (Brooke Bond) followed by another company (Hindustan Lever) engaged in production of consumer goods, mostly agro-based. Out of total exports undertaken by subsidiaries, if one isolates the major items of their exports, one finds that tea, coffee and leather products (all of these happen to be traditional items of India's exports) account for more than half of exports by subsidiaries. India has for long been an important exporter of tea, coffee, hides and skins, tobacco, minerals and so on. It is no surprise that foreign subsidiaries like Brooke Bond, Numdung, Tea Estates and Makum Tea (all tea companies), Hindustan Lever, Food Specialities, Bata and ITC (formerly Imperial Tobacco Company) are seen to be prominent exporters. The place of industrial manufacturers or non-traditional products is very limited.

Table 13.7 shows the distribution of 133 foreign subsidiaries according to industry classification and export performance in terms of overall annual turnover. The most important export-oriented companies, judged on exports to turnover percentage and the value of exports, are seen to be the ones engaged in tea. The next important group of companies falls under the category of "processing industries." The classification of the companies, however, has serious limitations, as pointed out earlier.

Table 13.7

Showing Exports in Relation to Turnover on an Industrial Classification Basis for Subsidiaries (1975-76)

(₹ Million)

Sl. No.	*Industrial Classification*	*Number of Subsidiaries*	*Turnover*	*% of Total Col. 3*	*Exports*	*% of Total of Col. 5*	*% of Col. 5/3*
1		*2*	*3*	*4*	*5*	*6*	*7*
1.	Tea	4	15.28	6.0	3.18	26.4	20.8
2.	Mining and Quarrying	Nil	Nil	-	Nil	-	-
3.	Processing and manufacturing foodstuffs, textiles, metal, leather and chemicals	103	228.98	90.8	8.54	70.8	3.7
4.	Construction and Utilities	1	3.88	1.5	0.06	0.5	1.6
5.	Commerce (Trade and Finance)	21	3.58	1.4	0.23	1.9	6.4
6.	Transport and Communication	1	0.06	Neg.	0.02	0.1	32.6
7.	Community and Business	2	0.16	Neg.	Neg.	Neg.	Neg.
8.	Personnel and Others Services	1	0.01	Neg.	Nil	-	-
	Total	133	251.95	100.00	12.04	100.00	-

Source: The classification of companies is as per the Research and Statistics Division, Department of Company Affairs, Ministry of Law, Justice and Company Affairs, Government of India, New Delhi, and the data have been collected from company annual records.

While discussing export performance of foreign subsidiaries in the country, one needs to also keep in mind that India has a good number of bilateral agreements, under which Indian industrial products receive a preferential treatment for purposes of imports. For instance, when some of the socialist countries India have rupee payment arrangements; a direct consequence of it is that some of the Soviet and East European countries buy Indian goods against which India does not receive hard currency. But this enables the country to import goods needed for implementation of its plan programmes. Similarly, some of the oil producing countries have signed trade protocols under which India-based production units receive a ready market. The need for enhancing trade among developing countries is being accepted by more and more countries. One immediate result of these developments is the enlarged demand for Indian exports in the third world in general and countries of the socialist block in particular. It is an interesting phenomenon that at one time while some of the Arab countries had boycotted goods manufactured in some of the pro-Israel countries, products of the subsidiaries of companies from these very countries, located in India or in other friendly countries, were purchased. Similarly, because of cooperation amongst a socialist and friendly country and India, bulk orders for supplies have been placed in this country. The export performance of foreign subsidiaries, when viewed in this perspective, would appear to be much lesser than otherwise. More detailed examination in this direction is an obvious necessity.

Transfer Pricing and Exports

An important aspect of exports undertaken by foreign subsidiaries particularly TNCs is their indulgence in transfer pricing practices. It is a difficult area of examination. Transfer pricing practices have, however, been discovered in some cases in India. For instance, the MRTPC in its two reports on Philips India Ltd. has shown that the company exported its products from India to its holding and associate companies abroad at a much lower price than the cost of production. The commission calculated that one US dollar earned by Philips India Ltd through its exports cost ₹ 10.14, ₹ 10.35 and ₹ 13.46 during 1971, 1972 and 1973, respectively. The official exchange rate has been around ₹ 8 per US dollar. The Commission observed:

> One important feature of the exports made by PIL (Philips India Ltd.) is that in most of the items exports are being made at much less. Except in one or two items the loss as compared to the exfactory cost appears to be significant and it is found to be even larger if the total cost of production of the items is considered. Only in a few items—constituting a small value of exports—is the loss as compared to cost lower than 20 per cent; in some other small and not so small items the loss exceeds 50 per cent; **and even in items that constitute a large proportion of the total Philips India Ltd. exports, the loss varies from 30 per cent to 50 per cent of the cost of production**[12] (emphasis added).

A specific case of transfer pricing practices as resorted to by TNCs is provided by the Public Accounts Committee of India in the Parliament. This relates to International Business Machine (IBM) and International Computers Ltd. (ICL) operations. The committee observed:

> There is more than enough evidence that the multinationals in the field of computer and data processing such as IBM with its near monopoly position in India, have defrauded the country of enormous revenues by resorting to various unfair practices **like transfer pricing under the garb of inter-company billing system**, misuse of import entitlement, exaggerated claims of draw back under-payment of excise duty, exaggerated claims of depreciation, development rebate, head office expenses, etc. All these practices have enabled them to reap high profits at the cost of the exchequer as well as the technological development of the country[13] (emphasis added).

With regard to the ICL, the committee observed:

> The Committee noted that the ICL follow different conversion factors in the matter of transfer of machines and equipment from the parent foreign company to the Indian branch; the rate ranging, for some extra-ordinary reason, from one = Rs. 8.3 to one = Rs.19.25. This must be a clever mechanism which must be fully probed by Government and action taken accordingly, so that all detriment to the country's interests can be avoided.[14]

To show the mechanism of transfer pricing in actual operation the committee observes:

---

12. Report of the Indian MRTPC commision on "Philips India Ltd. for Establishing a New Undertaking for the Manufacture of Medical Electronics Equipment". October 1974. Delhi (unpublished but placed on the table of the House of Parliament) para 1.34.

13. Lok Sabha (Parliament of India), *Public Accounts Committee: Report No. 221*, Fifth Lok Sabha, on "Computerization in Government Departments". April 1976. New Delhi. p.255.

14. Ibid.: 244.

> The investment made by IBM in the Indian plant for the manufacture of data processing equipment are mostly used for exports. These exports to IBM's related companies. The inter-company billing price for exports does not cover even the relevant head office and New York costs properly allocable to it. Exports, thus, results in losses to India operations. However, as equipments are sold in the importing countries at uniform international prices the profits on these machines exported from India are reflected in the respective IBM's organizations in the importing countries.[15]

The foreign subsidiaries are known to be exporting their products to their parent and associate companies. The practice of exporting goods to associates at a loss is obviously an indirect method of transferring resources from India, and the motivation for accelerating such exports is to defeat the spirit of foreign exchange regulations, and not to promote the Indian national interests. More specific studies in this area need to be undertaken. However, there does appear to be a *prima facie* case for further inquiry on a larger base. It may be added here that 'transfer pricing' practice may not be easily known to host country administrations—as one knows that the administrative competence of most of the developing countries continues to be far below the level required to regulate modern corporations of the developed world. Even if a company is discovered to have clearly been guilty of transfer pricing practice, it may not be a legal offence as per the legal system of the country concerned. Additionally, policy makers in host countries may, consciously, decide to opt for soft action against the offender corporation to avoid public controversy which could lead to an adverse climate for foreign capital.

Foreign Exchange Utilisation

While the foreign exchange earnings through exports are important by themselves, it is equally important to examine the foreign exchange utilisation by foreign subsidiaries during the same period. The 133 foreign subsidiaries utilised foreign exchange of India to the tune of ₹ 2,220.14 million during 1975-76.

A general impression carried by policy makers in India has been that foreign companies undertake high profit remittances and, therefore, a main cause of foreign exchange drain on the Indian economy was in dividends

15. Ibid.: 177.

remitted by foreign companies. To plug the loophole, the government enacted FERA under which the foreign subsidiaries and branches of foreign companies have been directed to dilute the extent of foreign equity to a level of 40 per cent. Similarly, the government policy has been to announce a variety of restrictions on payments for know-how, royalty and travelling abroad.[16] None would dispute the importance of regulating foreign exchange utilisation in a developing economy. However, the policies must have a realistic understanding of the relative significance of the different components of the total foreign exchange budget as utilised by the corporate sector in general and the foreign companies in particular. For this purpose, we have examined the pattern of the foreign exchange utilisation by the foreign companies in India, for the year 1975-76.

Pattern of Foreign Exchange Utilisation Dividends

Table 13.8 shows the pattern of foreign exchange utilisation by 133 foreign subsidiaries and 189 foreign-controlled companies (inclusive of the 133 subsidiaries) for 1975-76. It is observed that in the case of 133 foreign subsidiaries, the remittances abroad, as dividends, accounted for ₹ 110.30 million out of the total foreign exchange burden of ₹ 2,220.1 million. The significance of dividends was 4.97 per cent for foreign subsidiaries and 4.76 per cent for 189 foreign-controlled ones. The impact of equity dilution (described as Indianisation) under FERA could be only marginal even if all the subsidiaries are forced to bring down their foreign equity to 40 per cent level.

Know-how and Royalty

The importance of payments against supply of know-how was only 0.88 per cent of the total. This may be the result of the stringent policies pursued by the government; however, even if there were no serious restrictions on payments for know-how or transfer of technology, the total cost to the Indian economy, in terms of foreign exchange burden, could not be very large. The same seems to hold true of 'royalty' payments. The insignificance of 'interest' payments should be taken as an indicator of

16. Policy statements, on each one of the aspects of foreign exchange regulation, are made from time to time: See: INDIA (Department of Industrial Development), *Guidelines for Industries: 1975-76*, Delhi, 1975.

Table 13.8

Showing Pattern of Foreign Exchange Utilisation by Foreign Subsidiaries (1975-76)

Sl. No.	Item	133 Foreign Subsidiaries (₹ Thousands)	% of Total (Col.2)	189 Foreign Controlled (₹ Thousand)	% of Total (Col.4)
	1	2	3	4	5
1.	Capital Goods (machinery)	65,401	2.95	2,14,900	8.26
2.	Raw Materials (of which oil imports)	19,02,793 (7,17,019)	85.71 (32.29)	20,47,400 (7,17,019)	78.26 (27.55)
3.	Spares	47,612	2.14	1,09,400	4.20
4.	Interest	13,616	0.61	16,300	0.63
5.	Dividends	1,10,298	4.07	1,23,800	4.76
6.	Know-how	19,581	0.88	21,800	0.84
7.	Royalty	7,991	0.34	8,400	0.32
8.	Travelling	2,457	0.11	2,700	0.10
9.	Commission	17,075	0.77	20,800	0.80
10.	Others	33,320	1.50	37,000	1.42
	Total	22,20,144	100.00	26,02,800	100.00

Source: Same as Table 13.1.

the very marginal assistance, offered by the parent companies, in raising foreign exchange loans.

Capital Goods

In a developing economy like India, which has embarked on a process of planned industrial development, one should imagine that one of the significant items under the heads of foreign exchange utilisation would be the import of capital goods and machinery. However, strangely enough though, the pattern of foreign exchange utilisation by the foreign subsidiaries shows that capital goods imports accounted for only 2.95 per cent of total expenditure. In the case of the other foreign-controlled companies, the machinery imports were relatively more important. It is, however, important to note that 'spares and components' accounted for nearly 70 per cent of the value of capital imports by foreign subsidiaries.

Is it a method of replacing old machinery? Or it is due to transfer pricing practices spares would naturally have to be obtained from parent companies or original machinery suppliers.

Raw Materials

The most important single factor responsible for 85 per cent of foreign exchange utilisation by foreign subsidiaries was the import of raw materials. Before drawing any conclusions, one must underline that while examining the imports by subsidiaries, one should, for obvious reasons, exclude 'oil' imports. If we exclude oil imports, the total figure of direct raw material imports would stand at ₹ 1,185.77 million (see Table 13.8).

Imports by the STC

In India, a good number of import items are canalised through public sector organisations. The imports made by the public sector and supplied to industrial units, strangely enough, are treated as indigenous goods and raw materials. It is understood that the major recipients of goods imported by the State Trading Corporation were large enterprises, including some TNCs. If this fact is taken note of, the total foreign exchange burden imposed by foreign subsidiaries would work out to be much higher. There is need to study the pattern of allocation of imports by public sector importing agencies.

It is, however, seen that value of cost, insurance and freight (CIF) imports was ₹ 855.5 million (excluding oil imports). Table 13.9 shows distribution of foreign subsidiaries according to the size of CIF imports undertaken by 132 foreign subsidiaries (one, the Caltex being excluded as the company imported crude oil only). Of the total CIF imports, it would be seen that the top 10 subsidiaries accounted for more than half of imports. It has already been mentioned that there is suggestive evidence of the existence of transfer pricing practices, resorted to by foreign subsidiaries while exporting goods to their parent and associate companies. The transfer of resources was possible both by exporting goods from India at a low price and by inflating prices by parent companies while exporting goods to their subsidiaries in India. The CIF value of imports does suggest an area of further inquiry for identification of the precise extent of transfer pricing practices.

Table 13.9

*Showing Distribution of Foreign Subsidiaries in India according to CIF Value of Imports (1975-76)**

(₹ Million)

Sl. No.	Size of CIF (₹ Lakh)	No. of Companies Total	CIF	% of Total
1	2	3	4	5
1.	500-1,000	3	206.0	24.1
2	250-500	7	255.0	29.8
3.	100-250	12	195.7	22.9
4.	50-100	13	9.89	11.6
5.	10-50	34	8.35	9.8
6.	Below 10 lakhs	35	1.64	1.9
7.	Nil	28	-	-
	Total	132	855.5	100.0

Note: *The above data do not include 'Caltex' as it has been nationalised.

Source: Same as Table 13.1.

Net Impact on Balance of Payments

So far we have shown foreign exchange earnings and the pattern of foreign exchange utilisation by 133 foreign subsidiaries and 189 foreign-controlled companies (inclusive of the 133 subsidiaries). One must examine the net annual impact of the operations of foreign subsidiaries on the balance of payments situation of India. The value of total foreign exchange utilised by 133 foreign subsidiaries during 1975-76 was ₹ 2,220.1 million, and the total foreign exchange earnings, for the same period, were of the order of ₹ 1,235.8 million. This means a net deficit of ₹ 984.34 million in one year. However, if one takes the net foreign exchange burden, after excluding oil imports, the net direct foreign exchange loss works out to be ₹ 200.74 million in one year. Even if one takes the group of 189 foreign-controlled companies, the net foreign exchange contribution of the foreign companies, during 1975-76, was negative, i.e., a loss of nearly ₹ 139 million. In brief, all the efforts at exports in the form of concessions, rebates and policy exemptions made to foreign private capital in India, in the hope of expanding exports, have yielded negative result, a minimum net loss of ₹ 200 million of foreign exchange during one year, 1975-76 (even after excluding oil imports).

Number of Net Earnings and Net Losing Subsidiaries

Out of 133 foreign subsidiaries, 11 were such which neither earned nor placed any foreign exchange burden on the Indian economy. The net foreign exchange earning subsidiaries were 46, while the net contribution of the 76 foreign subsidiaries was negative. Table 13.10 shows that more than half the 46 net earning subsidiaries was accounted for by one single tea exporting company, namely, Brooke Bond. There were only 17 subsidiaries, which made a net contribution of ₹ 1 million and more, each. The contribution of 46 'net earning' companies in 1975-76 was ₹ 623.67 million.

Table 13.10

Showing Size-wise Distribution of Foreign Subsidiaries in India according to Net Earnings of Foreign Exchange (1975-76)

Sl. No.	*Size of Net Earnings (₹ Million)*	*No. of Companies*	*Net Earning (₹ Million)*	*% to Total of Col. 3*
	1	*2*	*3*	*4*
1.	Below 1 Million	13	3.65	0.59
2.	1.0-2.5	8	15.53	2.49
3.	2.5-5.0	8	26.83	4.30
4.	5.0-10.0	6	46.42	7.44
5.	10.0-50.0	9	186.97	29.98
6.	50.0 and above	2	344.28	55.20
	Total	46	623.68	100.0

Source: Same as Table 13.1.

A majority of the foreign subsidiaries were net losers of foreign exchange for the country, during 1975-76. Table 13.11 shows the distribution of 'net losers'. If one excludes the oil-importing foreign subsidiary, the total net loss of foreign exchange by 75 of the foreign subsidiaries was ₹ 887.47 million.

Table 13.11

Showing Size-wise Distribution of Foreign Subsidiaries according to Net Loss

S. No.	*Size of Net Loss (₹ Million)*	*No. of Companies*	*Net loss (₹ Million)*	*% to Total of Col.3*
	1	*2*	*3*	*4*
1.	Below 1 Million	25	8.88	0.55
2.	1.0-2.5	9	15.43	0.96
3.	2.5-5.0	6	21.00	1.31
4.	5.0-10.0	10	71.25	4.43
5.	10.0-50.0	22	478.85	29.78
6.	50.0 and above	4	1,012.57	62.97
	Total	76	1,607.99	100.00

Source: Same as Table 13.1.

14 The New International Economic Order and Transnational Corporations[1]

Introduction

The Declaration and Programme of Action for establishment of the New International Economic Order (NIEO), as adopted by UN General Assembly in May 1974 suggests that developed countries should (i) respond favourably to requests of developing countries for financing of industrial projects and (ii) encourage investors to finance industrial production projects in developing countries. At the UN Conference on Trade and Development I (UNCTAD-I) held at Geneva in 1964, developed countries had, in fact, committed to provide one per cent of their gross national product (GNP) as developmental aid. Later the Pearson Commission and the Brandt Commission also argued for large capital transfers to poor nations. In response to the pressures and demands at various international fora, developed countries have generally argued that while it was not possible to set aside desirable levels of governmental aid—in view of internal demands on budgetary resources—there was large scope for transfer of capital through direct private investments. Therefore, the view has been that developing countries should provide adequate incentives, security and opportunities to attract foreign private investments. It is also argued that there was a need to get rid of a variety of imaginary fears and ideological stances taken by some of the underdeveloped countries on the question of transnational corporations (TNCs). It is, however, agreed that there should be a voluntary code of conduct and host governments should regulate TNC activities in the overall framework of their national development plans.

The above framework is based upon the basic assumption that the present level of underdevelopment and poverty in developing countries was

1. *Corporate Studies Group Working Paper* 5, 1982. Also published in *Secular Democracy*, Non-Aligned Summit Special Annual Number, 1983.

a direct consequence of the 'capital scarcity.' Secondly, the most important development issue for developing countries was the size of investment and not the structure or pattern of investments. This assumption seems to be of a very questionable nature. It can be demonstrated that the main causes of continuing injustice, inequality and poverty in developing countries are not the scarcity of physical and financial capital. These lie somewhere else, namely, in the existence of irrational, illogical and unproductive social, economic, political and administrative structures on the one hand and the inadequate and inconsistent efforts at planned development to effectively protect and promote their national self-interest. The issues of development in the poor countries have to be solved basically by poor nations themselves through establishment and strengthening of a new internal order. The role of external factors (aid, trade and investments) is much lesser than many a time assumed. This, however, does not mean that with appropriate assistance, the internal processes of development cannot benefit from the outside world. In fact, it can be shown that emergence of internally stable, enlightened and consistent governments in the poor economies can alone pursue genuine developmental policies and provide the building blocs for the realisation of the NIEO wherein poor nations would be able to take advantage of modern technologies for the liquidation of human misery and poverty. We discuss this with reference to TNCs and governments of developing nations.

II

TNCs have come to occupy an important and strategic role in the world economic system of today. These are privately owned organisations with global operations and are guided by the principle of 'maximisation of global profits.' TNCs enjoy control over modern and sophisticated technologies, vast financial and physical resources in large parts of the advanced world and many of the underdeveloped nations. Most TNCs have developed their own national and international systems of communication, consultation and coordination, which operate far more efficiently than any govenmental system. Their capabilities at offering lucrative employment opportunities cannot be matched by that of the governments. The fact that TNCs operate at the global level makes it also obvious that they have rich, varied and accumulated experience of dealing with governments which profess adherence to varying faiths and shades in their ideological commitments, countries with different levels of effectiveness in their techno-legal regulatory systems as also economies at different stages in development. Most TNCs are products of market-oriented and industrially advanced economies. The home countries cannot but have a stake in their growth and expansion. TNCs may not bring large and immediate surpluses but these do create long-term assets for home economies. Therefore, it should be no surprise if TNCs enjoy influence in and political backing of home governments both at the level of internal and foreign policies. It is also not very often appreciated that TNCs are neither industry-specific nor country-specific. And further, since TNCs are business organisations, these organisations are fully conscious that they stand to benefit more under monopolistic positions rather than under open business confrontations. This awareness brings TNCs, even those belonging to otherwise unfriendly countries, together to share national and international markets through mutual agreements. These are some of the characteristics of TNCs—each having a bearing on the role of TNCs and the manner and style of their operations.

Do governments in developing countries have adequate appreciation of these characteristics of the institution of TNC? It would be easier to formulate policies and build objective expectations, if governments in the Third World were fully conscious of the various characteristics of TNCs. Unfortunately, this does not appear to be the case. Developing countries have yet to have an objective basis to evolve meaningful policies towards foreign private capital. Consequently, poor nations either do not have adequate mechanism to regulate, and if there is one, it is weak and based on unrealistic assumptions. We demonstrate this point with the help of Indian experience.

III

The role of TNCs in development and the associated dangers has been under discussion for nearly two decades at various international fora. India has actively participated in these discussions. The Eminent Persons Committee of the UN to study the impact of TNCs on world development was indeed chaired by an Indian. It is also generally believed that India is one of the more successful Third World countries which have been able to effectively regulate and control the entry and operations of TNCs. The cases of Coca Cola and the International Business Machine (IBM) are often cited as illustrations to underline the efficiency and the stringent character of measures that India was able to take against the powerful international giants who declined to fall in line. In this background, it appears necessary to examine the Indian regulatory system with regard to TNCs. Any administering system to be effective requires a clear legal definition of the area and its coverage. What is the legal definition of a TNC/MNC (multinational corporations) in India? While there has been a considerable degree of interest and assertion regarding TNCs in the policy making circles and parliament, the fact remains that Indian government has yet to evolve a legal definition of a TNC. In India, companies having substantial direct involvement of foreign capital are categorised under three heads: one, branches of companies incorporated abroad; two, Indian subsidiaries of foreign companies (having majority equity held by one foreign company); and three, Indian companies in which foreign-held equity is more than 40 per cent. Since there is no official definition of a TNC, in practice all companies covered by Foreign Exchange Regulation Act, 1973 (FERA), are referred to as TNCs. The Company Law Department, the main source of information and data on the corporate sector, however, for long has been treating only branches and subsidiaries of foreign companies as TNCs/MNCs.

Parliament members have, from time to time, been expressing their concern over the growth of transnationals in India and asked the government to give facts on the growth of TNCs. Table 14.1 provides the information furnished to the Parliament. From the official replies given to the highest forum of the country, it would appear that:

(a) the actual number of multinationals operating in India has declined substantially—branches from 481 to 315 and subsidiaries from 171 to 118;

(b) the combined sales turnover of the two categories of companies (called multinationals) witnessed a decline from ₹ 38,785 millions in 1975-76 to ₹ 29,657 millions in 1978-79; and

(c) on the assets side, the increase was from ₹ 17,622 to ₹ 23,738 million (for branches) and from ₹ 16,149 million to ₹ 18,966 million (for subsidiaries) during 1975-76 to 1979-80. The average rate of asset growth does not work out to be more than 6.6 per cent per annum.

Table 14.1

Foreign Branches and Subsidiaries in India: 1975-76 to 1979-80

Particulars	*1975-76*	*1976-77*	*1977-78*	*1978-79*	*1979-80*
1	*2*	*3*	*4*	*5*	*6*
Branches of Foreign Companies					
1. Total No. of Branches	481	482	473	358	315
2. Data Available for	259	220	177	141	247
3. Assets (in India)	1,762.2	1,626.7	1,836.4	2,011.4	2,373.85
4. Turnover	1,380.4	642.0	690.0	418.7	N.A.
5. Profits before tax	57.9	89.4	50.1	15.9	N.A.
Subsidiaries of Foreign Companies					
1. Total No. of Subsidiaries	171	161	146	125	118
2. Data Available for	161	142	137	113	118
3. Assets	1,614.9	1,619.7	1,379.1	1,662.8	1,896.64
4. Turnover	1,498.1	2,712.7	2,730.6	2,547.0	N.A.
5. Profits before tax	219.5	257.7	267.0	256.5	N.A.

Source: Information furnished in the Parliament in response to R.S. Unstarred Question 683 on February 23, 1981, and L.S. Unstarred Question No. 4153 on December 16, 1981.

On the basis of this data, one gathers the general impression that the Indian government has been very successful in keeping the growth of foreign private capital under stringent control, which has an empirical base.

The above account on the growth of TNCs is an erroneous one. The fact that the number of branches and subsidiaries of foreign companies operating in India has declined does not mean closure, takeover or exit of TNCs from the country. The factual position has got hidden under the process of implementation of the enactment of FERA. A large number of foreign companies have diluted the percentage of foreign-held equity to a level that makes them not to be classified as 'subsidiaries.' Therefore, the number of TNCs operating in India today, as against 1975-76, appears to have declined in a significant manner. The same holds true of such companies who have reduced their foreign equity to the level of 40 per cent or below. The number of FERA (and therefore TNCs in the legal sense) companies has also witnessed a significant decline.

The moment a TNC reduces the percentage of the foreign-held equity to 40 per cent or less, it establishes a claim to be classified as an Indian national company for all policy purposes and gets out of the obligations which a TNC is obliged to live with. Table 14.2 gives a list of some of the well-known transnationals which due to equity dilution have got excluded from the official list of TNCs operating in India. Philips, Colgate-Palmolive, British American Tobacco, Cadbury, Ponds, Nestles, Horlicks and so on are all Indian companies now. This fact of their 'acquired nationality' is underscored by company managements for national consumers. One has only to have a look at the advertisements in the mass media to convince oneself of the change that has been brought about.

Table 14.2

Illustrative List of Foreign Companies which became 'Indian' after Equity Dilutions under FERA

S. No.	*Name of the Indianised Company*	*Name of the Parent Company*	*Percentage of Foreign Equity after Dilution*	*Assets in 1981 (₹ Crores)*
1	*2*	*3*	*4*	
1.	Bata (I) Ltd.	Leader, AG, Switzerland	40.00	47.07
2.	Britannia Biscuit Co.Ltd.	Control Nominees, UK	38.00	25.88
3.	Brooke Bond (I) Ltd.	Brooke Bond Liebig, UK	39.90	75.41*
4.	Cadbury (I) Ltd.	Cadbury Schweppes Overseas, UK	40.00	17.06
5.	Colgate-Palmolive (I) Ltd.	Colgate-Palmolive Co., USA	40.00	18.11
6.	Crescent Dyes & Chmls.Ltd.	Imperial Chemical Inds., UK	40.00	13.82
7.	Food Specialities Ltd.	Nestle Holdings, Bahama Islands	40.00	17.86
8.	HMM Ltd.	Horlicks Ltd., UK	40.00	27.14
9.	ITC Ltd.	British American Tobacco, UK	39.90	181.65
10.	Indian Oxygen Ltd.	British Oxygen, UK	39.90	65.48
11.	Intl.Computers Indian Mfrs.	Intl. Computers, UK	40.00	17.57
12.	Parke Davis (I) Ltd.	Parke Davis & Co., USA	40.00	9.79
13.	Peico Electronics & Electricals Ltd.(Philips)	Philips, Holland	39.70	96.49
14.	Reckitt & Colman of(I) Ltd.	Reckitt & Colman, UK 39.90 11.23		
15.	Sesa Goa Ltd.	Finsder, Italy	40.00	16.39
16.	Tube Invt. Co. of(I) Ltd.	Tube Investment, UK	39.92	31.00
17.	WIMCO Ltd.	Swedish Match Co., Sweden	39.50	50.21

Note: * Indicates the figure for the year 1980.

Source: Corporate Information System, Indian Institute of Public Administration (IIPA), New Delhi.

If dilution of foreign-held equity resulted, or could result, at a later date, in transfer of control of the enterprises to Indian hands, one could find a justification for the company being treated as Indian and not a foreign one. But the official policy has not been to change control over the managements. In fact, the government has permitted legal agreements which ensure that minority equity holding companies (located abroad) continue to enjoy the rights to appoint key management persons as long as the foreign equity holder had a certain percentage of interest in equity shares (see Table 14.3). It is a very different issue if such agreements (which give disproportionate authority to foreign minority shares *vis-à-vis* the majority of the Indian shares) are in conformity with the basic principles of corporate democracy but the fact remains that a TNC does not remain a TNC, according to the official approach, even though its control and management is being directed and influenced from abroad.

A direct consequence of equity dilution would be that the share of gross profits to be remitted abroad would be lower than what the TNC headquarters would have received if the dilution had not taken place. The percentage share being low for an investor, however, does not mean that the absolute amount of profits would also be necessarily lower. In fact, it appears to have been just the reverse in actual practice, as dilution of equity has invariably been accompanied by widening of the equity base.

The enactment of FERA is described by many as a landmark in the attempts to control direct foreign private investments. The equity dilution strategy of the act was, apart from the objective of having a majority for the Indians, based on the assumption that since TNCs were making very high profits in India, a reduction in the foreign-held equity would reduce the continuing drain on the limited foreign exchange resources of the economy. If the overall objective of the enactment was to conserve foreign exchange resources, a preliminary question requiring empirical verification would be: How significant are profit remittances by TNCs in the overall quantum of the foreign exchange utilised by them. Table 14.4 shows the pattern of foreign exchange utilisation by subsidiaries of foreign companies in India. It would be noticed that 'dividend remittances' accounted for less than 5 per cent of foreign exchange utilised by TNCs during 1975-76.

Table 14.3

Showing an Illustrative List of Companies which Diluted Foreign Equity under FERA, 1973, with Rights to Appoint Directors held by the Parent Company

S. No.	*Indian Affiliate*	*Parent Company*	*Minimum share holding needed to exercise right*	*Right to Appoint or Remove*
	1	*2*	*3*	*4*
1.	Abbot Laboratories (I) Ltd.	Abbot Laboratories, USA	25	One third (including Managing Director) of the total Board of Directors.
2.	Colgate-Palmolive (I) Ltd.	Colgate-Palmolive Co.,USA	20	do
3.	Corn Products Co. (I) Ltd.	CPC International Inc. USA.	..	Chairman and Vice-Chairman
4.	Davy Ashmore (I) Ltd.	Davy Ashmore (I) Ltd., UK	26	One third (including Managing Director) of the total Board of Directors.
5.	E. Merck (I) Ltd.	Chemitra Gmbh	26	One third (non-retiring including Managing Director) of the Board.
6.	Fulford (I) Ltd.	Schering-Plough Holdings Ltd., UK.	10	One third (including Chairman) of the Board of Directors.
7.	Lipton Tea (I) Ltd.	Unilever Ltd., UK	26	Managing Director
8.	Malayalam Plantations (I) Ltd.	Malayalam Plantations (Holding) Ltd., UK.	26	One third (including Managing Director) of the total Board of Directors
9.	Mather and Platt (I) Ltd.	Mather & Platt Ltd., UK.	26	Chairman and Managing Director
10.	May & Baker (I) Ltd.	May & Baker Ltd., UK	26	One third (including Managing Director) of the total Board of Directors
11.	Nicholas Laboratories (I) Ltd.	Aspro-Nicholas Ltd., UK	..	Chairman and Vice-Chairman
12.	Parke-Davis (I) Ltd.	Parke-Davis & Co. Ltd. USA	..	Chairman and Vice-Chairman
13.	Pieco Electronics & Electricals Ltd.	Philips, Holland	26	Managing Director
14.	Pfizer Ltd.	Pfizer Corporation, Panama	..	Managing Director
15.	Sesa Goa Ltd.	Finsider, Italy	26	Chairman
16.	Thomas Cook (I) Ltd.	Thomas Cook Overseas Ltd.,UK	..	Chairman & Managing Director

Source: Cols. 3 and 4 are based on information given in Prospectuses of respective companies.

Table 14.4

Showing Pattern of Foreign Exchange Utilisation by Foreign Subsidiaries (1975-76)

S. No.	Item	133 Foreign Subsidiaries (₹ Thousands)	% of Total (Col. 2)	189 Foreign Controlled (₹ Thousands)	% of Total (Col. 4)
1.	Capital Goods (Machinery)	65,401	2.95	2,14,900	8.26
2.	Raw Materials (of which oil imports)	19,02,793 (7,17,019)	85.71 (32.29)	20,47,400 (7,17,019)	78.26 (27.55)
3.	Spares	47,612	2.14	1,09,400	4.20
4.	Interest	13,616	0.61	16,300	0.63
5.	Dividends	1,10,298	4.07	1,23,800	4.76
6.	Know-how	19,581	0.88	21,800	0.84
7.	Royalty	7,991	0.34	8,400	0.32
8.	Travelling	2,457	0.11	2,700	0.10
9.	Commission	17,075	0.77	20,800	0.80
10.	Others	33,320	1.50	37,000	1.42
11.	Total	22,20,144	100.00	26,02,800	100.00

Source: Goyal, S.K. (1979). "The Impact of Foreign Subsidiaries on India's Balance of Payments," A study prepared for the Joint CTC-ESCAP Unit (*mimeo*). Public Policy and Planning Division, Indian Institute of Public Administration, New Delhi.

With regard to the official Indian approach towards TNCs for purposes of regulations, one has underlined the weakness of the very definition of what should be treated as a TNC, and secondly, that the basic assumptions of the regulatory legislation i.e., FERA was only too weak to provide any meaningful comfort to the country on account of the foreign exchange situation. One could probably show that the FERA has proved to be a blessing for TNCs as they have gained national acceptability not only with consumers but also with the government and policy makers without any loss of freedom or control over their investments.

It is a widely accepted view that the only comprehensive policy statement on the role of foreign private capital was made in 1949 by the then Prime Minister Jawaharlal Nehru. The official expectations were that foreign private capital would:

(a) supplement domestic savings,

(b) provide requisite sophisticated technology, and

(c) provide the foreign exchange component of capital outlay of projects.

These assumptions emerge from the 'priming the pump theory'—very similar to the recommendations under the Programme of Action for establishment of the New International Order of the UN General Assembly for capital transfers from developed to underdeveloped countries. By now there is sufficient evidence to indicate that all the three expectations have proved to be misplaced ones. Government-sponsored financial institutions in India have extended large rupee as well as foreign exchange loans to TNCs and this too at low rates of interest. Additionally, TNCs have been granted special advantages and preferences in accommodating against loans granted to India at cheap and convenient terms. No substantial capital transfers have taken place over the past three decades. Probably, the net contribution of TNCs has been a negative one. With many TNCs acquiring Indian nationality, there could be reasons to expect that there would be a net outflow of capital from India under the plea of joint ventures abroad—more so under the South-South collaborations, ITC from India establishing production capacities in Nepal, Philips of India to Africa and so on. The other interesting feature of India's policy is that while on the one side there was expectation that private foreign companies would bring capital from abroad (by way of investments, loans and credits), there are stringent rules prohibiting entry of TNCs as well as other Indian companies into the world capital markets.

During the past many years, India's policy has been to promote exports on a priority basis so that the country can meet enhanced costs of oil imports and obtain other crucial industrial goods required for her development and defence. In recognition to the hard reality that the market structures in developed economies are controlled by TNCs, it is suggested that TNCs alone can help India to step up her exports by offering access to home trade channels. How far this assumption has empirically been proved to be a valid one needs to be assessed. But it seems that the TNCs would indeed be willing to help India step up her exports provided India also allows the TNCs to import liberally—capital goods, raw materials and so on. It is only logical that TNCs should enhance the overall size and proportion of India's foreign trade being routed through them. It should have been understood by policy makers that TNCs cannot promote any one country's interests—e.g., Indian exports. TNCs as global institutions have to keep in mind the interests of all of their subsidiaries in whichever country they operate. Thus, the policy assumption that TNCs can prove to be net earners of foreign exchange through promotion of Indian exports abroad seems to be an exaggerated, and probably, an equally misplaced one.

Let us take another example from the Indian policy framework of TNC regulations. The general policy pursued by India is that it does allow foreign investments in only such areas wherein the country does not possess the necessary technology. Thus, all foreign investors would have had, from the day of their entry, a monopoly position in the product area of their operations. TNCs, as a rule, therefore, would enjoy a dominant market position in the country. By this logic, all foreign companies should normally be registered under the Monopolies and Restrictive Trade Practices (MRTP) Act. This is not a reality. In fact, the legal provisions of the MRTP Act are such that these leave even many of the world giants, which are operating in India, outside the MRTP Act scope. Table 14.5 provides an illustrative list of TNCs which are not even registered under the Indian MRTP Act.

Table 14.5

Showing an Illustrative List of Foreign Companies which are not Registered under MRTP Act

1. Bayer India Ltd.
2. Cadbury India Ltd.
3. Colgate-Palmolive Ltd.
4. Ponds India Ltd.
5. Molins India Ltd.
6. Roche Products (India) Ltd.
7. Sandoz India Ltd.
8. HMM Ltd.
9. Food Specialities Ltd.
10. Parke-Davis Ltd.
11. Warner Hindustan Ltd.
12. Polydor India Ltd. (Now Music India Ltd.)
13. Fibreglass Pilkington Ltd.
14. Goodlass Nerolac Paints Ltd.
15. Duphar Interfran Ltd.

It is not only that many TNCs are outside the scope of investigations under the MRTP Act, what one finds equally interesting is that a good number of TNC subsidiaries operating in India had in fact been registered as small-scale industries. These foreign companies did not obtain any industrial licence and were able to take advantage of cheap finance, priority allocation in raw materials, power, subsidised infrastructural facilities and avail of a variety of fiscal concessions—all as small-scale units. Table 14.6 provides an illustrative list of such cases.

Table 14.6

Illustrative List of Multinationals which had Small-Scale Units in India

S. No.	*Name of the Multinational Company*	*Remarks*
	1	*2*
1.	Avery Co. of (I) Ltd., Delhi	Foreign Subsidiary (1966)
2.	Britannia Biscuit Co. Ltd., Delhi	do
3.	E. Hill & Co., P. Ltd., Mirzapur	do
4.	Tyresoles Concessionaires P. Ltd., Delhi	do
5.	East India Distilleries & Sugar Factories Ltd., Kottayam	The company later became E.I.D. Parry (I) Ltd. Foreign Branch (1966)
6.	Getz Brothers & Co., Calcutta	Foreign Branch (1966)
7.	Minimax Ltd., Ranchi	do
8.	Monotype Corpn., Bangalore	do
9.	West's Patent Press Co. Ltd., Aligarh	do
10.	Cambridge Instruments (I) Ltd., Bombay	FERA
11.	Chelpark Co. Ltd., Madras	do
12.	Crompton Engg. Co. Ltd., Madras	do
13.	Eastern Scales P. Ltd, Calcutta	do
14.	Eastern Assam Tea Co. Ltd. (Group Workshop), Lakhimpur	do
15.	Fordham Pressing (I) Ltd., Bombay	do
16.	Hindustan Klockner Switchgear Ltd., Bombay	do
17.	Travancore Tea Estates Co. Ltd. (Peermade Foundry)	do
18.	Sharpedge Ltd., Delhi	Promoted by Hindustan Lever and Escorts.
19.	Bluemount Ceramic P. Ltd., Matham Palayam	Was registered under MRTP Act GEC House

contd...

...contd...

S. No.	*Name of the Multinational Company*	*Remarks*
	1	*2*
20.	Sankar Electricals P. Ltd., Madurai	do
21.	Pandiyan Press Ltd., Madurai	Was registered under MRTPA, Madura Coats House.
22.	A.L.A. Chemicals Ltd., Bombay	FERA
23.	C.E. Fulford (I) Ltd., Bombay	do
24.	Carter Wallace P. Ltd., Goa	do
25.	Ethnor Ltd., Bombay	Subsidiary of Johnson & Johnson Ltd. (a FERA Co.)
26.	Indian Schering Ltd., Bombay	FERA
27.	J.K. Helen Curtis Ltd., Bombay	do
28.	Nicholas of (I) Ltd., Bombay	do
29.	Roussel Pharmaceuticals Ltd., Bombay	Subsidiary of Hoechst Pharma ceuticals Ltd. (a FERA Co.)
30.	Smith Kline & French (I) Ltd.,Bombay	FERA
31.	Whiffens (I) P. Ltd., Bombay	do
32.	Indian Transformers Ltd., Alwaye	Was registered under MRTPA, under GEC House
33.	Precision Tools India Ltd., Calcutta	Was registered under MRTPA, under Macneill Magor House
34.	Ascu Hickson Ltd., Calcutta	FERA
35.	Beclawat of (I) Ltd., Karamsad	do
36.	Shah Medical & Surgical Co. Ltd., Baroda	do

Note: Sl. No. 1-18 were listed in the Federation of All India Small Scale Industries (FASII) All India Directory and Hand Book of Small Industries, 1966, published by the Federation of Associations of Small Industries in India.

Sl. No. 19-21 were listed in the Directory of Small Scale Industrial Units in Tamil Nadu; Supplement to the Second Edition (From 1164 to 311267), 1969, published by the Director of Industries and Commerce, Tamil Nadu.

Sl. No. 22-31 were listed as small-scale manufacturers who are members of Basic, Chemicals, Pharmaceuticals and Cosmetics Export Promotion Council in the Thapar's Indian Industrial Directory & Export & Import Directory of the World, 198081.

Sl. No. 32-33 were registered for government purchases being small-scale units. See Directory of Small Units Enlisted for Government Purchases, 1976, published by the National Small Industries Corporation Ltd.

Sl. No. 34-36 were registered for government purchases being small-scale units. See Directory of Small Units Enlisted (Under Single Point Registration Scheme) for Government Purchases, 1980, published by the National Small Industries Corporation Ltd.

FERA in Col. 2 indicates that the company was one of the applicants which applied to the Ministry of Finance under the Foreign Exchange Regulation Act.

Quite apart from weaknesses in regulatory policies, misplaced expectations and absence of effective coordination, there are a host of issues emerging from the weak and inadequate legal systems in the developing countries which are fully taken advantage of TNCs. The widespread resort of TNCs in pharmaceutical and drugs to harmful and unethical practices has already received worldwide attention. To expect that a TNC would not take advantage of what the local laws permit would be asking for only too much. TNCs are in business and not in the promotion of social welfare. This explains the Indian experience with TNCs in matter of industrial licensing (see Table 14.7). Even though the number of foreign companies operating in India is a small one, nearly half of the total cases of gross violation (i.e., more than 100 per cent excess production over the authorised capacities) were that of TNCs and their associates. One can cite a large number of instances where TNCs have openly flouted the spirit of regulations, but by and large nothing can be done against them legally. For instance, much has been said about the exit of IBM from India. But very few would know that a parliamentary committee had discovered that IBM was involved in clear cases of illegal 'transfer pricing practices.' The company would have faced legal action and it would have been embarrassing; as an alternative, it chose to exit on the plea of declining to accept the demands under FERA. Incidentally, IBM is back in business under a new name.

It is our contention one should not place the entire blame on TNCs for their practices if these happen to be unethical or if TNCs do not come up to the expectations of host countries. A more purposive approach would be to have a hard look at the regulatory policies and assess weakness in operating mechanisms. This should be done with an objective and critical appreciation of the institution of TNC. Unless these exercises are undertaken by the developing countries themselves, no amount of internationally agreed norms or codes of conduct can be of much help. In this, there is need to extend and promote empirical studies in the areas of regulations and undertake policy research—particularly, for the lead sector of the developing economies, i.e., industrial and organised sectors. There was also a need to study the effectiveness of various regulatory enactments in order to identify the areas wherein the regulatory mechanisms need strengthening or rationalisation. It needs also to be assessed if the

Table 14.7

Showing the Distribution of Licences Utilised in Excess of Licenced Capacity according to the Licensee Category and Level of Utilisation

S. No.	Licensee Category	No. of Licences in Excess Utilisation Range			Excess Licences Utilised	
		Upto 25 (%)	25-50 (%)	50-100 (%)	100 and above(%)	Total
	1	2	3	4	5	6
1.	MRTP Companies	112 (61.5)	44 (67.7)	21 (50.0)	36 (56.3)	213 (60.3)
2.	Dominant Undertakings	45 (24.7)	11 (16.9)	6 (14.3)	6 (9.4)	68 (19.3)
3.	Large Houses (CIS Classification)	134 (73.6)	50 (76.9)	28 (66.7)	46 (71.9)	258 (73.1)
4.	Other Groups (CIS Classification)	16 (8.8)	4 (6.2)	6 (14.3)	2 (3.1)	28 (7.9)
5.	Companies presently under public management	1 (0.5)	0 (0.0)	1 (2.4)	0 (0.0)	2 (0.6)
6.	Former Branches, Subsidaries (ILPIC) and FERA companies (1974)	55 (30.2)	23 (35.4)	15 (35.7)	31 (48.4)	124 (35.1)
7.	Others with Foreign Equity above 25 per cent	16 (8.8)	8 (12.3)	3 (7.1)	3 (4.7)	30 (8.5)
8.	Others with Foreign Equity between 10-25 per cent	10 (5.5)	2 (3.1)	1 (2.4)	1 (1.6)	14 (3.9)
9.	Joint Sector Companies	7 (3.8)	1 (1.5)	0 (0.0)	3 (4.7)	11 (3.1)
10.	Other Companies	32 (17.6)	11 (16.9)	7 (16.7)	16 (25.0)	66 (18.7)
	All Companies	182 (100.0)	65 (100.0)	42 (100.0)	64 (100.0)	353 (100.0)

Notes: 1. The column totals will not agree as there is overlapping of companies in the above groupings. A company may be a FERA one and also MRTP Act registered one. Therefore, each group of companies has to be treated as such.

2. Figures in brackets are percentages calculated with respect to the total number of licences in each utilisation range.

3. CIS: Corporate Information System Classification; ILPIC: Industrial Licensing Policy Inquiry Committee.

Source: Corporate Information System, IIPA, New Delhi.

monitoring of the corporate sector in general and operations of the TNCs in particular can be effectively achieved on the basis of the traditional systems of data collection, compilation and analysis. The results of such inquiries can not only help the individual countries but also assist in evolving realistic policy alternatives in development for developing countries in general. India's experience by itself may have relevance for a number of the developing economies in the spirit of the NIEO.

15 Multinational Corporations and Indian Policy Framework[1]

The new industrial and foreign investment policy announced on May 31, 1990, proclaims to release Indian industry from "unnecessary bureaucratic shackles by reducing the number of clearances required from the government." As a part of this objective, it is proposed to allow foreign investment upto 40 per cent on an automatic basis subject to a 30 per cent restriction on the import of capital goods. Similarly, larger freedom to Indian entrepreneurs in the matter of technology imports is in the offing. The policy explains that these and other proposals would be applicable to all manufacturing units in a 'specified list' to be announced later.

Predictably, the announcement generated a great deal of discussion at various fora. However, neither the policy statement nor the subsequent official clarifications throw light on the empirical basis for the decisions with regard to foreign investment and technology. Nor do they reveal any understanding of the nature of foreign private capital already existing in India. Significantly, the likely impact on the balance of payments, self-reliance, indigenous research & development (R&D), employment, India's stand on multinational corporations (MNCs) in the Third World fora and India's social and political spheres have not been spelt out clearly. Is it because the policy makers are not aware of the basic characteristics of the institution of MNC and the long-term implications of the open door policy for foreign private capital and technology? The answer might be in the affirmative for the political leaderships but could not be so for the high profile economic advisers.

When it is decided to invite, permit or encourage large private corporations from outside the country to find a solution to Indian societal problems on the belief that MNCs would help solve India's major problems—may it be foreign exchange, inflation, unemployment, interpersonal inequities or regional imbalances it is of importance to discuss direct and indirect

1. *ISID Working Paper*, 1990.

implications of the new policy initiatives. First of all, one must recognise that MNCs are private corporations primarily guided by the philosophy of profit maximisation. MNCs are not in social service. There is a need to understand that societal problems cannot be the concern of private business. If one places faith on a wrong institution or instrument, one has only to wait for the day of disillusionment.

Secondly, we need to recognise that MNCs operate worldwide. Most of the largest MNCs originated from the USA, the UK and West Germany and have their headquarters located in one or the other part of the industrialised world with market orientation. In operational terms, however, no large MNC has one nationality. MNCs may not be country-specific but are economic system-specific. It would be difficult to say in India if Nestle (Food Specialities) should be treated as a Swiss company or a Bahamas' one. Similar would be the case with Pfizer whose foreign shareholder is registered in Panama, while the ultimate parent is located in the USA. Legal provisions differ from one country to another. It could be that a large MNC is treated as an Indian national company in India, but a foreign one in the UK, France or Japan. MNCs are not nationality-specific. Therefore, the top executives have no national hang-ups.

MNCs represent a network of private business enterprises having operations in large many geographic locations. For any network, the success or failure is not judged by the performance or profit of any single wing or business in a country. MNCs business perspective has to be global. It does not fall in the realm of objectivity to expect that MNCs would promote interests of any one nation. It is just not in their character. However, to the extent promotion of exports from a country served their objective of global profit maximisation, the MNCs would most certainly do so.

Thirdly, MNCs are in private business, and business means all activities that give a net advantage to them. Their choice of activity would depend on their understanding and assessment of market potential. MNCs would engage themselves in any activity that requires investment, market knowledge and experience, business connections, legal rights in tangible or non-tangible assets (ownership of patents, trade marks or monopoly rights) from where the corporation can extract economic return. MNCs, therefore, are neither activity- nor industry-specific. Anything would do. If it was a tobacco company initially, it could take up hotel business or sale of vegetable oils later on. To shift the nature of business operations is normal as long as the new business offers higher return than the traditional industry. If the policy makers of the country develop a misplaced belief that MNCs would help India bridge technology gaps in hi-tech areas or any other industry, the fault does not lie with MNCs. For lack of one's own understanding of business logic and reality, the business enterprises cannot be justifiably accused.

In the modern age, it is well accepted that the institution of state has direct responsibility to lay down rules of the game even for the private business. Public interventions are a pre-requisite for smooth functioning of even the market-oriented economies. In the Third World countries, however, the state has to play even a more important role. Many of the Third World countries have adopted regulatory mechanisms. From the viewpoint of business promotion, MNCs are bound to take measures that would reduce the intensity of regulations for them. It would be considered a very legitimate action if an MNC decides to cultivate 'mutually profitable' relationships with those who control levers of political and administrative power. Investment in politics could be risky but also extremely remunerative. World history is full of instances when MNCs have not hesitated to sponsor coups against political leaderships who posed a threat to MNC business interests.

MNCs must aim at diversification in the long run though. Thus, to gain entry, if the host country insists on the MNC manufacturing certain products, such conditions would be acceptable as long as the host country regulations do not forbid diversification, new investments and expansion. If the host country, on its own, awards them Indian nationality and help build their business image, why should an MNC object? The policy makers in India have made the people believe that enactment of Foreign Exchange Regulation Act (FERA), imposing export obligations and insistence on diversification is some sort of an unpleasant conditionality.

Let any one examine the record of large private corporations in India or abroad to find out how MNCs have been itching to engage themselves in export, of course, combined with rights to import. No MNC would like to invest in a country for the sake of dividends, technology payments or high salaries to the host country executives. MNCs being a part of international network of business activities cannot afford any one country unit (company or a branch) to live in isolation of the rest. Business autonomy is not a rule of the MNC institution.

MNCs can certainly be depended upon to promote exports as well as imports. Movement towards globalisation is their business philosophy. Can one place a faith in an international private business institution (the MNC) to earn net surplus of foreign exchange for India or any one country? To the extent exports are of raw materials and products that can only be produced in India, comparatively at cheaper prices, MNCs would export from India. The question, however, is not of sheer exports, an equally important issue is of the export prices. If an MNC is buying from five countries, it is but natural that it would buy from the country that offers the lowest price. It has been widely recognised that the buying locations can shift as a business strategy to take advantage of the lowest price. To have a better appreciation of this aspect of international trade and capacity of MNCs, one needs to understand today's reality where in a number of commodities, MNCs enjoy a near monopsony status. In absence of producer country alliances, buyers dictate the prices. MNCs can comfortably pitch one country suppliers against another.

Yet another fact to be understood is that MNCs are large international business networks with control over vast finances, massive framework of distribution and sales outlets in industrially advanced countries, advertising resources, press and communication systems; employing the best and the largest army of attorneys and lawyers, auditors and accountants, researchers and public relations men; and enjoying legal protection to monopoly rights on thousands of basic inventions, industrial processes, patents, trade marks and designs. The network of international information and the speed at which it operates cannot be matched by any one governmental system including the USA not to speak of India or any other Third World country. While formulating policies with regard to such a powerful business institution, policy makers cannot be casual and project their own illusions. The national costs can be high.

MNCs belong to a category of giants in relation to individual governments of many a country like India. If India wishes to harness and benefit from the powerful, we need to understand the natural aptitudes, the motivations, the capacity and other characteristics of MNCs. What we need to also appreciate is that MNCs are invariably aware of their own weakness and incapacity to fight against nationalism and ideologically committed national public systems. The only thing the MNCs yield to is public pressure. To them, public means consumers and consumers cannot be easily brushed aside.

With fast changes in the global system of production, the MNCs would change their business strategies. For instance, instead of seeking to engage themselves directly in production (and make investments), MNCs may increasingly go in for marketing of goods manufactured by others. This could help avoid direct conflicts with labour. What the MNCs, however, insist upon would be the right to brand names. To strengthen this, MNCs would tend to emerge as the biggest patrons of mass media—TV, radio and the press. To remain dominant, it would be only expected that MNCs would insist on having legal and administrative support for patents and other forms of intellectual property rights. Trade and trading activity is a service industry. Expansion of specialised services is the new area, and it should surprise none if the US and other advanced economies are asking for grant of entry of foreign private capital into insurance, construction, banking, consultancy and trade—external and internal. Given these likely trends, the pressure on the Third World countries would be mounted for lowering of regulations on national currencies.

To meet the challenge of nationalism and related sensitivities, MNCs invariably try hard to wear related host country nationality caps and project their enterprises as promoters of local culture, music and traditions. It helps. Of late, MNCs have become more conscious that while avoiding direct political patronage in any host country, it is far more effective to find local partners who have high political clout and influence on national governments. This probably explains the recent growth of Birla-Yamaha, Tata-Unisys and Modi-Xerox type of joint ventures (see Annexure A-15.1 for an illustrative list). No wonder, today the very Indian big business who opposed British capital and took a nationalist stance with the Congress and Gandhiji is finding it more profitable to be associates of MNCs. Can one be surprised if the Federation of Indian Chambers of Commerce and Industry (FICCI) and the Associated Chambers of Commerce and Industry of India (ASSOCHAM) have become the most vocal and loud supporters of MNC entry into India? Who controls FICCI or ASSOCHAM?

While these are some of the main characteristics of MNCs, we in India in general and policy makers in particular seem to have felt shy in recognising them. We did not attempt to debate and understand the multifaceted institution known as MNC. It is also possible that we preferred to ignore the reality and chose to follow haunches, beliefs and motivated suggestions. The state of affairs with regard to policy towards MNCs is best illustrated by the fact that the Indian legislations do not recognise even the concept of multinational corporation. While the government has not found it necessary to undertake an exercise on the identity of the institution of MNC, it has not hesitated to take the 40 per cent equity limit, fixed for the applicability of FERA to permit open entry. As a result, associates of a number of well-known multinationals are treated on par with wholly owned Indian companies. The beneficiaries include: Unilever, Philips, Kodak, BAT Industries, Swedish Match, Nestle, Hoechst, Ciba-Geigy, Alcan Aluminium, Pfizer, Singer, etc.

The fact also remains that control is being exercised by MNCs not only through the ownership of equity capital, but also with the help of management rights which they bestowed upon themselves with the government's explicit consent and legal stamp of approval. In many cases, MNCs wield 100 per cent control while owning far less than 40 per cent foreign equity (see Annexure A-15.2). Given such extensive control over the affairs of the company, it is obvious that the foreign shareholder would decide what to produce, where and to whom to sell and at what price, where to import from and at what price, which technologies to pursue and which products to promote. One needs to ask: would such a high degree of control in foreign hands be beneficial or inimical to self-reliant and independent development? If not, do we have the necessary instruments to make them work to the advantage of the country or are we voluntarily surrendering national regulatory rights to intervene?

Coming back to the recent policy announcement, even if one accepts the official explanation that automatic entry of foreign investment up to 40 per cent is allowed only in specific areas, would such a policy continue to be applicable to existing MNCs? In other words, would such 40 per cent foreign equity companies be restricted to product areas for which they apply to enter India initially or they would have the same freedom as enjoyed by non-FERA national companies? The scenario is not very difficult to imagine. Since the foreign equity would not exceed 40 per cent, the new entrants would straight away qualify to be non-FERA national companies. It is quite a common knowledge how ex-FERA companies are now expanding into a variety of consumer goods both through direct manufacturing and through marketing of products manufactured by small-scale units in the former's brand names. There is no instrument with the government to restrict non-FERA companies (whether old or new entrants to India) to 'specified lists'. Annexure A-15.3 gives an illustrative list of low technology/ low priority consumer products manufactured/marketed by MNCs who are otherwise supposed to be engaged in hi-tech production processes.

Another anomaly which has not been given the due attention it deserves is with regard to the small-scale sector. The policy relaxations are in contradiction with the expectations from the sector. Given the freedom to conclude foreign collaborations, would the small scale or for that matter any entrepreneur insist on exports which the foreign collaborator is known to resist? Secondly, wouldn't the resultant excessive dependence on foreign technology alter the character of the small-scale sector to make it more capital intensive and reduce its potential for employment generation? Thirdly, can we rule out the possibility of MNCs entering directly in the small-scale sector in the absence of any clear-cut guidelines with regard to foreign equity in the small-scale sector? Would an MNC-owned small-scale company satisfy in any way the objective behind protecting and promoting small entrepreneurs?

One is not aware of any official study to assess whether existing collaborations are borne out of genuine felt need for technology or were intended to blunt the edge acquired by the competitors through foreign brand names and trademarks. Such competition would without doubt lead to increased dependence on external sources for technology, machinery and raw materials.

It is debatable if the country ever really tried to restrict the operations of MNCs. While a feeble attempt has been made to restrict their operations to the so-called Appendix-I industries, the Appendix itself has been expanding continuously. While FERA companies number about one hundred, the restrictions on their trading activities have been relaxed on the plea of export promotion. It is no surprise that a number of the important FERA companies have turned themselves into export/trading houses. To what extent the MNC exports comprise of the products manufactured by them?

The plight of Third World countries in the present international context is aptly described by the South Commission when it said:

> A network of relationships has been built up among private entities—banks, investment houses, transnational companies—in the leading developed countries. This has served to strengthen the influence of decisions made by private bodies on world economic activity, and to that extent to limit the effectiveness of governmental policy decisions. For the South the result is even further marginalisation and greater powerlessness.

Strengthening India's own administrative frame and building the capacities to pick what we need and at a price not only that India can afford but that is the lowest in the international market is the first step in the right direction. It is only through a strong public system, one can attempt to keep the MNCs under check.

Annexure A-15.1

Illustrative List of Joint Ventures

Beacon Kone	Mafatlal Zinser Engg
Beacon Neyrpic	Mahindra British Telecom
Beacon Rotork Controls	Mahindra Owen
Beacon Tileman	Mahindra Ugine Steel
Beacon Weir	Modi Champion
Birla Yamaha	Modi Olivetti
Birla 3M	Modi Telematics
DCM Toyota	Modi Xerox
Essar Brown Root	Murugappa Morganite Ceramic
Essar Forasol	Nagarjuna Signode
Fuller KCP	Nava Bharat Parker Drilling
EIMCO KCP	Nicco Hambro Financial
Escorts JCB	Furmanite Nicco
Great Atwood	Nicco Helifusion
Greaves Dronsfield	Shriram Honda Power Equipt
Greaves Foseco	SRF Nippondenso
Greaves Midwest Engg	Tata Bradbury Wilkinson
Crompton Greaves	Tata Honeywell
David Brown Greaves	Tata Klockner Indl Plants
Drayton Greaves	Tata Korf Engg Services
Hero Honda	Tata Timken
Hindustan Textronix Inst.	Tata Robins Fraser
J.K. Helene Curtis	Tata Unisys
J.K. Satoh Agricultural	Tata Yodogawa
Khatau Junker	Sundaram Abex
Kinetic Honda	Sundaram Clayton
Kirloskar Rateau	TVS Suzuki
Kirloskar Warner Swassey	TVS Whirlpool
Kirloskar Cummins	Lucas TVS
Kothari General Foods	Harita Grammar
L&T Gould	United Van Der Horst
Lohia Starlinger	

Note: Besides these are many others like Hitech Drilling Services, Eicher Motors, Digital Equipment India, Vespa Car Co., etc.

Source: Information System, Institute for Studies in Industrial Development, New Delhi.

Annexure A-15.2

Illustrative List of Companies in which Foreign Shareholders were Allowed to Appoint Managerial Personnel/Exercise Veto Powers by the Government of India

Abbott Laboratories India
Astra-IDL Ltd.
Automotive Axles Ltd.
Axles India Ltd.
Bihar Sponge Iron Ltd.
Birla Yamaha Ltd.
Boehringer-Knoll Ltd.
Burroughs Wellcome & Co. (I)
Cadbury India Limited
Carrier Aircon Ltd.
Cemindia Co. Ltd.
Colgate Palmolive (I) Ltd.
Corn Products Co. (I)
DCM Toyota
Digital Equipment (I) Ltd.
E Merck (I) Ltd.
ESAB India Ltd.
Eskayef Ltd.
Fulford (I) Ltd.
Fuller KCP Ltd.
Gabriel India Ltd.
German Remedies Ltd.
Glaxo India Ltd.
Godfrey Phillips India Ltd.
Gramophone Co. of India Ltd.
Hinditron Tektronix Instruments
Hindustan Ciba-Geigy Ltd.
Hindustan Powerplus Ltd.
Hoechst India Ltd.
Incon (I) Ltd.
IND-Suzuki Motorcycles Ltd.
Indian Duplicator Co. Ltd.
India Nippon Electrical
India Photographic Co. Ltd.
Indian Sewing Machine Co. Ltd.
Indian Shaving Products Ltd.
Indian Xerographic Systems
Indo-Asahi Glass Co. Ltd.
Indo Matsushita Appliances
Indrol Lubricants & Specialities Ltd.
Infar India Ltd.
International Computers Indian Mfrs. Ltd.
Invel Transmission Ltd.
Kalyani Brakes Ltd.
Kanthal Bimetals India Ltd.
Kirloskar Warner Swassey
Kothari General Food Corpn
Lipton India Ltd.
May & Baker India Ltd.
Miles India Ltd.
Modi Champion Ltd.
Modi Olivetti
Modi Xerox Limited
Monotype India Ltd.
Moran Tea Co India Ltd.
Nagarjuna Signode Ltd.
National Peroxide Ltd.
Nicco Batteries Ltd.
Nicholas Laboratories India
PCS Data General India Ltd.
Padmatex Engineering Ltd.
Peico Electronics & Electricals Ltd.
Perfect Circle Victor Ltd.
Pfizer Ltd.
Pond's (I) Ltd.
Revathi-CP Equipment Ltd.
SRF Nippondenso Ltd.
Sesa Goa Ltd.
Steelage Industries Ltd.
Stormac India Ltd.
Sulzer India Ltd.
TVS Whirlpool
Tata Burroughs Ltd.
Tasta Honeywell Ltd.
Telemechanique & Controls (I)
Thomas Cook India
Tri-Sure India Ltd.
Uni-Abex Products Ltd.
Uptron Colour Picture Tubes
Utility Engineers (I) Ltd.
Vespa Car Co. Ltd.
WG Forge & Allied Industries
Wendt (I) Ltd.

Source: Prospectuses of respective Indian associates for different years available in the Information System of the Institute for Studies in Industrial Development, New Delhi.

Annexure A-15.3

Illustrative List of MNCs in Indian Economy Operating in Consumer Goods Industries

Name of the MNC	*Consumer Goods Produced/Marketed*
Agfa Gaevart India	Cameras, Camera Films
Asian Agro Farm India	Poultry
Bata India	Shoes, Socks, Readymade Garments, Leather Bags
Berger Paints India Ltd.	Paints
Brooke Bond India Ltd.	Tea, Coffee, *Masalas*, Leather
Cadbury's India Ltd.	Chocolates, Biscuits, Ice Cream
Carrier Aircon	Domestic Air conditioners
Ceat Tyres of India	Marine Products
Colfax Laboratories India	After Shave Lotions, Shaving Cream
Colgate-Palmolive India	Tooth Paste, Tooth Powder, Tooth and Shaving Brushes, Shaving Cream, Soaps, Cold Creams
Corn Products Co. India	Jelly and Custard Powders
Crompton Greaves	Domestic Electric Fans, Electric Lamps
Duphar Interfran	Cosmetics and Toiletries
Eskayef Ltd.	Iodex Pain Balm and sprays
Ethnor Ltd.	Marine Products
Eureka Forbes	Vacuum Cleaners
Fiskars India	Scissors
Funskool India Ltd.	Toys
General Electric Co.	Domestic Fans, Electric Lamps
Geofrey Manners India	Tooth Paste, Tooth Brush
Glaxo India	Baby Foods, Glucose
Godfrey Phillips India	Cigarettes, Tea
Goodlass Nerolac Paints	Paints
Gramophone Co. of India	Records, Pre-recorded Cassettes
Guest Keen Williams	Safety Pins, Nuts, Bolts
Hero Honda	Motor Cycles
Hindustan Lever	Soaps, Tooth Paste, Margarine, Shampoos, Detergents, Cleaning Powder, Carpets, Readymade Garments, Marine Products, Leather Goods, Carpets
Hindustan Ciba-Geigy	Tooth Paste, Tooth Powder, Tooth Brushes, Creams
HMM Ltd.	Dairy and Milk Products, Hair Cream, Biscuits
ICI India Ltd.	Paints
India Photographic Co.	Cameras, Camera Films

contd...

...contd...

Name of the MNC	*Consumer Goods Produced/Marketed*
Indian Shaving Products	Blades, Shaving Brush, Razors
Indian Sewing Machine Co.	Sewing Machines, Kitchenware and Domestic Appliances
Indo-Matsushita Appliances	Rice Cookers
Indo-National Ltd.	Dry Cells
Ion Exchange India	Water Filters
ITC Ltd.	Cigarettes, Hotels, Vegetable Oils, Carpets, Marine Products
J L Morrison	Tooth Paste, Feeding Bottles, Face Cream
J K Helene Curtis	Cosmetics
Johnson & Johnson	Ear Buds, Baby soaps, Baby Talcum Powders, Baby Lotions, Sanitary Napkins
Kelvinator India	Domestic Refrigerators
Kinetic Honda	Scooters
Kissan Products Ltd.	Jams, Sauces, Squashes, Biscuits
Kothari General Foods	Coffee, Soft Drink Concentrates
Lakhanpal National	Dry Cells
Lipton India Ltd.	Tea, Fruit Juices, Soft Drinks, Vegetable Oils
Madura Coats	Threads, Readymade Garments
Metal Box	Metal and Plastic Containers
Modi Carpets	Carpets
Nestle India	Coffee, Tea, Baby Foods, Dairy Products, Noodles, Ketchup
Pieco Electronics & Electricals	TVs, Radios, Tape Recorders, Intercoms, Marine Products
Pepsi Foods	Potato Chips, Soft Drinks
Pond's India	Toilet Soaps, Talcum Powder, Cold Cream, Leather Goods, Marine Products
Procter & Gamble	Balm, Chicklets, Digestive Tablets
Punjab Anand Lamp Inds	Electric Lamps
Rallis India	Fans, Readymade Garments
Reckitt & Colman India	Boot Polish, Antiseptic Lotion, Soaps, Detergents, Barley
Sylvania Laxman	Electric Lamps, Tube Lights, TVs
Thomas Cook	Travel agents
Tube Investment of India	Bicycles
TVS Suzuki	Motor Cycles, Mopeds
Union Carbide India	Dry Cells
Vespa Car Co.	Scooters
VST Industries	Cigarettes
WIMCO Ltd.	Matches, Salt, Marine Products

Source: Information System, Institute for Studies in Industrial Development, New Delhi.

16 Transnational Corporations and the Third World[1]

Transnational corporations (TNCs) occupy a unique place in the global economic system. The fact that TNCs control vast and varied resources[2] places them in a position where from they can exercise effective influence at various levels of policy-making systems, besides their fast growing capacity to play a decisive role in determining the life styles and consumption patterns of the present day consumers. Their visibility is becoming more pronounced. TNCs are admired by many, and the same is true of TNC critics. One does, however, find an abundant degree of misinformation and untrue assumptions about TNCs. There is plenty of ignorance even on basics about TNCs. Here we attempt to bring out a few of these and raise some questions.

The first clarification needed is with regard to the very nature of the TNC. TNCs are private corporations, most of them originating from the industrialised countries,[3] endeavouring to optimise their global advantage. All operations of theirs have to be judged in terms of net economic

---

1. *ISID Working Paper*, November 1995.

2. Except for Brazil, Argentina, Mexico, Venezuela, Saudi Arabia, Iran, Iraq, Turkey, Indonesia, India, Republic of Korea, Hong Kong and Taiwan none of the countries in the developing world had a gross domestic product (GDP) of more than $50 billion in 1991. Obviously the number would be much smaller if one keeps out the oil exporters. On the other hand, there were at least 21 TNCs with total sales exceeding this amount during the same year. Looked in a different way, total sales of General Motors were lower than the GDP of only Brazil, Mexico, Iran, India, Republic of Korea and Taiwan in the developing world. See: table 6.1 in UN Conference on Trade and Commerce (UNCTAD), *Handbook of International Trade and Development Statistics*, United Nations, Geneva, 1994 and table 1.2 in UNCTAD, *World Investment Report 1994: Transnational Corporations, Employment and Workplace*, United Nations, Geneva, 1994.

3. During 1985-1989, the developed countries accounted for 96.8 per cent of total foreign direct investment (FDI) outflows with the USA, the UK, Japan, FRG and France accounting for as much as 69 per cent. See: United Nations Centre on Transnational Corporations (UNCTC). *World Investment Report: The Triad in Foreign Direct Investment—1991*, United Nations, 1991.

advantage and profit. Thus, the expectation that TNCs could promote national interests of anyone host country, especially *vis-à-vis* their parent enterprise or home country, would be wholly a misplaced one. TNCs are in business of making profit and generating maximum surpluses for themselves; it is not their concern to promote development of the host countries. However, to the extent they stand to benefit from the growth and development of the host country, they would not hesitate to project themselves as the real promoters of development in the country of their operation. TNCs would seek and pursue all such opportunities that give them economic advantage. The task before host developing countries on the other hand has to be to identify which transnational offers the best and costs the least. A transparent system of business requires information to be shared openly. It so happens, however, that a great deal of detailed economic information is made public by governments and comes to stay as public knowledge; the same is not true of TNCs. Information and data on their operations are extremely limited, and this too is released with extensive window dressing. A consequence of this is that private corporations hold discussions with full knowledge of the government's stand but government negotiators have extremely limited information, and this too is a tutored one, at their command.[4] The nature and direction of the flow of advantages should be only too obvious. The primary point being made is that TNCs have to be viewed as business organisations and one should not expect them to be in social service. Also, when faced with a choice of preferences, they are obliged to promote and place higher priority to the interests of their parent country and parent corporation.

Secondly, one often assumes that each TNC has an industry/area specialisation. May be it was so in the early stages of TNC development. It holds true no more. TNCs are in business and are not wedded to any one industry, one type of activity or one nation. Like any shrewd businessman, TNCs stay in an industry as long as it gives them extra advantage. If their activities do not offer special premium, they must shift and move to better alternatives. This is understandable business logic. For policy makers, therefore, it should be clear that TNCs cannot have any special love for

---

4. The manner in which the foreign investors came prepared to reduce the costs of power projects after the Enron fiasco is a clear indication of the extent of naivete displayed by the Indian side in negotiating these projects.

any one location. Their decisions have to be impersonal. One should not, therefore, take any moral stances while dealing with TNCs. One does visualise that transnationals would attempt to enhance their capacity to move from one activity to another.

Mobility shall be the keyword for TNCs to follow. This implies that TNCs must keep their own investments to the minimum, especially in the fixed assets that would restrict their mobility. What would be the best economic activity that TNCs should take up, if the mobility logic is accepted? There appears to be a clear area in which TNCs should be seen as major actors. For instance, if a TNC takes up trading operations, the corporation can enter in any market with a big bang due to the very large financial resources at its command. Here, one is not referring to trading of the traditional type. In the present day world, trading means bridging the gap between the consumer and the producer—the role often assigned to intermediaries. The essential component of the activity is to service the end-user. In the modern trading, one would include all that goes under the name of packaging and developing consumer acceptability.

The new role of TNCs—the same should hold true of large national corporations—would be in trading and for this, there are many reasons. By confining to trade and distribution services of what has been manufactured by others, one avoids all problems of direct confrontation with labour and other regulatory bodies. One has only to ensure that goods supplied are of a 'standard' determined by the corporation. There can be as many suppliers as the situation demands. The entire responsibility for manufacturing is outside the liabilities of the large corporation. Instead of depending on one or only a few suppliers, it would be of advantage if the suppliers are many and the buyer is only one. To achieve such a situation, one should expect that there would be insistence by the corporation to have exclusive rights on all output of the manufacturer. Secondly, the supplier is not granted any rights to place any identification marks or brand names different from what is given by the corporation.[5] There has to be strict adherence to the norms. But, the end price or brand name has to be of no

---

5. A host of popular consumer goods marketed by TNCs in India are indeed manufactured by local small-scale units. Tooth paste, tooth brushes, shampoos, talcum powder, creams, lotions, pomades, etc., sold under the brand names of Colgate, Hindustan Lever, JL Morison, Ponds and Ciba-Geigy are only a few examples of this practice. See: Chandra Shekhar, *Political Economy of India*, Vikas, Delhi, 1992.

concern of the manufacturer. The system gets perfected as the ownership of 'brand names' and their popularisation through massive advertisement campaigns is taken up by the intermediary corporation.[6] Thanks to the new laws relating to 'intellectual property rights' gaining support of increasing number of countries, tendencies at emerging trade monopolies would get strengthened. One knows it too well that any monopoly (or monopsony) situation gives advantage to the more powerful and the privileged than the average consumer. The future trend, one should expect, would be for TNCs to be seeking to hold widest possible legal rights on manufacturing technologies and processes and brand names. If this was not to be so, TNCs would lose their special position. Viewed from the basic logic and merits of a competitive world, can one assert that the above trends would promote competition that leads to reduction of costs to the benefit of the consumer?

Third, a widely promoted assumption is that entry of TNCs in the developing countries can help the host countries to meet balance of payments problem. For this, it is argued that their direct business linkages in home markets (which are the industrially advanced nations) and control over domestic distribution networks can provide the opportunity to enhance host country's exports. Added to this is a long and winding argument that TNCs would transfer capital resources without placing any burden on the

6. From the aggregate level data brought out by the Reserve Bank of India (RBI), it can be seen that relatively speaking TNC subsidiaries and affiliates in India spend double the amount on advertisement in relation to their sales compared with large companies in the Indian private corporate sector. If one excludes the foreign sector from the latter category, relative expenditure on advertisement by TNCs would work out to be much higher. Though somewhat of an extreme case, Unilever Group in India offers a telling example of how TNCs build up their market power. For instance, Hindustan Lever Ltd. and its wholly owned subsidiary together reported an advertisement expenditure of about ₹ 125 crores during 1987-1990. See: ibid.: 66. No wonder even a long established company like Tata Oil Mills succumbed to the brand strength of the Levers. Looking in a different way, we find from our database on company finances that out of the top 15 spenders on advertisement in 1990-91, as many as 11 were TNCs. A similar situation emerges if one looks at the top brands in the country. See: "India's Top Brands", *A & M*, October 13, 1995, pp.42-64. In many consumer goods industries, the fight for top market shares is now gradually turning into TNC *versus* TNC to the complete exclusion of domestic companies.

exchequer.[7] TNCs are also supposed to be the carriers of new and modern technologies that would help improve quality of goods produced and lower production costs; all these associated developments lead to ending of inefficient, high cost, low quality private national monopolies. One needs to critically examine the truth and actual experience of the recent past. Has it happened that TNCs have indeed exported larger percentage of their own production? One needs to go case by case. The empirical evidence, at least in India, does not seem to place the TNCs as earners of net foreign exchange.[8] Even in 1990-91, as is evident from Table 16.1, TNCs in engineering and chemical industries—which are regarded as high technology based and in which TNCs have an in-built advantage over domestic companies—have proved to be heavy losers of foreign exchange. It can also be seen how payments for technology and dividend remittances have further worsened the already adverse trade balance.

---

7. Though initially the argument may sound convincing, the long-term burden of TNCs on a developing country's balance of payments can often be substantial. As we shall see later, the net direct impact of TNCs on the bottom of the pyramid (BOP) front has been substantially negative. Indeed, much of the risk capital owned by TNCs in India has been created out of profits generated within the country. For instance, 93.53 per cent of the capital held by Unilever in its Indian subsidiary at the end of 1990 was created out of the profits generated in India. In spite of the repatriation of capital in 1978, 99.88 per cent of Colgate, the USA's share in Colgate Palmolive India was on account of bonus shares issued to the former. Other notable cases in this respect are: Geoffrey Manners, Kirloskar Cummins, Bata, MICO, Chloride, Johnson & Johnson, Boots, Otis, Nestle, Union Carbide and English Electric. As time progresses dividend outgo too will increase in line with the increase in the foreign-owned capital.

8. A number of studies have shown this to be the case. For instance, an empirical study of the operations of foreign subsidiaries in India observed that foreign subsidiaries have been net losers of foreign exchange. The study also highlighted the importance of raw materials in foreign exchange outflows on account of foreign subsidiaries. See: S.K. Goyal, *Impact of Foreign Subsidiaries on India's Balance of Payments*. Indian Institute of Public Administration, 1979. The study was prepared for the Joint Centre on Transnational Corporations-Economic and Social Commission for Asia and the Pacific (CTC-ESCAP) Unit, Bangkok. Another study showed how the TNC subsidiaries managed to show a somewhat better performance at exports and net foreign exchange earnings by resorting to exports of unrelated and bought-out items under the export and trading houses route. It is interesting to find that garments, marine products, leather goods and such other items form part of the export basket of many trading houses. Can one ever associate Philips with export of marine products? It is, however, a reality in India. See: Pitou van Dijck & K.S. Chalapati Rao (1994). "India's Trade Policy and the Export Performance of Industry", *Indo-Dutch Studies on Development Alternatives* No. 12. Delhi: Sage.

Table 16.1

Net Earnings of Foreign Exchange by Foreign-controlled Rupee Companies Manufacturing Engineering and Chemical Products (1990-91)

	Item	*Amount (₹ Cr.)*
	(1)	(2)
A.	Earnings in Foreign Exchange	
	Exports	1,124.42
	Other Earnings	10.64
	Total Earnings	1,135.06
B.	Expenditure in Foreign Exchange	
	Imports	1,222.31
	Other Expenditure in Foreign Exchange	174.45
	of which,	
	(a) Dividends	81.12
	(b) Royalty and Technical Fee	32.54
	Total Expenditure	1,396.76
C.	Net Earnings (A-B)	261.70

Source: Based on data provided in "Finances of Foreign Controlled Rupee Companies, 1988-89 to 1990-91", *Reserve Bank of India Bulletin*, Vol. XLVIII, No. 11, November 1994, pp. 1395-448. The data presented in the table refer to 189 companies.

Further, one would observe that TNCs are increasingly opting and restricting themselves to soft technology areas and are indeed avoiding capital investments.[9] More and more collaboration agreements and investment proposals are to assemble and market under brand names. As a consequence, the visibility of TNCs has become more pronounced but actual transfers have been very limited.

If one examines the nature of capital flows from abroad, one also observes that in most developing countries a good part of the new investment is directed to gain management control over the already existing

9. Besides the cases involving takeovers and consolidation of control, one finds that implementation was quick in low technology, elite-oriented consumer goods industries. Notable among these is the liquor and beverages industry. It can easily be seen that international companies like Seagram, United Distilleries, International Distillers and Hiram Walker have already established their presence in India. The same is true of Kellogg's corn flakes, Perfetti's chewing gum, Kentucky's chicken, Sony and National Panasonic's televisions and garments of Pierre Cardin, Benetton, and Levi Strauss.

enterprises. These are through mergers and takeovers.[10] The privatisation drive inspired by the multilateral agencies is only increasing the scope for such takeovers of public sector companies by the TNCs. Viewed differently, one also finds that TNCs have become more active in stock exchanges of the developing countries. Indeed, in the Indian case, foreign portfolio investments far outstripped direct investments (see Table 16.2).

As for the experience of India, one finds that stocks of major Indian corporations can be easily cornered and introduce speculative trading on the exchanges. Again, portfolio investments, with the regime of free convertibility, can hardly be taken as a basis for stable industrialisation of the country. The stock exchanges should, if the trends continue, become a major field for TNC operations. The simple reason for it is that investment in shares helps to sustain the highest degree of mobility.

10. It has been observed that new foreign investment proposals involving increase in foreign equity in existing companies accounted for more than one-fifth of the amount involved in implemented projects. Indeed, the share of equity hike cases in actual inflows under the automatic approval scheme was as high as 53.8 per cent of the total. Notable among the equity hike cases are: Colgate, ABB, 3M, Carrier, Hoechst, Cadbury, Corn Products Co., Coats Viyella, Nestle, Philips, Pepsi, Procter & Gamble, Castrol and Whirlpool. More importantly, many of these acquired the additional shares at prices far lower than the prevailing prices in the stock market. Even in other cases, it can be seen that the so-called new proposals were nothing but disguised takeovers as the existing manufacturing units/operations were transferred to the joint venture. Apart from the well-publicised re-entry of Coca Cola on the foundations of Thums Up, mention can be made in this regard of the joint ventures between: (i) Godrej and Procter & Gamble, (ii) Premier Automobiles & Peugot, (iii) Kirloskar & Snydergeneral Corp., (iv) Ballarpur Industries and Owens Illinois, and (v) public sector companies and TNCs like Caltex, Mobil and Shell. In a few other cases, the foreign collaborator had sold off in the existing ventures but immediately returned in another form through setting up of wholly owned subsidiaries with undisputed control. One can cite Turner Newall and Black & Decker which respectively terminated their collaboration with Hindustan Ferodo and Kulkarni Black & Decker to set up the new ventures. Unless these factors are taken into account, one will only get a distorted picture of the foreign investments in the new policy regime. See S.K. Goyal, *et al.* (1991). *Foreign Investment Approvals & Implementation Status: A Review* (August 1991 to December 1994). Delhi: Institute for Studies in Industrial Development. The report was submitted to the Ministry of Finance.

Table 16.2

Foreign Investment Inflows since the Liberalisation of Industrial Policy

(US$ million)

	1991-92	*1992-93*	*1993-94*	*1994-95# (Apr-Dec)*
(1)	*(2)*	*(3)*	*(4)*	*(5)*
A. Direct Investment	**150**	**341**	**620**	**756**
a. RBI Automatic Route	-	42	89	81
b. SIA/FIPB Routs	87	238	315	380
c. NRIs (40% and 100%)	63	61	217	295
B. Portfolio Investment	**8**	**92**	**3493**	**3141**
a. FIIs	-	1	1665	1195
b. Euro Equities	-	86	1463	1726
c. Offshore Funds and Others	8	5	365	220
Share in Inflows (%)				
A. Direct Investment	94.94	78.75	15.07	19.40
B. Portfolio Investment	5.06	21.25	84.93	80.60
Total (A+B)	158	433	4113	3897

Note: # Provisional; SIA: Secretariat for Industrial Assistance; FIPB: Foreign Investment Promotion Board; FIIs: Foreign Institutional Investors; NRIs: non-resident Indians.

Source: Based on: India, Ministry of Finance, *Economic Survey*, 1994-95: 90, table 5.3.

For long, the critics of TNCs used to insist that TNCs must be made to undertake exports. The critics, obviously, did not know what they were asking for. TNCs are international business networks. Transnationals, therefore, have an inherent advantage in the area of international trade. For undertaking exports or imports, one needs to have an international network for gathering business intelligence and a regular and reliable infrastructure. Entry into the field of international trade is not as open as is many a time assumed. Contrary to the general perception, international trade is not amenable to free competition. This realisation, one is afraid, has yet to come to policy makers in the developing countries. It is because of these realities that one finds that there is a high degree of concentration in imports, as also exports, when viewed from the identity of the trade actors. The number of the largest importers/exporters for a country of India's size is not more than 200 or so.[11] Foreign trade is controlled by small numbers and there is domination by the TNCs or their associates.

The fact that policy makers in developing countries start asserting that TNCs must raise national exports, fits well with the strategy of transnationals. It is obvious that no government would expect a corporation to be only engaged in exports. Those who export will have to be given the rights to import.[12] The logic is simple. In practice, however, it is seen that imports rise at a much higher pace than exports thereby making the balance of trade more unfavourable. This aspect has been dealt by many. We wish to underline the hard reality that imports and exports by TNCs are not what one would believe as foreign trade. TNC trade activities are essentially in the nature of inter-branch transactions. Most of the imports are sourced from their associates, and similarly, exports are made to TNC

11. A study of India's imports during 1990-91 through the major entry points of Bombay, Calcutta, Madras and Delhi revealed that there were only about 1,480 private sector importers who imported at least ₹ 1.00 crore worth of goods. Further, just 330 out of these accounted for almost two-third of the imports on account of private sector. There were indeed less than 150 importers with ₹ 10 crore or more of imports during the period. See: S.K. Goyal, *et al.* (1991). *India's Imports and Exports: Some Insights* (An Analysis of Daily Trade Register Data). Delhi: Institute for Studies in Industrial Development. The report was submitted to the Ministry of Finance.

12. The case of Japanese investment in Thailand provides a telling example of the dependency that gets developed between a host developing country and the home country of the TNC investors.

    The data suggests that there is a strategic coupling between Japanese trade, DFI, capital transfer and technological transfer. It seems to be a coordinated economical penetration of Thailand by Japan. The interest of Japan and Japanese companies being central ... Thailand seems to be forced to export more and more, in which the terms are determined less and less by the needs of Thailand, or even by the demands of the world market, but instead by the needs of one country: Japan. In doing so the proceeds of industrial goods are nullified by the costs of the required imports to export, as well as by the associated capital outflow in the form of profit and dividends. Due to the Thailand's industrial structure it is becoming more dependent on Japan, but not Japan on Thailand. Thailand is for Japan and Japanese trade and industry...

    See: Ed Aerts & Luuk Knippenberg (1991). "Japanese Investments in Thailand: A Network of Dependent Relations?", Paper Presented at the *Workshop Internationalization of National Economies: The Role of International Firms*, Organised by the Third World Centre, University of Nijmegen, and NICCOS, Nijmegen, December 18-20.

associates.[13] This is the unique advantage that TNCs have. Also, it is very rarely that one is able to grasp the full extent of transfer pricing under TNC operations.[14] Most developing countries do not have adequate legal framework or administrative capabilities to uncover the practice of transfer pricing or a variety of unethical trade practices. The unfortunate reality is that most policy makers in the developing countries are so busy and tired that they have little time to think and evolve an appropriate system for national policies. It comes easy to follow ready-made policy prescriptions than enter into long debates.

We have made an attempt to underline—more by way of illustration than claiming exhaustive critique—the policies and assumptions in debates relating to TNCs. The attempt is directed to assert that there is need to have more active debate based on empirical data than what often happens to be the case. Developing countries need to learn from their experiences and evolve a relevant policy framework best suited to their conditions.

---

13. For instance, intra-firm flows represented 63 per cent of the US manufacturing industry imports. On the exports side, the corresponding share was about 40 per cent. See: Charles-Albert Michalet (1991). "International Trade and Multinational Enterprises Activities", Paper Presented at the *Workshop Internationalization of National Economies: The Role of International Firms*, Organised by the Third World Centre, University of Nijmegen, and NICCOS, Nijmegen, December 18-20.

14. The study of India's imports also revealed that Mahindra Nissan was importing almost entirely from its Japanese partner Nissan. Similarly 85 per cent of imports of Kinetic Honda and Hero Honda were from Honda Motor Co., Japan. Rank Xerox along with its worldwide subsidiaries and associates was meeting 80 per cent of the import requirements of its Indian affiliate Modi Xerox. Philips India was getting nearly 60 per cent of its imports from its parent company Philips, Holland and its affiliates spread over Japan, Latin America, Europe, USA and Singapore. In such a situation could it be said that the prices will be decided by market forces or to the overall advantage of the TNC? See: S.K. Goyal, *et al.*, *India's Imports and Exports*, *op. cit.*: Table 24.

17 Multinational Corporations and Self-Reliance

An important element in India's struggle for independence from British colonial rule lay in the desire to establish a self-reliant society free from all forms of external dependence, domination or control. *Swadeshi* was not a matter of faith and creed with Gandhi ji alone, it was equally shared by all nationalist forces—economic and political. The existence of foreign capital was identified as a cause of many of the country's economic ills. The national sentiment was marked by hostility towards foreign capital. The attitude towards foreign private capital, however, underwent a marked shift within a couple of years of the establishment of a national government. Initially, the change in approach was from outright hostility to conditional acceptance, but with each successive period the attitude got further softened. Of late, there is plenty of evidence to suggest that the official policy towards foreign investments has reached a phase when it could certainly be characterised as that of 'cordiality', if not of preferential treatment.

The rationale, as spelled out in official statements, for allowing entry of foreign private capital into the Indian economy, has been changing with time. In the official policy statement of 1949, it was visualised that foreign private investments would complement the limited national resources to achieve a higher rate of investment, as also bring with it advanced technology and capital equipment without strain on scarce foreign exchange. In the mid-1950s, the main policy emphasis was on undertaking industrial investments with a view to promote 'import substitution' in collaboration with foreign capital. The primary justification for allowing an extended role to foreign capital and confessional treatment, under Foreign Exchange Regulation Act (FERA), was in terms of the supposedly superior capabilities of foreign companies in promoting sale of Indian goods abroad.

Presently, one finds a variety of other arguments being put forth in favour of an enlarged role for foreign private capital in India. The Union Minister of Commerce Pranab Mukherjee argues that "MNCs could impart their advanced marketing know-how and skill to the developing countries for boosting exports" (*Economic Times*, Bombay, February 18, 1980). Jyoti Basu, Chief Minister of West Bengal (with a Marxist Party in power) openly welcomed multinationals on the plea that "we want latest technology, no matter who supplies it" (*Economic Times*, Bombay, October 14, 1979); Vice-President of India Hidayatullah observed that "the more we shut foreign competition out, the more shall we be shut out also" (*Financial Express*, Delhi, February 22, 1980). The Minister of State for Finance, in a recent policy statement, announced that India would welcome foreign investments and technology as "this was necessary for up-dating its existing know-how and for making new products" (*Economic Times*, Delhi, November 21, 1981). The shift in policy towards foreign capital has been clearly brought out by the government itself in the official note submitted to the International Monetary Fund (IMF). The change in the tone and content of national policies is obviously influenced by considerations of obtaining a large loan from the international financial institution.

The change has been gradual but always in the direction of opening the economy more and more to foreign private investments. Quite apart from changes in the overall policy, it may prove quite helpful if one could prepare a catalogue of reasons assigned to approve individual cases of entry of foreign companies into the Indian economy. For instance, in one case, entry was justified on the ground that it was necessary to break the monopoly hold of an Indian company on the national market. In another, the approval was related to political considerations and India's long-term interests. In fact, any plea is considered good enough to justify the role of foreign capital in India.

The softening attitude towards foreign private investments gives an impression that a large variety and number of foreign investors are likely to come to India and as a consequence the process of industrialisation would get accelerated. Such a belief is not objectively based. The general policy of concessions to foreign private capital is *de facto* to be availed of by a handful of international companies, i.e., a few multinationals. This is evident from the fact that while the total number of foreign subsidiaries in India was 171 in 1977, nearly three-fourth of the total assets of the subsidiaries was held by only 32 of them. Again, if one were to group foreign subsidiaries operating in India, according to their parentage, the number of multinationals of significance operating in India would be less than 20. The policy towards foreign private capital should, therefore, be defined as the policy towards multinationals.

The policies which permit entry of new multinationals and assign an announced role to existing ones, and their implications with reference to the country's objective of achieving self-reliance, can be better understood if the basic characteristics of multinational corporations (MNCs) are kept in mind. In the absence of an objective assessment of the very nature of the institution of the MNC it is not possible to have a correct perspective. It is with this view that we bring out some of features of the MNCs particularly those which are related to the question of self-reliance.

Firstly, MNCs are privately owned corporate bodies operating in a large number of countries. These subscribe to the philosophy of free enterprise and profit maximisation. By their very philosophy, MNCs stand against all forms of governmental intervention, particularly those which place restrictions on the freedom to determine and implement investment priorities as determined by the corporate sector in response to market conditions. MNCs and the national private sector would have the same attitude towards governmental regulations and controls. In a country like India, where the pattern of land holdings, corporate wealth and other means of production is ridden with extreme disparities, absence of regulations on the limited investible resources of society would imply that the new investments would flow in the direction that satisfies the needs of the few—who happen to have control over the large part of national wealth and incomes. It was in appreciation of these realities that India opted for a process of planned socioeconomic development instead of accenting the philosophy of free enterprise. The enhanced role for the MNCs in the Indian economy as also of the national private sector, therefore, would have serious implications for the process of Indian planning. Since planning in India had the specific objective of taking the country on the path towards self-reliance, any weakening of the planning process would make the achievement of the objective more difficult.

It is quite common to come across an argument that national monopoly capital, if encouraged and protected, would enable the country to keep MNCs away. The strengthening of national private capital, it is sometimes argued, because of its patriotic attitudes, would be the surest guarantee against international private capital and the MNCs. Thus, it is suggested that national monopoly houses in India should be encouraged in all possible manners in the interest of establishing a 'self-reliant' national economy. The assumption in this argument is that the sentiment of nationalism is more powerful with the Indian private industrialists and businessmen than their faith in the philosophy of free enterprise. That all such assumptions are wholly misplaced is well demonstrated by a variety of developments in India during the last three decades. Indian private large enterprises and monopoly houses have lost all pretentions to being industrialists of this country alone. Very true to the private corporate philosophy, Indian industrialists are only too ready to adopt the same techniques for their expansion in the world economy as that of the USA of any other country-based MNCs. For matters of economic policy, there cannot be any distinction between Indian large industrial houses or that of MNCs. Their corporate interests direct them to oppose national planning as a system and all forms of governmental controls and regulations which restrict business freedom. The objective of national self-reliance, by its very nature, places restrictions on the international growth of Indian houses. This would not be acceptable to them. The private corporate philosophy does not, therefore, lend itself to the ideals of national self-reliance—which could be an objective for individual developing countries of the Third World.

Secondly, MNCs are international business organisations and these are steadily losing their national identities. While it is true that most of the MNCs have had the US as the parent country, recent trends suggest that MNCs are emerging as world institutions having multiple points for central coordination and with no special love for any one country. The objective of MNCs cannot be to remit all surpluses to their respective parent country. Their approach has to be global. It would be in the direct interest of MNCs to work for an international order that enables them to operate freely in different countries of the world. Thus, the logic and motivation of MNCs would be in promotion of such international relationships which make different parts of the world more interwoven and interdependent rather than any one group of countries pursuing the ideals of self-reliance. 'Self-sufficiency' in food and other basic national needs, for instance, could be a rightful objective of the Third World countries, but in this process, MNCs are bound to see a shrinking role for themselves. If India could achieve self-reliance in the area of science and technology, the main argument for their entry to the Indian market would not hold true.

Thirdly, MNCs are foreign-controlled private organisations and to do business is their business. These are not charitable organisations established to enable the developing countries to achieve economic independence. Whether a country has large degree of poverty and only a few have large wealth and control over national resources cannot be a matter of any concern for business institutions. What matters for them is that resources under their control should grow. It is in this context alone that MNCs would pursue such policies that enhance their global economic benefits, irrespective of the social costs to any society. The MNCs would very naturally argue that pursuance of social objectives was the concern of the national governments and not theirs.

Fourthly, MNCs are business organisations and, therefore, their interest cannot remain confined to any one industry. Given a choice to invest in a wide range of alternative industries, locations and countries, their decisions on size of investment and the selection of industry would depend on the comparative economic returns and not on what the host country may require the MNC to promote for protecting or furthering of her national interest. It is true that many foreign companies in India were associated with specific industries, but one is already witnessing a fast growing tendency towards diversification. For instance, Imperial Tobacco Company (ITC), later known as ITC, has already acquired an important status in the country's hotel industry; Union Carbide has gone in for marine fishing and shrimp exports, and Brooke Bond has taken over the promotion of blades and a host of other consumer items in the Indian market. The diversification plans of Hindustan Lever are well known. The limited point in mentioning these cases is to highlight that MNCs in any country would not like to be pegged down to only one industry. Whichever industry offers better economic returns would be considered good for their exploitation. On similar considerations, while taking investment decision at the global level, the choice of country and location would be governed by weighing the comparative advantages of investing in different countries. MNCs will have to operate in a manner that would help them reap the most profitable mix in manner that would help them reap the most profitable mix in their global economic activities. Added to the pure economic considerations, it also follows that MNCs would like to diversify their activities to the widest possible extent for reducing risks associated with total involvement in one industry or one country. Viewed in this framework, MNCs and 'self-reliance,' from the viewpoint of anyone nation, do not go together.

Fifthly, the roots of the MNCs have been in western and developed capitalist societies. A major source of their strength lies in the fact that the MNCs have been able to (i) perfect their marketing techniques, (ii) develop enormous competence to influence consumer choices and (iii) operate in a systematic manner to quietly obtain favours from all those who happen to be in power. MNCs have been very successful in establishing an image that they represent the most modern and advanced sector of the world economic system. Whichever project is offered by them is always of better quality. Because of such an image, MNCs are able to have easy and quick access to consumer and capital markets in developing countries. These assertions have to be seen in the light of the fact that, for a large many consumer products in the West, MNCs happen to have an already dominant place in manufacturing capacities. Most MNCs have brand names and patents which are promoted and protected through mass advertisement campaigns. MNCs have indeed introduced a large many new consumer items in the Third World. For instance, Dalda and Coca Cola for the large part of India's population represent a commodity and not a brand name. MNCs through their cooperation promote a large many new items and through it a new consumption pattern in the host countries. In this process, MNCs encourage and support western capitalist value systems. In India, one can easily trace that the influence of MNCs has been significant, not only in matters of industrial manufacture but also in the realm of food habits, clothing styles and patterns of buildings and other construction activity. Since the new consumption patterns, evolved in the West, also involve a considerable import component, host countries allowing free operations to MNCs get tied down to large amounts of regular but avoidable imports.

Such developments are bound to make it more and more difficult for a country like India to become self-reliant. The acceptance of new consumption norms and life styles also bind the country to developments and trends abroad.

Sixthly, MNCs are associated with high technology and large efforts at research and development (R&D). Suppose, for the sake of argument, the research staff of an MNC in India is able to develop a very efficient industrial process that would not only reduce costs of production but also make the imports of raw materials from the parent company in Europe unnecessary. Would the management of the MNC be expected to support adoption of the new technology and cancel all imports from the parent company? If one accepts that the final verdict, in matters of all important business policies for an MNC, rests with the central head quarters, it is obvious that the Indian subsidiary of the MNC would have to drop her plans for adoption of the new technology developed by the Indian research staff. It may be in national interest of India but one cannot expect the subsidiary of an MNC to adopt policies which run contrary to the business interests of the parent company. The objective of all R&D carried out by MNCs in the Indian market can be anything but achievement of self-reliance.

From the high points of the central offices of MNCs, the world scene presents itself in the form of clearly demarcated national markets, each having a differing level of standard of consumption and consumer behaviour pattern. The countries of the world can not only be grouped according to the size and other similarities in market conditions, but can be divided according to the stages of technological developments, the character of sociopolitical systems and the levels of maturity and stability of the ruling elites. Given their position of vantage in the world economic system, MNCs possess a far better historical and global perspective than governments and national leaderships, particularly those in the Third World. MNCs with a sharper and broader perspective of the world economic system are able to intervene much more effectively to promote their interests than any national government. If it suits them, the national sentiments of a country can be aroused and local politics manipulated with ease.

MNCs have control over a wide variety and levels of technologies. The most advanced technologies have to be adopted by them in the developed countries since each MNC faces direct competition from other MNCs in the industry. In developing countries, the situation is quite different. Invariably,, the national market for a commodity or group of commodities is the monopoly of one MNC. To maintain the monopoly position of a MNC, the local laws are generally quite helpful. In protected markets of the Third World, there cannot be market pressures to adopt the latest and most efficient technologies that the same MNC may be employing in advanced countries. For MNCs, therefore, it is quite normal to employ differing levels of technologies at the same time in different countries. The situation is like differing levels of Mechano children building blocks. For each age group, representing a level of mental maturity, there is a separate set. The higher the age group, the more advanced is the Mechano number. If a country has matured to technology level 'A,' the MNC can adopt technology level 'B.' The process can continue. The MNC would always be able to retain the image of a provider of better technology to the host country. One cannot, however, place the entire blame on MNCs for following such strategies and phased release of technologies. It is implied in the process of development. The real point is that if a nation develops her technologies and builds a large base for technology absorption, the process of updating can be faster. It is not necessary that each country should invent a wheel, but what can certainly be done is that a country can discover the application of the wheel in its own environment. The developing countries can identify and obtain only such parts of the technology and only import such critical capital goods which are beyond their capacities at a point of time. Such an approach to obtaining critical technologies would hasten the process of self-reliance. This, obviously, cannot be in the interest of MNCs. MNCs, therefore, cannot identify themselves with national efforts at R&D. MNCs would stand to gain if all national efforts at R&D can be frustrated. One should, therefore, expect that MNCs would follow a variety of policies to keep local scientists busy on minor areas of technologies or such programmes which bind them to their own scheme of technology relationships.

The above characteristics of the institution of MNC should be sufficient basis to see that MNCs and self-reliance for developing countries cannot go together. To the contrary, more involvement of MNCs can only make the developing economies more dependent on outside influences. MNCs are an integral part of the capitalist system of the developed countries. It is equally true that international financial institutions like the World Bank and the IMF are part of the same system. Both these institutions provide a support mechanism for each other. In this perspective, it should be easier to see the implications of the massive IMF loan that has been approved for India. The conditions attached to the loan are such that would make India accept a larger role for MNCs; adopt an export-led strategy and develop the Indian economy in response to the market demand of the developed countries instead of national needs; and make India a junior partner and sub-system—always dependent on "the magic of the market place" of the advanced capitalist world.

18

Foreign Private Investments in India

Myth and Reality

Consequences inherent in the existence of large foreign private capital in an economy are only too well known. Therefore, the need for evolving restrictive policies and for establishing administrative and other mechanisms to curb and regulate the operations of foreign capital in India was pleaded by all national political parties during the struggle for the country's freedom and was recognised by the national government. Soon after Independence, a comprehensive official statement on the role of foreign private investments was made.[1] The justification for inviting foreign private investments, as made out in the statement, was that (i) "Indian capital needs to be supplemented by foreign capital, as our national savings will not be enough for rapid development of the country" and (ii) "in many cases, scientific, technical and industrial knowledge and capital equipment can best be secured with foreign capital." During the last three decades, though a number of amendments to the 1949 policy statement have been made, the basic policy frame has remained unchanged.

The official policy, with regard to foreign private investments, is supposed to be 'selective.' For instance, new investments by foreign undertakings can only be made with the approval of the Foreign Investment Board, in addition to the processing of the proposals under the Industries (Development and Regulation) Act (IDRA), 1951. The processing of investment proposals is done to restrict the entry of foreign capital in areas where 'indigenous technology' is already available. The Foreign Exchange Regulation Act (FERA), 1973, is expected to reduce the level of remittances by foreign undertakings. Additionally, large and dominant undertakings (irrespective of their being Indian-or-foreign-controlled) are granted approvals for new investments only after the proposals have been examined

1. "Participation of Foreign Capital in Industries", the statement made by the Prime Minister Jawaharlal Nehru before the Constituent Assembly of April 6, 1949.

under the provisions of the Monopolies and Restrictive Trade Policy (MRTP) Act 1969. In brief, India would appear to have a comprehensive legislation, the requisite administrative system and a policy to regulate foreign investment in the economy effectively.

Actual Experience

The validity of the two assumptions made for inviting foreign private investments, namely, the transfer of (i) capital and (ii) the accompanying technology, needs to be critically assessed in the light of India's actual experience since Independence. The transfers of private foreign capital, as the world experience suggested, are never so substantial as to be seriously considered supplementary to national savings. In India, for instance, between July 1948 and December 1961, the net transfer of private capital are estimated at approximately ₹ 123 crore, i.e., nearly ₹ 10 crore a year.[2] A recent study conducted by Sudipto Chaudhry shows that "foreign sources contributed only 5.3 per cent to the growth of the transnational corporations in India during 1956-1975."[3]

The assumption of the 1949 statement that capital transfers would supplement India's resources to enable it to achieve a higher level of industrial investments has not come true. Whatever little capital appears to have got transferred has been primarily in 'kind' or in services (i.e., by way of supplying machinery, technical know-how or other services), against which the supplier companies were paid in the form of equity shares. In a situation in which the supplier is the parent company and the recipient is its subsidiary, the scope for inflating prices to show larger capital contribution to the Indian company is in-built. However, one would admit that some capital contribution by parent companies, while gaining initial entry through their subsidiaries, was indeed made. But this does not appear to be the case any more. The expansion of foreign subsidiaries and foreign-controlled companies is now entirely financed from rupee resources and in this respect, public sector financial institutions play the most important role. This fact is brought out in Table 18.1, showing the 'sources of finance'

2. Kidron, M. (n.d.). *Foreign Investments in India*, p.229.

3. Chaudhry, Sudipto (1979). "Financing of Growth of Transnational Corporations in India, 1956-75", *EPW*: 1431-35, August 18.

Table 18.1

Showing Sources of Finance for Industrial Expansion by TNCs and their Associates (An Illustrative List)

(₹ *in Lakhs)*

S.No.	Company	Associate Equity	Additional Equity	Loans from IFC,UTI,ET		Other Public institutions	Internal accruals	Total
				Rupee	Foreign exchange			
1.	Hindustan Lever (1977)	Lever (UK)	803.20 (29.06)	1,040.00 (37.62)	285.00 (10.31)	364.89* (13.20)	217.91 (0.80)	2,764.00 (100.00)
2.	Peico (1979)	Philips (Holland)	224.00 (5.38)	1,862.00 (44.78)	50.00 (1.20)	- -	2,024.00 (48.65(	4,160.00 (100.00)
3.	International Computers (1979)	GEC (UK)	130.00 (46.43)	150.00 (53.57)	-	-	-	280.00 (100.00)
4.	Welcome Hotel	BAT (UK)	65.00 (34.03)	32.50 (17.01)	-	85.00** (44.50)	8.50 (4.45)	191.00 (100.00)

Note: * Interest-free unsecured loan from West Bengal Industrial Development Corporation Ltd. (WBIDC) (₹ 334.89 lakh) and Central Government subsidy (₹ 30 lakh)

** Term loans from Rajasthan Financial Corporation (₹ 30 lakh), Rajasthan Industrial and Mineral Development Corporation (₹ 25 lakh) and Central Bank of India (₹ 30 lakh)

Source: Prospectus of the Companies.

for four industrial expansions, being undertaken by well-known foreign companies and their associates.

The companies included are for purposes of illustrating the phenomenon. Each one of the four companies is an associate or subsidiary of a well-known multinational corporation. Hindustan Lever is a subsidiary of Lever Brothers; International Computer is an associate of the GEC., Peico (Philips) was formerly a subsidiary of Philips N.V. Holland, and Welcome Hotel (S.B. Properties) is under the management of the ITC (an associate of British-American Tobacco). The expansion plans do not visualise any foreign exchange loan from parent companies.

The foreign exchange requirements are proposed to be met by the Industrial Credit and Investment Corporation of India (a financial institution which was promoted to help indigenous entrepreneurs who were not able to raise adequate capital from the market).[4] Hindustan Lever, a foreign subsidiary, with the largest turnover among the foreign-controlled companies, was granted by the central government a subsidy amounting to ₹ 30 lakhs to expand its industrial base in India. The long-term rupee loans were provided by the IDBI, Industrial Finance Corporation of India (IFCI), Unit Trust of India (UTI), Life Insurance Corporation (LIC) and other financial institutions at a concessional lending rate. As if this was not adequate, the State Industrial Development Corporations (promoted to assist medium and small industries, which could not be serviced by the national institutions) and other state-level promotional agencies have extended liberal loans. In the case of Lever Brothers, the WBIDC granted a loan of ₹ 3.34 crores without interest.[5] Another feature of the 'scheme of finance' is that in two cases, whereas the public sector financial institutions would provide the finance, as today, the company's own contributions (described as internal accruals) would be out of the future expected profits. In addition to the direct financial support at concessional lending rates, the foreign companies also take advantage of a variety of tax benefits and

4. ICICI, 1955-1965, "While giving a brief history of the 'Formatting and Resources of ICICI, it is stated that India did not have dearth of entrepreneurs willing to take calculated risks, but public offers of capital, except for well-established houses, were meagre..." The ICI was, therefore, expected to provide risk capital for those Indian entrepreneurs who were not well established and could not raise the requisite finance.

5. If a company was granted an interest-free loan for six years, in substance, it amounts to an outright donation of the principal amount.

other help from the central and state governments, available to other Indian industrialists. Such facilities have become easier after the enactment of FERA.

Low Level

The above account should be a good indicator of the low level of transfers of private capital. The foreign-controlled companies are expanding on the basis of Indian capital, which, too ironically, is provided by various government agencies at concessional lending rates. Ready, convenient and preferential access to the Indian institutional finance would clearly indicate that India would witness a much higher rate of expansion of foreign companies, particularly the ones which are the associates of the multinationals, than in the past. Table 18.2 shows the rate of growth of the 39 top Indian subsidiaries of foreign companies during 1969-1979.

Table 18.2

Showing the Growth of Foreign Subsidiaries during 1976-1978

S.No.	*Company*	*Year of incorporation*	*Assets (₹ crore)*			*Turnover (₹ crore)*		
			1969	*1977*	*Percentage*	*1969*	*1977*	*Percentage change*
(1)	*(2)*	*(3)*	*(4)*	*(5)*	*(6)*	*(7)*	*(8)*	*(9)*
1.	Hindustan Lever	1933	31.82	122.02	283.5	108.79	261.50	140.4
2.	Dunlop	1926	39.78	99.78	149.2	81.70	166.85	104.2
3.	Brooke Bond	1912	23.21	55.00	136.9	75.36	186.30	147.2
4.	Union Carbide	1934	35.24	68.18	93.5	44.13	106.85	142.1
5.	Indian Explosives	1954	51.05	79.96	56.6	15.13	91.59	505.4
6.	Indian Aluminium	1938	59.03	96.18	63.0	27.29	117.17	329.4
7.	Ashok Leyland	1958	22.30	61.51	175.8	29.11	97.41	234.6
8.	GKW (1972+1977)	1931	41.99	70.98	69.0	53.37	88.73	66.3
9.	Bata	1931	27.10	50.02	84.6	48.33	83.05	71.8
10.	Siemens	1957	18.02	47.95	166.1	19.98	77.74	289.1
11.	Goodyear	1962	14.08	23.98	70.3	28.84	52.16	80.8
12.	Philips	1930	24.18	55.64	130.1	32.23	82.04	154.5
13.	Metal Box	1933	21.82	32.58	49.3	25.97	54.20	108.7
14.	MICO	1951	15.85	40.90	158.0	14.59	61.14	319.1
15.	GEC	1911	23.87	34.72	45.5	17.98	58.60	225.9
16.	Alkali & Chemicals	1937	14.64	35.36	141.5	15.18	53.89	255.0
17.	Glaxo	1924	16.24	35.25	117.1	24.42	56.51	131.4
18.	WIMCO	1923	12.61	17.60	39.6	26.63	41.63	56.3
19.	Indian Oxygen	1935	15.73	33.75	114.6	15.86	48.10	203.3
20.	Ciba-Geigy	1947	-	21.16*	-	-	34.64*	-
21.	Pfizer	1950	12.51	25.09	100.6	15.89	41.29	159.9
22.	Britannia	1918	7.32	17.40	137.7	16.87	44.13	161.6
23.	Parry (1966+1977)	1975	7.44	46.05	518.9	-	108.89	-

contd...

...contd...

S.No.	Company	Year of incorporation	Assets (₹ crore)			Turnover (₹ crore)		
			1969	1977	Percentage	1969	1977	Percentage change
(1)	(2)	(3)	(4)	(5)	(6)	(7)	(8)	(9)
24.	Chemicals & Fibres	1961	12.79	23.05	80.2	25.05	39.18	56.4
25.	Chloride (I) Ltd. (1969+1973)	1947	7.57	9.25	22.2	6.77	16.76	147.5
26.	Bayer (I) Ltd.	1958	8.61	23.46	172.5	5.76	35.95	524.1
27.	Sandoz	1947	8.66	16.50	90.5	7.60	36.45	379.6
28.	Tube Investment (1966+1977)	1949	11.38	19.62	72.4	-	26.20	-
29.	Colgate Palmolive (1966+1977)	1937	2.88	13.17	357.3	-	32.62	-
30.	Asbestos Cement (1966+1975)	1934	5.93	10.32	74	-	17.02	-
31.	Hindustan Milk Food(1966+75)	-	1.46	6.48	343	-	16.67	-
32.	Cynamid (1966+1975)	1947	5.72	12.80	123	-	16.89	-
33.	Associated Bearing	1961	9.25	1.18	107.4	5.05	19.88	293.7
34.	Lucas TVs (1966+1975)	1961	4.74	14.74	210	-	15.14	-
35.	Food Specialities	1959	5.72	12.38	116.4	7.87	20.79	164.2
36.	Sandvik Asia	1960	5.85	17.25	194.8	4.81	14.65	204.6
37.	Goodlass Nerolac (1969+1976)	1920	3.41	8.07	136.6	5.39	18.29	239.3
38.	Otis	1959	5.77	12.01	108.1	2.63	8.07	206.8
39.	India Tyre (1966+1975)	-	1.11	2.80	152.0	-	12.38	-
40.	Abbot Laboratories (1966+75)	-	0.60	4.89	715.0	-	12.19	-
41.	Tribeni Tissues	1946	19.63	19.13	2.6	4.41	12.86	191.6
42.	Cadbury (1973+1977)	1948	6.45	13.40	107.8	9.79	16.89	74.1
43.	Reckitt & Colman	1951	6.23	8.28	32.9	7.17	11.86	65.4
44.	EEC	1957	6.01	11.69	133.3	2.15	16.58	671.2
45.	Atlas Copco	1960	2.75	6.79	146.9	3.75	11.61	209.6
46.	Hindustan Ferodo	1964	5.26	8.54	62.4	5.28	15.76	198.5
47.	Gramophone Co.	1946	3.60	10.94	203.9	3.97	11.34	185.6
48.	Merck Sharp (1966+1977)	-	2.98	6.73	125.8	-	11.60	-
49.	Boots	1944	2.51	5.10	103.2	3.49	11.98	243.3
50.	Shalimar Paints (1972+1977)	1902	4.37	6.77	54.9	6.85	12.50	82.5
51.	Roche (1966+1975)	-	3.81	6.70	75	-	9.84	-

Note: (1) Figures in brackets indicate the relevant years for which the data have been given.

(2) * the figures for 1975.

(3) - not available.

Source: Bombay Stock Exchange Official Directory.

Out of the 39 foreign subsidiaries listed in Table 18.2, 18 were able to expand more than double their assets, and 6 expanded their assets by more than 200 per cent in ten years. In terms of turnover (sales), but for 7, which experienced less than 100 per cent increase, each one of the remaining subsidiaries expanded at much higher rate.

The second expectation in inviting foreign private investments in India lay in the desire of the government to take advantage of modern technology available to the Indian economy. This expectation was based upon a number of unspecified assumptions, such as that foreign private investors would (i) be willing to employ the latest technology and industrial processes in their Indian establishments, (ii) freely share the technology with Indian entrepreneurs, (iii) be taken to utilise the indigenous resources and adapt their technology to local needs and (iv) identify themselves with India's national interests. Each one of the assumptions taken individually, when critically examined, would prove to be wholly misplaced.

A fact to be adequately appreciated by the Indian policy-makers is that international private investments in the present age can only be made by large corporations. Small entrepreneurs confine themselves to their own countries. Secondly, like any shrewd investor, no large corporation would consider it wise to put all its eggs in one basket. Given a situation, in which large international corporations have investments scattered in many countries (some developed and others at different levels of development), the private corporations would have to treat each country as a separate market. And to maximise their world gains, they would operate in a manner that would not be always in the best national interest of any one country. Therefore attempts to evolve national policies on assumptions that national interest can be promoted through foreign capital can only be described as naive.

Profitable Charity

Business, national or international, is run on considerations of profit maximisation; it cannot afford to be charitable. Even when some charity is given, it is with clear business objectives. It may be for image build-up or to oblige someone to seek favours or other considerations which would help to promote business. And secondly, a price charged for supplying goods or services is not determined on the basis of cost; it is particularly in an international market which is far from being a perfect one, a direct function of the comparative bargaining strength of the buyer and the seller. It is obvious that foreign private undertakings in India or elsewhere have primarily to be guided by their objectives to promote and protect the interests of their parent companies located elsewhere.

The initial assumption made in the statement of 1949 was that foreign investors would be willing to invest in India, as they would be able to have higher profits on their capital than what they earned in their home countries. It was, therefore, assured that foreign investing undertakings would face no discrimination and there would be adequate facilities for the remittance of dividends, profits and repatriation of capital. It was further assured that a fair compensation would be paid in case a foreign enterprise was compulsorily acquired. The logic for treating foreign and Indian enterprises on equal basis appears to have been in the belief that the transfer of foreign capital would also be accompanied with modern technology. Foreign capital and technology were not seen different from each other.

In practice, however, it is seen that in India, there is hardly any important foreign enterprise which has not remitted foreign exchange from this country as the payment of dividends and for obtaining technology from the parent company. There are multiple agreements between the parent and their respective subsidiaries. Indian subsidiaries pay for each bit of information shared, advice or service rendered and consideration shown. The holding companies owe no obligations. Any excuse can be good enough to place a charge on the subsidiaries. The amounts and terms of payment are dictated by the parent companies and it is for the Indian managers of the subsidiaries to justify and convince the Indian regulatory agencies of the 'genuine' and specially favourable nature of the demands of the holding company.

The transfer of technology from a parent company to its subsidiary has a different operational significance from that in a case when it is obtained by the government or an Indian private enterprise. In the former case, there is continued and direct supervision to ensure that is no secrets of technology are shared, processes disclosed or equipment copied so as to generate any likelihood of threat of future competition. The transfer of technology to a subsidiary only means a literal shifting of a production unit from the country of the parent company to a location in the country where the subsidiary is operating. If the subsidiary closes down, the transferred technology would also vanish. In a way, the transfer of technology to subsidiaries is a mechanism to build permanent dependency relationships. This is precisely what India is experiencing today. On the other hand, the transfer of technology to locally owned undertakings offers an effective means to exercise judgement and to weigh the cost and benefits of collaboration. It is not uncommon to see the outright purchase of technology for wider dissemination by the public sector institutions. This, however, is not to deny that many Indian private entrepreneurs had entered into agreements of technical collaboration, not so much for obtaining technology as for borrowing trade names and patents.

The policy pronouncements of the government have been to allow the entry of foreign undertakings only in economic activities in whose case indigenous technology was not available. However, if one examines the areas of industrial activity, in respect of which foreign subsidiaries are now operating, one finds that there are a number of products in which, on the one hand, foreign subsidiaries have come to enjoy an important place, the products are also being manufactured by a large number of Indian manufacturers. In fact, one even finds products which are declared to be reserved for cottage and small-scale industries, though foreign companies enjoy a dominant position in manufacturing them. For instance, tooth paste, paints and varnishes, leather footwear, cycle tyres and tubes, hand-tools, safety matches, a number of household electric gadgets, radios, etc., are reserved items for the small-scale sector. In each one of these, there exists a subsidiary or an associate of a multinational. Additionally one finds that for items reserved for manufacturing on a small scale, there are instances in which the installed and the actual production with the multinational subsidiary were in excess of the licensed capacity. For example, in the case of cycle tyres, Dunlop India is licensed for 11,224 thousand tyres, whereas the installed capacity is 14,030 thousand tyres and the actual production during 1976 was 15,368 thousand tyres, and another MNC Goodyear had licensed capacity of 20,00,000 but the actual production during 1976 was reported to be more than 23,00,000 tyres. Such examples can be multiplied.

The consequences of adopting a policy of reservation of products for the small-scale sector, while allowing continuance and even expansion of capacities to large foreign companies for the same products, is, it appears, not fully appreciated by the policy makers. While it may give satisfaction to the policy makers when the list of 'reserved' items for the small industries and the cottage-industries sector gets enlarged, *de facto* such reservations result in the provision of protection to foreign companies instead of help to the small-scale units. Extending the argument a little further, one could show that the foreign companies would, indeed, like to see the day when government would declare all items for the small-scale sector, particularly the products in which they have already made an entry. This declaration could ensure the continuance of 'monopoly position' and conditions under which the foreign undertakings can have a premium on their products and hope to liquidate the tiny units in course of time.

Belied Expectations

New foreign private investment in response to India's policy statement of 1949 was very meagre. For instance, out of the 46 top foreign subsidiaries on the basis of assets (1975), 28 were the ones registered before 1950. Of the remaining 18, from the information available in the official Stock Exchange Directory, only 5 can be said to have entered a new; 12 were floated by the companies already operating in India or were conversions from foreign branches into corporate entities. Thus, in substance, the invitation to foreign private investments was primarily an assurance to the then existing foreign companies for continued support for expansion in Independent India. Since a general assurance of non-discrimination between Indian and foreign investors was promised, by implication, the foreign undertakings became eligible for financial and other support from commercial banks, government and public sector institutions. There was no insistence at any time that rupee or foreign-exchange financial accommodation would not be granted to support the expansion schemes of the foreign companies. The policy pursued, particularly after the foreign-exchange payments for capital imports, services or know-how, the issue of equity shares, should be preferred. The long-term implications of the policy were never fully understood.

It is generally believed that an important and recent development for the regulation of foreign private investments is FERA. FERA places an obligation on all foreign branches operating in India to register themselves under the Companies Act 1956, and secondly, foreign subsidiaries and other foreign-controlled companies are directed to reduce the percentage of shares held abroad. FERA, on the face of it, can result in reducing the level of foreign exchange remittances by foreign companies, as the foreign equity holdings would get reduced to a lower percentage. The FERA strategy, obviously, lies in achieving the dilution of foreign equity. How far this strategy is a misplaced one becomes evident from Table 18.3, showing the pattern of utilising foreign exchange by 133 foreign subsidiaries (1975). It would be seen that dividend payments accounted for less than five per cent of the total foreign exchange utilised by the subsidiaries.

Table 18.3

Showing the Pattern of Foreign Exchange Utilisation by Foreign Subsidiaries (1975-76)

(₹ in thousands)

S.No.	*Head*	*Foreign exchange spent*	*Percentage*
	(1)	*(2)*	*(3)*
1.	Capital goods	65,401	2.95
2.	Raw materials (of which oil imports)	1,092,793 (717,019)	85.71 (32.29)
3.	Spares	47,612	2.14
4.	Interest	13,616	0.61
5.	Dividends	1,10,398	4.97
6.	Know-how	19,581	0.88
7.	Royalty	7,991	0.34
8.	Travelling	2,457	0.11
9.	Commission	17,075	0.77
10.	Others	33,320	1.50
	Total	2,220,144	100.00

Source: Compiled from company annual reports on foreign exchange earnings and utilisation by individual foreign subsidiaries.

MRTP Constraints

MRTP Act, 1969, could be considered another important legislation with reference to the regulation of foreign private investments. Under the MRTP Act, 1969, an undertaking which controls more than one-third of the production of a product has to get itself registered under the act. As mentioned earlier, private foreign investments were expected to be only in such industrial activity in which indigenous technology was not available. On this count one could, therefore, expect that a majority of the foreign subsidiaries, if not all, would be controlling more than one-third of production in their area of activity. However, only a few of the foreign subsidiaries are registered under the MRTP Act as dominant undertakings. This is not to say that these companies are not dominant; these get excluded because of the loopholes in the Indian laws and also the fact that foreign investments are indeed not confined to areas in which indigenous technology was not available. Thus the facts and the role expected from the foreign private investments are at two divergent ends.

Foreign private investments in India since Independence have not filled the capital or the technology gaps, and yet the size of the assets and the turnover under their control have expanded fast. This should be a matter of concern to the Indian policy makers. One way of dealing with foreign private capital would be to have a critical scrutiny of the appropriateness of the enactments, the policies and the mechanisms evolved to regulate the operations of foreign companies. Thus was the task of a full-time commission, the members of which have to be experts drawn from different disciplines. Another approach could be in the establishment of a monitoring system for foreign companies with the clear objective of protecting the national interest. The successful functioning of the monitoring agency would depend upon the organisational capacity and the clarity of the objectives along with adequate powers to secure the necessary information. A primary principle to be accepted is that a policeman on a cycle cannot keep an effective vigil or chase high-speed automobiles.

Section IV

Public Sector

19 Private Managements and Takeovers of Public-owned Companies[1]

Some Issues for Debate

During the last few months the shares of Delhi Cloth Mill (DCM) and Escorts have been in demand. As a consequence, the share prices of these companies have witnessed a sharp rise. In all, it is believed that the overall size of shares changing hands is nearly 4 per cent in the case of DCM and around 1 per cent for the Escorts. The continuing pressure for buying up of the shares of the two companies is seen as a clear bid to dislodge the present managements. It is widely believed that the takeover bid has been engineered by some non-resident Indians (NRI)[2] who have been offered special fiscal concessions to invest in India.

The Federation of Indian Chambers of Commerce and Industry (FICCI), The Associated Chambers of Commerce and Industry of India (ASSOCHAM) and individual representatives of Indian big business have sought government assurance and protection against the takeover bids of important and large private sector companies by some NRIs. A number of suggestions have been made to ensure that the recently declared fiscal concessions to NRIs do not pose any threat to the present managements of Indian private sector companies. Alongwith the argument of possible destability that the takeover bids could lead to, Indian industrialists also feel that unregulated investments by NRIs could result in the national private sector industry falling in the hands of such individuals who had relinquished Indian nationality and chose to stay outside India to make 'dubious fortunes' while 'we have been here' to work for the development

1. *Corporate Studies Group Working Paper* No 7, May 1983.
2. Person of Indian Origin: According to the Finance Bill, 1982, "a person shall be deemed to be of Indian origin if he or either of his parents or any of his grand parents was born in undivided India."

and progress of the country. It has been said that the NRIs are 'raiders' and their unscrupulous attempts to dislodge managements in the 'well-managed' companies should be thwarted in the overall interest of the Indian industrial development.

As a spokesman of the NRIs, Swraj Paul, a family member of the Apeejay Group of Indian enterprises, has described Indian industrialists as 'feudal' and the ones who continue to treat shareholders in a shabby manner. Indian industrialists are, according to Paul, paying extremely low returns on financial investments. It is argued that with enlightened and scientific management, Indian private industry can demonstrate a far higher level of performance than what the 'feudal' managements have delivered to the Indian economy. An argument being put forth is that though 'we left India for various reasons we are still Indians at heart.' We have struggled against all sorts of odds in the white-man-dominated world and in the process, equipped ourselves with the most modern and sophisticated management techniques. We would like to give the benefit of our knowledge, expertise and resources to our own country with which we continue to have strong family and emotional commitment.

Even a remote prospect of losing management control over large companies could make the present managements shiver. The dislodging could mean a near liquidation of their industrial empires and the power they have exercised to oblige and patronise: (i) a host of activities outside the legitimate business activity and (ii) persons and parties who would promote and defend the family interests. The fact that two companies are Delhi-based adds special lustre to their economic and political power. The fight between the Shriram and Nandas on one side and Swraj Paul of the Apeejay Group on the other is an open and a direct one. The issue is: the management control of DCM and Escorts. The FICCI and the ASSOCHAM are making out as if it was an issue of national honour. The present managements are pleading to the sensitivities of the Indians against the 'raiders' and dubious operators. The non-resident investors are talking of ending 'feudal system' and the need for scientific management. The contenders of power and the present family in power are both seeking public support. It is, however, a pity that the view point of the real owners of these private corporate sector entities (the DCM and the Escorts), over which the fight for control has been going on for the last one month, has never been known or discussed. It is only in passing that one hears of the substantial shareholding of public sector financial institutions in these companies. This is mentioned in such a manner and style as if public sector has no option but to support one or the other. The public sector financial institutions are taken for granted by the present managements.

It appears that the precise shareholding structure of the large private sector companies is not widely known. One feels that for an objective public discussion, it is necessary to know the magnitude of the shares held by public sector institutions. It is also necessary to know the pattern of risk sharing in large private sector companies.

Let us take the two companies whose management rights are supposed to be getting traded on the stock exchanges. The DCM has assets of ₹ 184.78 crore (1981) with an equity capital base of ₹ 20.06 crore. The total number of issued and subscribed equity shares is 80.25 lakh (each share value: ₹ 25.00). There are 17,538 shareholders of the company. Of the total equity shares, nearly 10-12 lakh are claimed to be held by the Shri Ram family, friends, associates, family trusts and educational institutions managed by the family and the other family-controlled enterprises. In sharp contrast, public sector financial institutions are holding 34.14 lakh (i.e., 42.54% of the total equity capital). With only 10-12 lakh shares (out of the 80.25 lakh shares), the Shri Ram family cannot control the company without the support of the public sector financial institutions. Another fact, well known to students of the corporate sector, is that in widely held companies a fairly large part of the shareholding is never involved in determining the character of the management. It is only the large shareholders who matter. For instance, the top 10 shareholders of the DCM accounted for 46.54 per cent of the total equity capital. Of the top 10 shareholders of the DCM, 7 are public sector institutions and the 3 private shareholders are: Madan Mohan Lal Shri Ram Pvt. Ltd. (7.85 lakh); Shri Ram Scientific and Industrial Research Foundation (1.62 lakh); and Shri Ram Education Foundation (0.58 lakh). The single largest shareholder was the Life Insurance Corporation (LIC) with 7.95 lakh shares. The above was the picture in June 1980. By December 1982, the shareholding of the public sector had actually increased. For instance, the LIC holding was 10.39 lakh in 1982 as compared to 7.95 lakh shares in 1980. From another angle, one can see that 90 per cent of the shareholders held only 16 per cent of the equity shares (each having shares worth less than ₹ 10,000 only). There is a high degree of concentration of the shares, and it is also obvious that if non-voting shares are excluded, the public sector would enjoy a clear majority at any annual general body meeting. The Shri Rams family cannot remain in control of DCM if it does not have the confidence of the Ministry of Finance who controls public sector financial institutions.

The case of Escorts is still more clear. The public sector financial institutions held more than majority equity in Escorts during 1980. What is the present size of public sector holdings? Informed business circles believe that the majority equity shares of Escorts are still with public sector institutions. The Nandas are in control of Escorts because the government has agreed to keep them in power. The Nandas cannot be dislodged even if someone was to acquire twice the number of Escorts shares as held by the Nandas, provided, however, the government continues to patronise them. On the other hand, with majority equity under control of public sector financial institutions, the government can help anyone (even with or without having a single share of Escorts) to takeover the company management. The Nandas control the Escorts by courtesy of the Ministry of Finance of the Government of India (GoI). They cannot continue to control Escorts even for a day without the political and official patronage of the government. Though there are more than 10,000 shareholders of the company, they cannot determine the character of Escort management.

The present controversy over the DCM and the Escorts should be taken as an opportunity to have a public debate on some basic questions about the: (i) real character of the Indian private corporate sector, (ii) the role of Parliament, (iii) the role of regulation by public sector financial institutions and (iv) questions relating to the government nominee directors on private sector companies.

How Private is the Indian Private Sector?

We give below an illustrative list of large private sector companies in which the public sector financial institutions hold more than 25 per cent of the equity shares. If one goes by the majority concept (i.e., public sector having more than 51 per cent of the shares), the Andhra Pradesh Paper Mill and Hastings Mills, now with Bangur House, should indeed be taken as government companies. Similarly, in terms of voting rights, the Central Pulp Mills, the Escorts, Kohinoor Mills, Poysha Industrial, Kirloskar Pneumatic, Hindustan Brown Boveri, Seshasayaee Paper, Andhra Valley Power, Mangalore Chemicals and Gujarat Alkalies and Chemicals are government companies, as majority risk capital is with the Indian public sector.

According to the Monopolies and Restrictive Trade Practices Act, 1969, one does not require more than 33.3 per cent of equity shares to qualify for being grouped under a house. If the public sector was also treated as a house (which it is in terms of the economic interests in industry, trade and services), all private sector companies in which the public sector held equity was more than 33.3 per cent should be treated as under public sector control. If, however, one was to recognise the business reality and classify companies according to the controlling interest (i.e., single largest group among the share holders or the criteria of 25 per cent as adopted by the Reserve Bank of India (RBI) for assessing foreign assets and liabilities), one would have a larger number of the private sector giants included in the government companies or government-controlled companies. But since these are being presently managed by individual families, it may be appropriate to group these companies as under private management by the courtesy of the government. One may choose any label, but the essential character should be known to public and Parliament.

Role of Parliament

While public sector holdings are not only large but of even a majority nature in a good number of private sector giant companies, Parliament has never been informed of the extent of public stake and the rationality of patronising present managements. This indeed is somewhat strange. If the government can inform Parliament about the Indian Explosives, British India Corporation and Machinery Manufacturers Corporation in which the direct shareholding of the government is less than 10-15 per cent, why should Parliament be kept in total darkness about those companies in which the public sector holdings are in majority? There is a need to discuss and debate the basic issue and for removing the veil of secrecy on issues of public importance. The need for introduction of some sort of public accountability is only too obvious. There could be a special board to coordinate the corporate plans of all large-sized companies in which public sector holds substantial shares. In fact, such a proposition had come from the Prime Minister of India as far back as February 1969 (at Faridabad).

Regulations by the Financial Institutions

There are a lot many loopholes in the regulatory mechanism of the GoI. The government has expressed helplessness in taking effective measures due to inadequate legal authority. The case in point is the absence of appropriate law to make the industrial licence holders respect the conditions as visualised at the time of grant of the licences. Why cannot the financial institutions ensure that the spirit of various legislations is respected by all such companies in which the private managements are wholly dependent upon their support for survival? There can be a policy regarding wages and a ceiling on salaries. It is obvious that there is something basically wrong when all adult members of a family get salaries in lakh of rupees a year, irrespective of their age, qualifications or experience while the major risk capital of the company is provided by public sector financial institutions. There is need to rationalise the large purchases and sales as also other practices which transfer benefits to friends, relatives and other associates. A whole lot of reforms needs to be affected. Why can't a beginning be made with all large size compaies (each having assets of at least ₹ 10.0 crore) and the ones in which public sector holdings were the largest as a block or above 25 per cent in the equity?

Government Nominee Directors

There is need to rationalise the system of government directors. Presently, a good many senior civil servants are being appointed on large private sector companies. When a secretary to the government attends board meetings being presided over by private sector industrialists, there can be a variety of serious implications. Similarly, when retired civil servants get nominated as directors, there are possible dangers about which one needs to be fully aware of. Apart from this, what role does one expect the nominee directors to play in the companies? This is yet not clear.

Concluding Remarks

The issues raised here are of a basic nature. The data provided are only illustrative; one is sure to discover a far more serious public sector involvement in the private sector. Also, to be on the safe side and to avoid overstatement of the case, we have confined to equity shareholding structure. If one were to take note of preference and debenture shares, the responsibility of the government and Parliament in the private sector of India would work out to be far more significant.

Table 19.1

An Illustrative List of Large Private Sector Companies in which more than 25 per cent of the Equity is held by Government and Government-Sponsored Financial Institutions

Sl. No.	*Name of the Company*	*Public Sector Share in Equity (%)*	*Assets (₹ Crore)*
	1	*2*	*3*
AMIN			
1.	Jyoti Ltd. (23.9.82)	46.29	35.45
ACC			
2.	Associated Cement Co.Ltd.(17.12.82)	37.31	201.70#
ASHOK LEYLAND			
3.	Ashok Leyland Ltd.	27.75	236.33@
BANGUR			
4.	Andhra Pradesh Paper Mills Ltd. (29.12.82)	59.87	36.05@
5.	Shree Digvijay Cement Co.Ltd. (29.6.82)	32.15	45.41@
6.	Shreeniwas Cotton Mills Ltd. (28.6.80)	46.97	17.43#
7.	Bengal Paper Mills Co.Ltd. (21.7.82)	26.86	17.09@
8.	Shree Synthetics Ltd. (30.12.82)	26.86	33.48
9.	Fort Gloster Inds. Ltd. (30.9.78)	49.15	9.72@
10.	Graphite India Ltd.	41.82	36.03@
11.	Hastings Mills Ltd. (6.11.79)	53.76	16.80@
BIRD HEILGERS			
12.	Titaghar Paper Mills Co. Ltd. (1979)	45.61	40.78
BIRLA			
13.	Kesoram Inds. & Cotton Mills Ltd. (31.5.82)	38.64	74.58
14.	Bharat Commerce & Inds.Ltd. (23.4.81)	33.06	31.77@
15.	Electric Construction & Equipment Co.Ltd. (7.4.81)	44.31	25.49@
16.	India Steamship Co.Ltd.(30.12.82)	30.82	108.55
17.	Jayshree Tea & Industries Ltd. (1980)	25.94	53.56
18.	Sirpur Paper Mills Ltd. (29.12.79)	42.56	25.39@
19.	Texmaco Ltd. (28.4.77)	31.50	42.33#
20.	Zenith Steel Pipes & Inds. Ltd. (3.10.80)	30.80	56.29

contd...

...contd...

Sl. No. Name of the Company	Public Sector Share in Equity (%)	Assets (₹ Crore)
1	2	3
BOMBAY SUBURBAN		
21. Bombay Suburban Electric Supply Co. Ltd. (23.9.82)	66.43	108.06
CENTRAL PULP		
23. Central Pulp Mills Ltd. (27.3.80)	53.67	21.19@
DLF		
24. Industrial Cables (I) Ltd. (1979)	46.44	26.02*
ESCORTS		
25. Escorts Ltd. (26.6.80)	54.04	104.50@
ELCON ENGG.		
26. Elecon Engg.Co. Ltd. (29.6.82)	26.33	57.09@
ITC		
27. Tribeni Tissues Ltd. (30.4.82)	26.50	27.81@
28. ITC Ltd. (30.8.79)	28.02	210.18
FCC		
29. Calcutta Electric Supply Corpn. (I) Ltd. (24.9.82)	38.46	273.24
30. Dunlop India Ltd. (30.10.82)	33.74	163.82@
31. Indian Aluminium Co.Ltd. (29.4.80)	27.26	155.61@
32. Metal Box India Ltd. (30.12.82)	28.07	103.39@
33. Simon Carves (I) Ltd. (4.6.82)	25.08	13.02@
GV NAIDU		
34. South India Viscose Ltd. (27.6.79)	26.29	36.31
35. Lakshmi Machine Works Ltd. (31.12.82)	47.02	41.86@
ICI		
36. Indian Explosives Ltd. (17.2.81)	25.19	164.08@
37. Alkali & Chemical Corpn. India Ltd. (19.2.82)	29.54	50.52@
38. Crescent Dyes & Chemicals Ltd. (9.2.82)	40.16	13.82@
INDIA CEMENTS		
39. India Cements Ltd. (28.9.79)	48.69	33.04
KAPADIA		
40. National Rayon Corpn. Ltd. (23.6.82)	35.37	55.86@
41. Kohinoor Mills Co. Ltd. (29.9.80)	71.68	15.82@
42. Ahmedabad & Electricity Co. (20.9.79)	38.34	112.97
HN KAPADIA		
43. Poysha Industrial Co.Ltd. (1980)	50.29	17.00
KAMANI		
44. Kamani Engg. Corpn. Ltd. (16.5.80)	49.13	58.24@
KHATAU		
45. Khatau Makhanji Spg.& Wvg. Co.Ltd. (16.10.79)	31.85	25.48@

contd...

...contd...

Sl. No.	*Name of the Company*	*Public Sector Share in Equity (%)*	*Assets (₹ Crore)*
	1	*2*	*3*
KIRLOSKAR			
46.	Kirloskar Electric Co.Ltd. (21.1.83)	38.11	46.28@
47.	Mysore Kirloskar Ltd. (1980)	41.92	22.88@
48.	Kirloskar Pneaumatic Co.Ltd. (1979)	60.42	28.36@
49.	Kirloskar Oil Engines Ltd.	30.79	57.33@
KOTHARI G.D.			
50.	General Indl. Society Ltd. (3.4.80)	30.13	21.86@
KOTHARI D.C.			
51.	Kothari (Madras) Ltd. (22.12.79)	27.57	50.45@
LARSEN & TOUBRO			
52.	Larsen & Toubro Ltd. (24.4.81)	34.74	142.21@
53.	Hindustan Brown Boveri Ltd. (23.10.80)	63.93	50.50
LALBHAI			
54.	Atul Products Ltd. (24.4.80)	34.03	64.44@
55.	Arvind Mills Ltd. (23.6.82)	27.40	46.24@
MAHINDRA			
56.	Mahindra & Mahindra Ltd. (23.4.82)	44.10	129.50
57.	Mahindra Ugine Steel Co. Ltd. (1979)	28.24	86.41@
MODI			
58.	Modipon. Ltd. (31.8.77)	27.14	68.11
59.	Modi Rubber Ltd. (30.4.82)	39.84	93.78@
PARRY			
60.	EID Parry (India) Ltd. (25.6.82)	28.17	57.55@
61.	Herdilla Chemicals Ltd. (16.4.80)	26.92	23.63@
62.	Coromandal Feertilizers Ltd. (2.6.82)	36.64	66.32@
PODAR			
63.	Podar Mills Ltd. (1979)	45.31	13.41#
RAUNAQ SINGH			
64.	Bharat Steel Tubes Ltd. (5.11.82)	42.94	32.96
65.	Appollo Tyres Ltd.	31.64	33.92@
RAJASTHAN SPG.			
66.	Rajasthan Spg. & Wvg. Mills Co.Ltd.	37.88	25.70@
SPIC			
67.	Southern Petro Chemical Inds. Ltd. (23.12.81)	42.59	168.79@
SHRIYANS PRASAD JAIN			
68.	Dhrangadhra Chemicals Works Ltd. (28.9.79)	30.28	29.25
SCINDIA			
69.	Scindia Steam Navigation Co.Ltd.(1980)	34.54	205.13
SHRI AMBICA			
70.	Shri Ambica Mills Ltd. (9.6.80)	31.87	66.03@
SESHASAYEE			
71.	Aluminium Inds. Ltd. (25.9.82)	42.22	34.86
72.	Seshasayaee Paper & Boards Ltd. (21.9.79)	56.73	31.71

contd...

...contd...

Sl. No.	*Name of the Company*	*Public Sector Share in Equity (%)*	*Assets (₹ Crore)*
	1	*2*	*3*
SHRI RAM			
73.	Jay Engineering Works Ltd. (27.8.80)	30.71	28.16@
74.	Delhi Cloth & General Mills Co. Ltd. (28.12.82)	42.54	184.78@
SINGHANIA			
75.	J.K. Industries Ltd. (28.7.80)	35.31	71.28@
76.	Sevenseas Transportation Ltd. (26.5.82)	31.52	17.19
TATA			
77.	Voltas Ltd. (10.2.82)	45.73	126.44@
78.	Tata Engg. & Locomotive Co.Ltd. (24.8.82)	44.84	605.23
79.	Tata Iron & Steel Co. Ltd. (17.8.82)	42.25	687.52
80.	Tata Power Co.Ltd. (23.9.82)	38.40	116.09
81.	Tata Hydro Electric Power Supply Co.Ltd. (24.9.82)	33.92	65.46
82.	Ahmedabad Advance Mills Co. (25.5.81)	42.52	40.20
83.	Svadeshi Mills Co.Ltd. (8.5.79)	37.14	18.17#
84.	Tata Oil Mills Co.Ltd. (1979)	33.89	86.81#
85.	Andhra Valley Power Supply Co.Ltd. (24.9.82)	51.18	93.59
THAPAR			
86.	Ballarpur Inds. Ltd. (22.12.80)	27.00	124.79@
87.	Greaves Cotton & Co.Ltd. (10.12.79)	28.28	49.72@
VISSANJI			
88.	Laxmi Vishnu Textile Mills Ltd. (20.5.80)	28.74	14.70@
VR NAIDU			
89.	Madras Aluminium Co.Ltd. (12.6.80)	33.61	31.81@
WALCHAND			
90.	Premier Automobiles Co.Ltd. (1980)	25.83	50.66
WALLACE			
91.	Bombay Burmah Trading Co. Ltd. (19.3.80)	34.00	20.65@
OTHERS			
92.	Mangalore Chemicals & Fertilizers Ltd. (28.7.82)	52.09	81.48@
93.	Gujarat Alkalies & Chemicals Ltd. (29.9.82)	50.57	24.94
94.	Sayaji Mills Ltd. (1982)	25.93	15.76
95.	Jain Tube Co.Ltd. (29.4.78)	27.05	15.56@
96.	Star Paper Mills Co.Ltd. (26.9.79)	27.88	19.40
97.	Gujarat State Fertilizers Ltd. (31.12.82)	74.12	178.96@

Note: 1. Date in brackets in col.1 given alongwith the name of company indicates the date of the 'Share Distribution Schedule.'

2. Assets data in col.3 : Unless indicated otherwise asset data are for the year 1982; * indicates data for 1979; # for 1980; and @ for 1981.

3. FCC indicates foreign-controlled companies.

4. The house classification is as per the Corporate Information System (CIS) of the Indian Institute of Public Administration (IIPA).

20 Public Accountability of Deemed Government Companies[1]

Under Section 619(B) of the Companies Act, 1956, companies in which more than 51 per cent of equity shares are held, singly or jointly, by one or more governments and government companies or corporations have to be treated as 'deemed government companies.'[2] These companies fall within the purview of the Comptroller and Auditor General of India (C&AG). This is to ensure a certain degree of public accountability. For purposes of the audit of accounts, the 'deemed' government companies have to be dealt in "the same manner as adopted for government companies."[3]

The C&AG since 1978, in its annual report, has been listing the names of all such companies in which majority equity is held by the central government and/or central government companies and corporations. According to C&AG, "on 31st March 1977 there were 40 companies coming within the provisions of Section 619(B) of the Companies Act

---

1. *Corporate Studies Group Working Paper* No. 8, August 1983.
2. *Report of the Comptroller and Auditor General, 1980* (Commercial : Part I), p.iii.
3. Section 619(2) of the Companies Act, 1956, which is applicable to government companies as defined under Section 619(B) provides that:

   "The auditor of a Government Company shall be appointed or re appointed by the Central Government on the advice of the Comptroller and Auditor General of India."

   Further the Section 619(3) states that:

   "The Comptroller and Auditor General shall have power

   (a) to direct the manner in which the company's accounts shall be audited by the auditor appointed in pursuance of sub section (2) and to give such auditor instructions in regard to any matter relating to the performance of his functions as such;

   (b) To conduct a supplementary or test audit of the company's accounts by such person or persons as he may authorise in this behalf; ...."

1956."[4] For the year 1982, the number of companies falling under Section 619(B) were only 53. The full list is given in the Appendix A-20.1. The *Company News and Notes*, an official monthly journal of the Department of Company Affairs, reports names of the companies in which auditors are appointed by the Government on the advice of the C&AG. The list, prepared on the basis of the *Company News and Notes*, includes 115 companies which are more than twice the number of companies reported by C&AG. This raises a question: By which information source should one rely on: C&AG or Department of Company Affairs?

A related question is what has been happening to the 'audit reports' of 'deemed' government companies? Why did the C&AG not comment on these according to its own understanding? "These have to be treated in the same manner as the government companies." The C&AG gives only the names of the companies covered under the provision and does not show whether the annual accounts have been received or not. For instance, the main information on 619(B) companies for the year 1982 is that out of the 53 companies falling under Section 619(B), the accounts for 1980-81 were received only from 35. Why have the accounts not been received for rest of the companies?

In the recent controversy over the takeover bids, it has been admitted by the government and company management that majority equity shares in Escorts are held by public sector financial institutions. A list of companies in which public sector institutions held more than 25 per cent of the equity capital had been included in an earlier study of ours.[5] The study showed that there were 12 companies in which the public sector and government holding was more than 51 per cent. The names of these companies are given in Table 20.1.

Out of the 12 companies listed in the table, strangely enough, only one company finds a place in the C&AG Report or in the information published by the *Company News and Notes*. Why have auditors not been appointed by the government in these companies in consultation with the C&AG? This becomes particularly relevant because each one of the companies included

---

4. Ibid.: 50.
5. Goyal, S.K. (1983). "Private Managements and Takeovers of Public Owned Companies Some Issues for Debate", Working Paper No. 7, Corporate Studies Group, Indian Institute of Public Administration, New Delhi. May.

Table 20.1

An Illustrative List of Companies in which Public Sector Financial Institutions held more than 51 per cent Equity

S. No.	Name of the Company	Year	% Equity held by by Public Sector	Assets (₹ Crore)
	1	2	3	4
1.	Andhra Pradesh Paper Mills Ltd. (Bangur)	1982	59.87	36.05 (1981)
2.	Hastings Mills Ltd. (Bangur)	1979	53.76	16.80 (1981)
3.	Bombay Suburban Electric Supply Co. Ltd. (Bombay Suburban)	1982	66.43	108.06 (1982)
4.	Central Pulp Mills Ltd. (Central Pulp)	1980	53.67	21.19 (1981)
5.	Escorts Ltd. (Escorts)	1979	54.04	104.50 (1981)
6.	Kohinoor Mills Co. Ltd. (Kapadia)	1980	71.68	15.82 (1981)
7.	Kirloskar Pneumatic Co. Ltd. (Kirloskar)	1979	60.42	28.26 (1981)
8.	Hindustan Brown Boveri Ltd. (Larsen & Toubro)	1980	63.93	50.50 (1982)
9.	Seshasayee Paper & Boards Ltd. (Seshasayee)	1979	56.73	31.71 (1982)
10.	Andhra Valley Power Supply Co. Ltd. (Tata)	1982	51.18	93.59 (1982)
11.	Mangalore Chemicals & Fertilizers Ltd.	1982	52.09	81.48 (1981)
12.	Gujarat State Fertilisers Ltd.	1982	74.12	178.96 (1981)

Source: Corporate Information System (CIS) of the Indian Institute of Public Administration (IIPA).

in the above list is a large one—the smallest undertaking having assets of ₹ 15.82 crore in 1981. It is not a technical and formal question whether the audit has been conducted by the auditors appointed by the C&AG or the ones appointed at the company's annual general meeting. One does believe that in both the situations, the auditors would be constituted from among a group of independent professionals. The real difference in this is that if the C&AG does not report on these companies to Parliament, the Public Accounts Committee (PAC) would have no jurisdiction in the matter. The PAC does not concern itself to the spheres not audited by the

C&AG. Thus, by keeping some of the large companies, in which public sector holding is in majority, outside the Section 619(B) of the Companies Act, 1956, Parliament is being denied the opportunity to ask any questions about 'deemed government companies.' In short, a large part of the public investments in the private sector remains outside the domain of public accountability.

The companies involved are large sized ones. Therefore, it is inappropriate to ignore the exclusion of these from the purview of the C&AG. An equally important aspect of the exclusion of the companies, from the applicability of the Section 619(B), is that each one of these 12 companies happens to be managed by one or the other large private sector industrial house as registered under the Monopolies & Restrictive Trade Practices (MRTP) Act, 1969. One could understand if a 'deemed government company' was placed under a group of management professionals with all autonomy required for efficient management of the enterprise. But there are cases where undertakings are continuing as family-owned undertakings as if the public sector, the government or the people of India have no stake or right to ask questions as to how the public assets were being controlled and managed. Viewed from another angle, it appears as if certain public assets have been left under private control of some families who find favour with the government of the time. There are a variety of political implications arising out of this situation.

A careful reading of the C&AG reports shows that the list of companies, covered by the C&AG under 619(B), is restricted only to companies in which "central government companies and corporations had dominant shares." This is a limited interpretation of the Section 619(B). The provisions of the Section 619(B) cover investments in equity held both by central and state governments and their corporations and companies. By excluding the state public-sector-held equity shares, the spirit of the legislation is bound to get defeated. It is, probably, because of this that many of the private managements have been able to avoid public accountability by manipulating the equity holdings in such a manner that the central or state sector, when accounted individually, does not have 51 per cent or more shares in companies controlled by them. Under the presently adopted practice, if 49 per cent shares in a company are held by the LIC and another 49 per cent are held by a State Industrial Development Corporation, the company would remain outside the purview of the C&AG—even though the combined stake of the public sector in the risk capital of the company was as high as 98 per cent. This may be a hypothetical case, but one does find the existence of a good number of such cases where the combined share of the central and state public sectors is more than 51 per cent and none of these is subject to review by the C&AG. An illustrative list of such cases is given in Table 20.2.

Table 20.2

List of Additional Companies with 51 per cent or more Equity Capital held by Public Sector Financial Institutions

S. No.	Name of the Company	Year	Public Sector	Assets (₹ Crore)
	1	2	3	4
1.	Bombay Wire Ropes Ltd.	1981	52.17	472.71 (1980)
2.	Banswara Syntex Ltd.	1979	82.15	1090.62 (1981)
3.	Gujarat Aromatics Ltd.	1979	52.02	1093.07 (1980)
4.	Madras Oxygen & Acetyleni Co. Ltd.	1980	57.11	
5.	Nagarjuna Steels Ltd.	1980	68.36	647.70 (1978)
6.	Orient Plywood and Veneering Inds. Ltd.	1980	57.58	
7.	Poysha Industrial Co. Ltd.	1980	52.86	1817.08 (1980)
8.	Refractories Specialities (I) Ltd.	1980	60.00	268.53 (1981)
9.	Siporex India Ltd.	1980	52.72	253.12 (1981)
10.	Shree Diguijaya Woollen Mills Ltd.	1979	50.40	939.38 (1981)
11.	Solid Containers Ltd.	1980	55.60	150.74 (1980)
12.	Uniloids Ltd.	1979	66.13	229.29 (1981)
13.	Vikrant Tyres Ltd.	1980	71.31	4336.51 (1981)
14.	W.S. Insulators (I) Ltd.	1980	64.19	1886.17 (1981)

Source: Same as Table 20.1.

Some of the instances mentioned in this may happen to be the cases of 'joint sector' enterprises—the undertakings in which the equity held by a State Industrial Development Corporation was 26 per cent and the private promoters are permitted to hold 25 per cent of shares. The intention in promoting the joint sector was that since the majority shares would be held by the private entrepreneur (the co-promoter) and the state-level promotional body, private management could remain assured of stability of management control. However, most of state-level joint sector enterprises, it is well known, have also been able to involve central public sector financial institutions. The participation of the public at large has been low. This has led to a situation where in the public sector (central and state) has the majority equity, but companies are able to avoid accountability to the C&AG, Parliament and state legislatures.

The exclusion of state public sector held equity shares, for determining whether the C&AG should be consulted for appointment of auditors, could have a variety of serious implications. There is need to have a clear policy in this regard. One could, for the sake of argument, take a view that establishment of the 'joint sector' was aimed to promote new entrepreneurs; and the enterprises in the joint sector are small in their operations. Therefore, the size of the assets involved, which remain outside the area of public accountability, could not be very large. Going by this reasoning one may accept that 'joint sector' and state promoted companies should be kept out of the public gaze during the initial period—or even during the subsequent period. It may appear to be a good, practical and business-like approach. The two assumptions in the above argument, however, are: (i) that the private promoter is a new entrepreneur and (ii) the size of the undertaking is a small one.

Will all the state joint sector enterprises satisfy the two criteria? Table 20.3 provides an illustrative list of state joint sector enterprises which the state governments have promoted in collaboration with well-known monopoly houses of the country. From the view point of size of the assets too, these can in no way be regarded as cases of marginal significance. There is, therefore, a need for a policy that would ensure public accountability of the joint sector enterprises, particularly when the combined stake of the central and state sectors happens to be a substantial one.

Table 20.3

Illustrative List of Joint Sector Companies Promoted by the State Industrial Corporations in Collaboration with Monopoly Houses

S. No.	Company	House	Assets (₹ Lakh)	Year
	1	2	3	4
1.	Bihar Air Products Ltd.	S.Mull Nagar Mull	100.00	1981
2.	Bihar Caustic & Chemicals Ltd.	Birla	240.05	1982
3.	Deccan Fibre Glass Ltd.	Goenka	131.67	1980
4.	Gujarat Aromatics Ltd.	K.Bhai L.Bhai	1093.08	1980
5.	Gujarat Carbon Ltd.	Goenka	894.45	1981
6.	IPIBEL Refractories Ltd.	Tata	679.47	1982
7.	Karnataka Oxygen Ltd.	TCI	180.08	1981
8.	LORCOM Protectives Ltd.	TTK	130.00	1982
9.	Maharashtra Scooters Ltd.	Bajaj	598.81	1982
10.	Mandovi Pellets Ltd.	Chowgule	7192.77	1981
11.	Mysore Petrochemicals Ltd.	Bangur	828.56	1981
12.	Punjab United Pesticides Ltd.	Tata II (Excel Industries)	331.41	1981
13.	Southers Petrochemicals Industries Ltd.	Chidambram	16879.93	1981

Source: Corporate Information System, Indian Institute of Public Administration (IIPA), New Delhi.

If one goes by the spirit of the Companies Act, 1956, it is obvious that whenever 51 per cent of shareholdings are mentioned, the reference is to the majority. It could not be the intention of Parliament or the law makers that 50.1 per cent does not make a majority but 51.0 per cent does. While interpreting the Companies Act, 1956, it appears that the Department of Company Affairs would take a technical position and insist on excluding companies like Gujarat Alkalies & Chemicals in which the public sector holding is 50.57. Similarly, this was the position taken by the government with regard to Jessop & Company where the government shareholding is 50.13 per cent.[6] The intent and purpose of the law would be better served if one took a more pragmatic view and sought to extend the scope of public accountability to all such companies in which public sector held 40 per

6. Morarka, R.R. (1971). "PAC—How to make It More Effective", *Public Accounts Committee (Parliament of India)*, 1921-1971, Golden Jubilee Souvenir, Lok Sabha Secretariat, p.41.

cent and more of equity and it also happens to be the largest shareholder. The logic of the cut-off point being at 40 per cent is well recognised and the Foreign Exchange Regulation Act, 1973, is based on this rule. The MRTP Act, however, has 33.3 per cent as the cut-off point. The Reserve Bank of India (RBI) had for long followed 25 per cent as the cut-off point for determining the character of foreign controlled companies. Incidentally, for determining if a company was a foreign-controlled one or not; the cut-off point in US is 10 per cent only. The limited point being made here is that one should have adequate public accountability for undertakings for which the single largest part of risk capital has been provided out of the public funds.

In India, this approach to public accountability has, however, been flouted by the government herself. Normally, one should expect that in a democratic set-up the government would enlarge the area of public accountability, but, strangely enough, the Government in India (GoI) has sought to reduce its own role and allow public assets to be managed by private individuals with no public accountability. In matter of Section 619(B) of the Companies Act, 1956, there is no distinction between public sector companies: whether owned by central or state governments, the control and ownership being under a statute or under the Companies Act, or the public sector organisation being a promotional, investment or any other type of undertaking. The essence is investments by the public sector; and hence the need for accountability to Parliament through the C&AG.

The C&AG in its report for the year 1980 (Part I, Introduction: Union Government: Commercial) has the following statement:

> Industrial Finance Corporation of India and Industrial Credit and Investment Corporation of India Limited which *were originally notified as institutions owned or controlled by central government were subsequently denotified by the Department of Company Affairs* (p.51) (emphasis added).

How and why should the Department of Company Affairs *denotify* a public financial institution for purposes of the Section 619(B)? It tends to become a mystery. The operational significance of the denotification lies in the unavoidable consequence that some of the companies which would have been covered under the C&AG would no more have the obligation to be treated under the Section 619(B). Table 20.4 shows how with denotification and by keeping some of the public investments outside, the private sector companies get excluded from the obligation to face audit by the C&AG.

Table 20.4

Illustrative List of Companies where Public Sector Financial Institutions held more than 51 per cent Share Holding Excluding the Institutions Denotified

S. No.	Company	Total Public Sector Holding (%)	Public Sector Share Holding	
			Excluding IFCI and ICICI (%)	Excluding UTI, ICICI, IFCI
	1	2	3	4
1.	Andhra Valley Power Supply Co. Ltd.	51.18	51.18	36.58
2.	Andhra Pradesh Paper Mills Ltd.	59.87	59.73	52.57
3.	Bombay Suburban Electric Supply Co. Ltd.	66.43	66.43	48.20
4.	Mangalore Chemicals & Fertilizers Ltd.	52.09	46.96	45.91
5.	Gujarat State Fertilizers Co. Ltd.	74.12	74.12	72.36
6.	Kohinoor Mills Co. Ltd.	71.68	71.68	71.68
7.	Hindustan Brown Boveri Ltd.	63.93	63.93	46.87
8.	Seshasayee Paper & Boards Ltd.	56.73	56.73	46.91
9.	Hasting Mills Ltd.	53.76	53.76	53.76
10.	Central Pulp Mills Ltd.	53.67	27.00	27.00
11.	Escorts Ltd.	54.04	54.04	48.02

Source: Same as Table 20.1.

It is not proper to suggest that there was a conspiracy by some in government to promote private interests. This, however, should not restrain the policy makers to openly acknowledge that the denotification would exclude same companies from the net of the public accountability. Which are these companies? It may make an interesting case study in governmental decision-making to ask: Who, during 1980, initiated the move to declare that Industrial Finance Corporation of India (IFCI) and Industrial Credit and Investment Corporation of India Ltd. (ICICI) are not government-controlled companies? And if the denotification had to be done, why feel shy of retaining the Life Insurance Corporation (LIC) or the Industrial Development Bank of India (IDBI)? Why exclude the shares held by Unit Trust of India (UTI)? These questions need to be probed and discussed. One would have to ask: Can one government department change the ownership and control category of an institution which was under control of another administrative ministry?

We have examined some of the available annual reports of the companies which, according to the spirit of the Companies Act, 1956, should have been brought under Section 619(B). In the case of the Escorts, though the public-sector held shares in 1980 were around 54 per cent, the company Annual Reports for 1977, 1979 or 1980 make no mention of the need to appoint auditors by the C&AG. In fact, the company does not even mention about the need to appoint the auditors by adopting a special resolution as required under Section 224(A) of the Companies Act, 1956, which is necessary if the public sector holdings were more than 25 per cent. Hindustan Brown Boveri, Seshasayee Paper, Andhra Valley Power and Mangalore Chemicals adopted a special resolution (as if the shares held by public sector were less than 51% but more than 25%) for appointment of auditors. There are, of course, instances wherein the managements inform the shareholders that a request has been made to the government to appoint auditors under Section 619(B). The Maharashtra Elecktrosmelt Ltd. is a case in point.

The need to have public accountability for all substantial public investments is only too obvious. For this, one could go by a certain percentage and fix any one cut-off point. It could be 25, 33 or 40 per cent. In addition to this, on operational considerations, one could confine C&AG audit for only large-sized companies, say, each with assets of ₹ 10 crore and more. Parliament could also introduce the element of size of the public stake by making it obligatory to have C&AG audit for companies in which more than ₹ 1.0 crore had been invested in the paid-up capital (PUC). One could evolve an appropriate method with the basic objective of ensuring that private managements of large companies are not allowed to play about with the public resources without any public responsibility or accountability which seems to be the case today.

A popular belief in government has been that whenever public sector investments are large or substantial, the government and public sector financial institutions should appoint institutional directors on the company boards. While for long it has been the practice to have nominee directors, it is time that one asked seriously if this institution has served much purpose. What role have the nominee directors been playing? How are they selected? What does one expect them to watch? To put it conversely, the nominee directors are a 'watch dog' for the institution or are they supposed to be officers in government who would ensure quicker disposal of the company files requiring government approval? Has the appointment of government directors helped to restrain the private boards to violate other regulatory laws and public norms? Is the institution of nominee directors seen, in the business circles, as an advantage or a handicap? Will not any large private sector company like to have, if possible, finance ministers on their board? Why do private companies have retired army generals and senior civil servants on their boards? These are questions which need to be examined dispassionately.

Another question with regard to public accountability is: what purpose does one wish to achieve by enlarging the coverage of public accountability. Is the intention to curb possibilities of organised frauds on public at large and the government? Or, the purpose of public accountability is merely to enable some questions being raised in Parliament and enhance restrictions on company managements? Such limited and narrow view cannot be the purpose of public accountability. The real objective of the public accountability would be to coordinate investments in an overall framework of planned socioeconomic development. The objective could also be to restrict anti-social activities by the private managements and promotion of healthy management practices. These are issues of public importance and need an open debate.

Appendix A-20.1

List of Companies Reported by the C&AG in its Annual Report 1982 to be covered under Section 619(B) of the Companies Act 1956

S.No.	*Name of the Company*
1.	Ashok Paper Mills Ltd.
2.	Andhra Pradesh Industrial and Technical Consultancy Organisation Ltd.
3.	Agricultural Finance Corporation Ltd.
4.	Bihar Industrial and Technical Consultancy Organisation Ltd.
5.	Banarhat Tea Co. Ltd.
6.	Coromandal Agro Products and Oil Ltd.
7.	Delta Paper Mills Ltd.
8.	Derco Cooling Coils Ltd.
9.	Hydrocarbons India Ltd. (Sub of ONGC)
10.	Hoolungoorea Tea Co Ltd.
11.	Indian Fine Blanks Ltd.
12.	Industrial Reconstruction Corporation of India Ltd.
13.	Industrial and Technical Consultancy Organisation of Tamil Nadu Ltd.
14.	J&K Industrial & Technical Consultancy Organisation Ltd.
15.	Kerala Industrial and Technical Consultancy Organisation Ltd.
16.	Madan Industries Ltd.
17.	Nagarjuna Steels Ltd.
18.	Neiveli Ceramics and Refractories Ltd.
19.	Orissa Industrial and Technical Consultancy Organisation Ltd.
20.	North Eastern Industrial and Technical Consultancy Organisation Ltd.
21.	Punjab Tractors Ltd.
22.	Shriram Pistons and Rings Ltd.
23.	Siporex India Ltd.
24.	Braith Waite Burn and Jessop Construction Co. Ltd.
25.	Mim Tea Co Ltd.
26.	Industrial Credit and Investment Corpn. of India Ltd.
27.	Universal Conveyor Beltings Ltd.
28.	U.P. Industrial Consultants Ltd.
29.	Vikrant Tyres Ltd.
30.	Wagon India Ltd.
31.	West Bengal Consultancy Organisation Ltd.

contd...

...*contd*...

32.	Allied International Products Ltd.
33.	Accumeasures Punjab Ltd.
34.	Associated Glass Industries Ltd.
35.	Brindavan Alloys Ltd.
36.	Bengal Assam Steamship Co. Ltd.
37.	Excellsior Plants Corporations Ltd.
38.	Gangawati Sugars Ltd.
39.	Gayday Iron and Steel Co. Ltd.
40.	Kohinoor Mills Co. Ltd.
41.	Mandovi Pellets Ltd.
42.	Nalanda Ceramics and Industries Ltd.
43.	Orissa Fertilizers and Chemicals Ltd.
44.	Pandayan Hotels Ltd.
45.	Protein Products of India Ltd.
46.	Shyam Properties Ltd.
47.	Textile Processing Corporation of India Ltd.
48.	Vidyut Steels Ltd.
49.	West India Chemicals Ltd.
50.	Webel Electro Ceramics Ltd.
51.	North Bengal Dolomite Ltd.
52.	Dishergarh Power Supply Co. Ltd.
53.	Vayudoot (P) Ltd.

21 Privatisation of Public Enterprises

Some Issues for Debate[1]

I

The Indian economy is a weak, though large, subsystem of the capitalist world. This, of course, is not to argue that it does not have unique features of its own. Nor is this to overlook the varied and meaningful economic and political association of the country with socialist societies. An overwhelming part of the country's foreign trade is with countries having market-oriented economic structures.[2] The main source of foreign aid is the industrialised west and the international institutions, like the International Monetary Fund (IMF), IBRD (World Bank) and International Finance Corporation (IFC) on which the country's development plans have depended substantially, are under direct control and domination of the countries of the capitalist world.[3] India has also foreign private interests in the form of direct investments by transnational corporations (TNCs) along with a very extensive coverage by technical, trade and financial agreements entered into by TNCs with India's influential private monopoly establishments, as also most of the central government-controlled public enterprises. In addition to all above, the inflow of information, ideas and values from the market-oriented societies is more frequent and intense than that from socialist societies. The channels of communication are

1. *Corporate Studies Working Paper* no. 11, Paper presented at an Institute of Public Enterprises-London Business School International Seminar on Public Enterprise Policy in the Eighties, February 11-14, 1985, Hyderabad.
2. The share of countries of Eastern Europe in imports was around 10-11 per cent and around 22 per cent in exports. See INDIA: *Economic Survey, 1982-83*, pp. 62-65.
3. Of the total external assistance during 1982-83, the share of the USSR and Czechoslovakia was 4.35 per cent as against 29.8 per cent of the Western market-oriented countries. IBRD and IDA accounted for 55.2 per cent. See ibid.: 152.

printed media (thanks to the English language being the language of the economic, administrative and social elite of India), conferences, seminars, lecture tours of distinguished scholars and, above all, the experience and participation of key Indian policy makers in international fora which are basically for promotion and development of an international order, that is conceived to primarily find solutions for the problems faced by the industrially advanced societies. In short, the Indian economy cannot be treated as independent of the economic developments and trends of thought in the advanced market economies.

In the UK, the policy of privatisation has been resorted to by the Thatcher government. The sale, however, has been mainly confined to profit-making public enterprises. While Jaguar, British Aerospace and some North Sea Oil enterprises have been already sold to private interests, the shares of the British Telecom were reported to be on sale. British Airlines, it is expected, would be also one sale in a few months. Thatcher government policy to privatise public enterprises has to be seen in the background of the successes with which the Reagan administration is claimed to have solved the US economic problems.[4] Whether it is described as Reaganomics, supply side economics or the contributions of Friedman, the fact does remain that in contrast to the earlier enlarged and expanding role of the state after the Second World War, it is being argued that the state should involve itself in the economic activity only if it cannot avoid it. Liberalisation of controls and deregulations are acquiring political respectability.

The discussion on the question of privatisation of public enterprises in India is of very recent origin. During the last few months, it seems to have become an issue of debate because many seem to believe that it is under active consideration by the Indian policy makers. While there is no official policy document to confirm the likely adoption of the privatisation policy, there do happen to be a number of significant press reports in this regard. Prakash Tandon, in his Nehru Memorial Lecture, 1984, posed the question:

> First and foremost we should decide whether we wish to keep it as public sector, as it is, a state sector. Today public has no say, no ownership, no control. It is owned and wholly run by the state, its political and

4. Fitchett, Joseph (1984). "Privatisation of British Phones" and "Privatisation for Better Result", *Times of India*, October 15-16.

> administrative set up and the public is rigidly kept out of it except, it might be argued, through Parliament.[5]

After making a frontal attack on the very philosophy of public sector and expressing a doubt on the capability and legitimacy of Parliament, he proposed privatisation of profitable public enterprises and the need to follow the management strategies of TNCs.

Nitish Sengupta following the lead given by Tandon argued:

> ... A start could be made selectively with about five to ten such enterprises... There would surely be an overwhelming response if companies such as STC, MMTC, HMT or BHEL make available some of their shares, say 24 per cent to the public... (This) will be desirable from the point of resources gathering...[6]

The suggestion for privatisation has been editorially supported by some of the leading financial dailies. While no concrete plan for privatisation of public enterprises appears to have been prepared, it would not be surprising if such policy proposals attract support from influential quarters.

II

The plea for privatisation of public enterprises should not be seen as an independent and isolated decision by itself. It falls in the overall framework of a policy of reduced public interventions, both direct and indirect, in order to direct and influence the structure and working of the economy. Withdrawal of direct government involvement in the economy implies a shift towards a philosophy and a belief that the pattern of new investments and deployment of national productive resources can be left to be determined by market forces of demand and supply, thus avoiding the distortions which allegedly follow state interventions. The privatisation policy has to be accompanied by withdrawal of administrative controls, licensing and other policies which restrict free interplay of market forces. The logic would also suggest that private monopolies, national and international, are in principle, desirable and necessary for efficient and low-cost production which, it is believed, can be harnessed only with the economies of scale of large industrial units.

---

5. *Economic Times*, August 31, 1984.
6. Sengupta, Nitish (1984). "The Case for Limited Private Share Holding", *Economic Times*, November 2.

The policy towards the reduced role of the state does also suggest that instead of adopting national plan exercises and undertaking large public outlays, the state should basically confine itself to its limited role of maintaining law and order, supplemented by appropriate fiscal and monetary policies to protect vulnerable sections or to achieve well-defined specific objectives.

Viewed from another angle, handing over of public enterprises to private managements can help to achieve what most democratic governments cannot. For instance, private managements would be able to close down such economic activities which were not remunerative. It may affect closure of units established for considerations of providing certain special opportunities for backward regions. It could order the closure of all airline services to hilly areas as well as of the running of train services on the loss making routes. Cutting down of the labour bill through retrenchment or withdrawal of certain financial payments and other obligations is more easily possible through the medium private managements than the public sector. Similarly, private managements can act faster and without much hesitation on questions of price escalation of output and services, and also implement the best product mix to reap full advantages of the market.

The basic difference between private managements and those of the public sector lies in the accountability of the formers' managements to a few (who are the dominant shareholders) rather than to the large many shareholders or to the public at large who may have no direct stake in the enterprise. In substance, 'privatisation' means shifting of the responsibility to take harsh and unpopular decisions from the public policy making quarters to a few, who have, direct vested interests in generating returns to their investments but have no pretensions to safeguard or promote public interest.

The post Second World War period witnessed the emergence of many new liberated countries. Also, at that time in the market-oriented group of economies, it was an unquestioned belief that 'state' has to play a direct and effective role in the reconstruction of the war hit economies. The socialist bloc of countries had always stood for an ever growing role of state in the restructuring of their economies. These trends in the market-oriented economies have come to be restricted by the experience of what is generally claimed as the success story of the US administration under Reagan. And the same is claimed to have happened in Britain under the stewardship of Margaret Thatcher. One may call this Reagonomics, supply side economics or the influence of Friedman. There is a clear thrust towards the reduction of economic intervention by the state in both the US and the UK. The influence of these two countries on internal economic policies of the other market-oriented societies is also clearly discernible. This is irrespective of the character of the political parties in power of, say, Sweden or France.

III

Quite apart from the limited discussion on privatisation as inspired by the happenings in the industrially advanced countries of the west, the public sector in India has been responsible for the establishment and promotion of enterprises which were later handed over to private parties. The process has, however, been confined to state-level public enterprises. Table 21.1 lists some of the government companies which got converted into non-government companies during the last one decade.

Table 21.1

Government Companies Converted into Non-Government Companies during 1973-1983

(i) India Tea & Restaurant Ltd.	1982-83
(i) Andhra Pradesh State Seeds Development Corpn. Ltd.	1981-82
(ii) Rajasthan State Seeds Corpn. Ltd.	
(iii) Rourkela Fabrications Ltd.	
(i) Andhra Pradesh Oil & Chemicals Industries Ltd.	1980-81
(ii) Hindustan Diamond Co. Ltd.	
(iii) Samachar Bharati	
(iv) Deccan Fibre Glass Ltd.	
(v) Andhra Pradesh Refractories Ltd.	
(vi) Utkal Foundry & Engg. Co. Ltd.	
(vii) Madhya Pradesh Vidyut Yantra Ltd.	
(viii) Orissa Tools & Engg. Co. Ltd.	
(ix) Malwa Cotton Seed Products Ltd.	
(x) Punjab Engineers Cuting Tools Ltd.	
(xi) Karnataka Blades Ltd.	
(i) Hyderabad Connectronics Ltd. (1)	1979-80
(ii) Transformers & Electricals Kerala Ltd.	
(iii) Gujarat State Machine Tools Corpn. Ltd.	
(i) Gujarat Aromatics Ltd.	1978-79
(ii) Punjab Breweries Ltd.	
(iii) Andhra Pradesh Rayons Ltd.	
(iv) Almora Magnesite Ltd.	

contd...

...contd...

(i) M.P. Agro Morarji Fertilizers Ltd. (2) (ii) Maharashtra Scooters Ltd. (2) (iii) Himachal Consultancy Organisation Ltd. (iv) U.P. Twiga Fibreglass Ltd.	1977-78
(i) Aravali Svachalit Vahan Ltd. (ii) Gujarat Alkalis & Chemicals Ltd. (iii) Jagannath Chemicals & Pharmaceutical Works Ltd. (iv) Fibre Foam Ltd. (3) (v) Orissa Concrete Products Ltd. (vi) Meghalaya Essential Oil & Chemicals Ltd. (vii) Industrial Papers Assam Ltd.	1976-77
(i) Andhra Pradesh Automobile Tyres & Tubes Ltd. (ii) Gujarat Carbon Ltd. (iii) Wagon India Ltd.	1975-76
(i) Manganese Ore Ltd. (4) (ii) Punjab Concast Steel	1974-75
(i) Punjab Tractors Ltd.	1973-74

Note: (1) Converted into a government company from a non-government company during 1977-78.
(2) Converted into government companies during 1976-77.
(3) Converted into a government company during 1974-75.
(4) Converted again into a government company during 1978-79.

Source: *Annual Reports on the Working & Administration of the Companies Act, 1956*, various issues.

In most of these cases, the initial industrial licence was obtained by a state industrial development corporation. It was argued by some state governments that initial establishment of these was necessary to promote the process of industrialisation in the state and to encourage local entrepreneurs. There is, however, some evidence to suggest that privatisation of many of such undertakings has been to benefit the already well-established industrial houses and not the local professionals or new entrepreneurs. Andhra Pradesh Rayon and Karnataka Blades Ltd. are cases in point. One needs to discuss the place and role of this process in which state governments bear the risk and nurture the enterprises, and only when the enterprises are on the threshold of making profits, the ownership and management gets transferred to private parties. What are the advantages of such a planned privatisation process? And who derives them?

The number of companies that have been privatised may not be very large. But another sector which generally goes without much attention is the joint sector. Appendix Table A-21.1 provides an illustrative list of joint sector companies which have been established by state governments in collaboration with one or the other national monopoly house.

In this respect, there is a need to underline that there are a large number of enterprises in which the majority or the main stake in the equity capital is that of public sector financial institutions. Table 21.2 gives an illustrative list of large private sector companies in which more than 25 per cent of the equity is held by government and government-sponsored financial institutions. We have listed here only large companies with assets or turnover of ₹ 10.00 crore and above. The number, otherwise, would be more than 300.

Table 21.2

An Illustrative List of Large Private Sector Companies in which more than 25 per cent of the Equity is held by Government and Government-Sponsored Financial Institutions

Sl. No.	Name of the Company	Public Sector Share in Equity (%)	Assets (₹ Crore)
	1	2	3
AMIN			
1.	Jyoti Ltd. (23.9.82)	46.29	35.45
ACC			
2.	Associated Cement Co. Ltd.	37.31	201.70#
ASHOK LEYLAND			
3.	Ashok Leyland Ltd.	27.75	236.33@
BANGUR			
4.	Andhra Pradesh Paper Mills Ltd. (29.12.82)	59.87	36.05@
5.	Shree Digvijay Cement Co. Ltd. (29.6.82)	32.15	45.41@
6.	Shreeniwas Cotton Mills Ltd. (28.6.80)	46.97	17.43#
7.	Bengal Paper Mills Co. Ltd. (21.7.82)	26.86	17.09@
8.	Shree Synthetics Ltd. (30.12.82)	26.86	33.48
9.	Fort Gloster Inds. Ltd. (30.9.78)	49.15	9.72@
10.	Graphite India Ltd.	41.82	36.03@
11.	Hastings Mills Ltd. (6.11.79)	53.76	16.80@
BIRD HEILGERS			
12.	Titaghar Paper Mills Co. Ltd. (1979)	45.61	40.78

contd...

...contd...

Sl. No.	*Name of the Company*	*Public Sector Share in Equity (%)*	*Assets (₹ Crore)*
	1	*2*	*3*
BIRLA			
13.	Kesoram Inds. & Cotton Mills Ltd. (31.5.82)	38.64	74.58
14.	Bharat Commerce & Inds. Ltd. (23.4.81)	33.06	31.77@
15.	Electric Construction & Equipment Co. Ltd. (7.4.81)	44.31	25.49@
16.	India Steamship Co. Ltd. (30.12.82)	30.82	108.55
17.	Jayshree Tea & Industries Ltd. (1980)	25.94	53.56
18.	Sirpur Paper Mills Ltd. (29.12.79)	42.56	25.39@
19.	Texmaco Ltd. (28.4.77)	31.50	42.33#
20.	Zenith Steel Pipes & Inds. Ltd. (3.10.80)	30.80	56.29
BOMBAY SUBURBAN			
21.	Bombay Suburban Electric Supply Co. Ltd. (23.9.82)	66.43	108.06
CENTRAL PULP			
22.	Central Pulp Mills Ltd. (27.3.80)	53.67	21.19@
DLF			
23.	Industrial Cables (I) Ltd. (1979)	46.44	26.02*
ESCORTS			
24.	Escorts Ltd. (26.6.80)	54.04	104.50@
ELCON ENGG.			
25.	Elecon Engg. Co. Ltd. (29.6.82)	26.33	57.09@
ITC			
26.	Tribeni Tissues Ltd. (30.4.82)	26.50	27.81@
27.	ITC Ltd. (30.8.79)	28.02	210.18
FCC			
28.	Calcutta Electric Supply Corpn. (I) Ltd. (24.9.82)	38.46	273.24
29.	Dunlop India Ltd. (30.10.82)	33.74	163.82@
30.	Indian Aluminium Co. Ltd. (29.4.80)	27.26	155.61@
31.	Metal Box India Ltd. (30.12.82)	28.07	103.39@
32.	Simon Carves (I) Ltd. (4.6.82)	25.08	13.02@
NAIDU GV			
33.	South India Viscose Ltd.	(27.6.79)	26.29 36.31
34.	Lakshmi Machine Works Ltd. (31.12.82)	47.02	41.86@

contd...

...contd...

Sl. No.	Name of the Company	Public Sector Share in Equity (%)	Assets (₹ Crore)
	1	2	3
ICI			
35.	Indian Explosives Ltd. (17.2.81)	25.19	164.08@
36.	Alkali & Chemical Corpn. India Ltd. (19.2.82)	29.54	50.52@
37.	Crescent Dyes & Chemicals Ltd. (9.2.82)	40.16	13.82@
INDIA CEMENT			
38.	India Cements Ltd. (28.9.79)	48.69	33.04
KAPADIA			
39.	National Rayon Corpn. Ltd. (23.6.82)	35.37	55.86@
40.	Kohinoor Mills Co. Ltd. (29.9.80)	71.68	15.82@
41.	Ahmedabad Electricity Co. Ltd. (20.9.79)	38.34	112.97
H.N. KAPADIA			
42.	Poysha Industrial Co. Ltd. (1980)	50.29	17.00
KAMANI			
43.	Kamani Engg. Corpn. Ltd. (16.5.80)	49.13	58.24@
KHATAU			
44.	Khatau Makhanji Spg. & Wvg. Co. Ltd. (16.10.79)	31.85	25.48@
KIRLOSKAR			
45.	Kirloskar Electric Co. Ltd. (21.1.83)	38.11	46.28@
46.	Mysore Kirloskar Ltd. (1980)	41.92	22.88@
47.	Kirloskar Pneaumatic Co. Ltd. (1979)	60.42	28.36@
48.	Kirloskar Oil Engines Ltd.	30.79	57.33@
KOTHARI G.D.			
49.	General Indl. Society Ltd. (3.4.80)	30.13	21.86@
KOTHARI D.C.			
50.	Kothari (Madras) Ltd. (22.12.79)	27.57	50.45@
LARSEN & TOUBRO			
51.	Larsen & Toubro Ltd. (24.4.81)	34.74	142.21@
52.	Hindustan Brown Boveri Ltd. (23.10.80)	63.93	50.50
LALBHAI			
53.	Atul Products Ltd. (24.4.80)	34.03	64.44@
54.	Arvind Mills Ltd. (23.6.82)	27.40	46.24@
MAHINDRA			
55.	Mahindra & Mahindra Ltd. (23.4.82)	44.10	129.50
56.	Mahindra Ugine Steel Co. Ltd. (1979)	28.24	86.41@

contd...

...contd...

Sl. No. Name of the Company	Public Sector Share in Equity (%)	Assets (₹ Crore)
1	2	3
MODI		
57. Modipon Ltd. (31.8.77)	27.14	68.11
58. Modi Rubber Ltd. (30.4.82)	39.84	93.78@
PARRY		
59. EID Parry (India) Ltd. (25.6.82)	28.17	57.55@
60. Herdilla Chemicals Ltd. (16.4.80)	26.92	23.63@
61. Coromandal Fertilizers Ltd.	36.64	66.32@
PODAR		
62. Podar Mills Ltd. (1979)	45.31	13.41#
RAUNAQ SINGH		
63. Bharat Steel Tubes Ltd. (5.11.82)	42.94	32.96
64. Appollo Tyres Ltd.	31.64	33.92@
RAJASTHAN SPG.		
65. Rajasthan Spg. & Wvg. Mills Co. Ltd.	37.88	25.70@
SPIC		
66. Southern PetroChemical Inds. Ltd. (23.12.81)	42.59	169.79@
S.P. JAIN		
67. Dhrangadhara Chemicals Works Ltd. (28.9.79)	30.28	29.25
SCINDIA		
68. Scindia Steam Navigation Co. Ltd. (1980)	34.54	205.13
SHRI AMBICA		
69. Shri Ambica Mills Ltd. (9.6.80)	31.87	66.03@
SESHASAYEE		
70. Aluminium Inds. Ltd. (25.9.82)	42.22	34.86
71. Seshasayee Paper & Boards Ltd. (21.9.79)	56.73	31.71
SHRI RAM		
72. Jay Engineering Works Ltd. (27.8.80)	30.71	28.16@
73. D.C.M. Ltd. (28.12.82)	42.54	184.78@
SINGHANIA		
74. J.K. Industries Ltd. (28.7.80)	35.31	71.28@
75. Sevenseas Transportation Ltd. (26.5.82)	31.52	17.19

contd...

...*contd*...

Sl. No.	*Name of the Company*	*Public Sector Share in Equity (%)*	*Assets (₹ Crore)*
	1	*2*	*3*
TATA			
76.	Voltas Ltd. (10.2.82)	45.73	126.44@
77.	Tata Engg. & Locomotive Co. Ltd. (24.8.62)	44.84	605.23
78.	Tata Iron & Steel Co. Ltd. (17.8.82)	42.25	687.52
79.	Tata Power Co. Ltd. (23.9.82)	38.40	116.09
80.	Tata HydroElectric Power Supply Co. Ltd. (24.9.82)	33.92	65.46
81.	Ahmedabad Advance Mills Co. Ltd. (25.5.81)	42.52	40.20
82.	Swadeshi Mills Co. Ltd. (8.5.79)	37.14	18.17#
83.	Tata Oil Mills Co. Ltd. (1979)	33.89	86.81#
84.	Andhra Valley Power Supply Co. Ltd. (24.9.82)	51.18	93.59
THAPAR			
85.	Ballarpur Inds. Ltd. (22.12.80)	27.00	124.79@
86.	Greaves Cotton & Co. Ltd. (10.12.79)	28.28	49.72@
VISSANJI			
87.	LaxmiVishnu Textile Mills Ltd. (20.5.80)	28.74	14.70@
NAIDU V.R.			
88.	Madras Aluminium Co. Ltd. (12.6.80)	33.61	31.81@
WALCHAND			
89.	Premier Automobiles Co. Ltd. (1980)	25.83	50.66
WALLACE			
90.	Bombay Burmah Trading Co. Ltd. (19.3.80)	34.00	20.65@
OTHERS			
91.	Mangalore Chemicals & Fertilizers Ltd. (28.7.82)	52.09	81.48@
92.	Gujarat Alkalies & Chemicals Ltd. (29.9.82)	50.57	24.94
93.	Sayaji Mills Ltd. (1982)	25.93	16.76
94.	Jain Tube Co. Ltd. (29.4.78)	27.05	15.56@
95.	Star Paper Mills Co. Ltd. (26.9.79)	27.88	19.40
96.	Gujarat State Fertilizers Ltd. (31.12.82)	74.12	178.96@

Note: 1. Dates in brackets in col. 1 given alongwith the name of company indicate the date of the 'Share Distribution Schedule.'

2. Assets data in col. 3: Unless indicated otherwise assets data are for the year 1982; * indicates data for 1979; # for 1980; and @ for 1981.

3. FCC indicates foreign-controlled companies.

4. The House Classification is as per the Corporate Information System of the Indian Institute of Public Administration (IIPA).

Source: Corporate Information System, IIPA, New Delhi.

IV

The process of fresh privatisation of central government undertakings may or may not get initiated. But in India, there are already a large number of private sector undertakings in which public sector has large investments. It is a situation that is very close to the post-privatisation conditions abroad. What should be the policy of the government with regard to these undertakings? What should be the form, degree or nature of public control in these undertakings? Should the responsibility to manage these undertakings continue with the present private managements who have only a marginal stake (say 5-10 per cent) in risk capital? If one is to accept the principle of profit maximisation for the private sector industrial enterprises, can one accept that the private managements with 510 per cent share of the enterprises' profit would have more at stake than the public sector financial institutions which have majority or the largest single bloc of shares? In whose interest would it be to keep such enterprises on the profit-making road? Financial institutions or private managements?

If there are government nominees, what should be their role? Or, alternatively, there can be a broad set of guidelines that no industrial house should be allowed to manage a company in which its own risk capital is less than half of the total equity. If privatisation has to have some of the advantages, then can one lay down some basic rules that private managements will not be allowed to direct company resources through 'transfer pricing' transactions with the management associated undertakings? Can there be strict rules for objective audits so that private managements cannot defraud public-owned companies? Can there be some degree of 'public accountability' (not necessarily limited to officials), of the large enterprises in which national resources of large size have got invested?

If, however, the plea for privatisation of public enterprises is to stall further expansion, oblige private industrialists or hand over management to some TNCs under international pressures, the above questions would appear irrelevant. On the other hand, if a group of experts get together with clear public purpose in mind, they must address themselves to the problems of large enterprises and seek policy measures to bring rationality in the process of decision making in these enterprises. At this level, the thin distinction between private and public enterprises would seem to have lost much of its meaning.

Appendix

Table A-21.1

Illustrative List of Joint Sector Companies Promoted by the State Industrial Development Corporations in Collaboration with Large Industrial Houses

S.No.	Company	Private Promoter	House Association
	1	2	3
1.	Arakonam Castings & Forgings Ltd.	K.C.P. Ltd.	Ramakrishna
2.	Asia Carbon Ltd.	Phillips Carbon Black Ltd.	Goenka K.P.
3.	Automobiles Corpn. of Goa Ltd.	TELCO	TATA
4.	Bihar Air Products Ltd.	(i) Asiatic Oxygen Ltd.	Soorajmull
		(ii) B.P. Industrial Corpn. (P) Ltd.	Nagarmull
		(iii) Amstar Investments Pvt. Ltd.	
5.	Bihar Caustic & Chemicals Ltd.	(i) Gwalior Rayon and Silk Mfg. (WVG) Co. Ltd.	Birla
		(ii) Hindustan Aluminium Corpn. Ltd.	
		(iii) Pilani Investment Corpn. Ltd.	
6.	Deccan Fibre Glass Ltd.	Phillips Carbon Black Ltd.	Goenka K.P.
7.	Gujarat Aromatics Ltd.	(i) Arvind Mills Ltd.	Kasturbhai Lalbhai
		(ii) Raipur Mfg. Co. Ltd.	
		(iii) Aruna Mills Ltd.	
		(iv) Cibatul Ltd.	
		(v) Ashoka Mills Ltd.	
8.	Gujarat Carbon Black Ltd.	Phillips Carbon Black Ltd.	Goenka K.P.
9.	IPIBEL Refractories Ltd. Belphar Refractories Ltd.	TATA	
10.	IPI TATA Ltd. Tata Iron & Steel Company Ltd.	TATA	

contd...

...contd...

S.No.	Company	Private Promoter	House Association
	1	*2*	*3*
11.	J & K Cigarettes Ltd.	Golden Tobacco Company Ltd.	Golden Tobacco.
12.	Karnataka Oxygen Ltd.	(i) M/s Lachhiminarain Company	
		(ii) M/s Ambica Textiles T.C.I.	
13.	Lorcom Protectives Ltd.	London Rubber Company Ltd.	TTK
14.	Madhra Pradesh Electricals Ltd.	Shakti Insulated Wires Pvt. Ltd.	Khatau.
15.	Maharastra Scooters Ltd.	Bajaj Auto Ltd.	Bajaj
16.	Mandovi Pellets Ltd.	(i) Chowgule & Co. Pvt. Ltd.	Chowgule
		(ii) Chowgule Steamships Ltd.	
17.	Mysore Petrochemicals Ltd.	Shekavati Invt. Corpn. Ltd.	Bangur
18.	Neptune Papers Ltd.	(i) Sirpur Papers Mills Ltd.	Birla
		(ii) Central India Inds Ltd.	
		(iii) Vimal Investments Ltd.	
19.	NICCO Orissa Ltd.	National Insulated Cable Co. Ltd.	Birla
20.	Noble Explochem Ltd.	Bengal Tea & Industries ltd.	Kanoria
21.	Orissa Synthetic Ltd.	Straw Products Ltd.	Singhania
22.	Phenol Chemical Corpn. of Gujarat Ltd.	Duncan Brothers & Co. Ltd.	Goenka K.P.
23.	Punjab United Pesticides Ltd.	Excel Inds. Ltd.	TATA (II)
24.	Southern Agrifurane Inds. Ltd.	South India Corpn. (Agencies) Pvt. Ltd.	Chidambaram, M.A.
25.	Southern PetroChemicals Corpn. Ltd.	South India Corpn. (Agencies) Pvt. Ltd.	Chidambaram, M.A.

contd...

...contd...

S.No.	*Company*	*Private Promoter*	*House Association*
	1	*2*	*3*
26.	Tamil Nadu Fluorine & Allied Chemicals Ltd.	(i) Hindustan Aluminium Corpn. Ltd.	
		(ii) Gwalior Rayon Silk Mfg. (WVG) Co. Ltd.	Birla
		(iii) Pilani Investment Corpn. Ltd.	
27.	Tuticorin Alkali Chemicals and Fertilizers Ltd.	Southern Petro Chemical Inds Ltd.	Chidambaram, M.A.
28.	Webel Jyoti Power Electronics Ltd.	Jyoti Ltd.	Amin R.K.
29.	Webel Telecommunication India Ltd.	Philips (I) Ltd.	Philips (FERA)
30.	West Bengal Alloy Steel Ltd.	Taxmaco Ltd.	Birla
31.	West Bengal Filaments & Lamps Ltd.	Bengal Assam Steamship Co. Ltd.	Andrew Yule
32.	West Bengal Pulp Wood Devpt. Corpn. Ltd.	Titaghur Paper Mills Co. Ltd.	Bangur
33.	Wiltech India Ltd.	Asian Cables Corpn. Ltd.	Goenka K.P.

Source: Corporate Information System, IIPA, New Delhi.

22 Joint Industrial Sector

Purpose and Form

The recommendation of the Industrial Licensing Policy Inquiry Committee[1] for the development of 'Joint Sector' rests on one basic consideration i.e., since in any case, a large proportion of the cost of major private sector industrial projects is being met by the public sector financial institutions, either directly or through their support, why should appreciation in the value of the assets and profits of the companies be not shared by the financiers i.e., the State. To give the suggestion a practical shape, the committee has suggested that the financial institutions should insist "on the whole or part of their assistance in the form of loans and debentures being convertible into equity at their option and, if necessary, the law should be amended to provide for this."[2] The committee has also mentioned the other resultant incidental advantages of the joint sector like restricting the emergence of huge private industrial empires with state support, thereby achieving the objective of curbing and restricting growth of concentration of economic power and also as a means to ensure that "public interest and not merely private profit would guide the operations of large industrial undertakings in the private sector."[3] The suggestion has been called as mischievous as it would amount to nationalisation of major private sector enterprises 'through the backdoor.'

Some representatives of the private sector consider that the concept of the 'joint sector' is a novel one, though it indeed is not so. Apart from a large many joint enterprises which function in a good number of foreign countries, India, itself, has a number of instances where some big industrial projects have been established with joint equity participation of

---

1. *Report of the Industrial Licensing Policy Inquiry Committee*, 1969, Manager, Publication Division. Henceforth referred to as *Report ILPIC*.
2. Ibid.: 186-87.
3. Ibid.

the government and the private sector. There were at least 12 undertakings in 1966-67 where the central government had substantial investments in equity without direct responsibility for management. The important examples are: Oil India (50% participation in equity) established in 1959, Manganese Ore (50.9% by central and state governments) in 1962, Bolani Ores (50.5%) in 1957 and Lubrizol (51%) established in 1966. There are others like Indian Explosives (1956) and Sikkim Mining Corporation (1960) where the government holds minority equity shares.[4] Thus, there is nothing novel in the concept. The idea was put un-ambiguously in the Industrial Policy Resolution of 1956. It was stated that financial assistance, "especially when the amount involved is substantial, will preferably be in the form of participation in equity capital."[5]

The difference between what is stated in the Industrial Policy Resolution (1956) and what the ILPIC has recommended is that what is true of the form of direct financial assistance by the state should also be true of the institutions which have been established for providing support to organised private industrial sector. This seems logical as assistance to large private sector projects by the state has been increasingly made available through the public sector financial institutions—many of which have incidentally been established after the announcement of the Industrial Policy Resolution of 1956. It would have, normally, been expected that even though financial assistance by the state to the Indian private sector was channelled through the financial institutions, the form of assistance would be essentially in line with the stated government policy (i.e., preferably, such assistance would 'be in the form of participation in equity'). A review of the form of financial assistance, provided by the public sector specialised financial institutions during the Second and Third Plan periods (excluding the State Bank and its subsidiaries) shows that nearly 67 per cent of the sanctioned, as well as disbursed, assistance was in the form of loans, the direct subscription in shares and debentures was nearly 4 per cent only.[6]

---

4. For more details see: INDIA (Ministry of Finance), *Working of Industrial and Commercial Undertakings of the Central Government: Annual Report, 1966-67*, New Delhi.

5. *Industrial Policy Resolution, 1956*, para. 10.

6. *Report ILPIC*, p.154.

Added to this is also the finding that the main beneficiary of the financial assistance has been the large industrial sector.

A curious feature of the operations of the public sector financial institutions has been in regard to their actual performance, at providing assistance to the private sector, in relation to the Plan targets. During the Second and Third Plan periods, these institutions were expected to provide ₹ 40 crore and ₹ 130 crore, respectively, i.e., ₹ 170 crore during 1956-1966.[7] However, the assistance disbursed was nearly ₹ 584.3 crore out of which the loans as such were of the order of ₹ 391.8 crore.[8]

The provision of more than the target amount by public sector financial institutions to the private sector industrial enterprises could not be questioned if the overall resources mobilised by the state were more than what were envisaged or if the state had no other priority projects which were postponed for lack of resources with the government. But one does not find any one of the two assumptions as valid. It seems, in fact, a mystery how these very financial institutions, during the Second and Third Plan, have consistently taken the stand that due to paucity of financial resources with them, they were confining their activities to the financing of the private sector only though these institutions were expected to finance public sector projects also.

The public sector financial institutions in India had no shortage of financial resources to assist the private organised sector. They provided overall assistance which was three to four times their expected operations. A question may arise: when the public sector in general have been facing the difficulty of finding resources for priority industries, how is it that the public sector financial institutions had always more than what they required to meet their plan commitments. Where from did this finance come? Very little has been said about the mysterious excessive funds, which according to a Reserve Bank of India (RBI) statement as circulated to the National Development Council in 1968, were creating a problem. And the institutions, not wanting to keep their resources idle, had to finance even non-priority industries in the private sector.[9]

---

7. *Third Five Year Plan*, p.465.
8. *Report ILPIC*. p.155 (table II, columns 2 and 10).
9. Papers circulated to the National Development Council, October 1968.

It is perhaps in this background of excessive resources with the public sector financial institution and their anxiety to help the borrowers that one would need to understand the part played by the Indian public sector financial institutions in meeting the project costs of the big private industrial units. Table 22.1 shows a list of such private sector projects where more than one institution had provided finance, in company with the Industrial Development Bank of India (IDBI) and the combined financial assistance was more than 50 per cent of the project cost. The

Table 22.1

Showing Percentage of Financial Assistance and Promoters' and Collaborators' Contribution to Total Project Cost by Institutions to 17 Companies

Companies	*House*	*Total Project Cost*	*Total Financial Assistance*	*Col. 4 as % of Col. 3*	*Promoters Collaborators' Contribution*	*Col. 6 as % of Col. 3*
(1)	(2)	(3)	(4)	(5)	(6)	(7)
Solid Container Ltd.	-	94.0	84.0	89.4	26.0	27.6
CTRMFG, Industries Ltd.	-	93.8	83.0	88.5	24.0	25.6
Incheck Tyres Ltd.	-	277.0	228.0	82.3	50.0	18.1
Bharat, Electrical Industries	-	36.0	29.0	80.5	-	-
Coromandel Fertilizers Ltd.	Parry	3674.0	2867.4	78.0	454.5	12.4
Shree Digvijay Cement	Bangur	365.0	278.5	76.3	-	-
Rammon & Demm Ltd.	-	186.3	141.7	76.1	60.9	32.7
Bombay Malleable Iron Castings & Allied Industries	-	120	86.0	71.2	32.5	27.1
High Quality Steel	Birla	895.0	604.3	67.5	205.0	22.9
Herdilla Chemicals	Parry	1009.0	644.5	63.9	221.0	21.9
C.I.M.C.O.	Birla	191.0	115.5	60.5	-	-
Raj Prakash Spg. Mills	-	66.6	39.0	58.6	13.0	19.5
National Co. Ltd.	Andrew Yule	140.0	80.0	57.7	-	-
Polyolefine Industries Ltd.	Mafatlal	977.2	546.5	55.9	242.4	24.8
Madras Alloy & Stainless Steel	-	800.0	433.0	54.1	122.0	15.2
Mahindra Ugine Steel Co. Ltd.	Mahindra & Mahindra	850.0	444.9	52.3	151.0	17.8
Tata Merline & Germ Ltd.	Tata	226.1	117.0	51.7	76.5	33.8

Source: *India, ILPIC Report*, pp.174-75.

share of the cost raised by the promoters and their collaborators is given in column 4. Table 22.1 shows that there were at least 17 private sector projects where more than half of the project cost was met by the state directly or indirectly. The contribution of promoters and collaborators has varied from nearly 12 to 33 per cent of total cost. The IDBI had assisted 33 companies in collaboration with other financial institutions. Aggregatively, the contribution of the promoters to the project cost was nearly 13 per cent only against the institutional support of nearly 40 per cent.[10] The proposal of the ILPIC for the 'joint sector' has, therefore, to be viewed in the background of these facts.[11]

One could, however, argue that the scheme of project finance cannot always be taken as a basis for deciding about the ownership of the project. A project may have to be in the private sector because the necessary technical know-how is non-existent in the public sector. And if the national interest requires the setting up of an industry, the over-riding consideration should be of ensuring quick implementation of plan projects and not whether it should be in the private sector or the public sector. This could be a somewhat reasonable argument if the required technical know-how was possessed by the private party proposing establishment of the project. Viewed from this angle, it can be said without much fear of contradiction that the possession of 'know-how' has not been the consideration for allowing major industrial projects in the private sector. Most of the big industrial projects have been based on foreign know-how. And in a majority of the large-sized industrial projects, the collaborations are technical as well as financial.

Another consideration for allowing a large industrial project in the private sector could be the possession of experience and talent of management in the execution of similar projects. Supposing it is so, the question would be whether their expertise cannot be availed on payment of the necessary regard. It would sound rather odd if one is to accept that

---

10. *Report ILPIC*, pp.174-5.

11. It may also be mentioned that the scheme of project finance, as given by the ILPIC, is the one as initially approved. The experience shows that there are substantial increases in the project costs when the projects are under implementation and the quantum of institutional assistance gets increased by a significant degree. Thus, the data analysed by the ILPIC are underestimates of the liabilities shared by the public sector financial institutions.

a group of good managers would not be willing to offer its professional services to the society on other than project ownership basis. Leaving aside the terms of exploiting talent or questions of professional ethics, it would bring the issue to realistic level if one attempts to find out the level of management expertise as it does exist in the Indian economy or question if the entrepreneurs who have bagged the bigger industrial projects had really done so on the strength of their professional competence in management and experience. This is a matter of individual knowledge and assessment whether the existing managerial talents in the Indian private sector are highly professionalised or not. But whatever one knows or is disclosed by inquiries conducted from time to time, it may be difficult for even few larger industrial houses to claim that they have already built up management cadres competent to manage large projects.[12] It may indeed be quite revealing if one could have an independent survey organised to assess the management potential, the practices followed and the degree of scientific working of, say 50, largest projects in the private sector—and especially the ones under the 20 larger industrial houses. In short, management capability is the last argument which can be considered as really strong about Indian larger industrial houses. Another argument as a possible justification for allowing large projects in the private sector is the risk element in the new and large ventures. If an entrepreneur takes the risk to 'swim or sink' with the project, there could be some good reasons to allow a large project in the private sector. The entrepreneur in the classical concept is the one who takes non-insurable risks of an enterprise arising out of the market fluctuations of demand and supply and competition from other producers. Theoretically, a reward for the risk bearing functions is considered as risk, and the one who takes the risk has also have to have the rights to manage and direct. The argument does carry some weight. But before accepting its application to the Indian conditions, one would like to question if the assumptions made in the argument are true in a planned and regulated economy as could be there in a market-oriented economy. May be that the regulations in India are not fully effective to accept India as a really regulated economy. But few would resent the role of planned investment, especially in the public sector—the quantum and pattern of which, by and large, are reasonably well known in advance. There are

12. c.f., *Ad-hoc Committee on Automobile Industry: Report*, 1964.

fairly good estimates of future demand for a large many products. In any case, demand fluctuations do not pose as serious a problem as in a free and market-oriented economy. Even if it happens that there is slackening of demand resulting in underutilisation of industrial capacities, the government is sensitive and is prepared to take such steps as would ensure a reasonable demand.[13] The public competition, either from within or outside, is not much of a headache as imports are restricted and protection granted to 'indigenous' producers as well as entry into the industries is regulated through licensing. The responsibility to establish the requisite infrastructure is borne by the state. In brief, the large industrial projects have not to experience the same kind of risks as are faced by the private sector in countries having no development plans.

In many ways the conditions for the private sector in India are rather unique. The demand for the products of large sector of the private industry is generated by the state many a time even directly. Take the case of the fertiliser industry in India. The initial breakthrough to popularise chemical fertilisers was made as a result of governmental efforts, and once the demand potential was built up, the industry has been thrown open to the private sector. In cement, the demand is directly linked up with the decisions to undertake major and medium multipurpose projects and other public construction activity. If it is the Indian automobile industry, the state has an expanding programme of road transport development in addition to the practice of granting subsidised loans to carry buyers.[14] In industries like aluminium and heavy transformers, the state has a direct interest both as the customer and for aluminium-conductor steel-reinforced (ACSR) conductors for power transmission and sheets and extrusions of the metal and alloys for air craft and nationalised road transport.[15] The contention here is not that the state has a plan for creating demand for the entire private sector activity. The emphasis is in regard to the demand for

---

13. The government action can take various forms ranging from reduction in excise duties, stepping up investment to create demand and subsidy for exports accompanied by other measures at creation of demand abroad. In extreme situations, the government can even be expected to take over private sector 'sick units' in public interest.

14. c.f. Goyal, S.K. "Car Industry—A Policy Framework". *National Herald*, September 22, 1969.

15. Planning Commission, *Programmes of Industrial Development*, 1956-61, p.32.

large industrial projects irrespective of their being in the private or public sector.

A pertinent question may be to ask: if there is no special justification for allowing large industrial projects in the private sector, to what factor can one account the past allocation of large industrial projects in the private sector. What is the contribution of those who in the private sector have been allowed to go ahead with large projects in the private sector? Perhaps a reasonably good answer to this is provided by the ILPIC itself.[16] The conclusion seems to be that influence and favour, at top political and administrative levels, have been the predominant factors in major decisions to allow large projects in the private sector in general and choosing of particular entrepreneurs is specific. Added to this has been the lack of clarity of vision and short-sighted attitude of those who were responsible for undertaking important decisions. And last, the ineffective and ill-equipped administrative machinery which was supposed to administer the Industrial (Development and Regulation) Act (IDRA) of 1952.

Most of the big private sector industrial projects were approved with a vague belief that large industrial houses have their own financial resources to undertake projects. And, a belief has also been current at significant points of decision making that the public sector has its own plate full to undertake any additional responsibility. And in the interest of speedy implementation, the projects, even if these were in Schedule A (industries for exclusive development in the public sector) or Schedule B (industries in which the State will establish new undertakings), were allowed in the private sector. It may appear odd, but it is a fact that some industrial projects which had already been processed for implementation in the public sector were passed on to influential large industrial houses under the sole argument that public sector did not have sufficient financial resources. The allocation of industries like aluminium, ferro-alloys and tools, fertilisers, synthetic rubber and chemical pulp to the private sector (which means large houses only) offers a good number of pertinent examples. As said above, a major assumption in sanctioning these big projects was that it would not place any financial burdens upon the government as the private sector

16. For this, one may profitably read Chapters V and VII in continuation of the *ILPIC Report*.

would find necessary resources for itself. The assumption has never proved to be realistic one.

Another consideration, sometime a pressing one, which led to granting of a big project to a private party has been the attraction that the necessary foreign exchange resources would be available if the project was assigned to the private sector. In a developing society faced with serious shortage of foreign exchange, it cannot be taken as a small consideration. But did we really examine the proposal from the viewpoint that recognition of such factors in deciding to deviate from the proclaimed national policies would have some political implications too? It is not to suggest that practical considerations and economic advantages when available should not be availed on dogmatic grounds. However, the intention certainly is to underline the question whether basic national policies should be sacrificed for some short-term gains which would come only if it is agreed to fall in line with political dogmas of those who can be donors of economic aid. The argument that foreign capital would be readily available if the national policies are 'marginally' modified is a matter which should be decided with full awareness of its implications, instead of simple executive decisions and likes and dislikes of the administration.[17]

It appears, in the desire to push through a vaguely defined bold programme of industrialisation, many a crucial deviation from the national economic and social objectives was accepted as 'pragmatic.' The overall perspective was of course the first victim of such pragmatic considerations. For example, it has not been fully realised that by following on easy course of obtaining foreign capital (more so in the private sector), a situation has arisen in which our capacity to introduce changes in the socioeconomic system has got weakened and some unhappy trends have been further strengthened. The point is well illustrated in the impact of foreign collaborations allowed for giant projects undertaken by Indian industrial houses.

---

17. During the foreign exchange crisis of mid Third Plan, the Government announced a number of concessions to the private foreign capital. The substance of the argument was that since foreign exchange is a pressing problem, any project, which did not place any additional burden on the government, should be welcome—irrespective of the project falling under Plan priority or otherwise.

The Mahalanobis Committee, as well as the Monopolies Commission, has specifically mentioned that one of the important factors contributing to the growth of concentration in the corporate sector has been the phenomena of foreign collaborations.[18] This point has been made more clear by the instances provided in Chapter VI of the *ILPIC Report*. One of very pertinent examples is that of the non-controversial Goa Fertilizer project of the private sector. This may be a good case to illustrate many of the processes which go underneath decision-making in government. The fertiliser industry according to the Industrial Policy Resolution of 1956 is such in which "the State will establish new undertakings." However, a deviation from this policy was made in the overall interest of raising national capacity to produce inorganic fertilisers (as India is importing fertilisers worth ₹ 75 crore annually),[19] and an exception was made to allow the private sector to set up fertiliser projects. The public sector projects, as contemplated and under preparation, were given a 'show down.'[20]

As each fertiliser plant, to be economic, has to be a large one, therefore, it is simple enough to accept that fertiliser projects could only be within the implementing capacity of large houses. Further because the technology required is complicated and sophisticated, foreign collaboration is unavoidable. Once all these points are conceded and formal clearance has been given by the government, the licencee parties turn back and demand priority in processing of their requests (many a time questioning the necessity of technical scrutiny or posing of inconvenient questions about what they wish to import) for blanket approval for import of capital and other goods (irrespective of the indigenous availability or otherwise), assurances of the government to build up special and speedy infrastructure, financial guarantees, etc. In view of the industry being a priority one, and the projects being included in the Plan industrial programmes linked up with hopes of agricultural prosperity, green revolution and more

18. *Monopolies Inquiry Commission: Report*, 1956, p.7.

19. According to Press Note issued by the Ministry of Petroleum and Chemicals, this decision was taken long back. See *National Herald* (Delhi edition) of January 22, 1970.

20. For the argument given for preference to the private sector, one may see Planning Commission, *Programme of Industrial Development*, 1956-61, pp.175-79. A similar and interesting comparison is in the case of aluminium industry in the above-mentioned two projects.

employment opportunities, everything becomes a smooth sailing. In brief, under the circumstances, it is for large houses to ask for what they want and for the society to pay the government to dutifully obey.[21]

The likely result of the process (what is happening to the fertiliser industry is not untrue of other industries) is that the country will be loaded with projects each employing a differing technology, paying high royalty (some claiming non-comparability of the know-how) and other payments in foreign exchange, and one wonders if the overall economics of the industry as it finally emerges would be anyway nearer the original assumptions and expectations. Undoubtedly, no one should hasten to reach conclusions without having the benefit of a full and technical scrutiny of the implications of having allowed multiple collaborations.

What, however, if *not* a secret is that the government is aware that in many a case-private parties and that too belonging to influential industrial houses have over-committed themselves and the country and made bad bargains. But by the time it is known, the government is left with no option but to swallow the bitter pill. Instances are also well known where Indian industrialists having overcommitted, did not hesitate to pressurise the government to accept otherwise unfavourable terms of collaboration in the interests of keeping the international private capital in good humour.

Apart from the doubtful economics of multiple and many of the private collaborations in allowing of the big industrial projects to be established in the private sector, there is another disturbing aspect which has so far gone unnoticed. This is in relation to the interlinking of international giants. When a large Indian house takes up a big project, very naturally, the house does not want to collaborate with insignificant parties abroad. The house would like to have dealings with collaborators who were important in their own country, and preferably the one internationally well connected. There are some obvious advantages in this choice. Firstly, such foreign collaborators have well-established reputation and prestige which comes in handy to meet any likely questions by the government agencies on the technical soundness of the proposal. Secondly, the association of an

21. Though the Indian licencees for fertiliser project have made a number of changes in their own proposals in regard to size, exchange requirements, terms of collaboration, costs and so on, yet the government is always held responsible for 'delays.' And surprisingly the government does not take offence.

international giant ensures a favourable and sympathetic consideration from the international financial institutions. And thirdly, the Indian collaborator comes to acquire a position where even the government representatives of the foreign collaborator's country would not hesitate to 'put in a word' here and there and to see that interests of the two collaborators are not adversely affected. In short, there are solid reasons for the Indian collaborating party to go after international giants. Such foreign collaborators are of course, not unaware of their importance. And they do play the game to their maximum advantage. Who can question the logic of the bargaining process?

A quick narration of the international interlocking process can appear as oversimplication to many. But for those who have witnessed industrial development closely during the last 15 years, it may only freshen up their memories and they may be able to make modifications to sharpen the narration. Viewed from another angle an aggregation of specific case studies may throw a lot of light on the processes of decision making to demonstrate how the so-called pragmatic considerations can lead the society away from the envisaged overall perspective. The present objective is, however, a limited one. And this is to underline that one exception made from the national policies did not have a limited result but had serious implications in regard to strengthening of concentration. It is no wonder that in India the growth of larger houses has been the direct result of such interlinking with international giants. Further, strengthening of the few large houses and private interests in the economic life of the country has its own implications.

The ILPIC had, it seems, these problems in mind when it came up with the recommendation that instead of allowing big industrial projects wholly in the private sector, it would be desirable to keep them in the 'joint sector.' The committee could not go into further details of their crucial recommendation—both, perhaps, it was pressed for time and it was beyond their term of reference. The committee, however, has provided some indication of what they had in mind. It is suggested that the financial institutions should have the right to convert their loans and debentures into equity. In this manner, the committee believes, the state would be able to share the advantages of capital appreciation and would be in a position to claim, on the strength of its substantial equity holdings, representation on the management boards of the projects assisted. The committee also adds that an apex financial agency like the IDBI should build up a group of professionals who could act as directors on the 'joint sector' companies.[22] But what is the precise 'purpose' of having these so-called 'institutional directors' on the private sector management boards? What shall they do? It is widely recognised that there are some private management boards which frequently resort to unfair business practices.

In such situations, these 'institutional directors' could perhaps ensure that unfair and unlawful management business practices were not resorted to. They could also attempt to bring in higher degree of professionalisation in 'joint sector' projects. Some improvements in the internal functioning of the enterprises could also be visualised if the institutional directors were more competent than the private sector directors. This could be an ideal objective in itself. No one can quarrel with these laudable objectives.

The committee has further suggested that presence of institutional directors could also ensure that "management of industry is conducted according to the overall policies laid down by government, and that public interest and not merely private profit would guide the operation of large industrial undertakings in the private sector."[23] This is where the recommendation of the ILPIC seems too casual and without much real meaning. Would an institutional director represent the government viewpoint on the board? Or, his first and foremost loyalty would be to the company in which he sits as a director? Supposing, there is a question of raising prices of the company products to reap larger profits to enable higher dividends to shareholders. What would be the institutional director's stand? Or, say, there is a proposal to expand production capacity of a company project which would place the company in a dominating position in the industry. Would the institutional director stand in the way of further expansion of the company as it goes against the government policy of not allowing a concern to have a dominant position? There is also a question likely to come up for approval of expenditure on 'public relations.' Would one take the position that no expenditure on public relations—especially with the government officials (though a painful reality and a necessity)

---

22. *Report ILPIC*, p.187.
23. Ibid.

should be allowed even if the company interests suffer? What precisely would be the 'public interest' to guard against?

One does not know what the committee would have to say. The experience of the existing 'joint sector' in India has not been reviewed so far. But the case of a government appointed director in a company is only too fresh in one's mind and one could narrate it here without being misunderstood. It is a case of the early 1960s. On receipt of some serious complaints about the mismanagement and misappropriation of funds in a company, the government appointed two directors on the company's board of management to keep a watch and report, in confidence, about the internal working of the company. One of the two gentlemen, after sometime, wrote to the government that since he was a director of the company and is morally and legally bound to protect the interests of the company, he was sending a report on the working of the company after its approval being given by the management board and that too through the chairman of the company. The confidential report was, of course, very good.

The institutional nominees on 'joint sector' companies would, in all probability, be from the regular service of the assisting financial institutions, the economic ministries or belonging to a new management cadre of the institutions. In that case, the private managements of the 'joint sector' projects could have a real advantage in having an efficient channel of communication through these directors in the government and public sector financial institutions itself. These directors, if in the government (would naturally be senior officials only), would be good contacts to protect and further the interests of the company. Any such possibility should be welcomed by the private sector, as it could be an effective way of ensuring preferential treatment to the company over the unlucky 'non-joint sector' companies. Even in the cases where the dealing officer in government or the institution was a different one, the director could, to expect the least, use his good offices to get a sympathetic (means what?) consideration from another member of his fraternity. Howsoever a cynical view this may appear to be, the instances are not in short supply where even some of the retired senior civil servants in India have been able to obtain substantial benefits for their employers from the government on the strength of their association and personal contacts. Very simply how else could one explain the hiring of retired civil servants by private firms at high salaries.[24]

The recommendation of the ILPIC on promotion of 'joint sector' also seems to be based on the belief that somehow, whether justified or otherwise, the large private industrial houses will have to be given a share in the big industrial projects. This is in the face of the reality that a large part of the finance for big projects in any case comes from the State and it is only with the active support of the government, directly and otherwise, that some of the larger industrial houses have been able to flourish during the last few years. The committee, though bitter about the deviations from the Industrial Policy Resolution (1956) which were made under political or administrative pressure and influence to accommodate a few powerful private interests, has gone over to suggest that the large houses may be given increasing participation in the 'core sector' (which mean even in industries included under Schedules A and B of the Industrial Policy Resolution of 1956). The possession of technical know-how has not been the strong point of large industrial houses in India.[25] Since the big projects are invariably conceived either to reduce imports or to meet the existing or growing shortages, the risk involved in new projects is extremely a limited one. Given those facts, it does not appear very clear why the committee considers that private large houses must be allowed to become partners in the 'core sector.'[26] The suggestion is, obviously, a concession to the private large industrial interests, if not, a scheme which in the name of pragmatism attempts to accommodate pressures from the national and international lobbies of the private sector.

24. It would perhaps be an exciting survey if one could have even a limited study about the number, positions and salaries obtained by retiring senior civil servants with the larger industrial houses of the country. The study could even be confined to the retired Indian Civil Service (ICS) officers. There are, however, well-known instances like the top position held by a retired Governor of the RBI and one of the companies under him having the highest degree of assistance to its total costs and another where a retiring Secretary to Ministry of Industry and Commerce landed up as Adviser to one of the largest industrial houses of the country. The examples can be multiplied.

25. And very few of them pay much attention to R&D of new industrial technology.

26. A variety of expressions like 'basic and strategic' priority, part of the core plan (used during The Second Plan period) essential industries and 'Core sector' (as used in the Fourth Plan) have been used by the planners in India. But at no time has anyone attempted to give a precise meaning. It is further interesting that the ILPIC has used the 'Core sector' to mean industries with large investments (internal as well as external) which is different from that of the Fourth Plan.

The logical recommendation of the committee would have been to clearly state that all large size projects, say of more than ₹ 10 crore investment, should in future be only established in the public sector. And if in a certain case it was felt that a private concern possessed good managerial talent, the concern should be invited to takeover or participate in management or implementation of the project on contractual basis. A joint sector could be where ownership is public and management is by a group which is professionally competent. No doubt there are even dangers in this approach as the management of important public sector companies could be monopolised by one or a few individuals or management houses. To meet the emergence of such tendencies, the government could follow a policy under which no management group was allowed to take over more than one project and all firms having their own private business could be kept out of such contracts.

Yet another form of 'joint sector' could be where a part of the equity was held by the workers of the enterprise and the rest by the government or public financial institutions. To encourage the workers to have a share in the ownership of the enterprise, they could be issued equity shares (may be non-transferable for some period) at a face value against a part of their salary or bonus. If felt necessary, the public financial institutions could gradually pull back from their financial involvement and the enterprise could wholly be owned by the workers. Such a phenomena could help to establish genuine industrial cooperatives which in any case would be a real 'joint sector' than the one proposed by the ILPIC. In contrast, it appears the joint sector proposal, as proposed by the ILPIC, is more a recommendation for formal financial collaboration of the big private interests and the government where the private interest would make best of both the sides.

As regards the establishment of some big projects where it is necessary to involve a foreign private enterprise or a government, the project should only be in collaboration with the government. The experience of the last 15 years provides abundant evidence of the implications of allowing private foreign firms to collaborate with the Indian private parties. A feature of the private collaboration has been in issuing equity shares at a face value to foreign collaborators as payment for the technical services and sharing of know-how. The practice being uneconomic in itself (as it binds the country to endless periodic transfers of foreign exchange) ends up in a big chunk of the equity shares being owned by the foreign collaborating firms. Supposing a private foreign collaborator has 40 per cent equity participation in an Indian project. One direct implication of this is that the Indian collaborator requires another 11 per cent to be in the control of the enterprise as long as he does not annoy his foreign partner. The equation between the foreign and the Indian partners in such situations is not that of equals. A foreign collaborator even with a minority holding can *de facto* enjoy control over policies and management of the so-called Indian projects. Supposing such a project was in the 'joint sector' as proposed by the ILPIC. The financial institutions would have a substantial equity participation. But the institutional directors would always be in a minority. In such situations, even though the project may be called a 'joint sector' one, it would only be a projection of an illusion.

The 'joint sector' proposal of the ILPIC can also be a good excuse to formalise the patronage granted by the government to large houses in India. The case in point is that of the Goa Fertilizers. The Goa Fertilizers is a project where majority equity interest is foreigner. The government or the financial institutions have no equity participation (as so far known), though the promoters and their sister concerns hold a small part of the total equity. Yet the management would rest with the Birlas. The majority equity is in the hands of foreigners. Correctly speaking, it is a foreign concern. It is not Indian. It is, of course, called a Birla project as Birlas are the junior partners. The Birlas would run the project under the advice or as desired by the US Steel, the technical and financial collaborators, whose continued support is basic for them to be in control of the project. 'What machinery' would be imported and at 'what price and 'who would supply' are questions which would be decided by the foreign collaborators. But ironically enough because two government directors would be appointed, according to the recent decision of the government, on the management board of the project, it is now justified as a 'joint sector' project. Naturally, the project would receive 'favourable' consideration at all stages as if it was a public sector project. A relevant question is how the appointment of two government directors reduces the significance of the project towards further growth of concentration in the Indian economy.

The proposal of the ILPIC to have 'joint sector', however, has a meaningful relevance to the already established big projects of the private sector where a large chunk of the project cost has been already met by the financial institutions. Table 22.1 has shown an illustrative list of big projects where more than 50 per cent of the project cost at the stage of project formulation was envisaged as support from the public financial institutions. One may as well repeat here that, invariably, the envisaged project costs, during the process of implementation, get increased (either the project is expanded or due to inflationary pressures and other factors the costs increase). The responsibility to foot enhanced cost is also generally that of the public financial institutions. Thus the picture given in Table 22.1 is most likely to be an underestimate of the financial support to the private projects and correspondingly an overstatement of the promoters' contribution. It would be seen that the contribution of the promoters and foreign collaborators varies between 12 and 33 per cent of the project cost. For the 33 companies assisted by the IDBI, jointly with other financial institutions, the promoters' contribution is about ₹ 39.35 crore, whereas the total cost of the projects was estimated at nearly ₹ 286.99 crore. The 33 big projects are private sector projects, belonging to the large industrial sector, though the financial contribution of the promoters has been less than 14 per cent of the cost of the 33 projects. These are indeed 'joint sector' projects with majority financial interest of the state. It would have made more sense if the ILPIC had suggested that all these projects should be treated as public sector projects under private managements. But, as it stands today, these cannot be treated so if one is to go by the pattern of the equity share holdings in these companies. The promoters' and foreign collaborators' contribution is generally in the form of equity participation which entitles them to claim the rights of ownership and management. The remedy to correct the prevailing anomaly is in expanding the equity base and treating the loans and other forms of financial assistance by the institutions as equity. A logical stand would be that after having the majority in the equity share of these companies, a serious thought should be given to examine whether the existing private managements have the competence and professional talent to administer the projects. In doing so the undesirable trends, which have developed due to lack of perspective and vision, would get corrected.

The 'joint sector' concept has also a significant meaning in relation to the public limited companies in which the financial institutions hold substantial shares. There has been no systematic study indicating the number of companies in which the financial institutions hold equity shares in different ranges. It could be easily done. It should also not be difficult for any individual scholar to get this information and compile a comprehensive list of companies showing in which companies the financial institutions hold more than 5-10 per cent of the equity shares jointly. The companies in which the institutions hold equity shares are invariably public limited ones, quoted in the stock exchange markets and big ones. The institutional shares would also be of substantial nature.[27]

In the absence of a readily available study on the joint equity holdings of the financial institutions in different companies, one can take the holdings of the Life Insurance Corporation (LIC) alone as an indicator of the degree of involvement of the institutions in the large private sector. This, of course, would be to say the least. According to the information given by the ILPIC, there were nearly 419 companies of the private sector, each public limited one, in which the LIC held shares as more than 30 per cent and in another 57, the equity shares held were between 20 and 30 per cent. If one takes the preference shares as such, the LIC held more than 30 per cent of the shares in 119 companies and between 20 and 30 per cent in another 65 companies.[28] While the interest of the LIC is substantial,[29] the LIC has nominated directors only in five companies.

In many a case, those who control the managements would not necessarily have more than, not to speak of majority, the block of equity shares held by the LIC. For example, the share-holding of the management

27. The stock exchanges maintain a list of top 10 shareholders of the quoted companies. On the basis of the information with the stock exchanges even a non-official study could easily be conducted. Another way of obtaining this information is to get the same from the companies directly by paying a nominal charge. Alternatively, the list of shareholders can be studied at the offices of the Registrars of the Joint Stock Companies.

28. Though the LIC is prohibited from holding more than 30 per cent of the equity shares in any one company, according to its Chairman, it held more than 30 per cent shares only in 2 companies during 1969; between 25 and 30 per cent in 25 companies; 10-25 per cent in 235 companies. Thus the LIC holdings are more than 10 per cent in 262 companies. See, Bhide, M.R. "LIC as Share-holder", *Commerce*, Annual Number, 1969. p.103.

29. Substantial means more than 10 per cent according to the Companies Act, 1956.

in the Ahmedabad Electricity (Killick House) is estimated as nearly 2 per cent; Atul Products (Kesturbhai Lal Bhai) 4 per cent; India Steamship (Birla) 5 per cent; Madras Aluminium (Naidu) 6 per cent; Tata Iron and Steel (Tata) 6 per cent; and National Rayon (China) 7 per cent only. The precise share-holdings of the LIC and other institutions in these companies are not known, but it is widely accepted in knowledgeable circles that the LIC alone holds in the Tata Iron and Steel nearly 15 per cent of the total equity. Similar appears to be the relative importance of the LIC in comparison to the holdings of the other management boards.[30]

A fairly large number of big private companies which have come to be accepted as exclusive preserves of large industrial houses are indeed not private companies, even if one takes the limited criteria of the pattern of equity holdings. The reason for their being treated as private companies is the voluntarily surrender of their voting rights by the public financial institutions and a conscious choice made to remain indifferent to the management problems and practices of the companies.[31] One, however, wonders if the position taken by the institutions to remain neutral is in reality so either. On the contrary, in practice, the institutions make their voting rights available to the existing management if there is a threat to their position. The recent example of the stand taken by the LIC in synthetic and chemicals is an exception. It would not be wrong to say that many a private management is continuing their advantageous position with the active support of the LIC and other financial institutions. In more than one way, all such companies, in which the institutions hold substantial shares, are the ones which are parts of the 'joint sector'—that exists and the one which may emerge after ILPIC recommendations are accepted.

Presently, however, there is no policy on the role of the financial institutions as dominant or substantial shareholders of the private

---

30. It may be pointed out that the estimate of the equity holding of the managements includes shares held by other house companies. If traced systematically, one would find that the share of the financial institutions works out to be still higher. This can be illustrated by the following example. Suppose there are two companies of a house and in each the institutions held 30 per cent shares. Also, company 'A' held 30 per cent shares in company 'B.' The interest of the LIC in 'B' may appear to be 30 per cent but in effect the LIC's position would be nearly 30 per cent if one takes 30 per cent share of 'A' in 'B' into account as in 'A' itself the institutions have 30 per cent shares.

31. See Bhide, M.R. "LIC as a Share-holder", *Commerce*, Annual Number, 1969.

corporate sector. The attitude adopted has, so far, been a narrow and limited one i.e., of a sleeping partner. The question requiring examination is if financial institutions should continue to play the same role of financing large projects without paying attention to the other implications of such help. Or, whether financial institutions can play a more purposeful role in regulating the direction and development of the private corporate sector in general and large enterprises in particular? More thought needs to be given on this aspect.

The least one can expect is that the strategic position of the financial institutions is used for achieving an effective coordination in planning, development and regulation of these 'joint sector' enterprises. For example, after identification of the companies in which the stake of the financial institutions is substantial and more than any other one single private interest, attempts could be made to have an overall plan of investments which would be more integrated in the plans of industrial development than the loose and global estimates of plan investment in the private sector as a whole. Secondly, efforts could be made to introduce, as a first step, modern techniques of management and public accountability. There could even be the sharing of experience and personnel in attempts to solve common problems of the various constituents of the 'joint sector.' Thirdly, a coordinated view of the large units in an industry could help to eliminate some of the wastes to reduce prices. There could also be common marketing, training and research programmes for development of industrial technology—which taken individually cannot be supported. The purpose of mentioning the above possibilities is only by way of illustration.

Viewed in this light, the 'joint sector' could be an effective instrument of regulating large enterprises, which are now under private managements, in line with social purposes. It would be a new responsibility and for effective discharge of this, building up of the requisite cadre which can provide a continuing perspective and the necessary meaning is fundamental.

The acceptance of 'joint sector' (not as visualised by the ILPIC but the *de facto* existing one) is all the more important when the managing agency system in India has been abolished and each large industrial unit has its own independent board of management. There has been a growing demand for some sort of public accountability of large private sector enterprises.

And this has come from the Prime Minister herself. By deciding to accept the position as a shareholder, the government could eliminate some of the unscrupulous private managements and help the rest of the private sector to improve its public image—which is not a very admirable one today. One could also hope in this process to achieve the objective of reducing the degree of concentration in ownership and control in the corporate sector.

Section V

Journalist Miscellany

23

FICCI and the Planning Commission

Strange Alliance against the Dutt Report[1]

Right from the time the *Report of the Industrial Licensing Policy Inquiry Committee* (ILPIC) was released, big business and its spokesmen have been up in arms against the recommendations made. The *Eastern Economist*, that very objective mouthpiece of the most affected business house, started its editorial on the subject by attacking the committee as Communist-inspired. This method of giving the committee a bad name for hanging its recommendations has been continued by big business spokesmen. The latest among these is the Federation of Indian Chambers of Commerce and Industry (FICCI), the organisation representing the top houses in the country. Mr Bharat Ram, in his speech at the Industrial Advisory Council on Saturday, has put together the various attempts of big business to malign the committee, to state the recommendations in a distorted form so as to confuse issues and put forward alternatives which would prevent any clear-cut steps being taken. A strange part of this effort is, as Mr Bharat Ram's speech indicates, that the FICCI has found an excellent ally in the Planning Commission.

Mr Bharat Ram as well as the FICCI have challenged the adequacy of the statistical data as well as the analysis based upon it. It would require a separate study to go into the details of this aspect. It should be pointed out, however, that the justification for the use of data about capital goods imports—not for the year 1966, as Mr. Bharat Ram says, but data for the whole 10 year period—as well as that for investment proposed was that only such data could provide the basis for aggregative analysis regarding licences issued for various commodities. With the enormous secretariat

1. By Economicus in the *National Herald*, September 21, 1969.

that the FICCI has, if it has a better methodology to suggest it would be interesting to know more about it.

Evidence of Undue Influence

Very cleverly, Mr Bharat Ram has appealed to the spokesmen of the government to make them the allies of big business in sabotaging the recommendations of the committee, by pointing out that licensing decisions are subject to scrutiny by a number of government authorities including ministers who, to quote him, "have been persons of highest integrity and political standing." He wants to make sure that the government will realise how dangerous it is for its own reputation not to permit this talk of undue influence to be sustained. The committee's report otherwise gives enough evidence of undue influence and the Commission of Enquiry proposed to be set up should provide even more evidence about the temptations put forward by big business and how people in government at various levels fall prey to them.

The idea that, after indicating industrial licensing as it has worked in the past, the committee has contradicted itself by suggesting that licensing should be made more pervasive is being consistently spread by not only big business and the monopoly press but even by a member of the Planning Commission. What really has the committee suggested?

Selected Licensing

In essence, the committee has suggested that the use of industrial licensing needs to be selective. It points out that licensing cannot but be *ad hoc* and arbitrary, except where good industry plans providing guidelines of industrial development are prepared. It points out that such planning for industry can only be possible in the 'core' sector. It, therefore, suggests that licensing in its full form should be confined to this sector.

The committee has also suggested not only the continuation but also the more rational application of the present policy of reserving certain industries for development in the small-scale sector. It suggests that where techno-economic examination indicates that production in the small-scale sector could be economical in the Indian circumstances, there should be a ban on the creation of capacity in large-scale industry.

Obviously, this measure will have to be accompanied by others such as financial and technical assistance. Similarly, it suggests that where the creation of capacity in a non-essential industry would make large drafts on scarce resources such as foreign exchange, and thus might affect essential industrial growth, there should be a ban on the creation of further capacity. The Planning Commission and the FICCI are in a strange alliance in opposing this recommendation. Both Mr Venkataraman and Mr. Bharat Ram are alarmed at the prospect that this would mean higher prices for the luxury goods and Mr Venkataraman speaks about this even having an inflationary impact. One can understand Mr Bharat Ram feeling agitated that luxury industries should not be permitted to grow, but one did not expect this of the Planning Commission.

Core Sector

The characteristic of industries to be included in the core sector has been indicated in the companies report. The principles which would help the government to decide on the industries further creation of capacity which should be banned are also spelt out. All that remains is covered by the middle or remaining sector. A number of critics are agitated that this area is not defined. Is it expected that such a committee, in addition to indicating broad principles, should also work out detailed lists? Is it not appropriate that this should be left to the Planning Commission and the government?

As regards this large middle sector, the committee's approach is very clear. Industrial licensing is to continue in this sector only for the purpose of ensuring the observation of two objectives of industrial policy: (i) the exclusion of certain top business groups from this sector and (ii) the observation of the bans as mentioned above. If the Company Law Department does its work properly—and does not go to sleep as it did after the Monopolies Inquiry Commission (MIC) Report—it should be able to keep track of the concerns and individuals connected with the top groups and should be able to advise in a matter of two or three weeks whether the applicant is connected with one of the top houses proposed to be excluded. Similarly, to decide whether the proposed production infringes the bans should not take much time for the Directorate General of Technical Development (DGTD). These decisions would be essentially of a routine character and should not take more than a month. As a matter of fact, once the decisions to exclude certain top houses and ban certain items are well known, the number of applications from such categories is likely to be rare. Otherwise there would be free licensing of anyone who wants to enter the field.

Top Business Houses

Why does the committee recommend the exclusion of top business houses from the 'middle' sector? The committee has provided adequate evidence to show that the top houses wield enormous influence at all levels of government. They also wield considerable influence with financial institutions. They command very large financial and other resources. If they are permitted freedom to develop industries in the areas outside the core, it would mean virtually a denial of freedom to the smaller business groups to develop these industries. While one can understand Mr Bharat Ram feeling agitated about it, should one not expect the Planning Commission as well as spokesmen of genuine private enterprise to support this approach? Does private enterprise only mean the top houses?

Whether the government should exclude the top 20 houses or only the top 15 or 10 is a matter that will have to be decided in the light of the assessment at the particular time about the capacity of other groups developing certain industries. The government may well start with excluding the top 10 and watch the result. But unless one assumes that all potential entrepreneurial capacity is concentrated in the top 10 or 20 groups, one cannot understand the opposition to this recommendation. Whether, as Mr Bharat Ram agitatedly asks, the sons and grandsons of top industrialists are to be excluded from the 'middle' sector depends upon whether they continue to work essentially as parts of the larger groups or independently. The sons and grandsons cannot have it both ways—obtain the advantage of inheriting the family fortune and business, and still call themselves independent and new entrepreneurs.

A deliberate confusion is being created by big business interests about the committee's recommendations regarding large houses by making out that the committee is against large techno-economically justified production units. The committee is not questioning the importance of large units being set up where necessary. It is only objecting to the top houses being permitted to expand in industries where their entry is not necessary for industrial growth. At the same time, it supports the use of managerial and technical talent as well as financial resources of top houses for the development of core industries, either independently or, as is more likely to happen, in cooperation with government through the joint sector. A project like Mithapur if approved could then be developed as a joint venture of the government and Tatas. The entrepreneurial ability of the Tatas can still be used. But the committee certainly recommends against the use of public money or building private empires. The committee also pointed out that top houses or foreign concerns may have in special cases to be permitted to operate in the 'middle' sector industries—provided there is real justification for it.

Joint Sector

The idea of the joint sector has been opposed on the plea that if this is done retrospectively for past loans, it will be a breach of contract. This is an unnecessary bugbear. The committee has nowhere recommended that past loans should be converted into equity. What it has said is that it should be possible in future for the loan assistance provided by public institutions to be convertible—whole or in part—into equity. When public institutions provide as much as 30 and 60 per cent of the project costs in different forms, what is wrong with a condition of this kind being laid down? Much is made of the importance of a proper debt-equity ratio. The committee's data about how public financial institutions provide both loans and a large part of equity through underwriting of new issues should prove how hollow this discussion about the capital structure is in practice.

The committee has suggested not a wholesale appointment of directors on all concerns in which public institutions hold significant equity. It has suggested that a cadre of professional directors should be built up over a period of time, the implication being that a start should be made by appointing such directors on the most important concerns, and the process should develop over a period of time.

The committee's emphasis on industry planning for the core sector has been criticised by the FICCI and the Planning Commission. One can understand the Planning Commission doing this as the new Planning Commission, like in many other respects, has disappointed people in this respect too. The Administrative Reforms Commission (ARC) has recommended that one of the essential requirements of better planning was that competent organisations should be created for the formulation of long-term perspective plans for the most important industries. Without such work, planning becomes merely target and financial jugglery. Nothing has been done by the new Planning Commission in the two years of its existence in this respect. What is the Planning Commission for and what kind of plans it can produce if long-term planning for the key sectors is not organised? Stating that technology is fast changing and, therefore, 10-15 years planning is not possible, stands ill in the mouth of a member of the Planning Commission.

Characteristically, Mr Bharat Ram's final plea is for another enquiry committee of "independent persons, economists and those who know something about industry." He dislikes this committee because it has only done the work assigned to it and not gone into the overall problems of industrial development. What he expects the new 'more expert and mature' committee to do apparently is to pay encomiums to the top houses for the great service they have performed, forgetting and overlooking the cost of their so doing, and then make a more detailed enquiry into the whole question of industrial development which should keep the committee busy for many years. In the meanwhile, let the process of delicensing continue, let the financial institutions be dominated by larger business houses, and let the top business groups expand all over the Indian economy. Amen.

24 India: The Economy and the Economists[1]

In the history of each nation, there are a few years which are seemingly not very significant but which are crucial from the viewpoint of changes in the institutional framework of the political, social or economic system. These changes, most of the time, fail to attract or cause sufficient excitement or even to result in well-informed discussion. To even the political leadership, the implications of such changes are not clear. This ignorance on their part would explain their insensitivity. In such situations, it is the responsibility of professional social scientists to give frank expression to their views to create the right type of awareness among the public in general and the leadership in particular.

On the Indian economic scene, today many in the top hierarchy of the government seem to suffer from great optimism on the agricultural front. An agricultural revolution is predicted by many to be around the corner. If it were so, one would wish them all success. But the question is: how can one predict a 'revolution' when better agricultural performance during the last year has been ascribed to the unusual kindness of the weather gods? Perhaps it needs to be understood that revolutions are 'man-made and not God-sent.' Optimism is good, provided it enhances the confidence of the doer. On the other hand, optimism can be dangerous if it results in the dismantling of the economic structure that was being built up (i) to meet contingencies and shortage and (ii) to pursue the broader objective.

Food Controls

For instance, the Planning Commission stated in 1951 that food controls had certain positive functions, such as safeguarding the minimum consumption standards of poorer classes, preventing excessive or

1. S.K. Goyal, also known as Economicus, wrote this article for the *National Herald* on August 31, 1968.

ostentatious consumption by the well-to-do and facilitating the country's programme of direct utilisation of unemployed manpower for investment. But with some little improvement in the food situation in 1953-54, the government took a decision practically to abandon all food controls. This step of the government, taken on the basis of the agricultural performance of two years, was quite contrary to the long-term needs of a planned economy. Very soon, the re-imposition of food controls became inevitable.

Once again a similar phenomenon is under way. Past experience seems to have taught us nothing. With the talk of agricultural breakthrough at many places, decontrol of foodgrains has been announced. How soon these will have to be reintroduced should be predictable. What have the professional economists to say about this? No one knows since they have not expressed themselves. Is it because taking rational positions is not always fashionable or popular? Or is it what they do not consider it of sufficient importance to strain their mental capabilities on such an issue? Or, is it their sense of being in isolation from the current economic life of the country? Or, may it be their honest belief that offering advice for reform was not their role?

Let us take the past one year during which a large many economic issues have been discussed in Parliament and at the levels of government. These issues did not become important all of a sudden. It is perhaps a coincidence that so many specific measures were proposed, each closely related to the other, in the last one year only. Soon these measure will be the 'law of the land.' A special feature of these bills is that these relate to a variety of substantial reform in the Indian economic system. One bill, now before the Joint Select Committee, is to curb monopolies and restrictive trade practices. The bill is the result of a decade of discussion on concentration of 'economic power.' The Mahalonobis Committee with a galaxy of top economists submitted Part I of their report nearly four years back (Part II is yet awaited, though another four years have passed). The Monopolies Inquiry Commission (MIC) submitted its report in October 1965. Only after three years, the government has been able to propose the Monopolies Bill in 1968. The motivation for this bill was to reform the 'economic system' as suggested in the Constitutional Directive so as to ensure that "the operation of economic system does not result in the concentration of wealth and means of production to the common detriment." No one can dispute that the issues involved are largely, if not wholly, economic ones. What was the involvement of the Indian economists in the framing of issues for this bill? What thought did they give to this important measure of economic reform? An indication of the extent of indifference of the economists is provided in the *MIC Report*. It says "Of the twentyone leading economists whom we addressed with the request to send their views only six responded....."

Social Control

The second bill of equal significance is seeking to bring financial institution under 'social control.' 'Social control' was the expression used to suggest that without the government taking over ownership, controls would be so designed as to achieve the same objectives through social control as were desired through bank nationalisation. The main argument for nationalisation of banks was to restrict the growth of concentration of economic power. The bill as introduced, however, has no reference to 'concentration.' It has a few provisions to ensure greater compliance of the Reserve Bank of India (RBI) directives by the commercial banks. How far has the bill provisions to make it an effective instrument of regulation? Will the proposed banking bill enable the government to ensure policies by the financial institutions which conform to the Plan objectives and priorities? These are questions which need to be analysed and discussed before the bill becomes a law. During the year, how many professional economists paid their attention to this aspect?

An equally important bill is regarding the abolition of the managing agency system in India. A special committee reported on this some time back. What has been the reaction of those who are students of the economic system and teach, day in and day out, industrial management? It would have been only proper if the alternative modes of management and organisation of the corporate sector were discussed in a dispassionate and analytical manner by the professionals. What organisational forms the vested interests of the managing agents can take when the managing agency system was abolished? Does the bill visualise 'abolition' only without suggesting other specific measures to check the continuance of the system under another garb? These are questions wanting a reply.

Donations

Parliament is soon to discuss the question of the banning of donations to political parties by companies. What are the economic implications of this bill? Will the bill help to restrict transformation of economic power into other forms? What part of the company donations goes out of government revenue? How does this effect investments of the companies? One needs to spell out the likely implications of this ban on the accounting practices. Similarly, there is a bill on patents. What will be its impact on the import substitution? Will it restrict foreign investment? These and many similar other are the questions the reply to which the economists can give. But unfortunately the silence of the economists on these vital issues seems to be, if not a calculated one, a throughly disturbing feature. The reference to the bills is only to illustrate the movement of the government, and the credit for this does not go to the Indian economists.

Some economists may, however, argue that it was not their function to interfere with the process of law-making. Granting this to be so, let us have a look at the other field, which one can be sure they would not disclaim. That is the field of national planning. The last year was continuance of another non-Five-Year Plan year—if not another year of 'Plan Holiday.' The Planning Commission was reconstituted and the 'Approach to the Fourth Plan' has been thrown open for discussion. What have been the reactions of the Indian economists as a class of professionals? How many of them have expressed themselves on this issue? The answer to this would lie in the papers written, seminars organised or the public lectures delivered by the top *elite* of the class of economists. Perhaps, it is not very appropriate to think of counting such things for the learned ones. Recently, a senior economist was complaining that before the Planning Commission made the Approach Document public, his views should have been asked. Now it was a public document and he had no obligation to comment on it.

Let us take another area in which there is scope for individual economists to make an impact, and yet, one cannot find even a couple of instances of economists' participation. The area is state Five-Year Plans. The state Plans in India account for nearly half of the National Plan. Each state Plan has to be formulated in accordance to the state's own geo-economic resources. It is well known that the expertise with the state planning departments is practically negligible, and yet in each state there are two or three universities, each having a professor of economics, supported by a few readers and lecturer-level staff. One often wonders why the state university economic departments do not consider it important to discuss, analyse and get interested in the problems of their home states. Is it a fact that each one in the states wishes to be a national economist as their national counterparts only think on international line? Home problems are not their business.

Financial Assistance

Another subject needing discussion by the Indian economists, especially during this year, should have been the principles of financial assistance to states as now being considered by the Finance Commission and the Planning Commission. The Finance Commission was constituted during the year. What the economists in the country could do, to expect the least, was to build up a theoretical framework for measuring the level of development in different states or to suggest ways and means of comparing regional disparities. This could have become a basis for determining the share of different states in the divisible pool. Once again, one does not find much proof of the alertness of economists to this task.

Another occasion for participation in national economic issues was provided by Dr R.K. Hazari's report on industrial planning. Undoubtedly, Parliament got engaged in the more explosive part of the report which dealt with the larger licences being given to one house. At this point, it was for the class of economists to emphasise that the real issue was much wider than the cornering of licences by one house. The Hazari report was basically an assessment of one of the instruments of industrial planning. What a pity that the report did not draw any interest of the professional forums of the economists in this country. No one would deny that the much condemned politicians were the only ones to take note of it.

Reasons

Why have the Indian economists neglected their role? One may mention a few of the probable reasons for such a state of affairs. One, the last few years have seen the exit of a few top economists from their professional role. A few of the old stalwarts, due to the phenomena of ageing, have taken the back seats. The process has been helped by the government by offering offices of power—may it be in the cabinet, commissions or administrative positions in the universities and other organisations. It is not our contention that economists should not take up such position. On the contrary, one would argue for more of participation in government decision making. But why the retiring ones only? Let the government think of inviting persons who have something fresh to offer than making offers to those who are wanting post-retirement assignments.

Two, there seems to be very little expression of confidence by the government in the younger economists. An indication of this is provided by the fact that opportunities for involvement in economic decision making are provided, again and again, to only the top few. One wonders if the monopoly of economic knowledge and advisory roles is the privilege of these alone. Under these conditions, no surprise, the younger ones have found themselves at a distance from the national economic current.

Three, some economists have, due to one or more reasons, chosen to accept more and more of international assignments. These assignments may not give them job satisfaction but there is more than due monetary compensation for that. A similar process is reflected in a section of economists which finds more rewarding to work on topics of international significance than the national ones. It is a different issue, if the topics they choose for study are also those which force them to make foreign visits frequently. How can the poor ones help it? But apart from this, frankly speaking, is it not a fact that national recognition in India is directly related to the number of foreign visits an economist makes in a year?

Dilemma

Leaving the individual attitudes aside, it must also be recognised that in India today, an average economist is really in a dilemma. In a mixed economy, which has resorted to planing, there is continuously a danger, if an economist writes on contemporary problems, of his sounding either a 'socialist' or a 'reactionary.' If he wishes to get his writings published in the economic dailies, he must adapt his views to the philosophy of the paper. Take the case of the two economic dailies published in India. Both follow policies of glorifying the private sector and painting the performance of the public sector as black. What does one do in the absence of an independent press? But for a stray weekly, here or there, the situation is no different from that of the dailies. The quarterly or bi-annual journals can obviously be no forum for such discussions.

From the employment angle also, a young economist is in a fix. What are the alternatives open to him? The teaching profession does not suit all, nor are the salaries very attractive. There are some research organisations managed by private business houses. Such private research institutions offer fairly high salaries, but an honest worker finds that he does not have faith in what he does nor does he have facts, leave aside the right to professional sense or fairness. Very similar may be the position of a business economist. The other alternative left to a young economist is to join government service. The Indian Economic Services (IES) is one such institution which has transformed in one stroke a large many potential economists into pure and simple administrators. If one decides to join government service, the professional limitations should be well clear. It falls to the lot of a government economists to provide arguments, wrapped in economic terminology, to oppose a decision knowing well that it was only a few months back that he himself was the man to suggest it. Many a time he does not have faith in what he does. But he cannot express himself openly lest it was a disclosure of a 'state secret.'

But are these sufficient reasons for the economists in general to remain indifferent to national economic issues? Should someone take upon himself the responsibility of organising, cajoling and pressurising them. Who should take this leadership role? How should he go about?

25 Approach to Fifth Plan

A Comment[1]

The Approach Paper envisages a reduction of 5 per cent in the monthly per capita consumption of the richest 30 per cent of the population. For this group of urbanites, the reduction envisaged is from ₹ 113.21 to ₹ 108.07 and for the rural rich, the proposed reduction is from ₹ 84.42 to ₹ 80.38. As a result of the Fifth Plan programmes and policies, the per capita monthly consumption of the poorest 30 per cent of the population would rise by 60 per cent in rural areas and 50 per cent in urban areas.

As at present, there are wide disparities in the pattern of national consumption. The estimates of the share of different fractile groups in total consumption for 1967-68 (see Table 25.1) indicate that the richest 5 per cent of urbanites shared a little less than 16 per cent of total consumption, whereas the share of the poorest 5 per cent was only a little above 1 per cent of total consumption. In the rural areas, the share of the richest 5 per cent was 13.2 per cent of total consumption as against 1.48 per cent of the corresponding section of the rural poorest. The richest 30 per cent shared a little more than 54 per cent of total urban consumption as against 12.38 per cent shared by the poorest 30 per cent of urbanites. If one takes the 1967-68 pattern of consumption as valid for the year 1973-74, it is obvious that a 5 per cent reduction in the total consumption of the richest 30 per cent, when wholly transferred to raise the consumption level of the poorest 30 per cent, could in itself mean a 20 per cent rise in the average level of consumption of the poorest 30 per cent. In this redistributive logic, the extreme degree of poverty experienced by the poorest can be appreciably reduced if one can impose a marginal sacrifice on the richest sections of the economy. The validity of this Approach Paper can be seen from the fact that a 5 per cent reduction in the consumption share of the top 5 per cent of the

1. This article was published in the *Young Indian* in 1973.

population, when fully transferred to the poorest 5 per cent, could mean by itself a rise in the level of consumption by nearly 60 per cent.

Table 25.1

Estimates of the Share of Different Fractile Groups in Total Consumption: 1967-68

Fractile Group	*Rural*	*Urban*	*Combined*
(1)	*(2)*	*(3)*	*(4)*
0-5	1.48	1.14	1.33
5-10	2.02	1.64	1.86
10-20	5.01	4.25	4.69
20-30	6.08	5.35	5.76
30-40	7.09	6.42	6.81
40-50	8.13	7.57	7.91
50-60	9.29	8.88	9.13
60-70	10.68	10.47	10.60
70-80	12.46	12.59	12.52
80-90	15.15	15.90	15.48
90-95	9.37	10.24	9.74
95-100	13.24	15.15	14.17
Total Population	100.00	100.00	100.00

Source: *National Sample Survey* (22nd Round), July 1967 to June 1968, based on a sample of 15,800 rural and 8,600 urban households.

Given the level of disparities even within the top 30 per cent of the rich sections of the economy, it would mean that for achieving a 5 per cent reduction, for the group as a whole, the top 10 per cent will have to reduce their consumption by a higher percentage than those whose consumption level is lower. On the assumption that 'the richer one is the higher cut he makes' probably, the top 5 per cent will have to reduce their consumption by more than 10 per cent and for the top 1 per cent would mean of a still higher order. It has to be accepted, however, that a 5 per cent reduction implying nearly a saving of 2.5 per cent in the national consumption would comprise of a variety of non-essential items of consumption, whereas the requirements of the poorest sections would be of an extremely different character. It is not a simple question of redistribution of the consumption goods within society. By implication, the desired change would suggest the need for raising production of those goods which comprise the consumption basket of the poorest. The existing productive system of the Indian economy has got built to cater to the consumption pattern that results from the extreme situation of inequalities of income and wealth. It has a certain product mix. While it does not have the productive capacity for providing the requisite amount of essential consumption goods, it is well organised to meet all varieties of non-essential and luxury consumption. It is but natural that one should ask what use would existing production capacities be put to? Many of us had the opportunity to visit the Asia 72. If one recalls the range of goods exhibited there, one would be able to visualise, very vividly, the nature of the production system that we have at the eve of the Fifth Five Year Plan.

To a marginal extent, it may be possible to adjust production capacities to suit new requirements. But a massive production base for essential goods of poor man's consumption requirement will need to be built up if the poorest have to be pulled out of the extreme levels of poverty. How will this be done? This question becomes all the more relevant in the face of the fact that, generally, the rate of profit on non-essential and luxury items is always higher than on items of poor man's consumption.

The task of bringing about a radical change in the production pattern, in an economy where large part of the investment decisions are governed by market demand, would become a near impossibility if, as a Fifth Plan policy (as enunciated in para 11 of pages 18-19), it is accepted that there would be higher rate of accrual of incomes with the well-to-do sections of the economy. The approach seems to be that "it is not accrual of income that has to be controlled" but the "disposition of accrued incomes." One would question the soundness of validity of such a formulation that seeks to mop up the entire additional incomes (100% marginal rate of savings), alongwith affecting a reduction in the existing level of consumption, through 'inducement' or 'the financial intermediaries.' What does this mean in concrete terms? Will we be able to have compulsory savings for richer sections?

This brings one to the policies regulating investments in the industrial sector. During the last few years, we have seen relaxation of the licensing policy in a variety of ways. Firstly, it has been seen that while targets for priority sectors have lagged behind, the planning process has allowed successive upward revisions of production and capacity targets for goods which do not have national priority. The developmental councils in various industries have industry representatives as well as official representatives on them. Industry representatives have normally pressed for adjustments of targets in a way that would increase profitability of their respective fields. Restrictions on new entrants can give high profits to the existing industrial units. In priority industries, the industry representatives want the targets to be set low, whereas for other items, they would want to enhance them as these targets enjoy good demand. In brief, the economic system of decision-making in relation to licensing of industries has always been adjusted to suit a demand pattern which caters to the upper strata of society. The same can be said about collaboration agreements. These points are well known. It will be necessary not only to apply breaks but undo what has been done in a number of industries catering to the needs of the richer sections. The licensing policy has also been relaxed as much larger investments can be undertaken without any social control or obtaining licences by new entrepreneurs. Diversion of limited resources to such fields which offer higher prospects for profit is very obvious. If a substantial part of the investment decisions is left to be determined by the market mechanism, there cannot but be tendencies for investment to flow in such fields for which there would be demand. The Approach Paper does not indicate the process by which maximum targets would get fixed for non-essential items of production. Would the commission suggest to the government to have more rigid physical controls on production and trade? Or, will it suffice to have a set of policies to ensure export of such production even when it involves a large degree of subsidy?

While one certainly has to talk about reducing essential consumption in the household sector, one cannot but point out to the pattern of public expenditure itself. There is a need to question the type of expenditure that is now being undertaken both in the government and the public sector enterprises. The public institutions have, in fact, to give a lead to the rest of the economy in setting up standards of austerity in consumption. If it is accepted, then one wonders how can one justify the provision of ₹ 280 crore for government servants as a loan for vehicles. One could possibly understand if this amount was provided for the purchase of bicycles. In this approach, isn't it necessary to have a serious look at the pay structure in the government, semi-governmental organisations like banking, insurance, etc., and the remuneration system (especially at top levels) in the organised corporate sector? One may also consider if the policy of encouraging foreign travel (through concessional tariff on Jumbos) and luxury living in five star hotels would fit in the pattern of society that we seek to build up or the type of austerity one expects the upper income strata to observe during the next five years. Similarly, do the public sector enterprises need to compete in having perquisites for staff at standards of affluent society?

There is one instance of public expenditure which needs to be mentioned by way of illustration to show how the pressures of the existing socioeconomic system lead the government, leave aside private consumption, to orient public expenditure with an eye to satisfy demands of a very small section of the population. This refers to the proposal for having nearly ₹ 120 crore plan for the expansion of television (TV) network in the country during the next five years. This is no place to go into the laudable objectives set before TV and what actually happens. One needs to only know the number of TV sets operating for the lower strata out of the nearly 80,000 sets now operating in Delhi. One also knows that the overall plan of investment on TV during the Fourth Plan was nearly ₹ 5 crore. The actual expenditure, however, would be roughly a double of this provision. With the given price structure, does one need to argue to which section of the society will this investment cater to? How do such trends fit in the vision that is sought to be projected in the Approach Paper? A related question to this is about the generation of demand for non-essential items through public media like Vividh Bharati. A look at the pattern of advertisements (see Table 25.2) is sufficient to convince the nature of demand that is being built up through the most powerful media of communication.

There is another very important aspect of national consumption which does not receive the necessary attention. This is regarding consumption in housing. One does not have any available data to give an idea of the magnitude of national resources which get diverted in building up of black assets in modern posh houses with large floor area and lavish furnishings. The Approach Paper not only avoids reference to the parallel economy, supported by black money, but also does not take note of the physical resources in cement, steel, industrial skills, etc., that can be brought to

Table 25.2

Products Advertised on Vividh Bharati (September 1971)

Items	*Net Amount per Month (₹ in thousands)*	*Per cent*	*No. of Minutes*	*Per cent*
Toiletries and Cosmetics	457.68	16.01	3,146	17.93
OTC Medicinals	496.06	17.35	2,632	15.01
Beverages	238.28	8.33	1,636	9.32
Fabrics and Apparels	216.94	7.60	1,336	7.61
Detergents and Deodorants	178.42	6.24	1,000	5.70
Confectioneries	157.63	5.51	868	4.95
Food Products	133.05	4.65	865	4.93
Films	135.66	4.75	682	3.88
Banks	91.23	3.19	597	3.40
Pesticides	102.76	3.59	571	3.25
Radios	73.05	2.56	474	2.70
Paints	65.29	2.28	419	2.39
Electrical Appliances				
Torches and Batteries	52.49	1.84	392	2.24
Cycles and Tyres	51.00	1.78	366	2.09
Shoes and Shoe Polish	37.51	1.31	279	1.59
Miscellaneous	371.90	13.01	2,284	13.01
Total	2,858.95	100.00	17,546	100.00

Source: Survey data.

augment socially desirable consumption and essential capital formation. Would the government be ready to place physical restrictions on floor area and new construction activity strictly in functional terms? Along with this, how would the government ensure utilisation of existing facilities to the functionally maximum limit and thereby eliminate the present forms of extravagance?

The Approach Paper does accept that basic plan decisions are political ones. One could even add that the will to implement will have necessarily to be demonstrated at the top.

26

A Critique of India's Fifth Plan[1]

The 'approach' document to the Fifth Five Year Plan was released to the public in the last week of January this year. It is, therefore, only natural that anyone would pick up a book like the one *A Critique of India's Fifth Plan* by Dr Sinha of the University of Bihar and eagerly go through it. The subject is of topical interest. This was the main reason why the reviewer got attracted towards this title. One expected that critique of the 'approach' would first underline the special features of the Fifth Plan approach to indicate how and in what manner does the approach to the next plan differ from the earlier ones. After this one hoped for a critical analysis of the assumptions, methodology and conclusions of the 'approach.' But here is a critique of the approach which takes the plan approach as the final Fifth Plan. The author is unable to distinguish between the approach paper and the Fifth Plan document which, according to the approach paper would only be ready by the end of the year. Probably, in his anxiety to be an early bird, Dr Sinha forgot that the most important part of the approach document was the strategy that has been put forth for future planning. The approach to the Fifth Plan indicates, for the first time, how the poorest 30 per cent of the Indian economy can look forward for a better level of living as also the extent to which the top 30 per cent of the population will have necessarily to reduce their level of consumption. Until now the plans did have an emphasis on growth but no plan had specifically stated the extent to which different income groups can hope to benefit as a result of planned economic development. This is a clear departure from the past practice and the most important feature of the Fifth Plan approach. But unfortunately, Dr Sinha has not been able to appreciate and understand the strategy of the approach of the Fifth Plan. While the first part of the book, comprising of 13 pages,

1. This is a review of *A Critique of India's Fifth Plan* by Laxmi Narayan Sinha, Bharat Book Depot, Patna, which appeared in the *Young Indian* in 1973.

contains vague short essays on rate of economic growth, saving, technology, rate of profit, wage and employment, the second part is supposed to be a technical appendix to the critique. But judging from the understanding of the writer, as reflected in Part I, it was obvious that it would be futile to waste time in going through Part II. However, the reviewer did go through, but only to prove to himself that his fears were genuine.

27 Planning comes to a Halt[1]

The Planning Commission, at its recent meeting, decided that no new plan projects should be initiated during the next financial year. The main thrust of plan efforts would only be to speed up completion of the projects on hand. This should not, however, be described as a plan holiday. Similarly, the public sector plan outlay would be stepped up from ₹ 15,109 crore to ₹ 17,417 crore in the next year and the government would compliment itself for having enhanced the outlay by about 15 per cent. But due to the price rise of nearly 18-20 per cent during the current year, the size of plan outlay during 1981-82 would actually be lower by 3-5 per cent. Is this what one can expect from a party that promised the country a 'working' and 'efficient' government?

Parallel Economy

There is admittedly a parallel black money economy. The size and extent of black money operations, however, remains unknown. The parallel character of black money operations is reflected in the fact that prices and interest rates in India are invariably of two types. In urban areas, all real estate business has a black money component. If the price of a house is ₹ 10 lakh, the white money price would probably be ₹ 3 lakh and the buyer would pay rest as black money.

Invariably two sets of prices are quoted for all the goods which attract sales and local taxes. For goods delivered, with a proper 'receipt,' the price is higher than that for unrecorded transactions. Interest rates on black money borrowings differ substantially from the rates charged by banks and other financial institutions.

---

1. *The Daily*, August 11, 1981.

Two Sets of Prices

For imported consumer goods, whether cigarettes or video systems, there are two rates—a much higher rate for legally imported goods and rates lower by 30-40 per cent for smuggled goods. For commodities manufactured within the country but having a larger demand than their supply (as in the case of commercial and private vehicles), the open market prices are substantially higher than the prices fixed by the manufacturers.

In brief, there are two sets of prices for most goods and services which carry high tax rates. The extent of black money in society is directly related to the extent of unaccounted transactions that take place in a year. What could be the extent of such transactions? If unaccounted transactions were only of the order of 1-2 per cent of the overall economic activity, the parallel economy would be of little significance. The crucial fact to be discovered is the size and the relative importance of the economic operations which evade fiscal obligations. It is difficult to assess the magnitude and relative importance of these activities. Little effort has been made towards its assessment. The more serious question is whether the extent of 'black money' supported activity is on the increase. The widely shared impression, confirmed by many in authority, is that activities under this head are growing fast—in any case much faster than the 'white money sector.'

It could be generally stated that hardly any black money supported economic activities are undertaken in the rural areas, in the unorganised sector and by low-income groups. Conversely, a high degree of consumption, production and trade is supported by unaccounted money in urban, organised, industry and high income groups: the elite of our society.

Locationally, the black money spread is restricted to a much smaller number of pockets in the country than often realised. The areas of economic activities, their geographical locations as also other distinguishing characteristics of the black money operated system are well known. By a process of elimination, it should be possible to encircle the pockets where black money is generated and appropriate policies could thus be evolved. But who would be interested in such exercises?

Would Indian political parties be earnestly interested in curbing the unaccounted sector and activities at the cost of depriving themselves of necessary resources for elections? It emerges from the above analysis that 'black money' is not a pool of financial resources but is a continuing process and a flow. By evading fiscal obligations, one is able to have unaccounted money. A part of it is utilised to support high levels of consumption and the rest diverted to support economic activity—whether it be manufacturing, construction or trade.

The root cause of the black money lies in the unaccounted economic activities, and therefore, any solution to the problem has to be in terms of liquidating the real cause. To do otherwise would be to treat the symptom and not the disease.

Illegal Activities

If this is accepted, occasional voluntary disclosure schemes, black money bearer bonds and floating of corporations to reduce liquid money in the market offer no solution. Any sincere government will have to think in terms of curbing unaccounted activities and taking punitive and stringent measures against all those involved. Given the broad characteristics of the group of persons who thrive on this activity, can one really expect that the people in authority would find it easier to act against those very people who are otherwise loyal and I obedient to their wishes?

28 Judging Public Sector Performance[1]

The public sector in India, according to the Finance Minister, had made a profit of ₹ 48.5 crore during the year as against the lose of ₹ 299 crore in the previous year. The number of undertakings making profits had risen from 139 to 170 in the same period. With each successive year, more and more undertakings are coming out of the red.

In the mind of the public, the level of profits made by an enterprise is the sole measure of its degree of success. While assessing the overall performance of enterprises, one needs to ask: if the only test of performance is in terms of profits—for private as well as public sector units—what is the logic of state ownership and management of business enterprises.

Their Logic

Is the objective of dragging the 'government into business' to provide job opportunities for the members of the Indian Civil Service (ICS)? Or, is it that state-owned enterprises are established to generate financial surpluses to supplement budgetary efforts at resource mobilisation? Alternatively, has one to find the logic of state enterprises in terms of providing infrastructural support and extension of public utilities? Or, is the expansion of public sector sought to introduce structural changes in the society?

What is it that provided the logic for the initiation of the public sector in India and why did the Five Year Plans place so much reliance on the expansion and growth of this sector? In which direction is India's public sector heading?

---

1. *The Daily*, January 1, 1982.

These are important issues, not only because one would be able to take a clear view on the question of profitability, but a discussion on these issues would enable us to evolve a better and overall perspective on some of the basic questions with regard to this important sector of our economy.

Let us first examine profits. Should the philosophy of the public sector be profit maximisation? If so, what would then be the difference between the private and public sector? For the sake of argument, let us assume that all public sector enterprises (PSEs) are given a directive to achieve the highest possible profitabilty. In that case, as good entrepreneurs, the public sector management would assess the existing market demand and frame their programmes of new investments as per demand estimates.

Market demand, in any country, is known to be a mirror reflection of the pattern of income and wealth distribution. Given the gross inequalities and wide disparities in income and wealth in India, public sector investment programmes would—in case the investments are only governed by market demand—be deployed to cater to the needs of a small section of the national population. Even if one goes by the official estimates, as quoted by the Sixth Five Year Plan, 48 per cent of the country's population is living below the poverty line. Obviously, in the situation, the poor half of the Indian people would have nothing to expect from enlarged investment in the public sector. The poor, by the very definition, are those who do not have adequate incomes to buy even the basic and minimum requirements at the prevailing prices. The rich, on the other hand, are those who have surplus to afford a much higher standard of living than what may be described as essential.

After Profit

If profit maximisation is decided to be the objective of public enterprises, in a short period, the Indian public sector can be expected to be wholly in the service of the rich economic elite. With the advent of time, those public sector units which are prone to incur losses or have relatively lower profitability would start getting liquidated. Conversely, the enterprises which earn high profits would be allocated larger public resources.

The next logical step would be that PSEs would play to go abroad in search of profits. This would imply a shift in their client group, that is instead of catering for the Indian rich, the enterprises would produce goods required by the elite in affluent societies.

It would be equally logical to expect that in search of more profitable markets, the public sector units may have to collaborate with both indigenious private sector units, as also the already established world market leaders identified as multinational corporations (MNCs).

The other direction in which public enterprises would have to move, given the objective of profite maximisation, would be towards closer cooperation with big business and multinationals in pleading for tax reliefs, fiscal concessions and adoption of such policies that would help them grow fast. To put it differently, the public sector would become a lobby for fewer governmental controls and demand freedom for business in order to allow the so-called free interplay of market forces.

It should be easy to predict that pressure from within would have more impact on the policies than when the government was reacting to pleas from the outside. In this approach it is also implied that each public sector management would seek more and more autonomy and lesser and lesser accountability to political institutions like Parliament and other elected bodies. Already a widely heard complaint is that in the presence of this Public Accounts Committee, no one can expect the public sector managers to take risk or business initiative.

On the question of autonomy, it is natural that in the logic of profit maximisation, these enterprises would object to their being pressurised to locate projects in backward regions, to provide housing, medical and other facilities to their employees, or to observe other labour welfare practices. It would be argued, with adequate reasoning, that the enterprises which happened to be owned by the state cannot be compelled to follow more liberal labour employment policies than what is being practised by the private sector.

Once we accept this reasoning, it should be also expected that more autonomy to public sector managements would have to be granted in matters of purchases and pricing. In India, it is not well appreciated that many of the PSEs have been in the red, not because of their inefficient managements but essentially because the enterprises have not been permitted to adopt pricing policies on the principle of what the market can afford. In fact, this is the single most important constraint on the public sector.

Commanding Heights

In India, as per the Industrial Policy Resolutions of 1948 and 1956, certain economic activities have been exclusively reserved for the public sector. In a sense, the public sector, in a large part of the economy, enjoys a monopoly position. Today, very few can dispute that the public sector has already acquired the commanding heights in the Indian economy. It is not only that public sector has expanded in public utilities, energy and banking, but it has also acquired a dominant position in many other areas of economic activity. From this monopoly position and by pursuing profit-oriented pricing policies, it should be an extremely easy proposition to make each unit a profitable one. If profit making has to be an important policy to be pursued by the Indian public sector, who can deny that from the commanding heights achieved, this is perhaps the easiest challenge that the public sector managements would be ready to accept.

In allowing more autonomy to public enterprises to fix prices that the 'traffic can bear,' the highest net returns would accrue in such products and activities which have inelastic demand. For instance, if the Food Corporation of India, was directed to adopt purchase and sale prices freely in response to market demand and supply—as any private trader would do—there is no reason why the corporation cannot make an easy profit of a thousand crore of rupees in a year. Similarly, if bus fares are allowed to be revised on cost-plus basis, the road transport corporations would all be making profits far in excess of what was needed for their normal expansion. One could take any one PSE, particularly the ones engaged in public utilities or enjoying monopoly positions and see that given the freedom to fix prices freely, each one of the units could make high net profits. Is it not true that the recent government policies have a thrust of this nature? Each unit is being asked to show profits. The Finance Ministry has come to an understanding with the International Monetary Fund (IMF) that it would reduce 'subsidies' to PSEs and allow more freedom to the public sector to adopt appropriate pricing policies. The new investments in the public sector are being made more to satisfy the needs of the top economic elite of the country than to create production capacities for goods which are needed by the poor. The public sector has now taken upon itself the task of exporting doctors and engineers to the Gulf countries without any regard for 'home needs.'

In this light, should not one ask: is this the public sector that the Indian 'public' needs. The performance of the public sector may be good or improving, when judged in terms of profits, but should not one also ask: for whom is the Indian public sector performing.

29 Small-scale Sector Sabotaged[1]

The protection and promotion of small-scale industries in India has always been assigned a high priority. The list of products reserved for exclusive development in the small-scale sector has been growing practically with each successive year. A variety of monetary and fiscal policies are also supposed to have a justification in the encouragement of the small-scale sector. Administrative structures at the central and state levels have expanded fast, all to help growth of the small-scale sector. There is also a degree of price preference: imported and other scarce raw materials are supposed to be available to small-scale units and special nominations are made to give adequate representations to the viewpoint of the small-scale in policy-making bodies. In brief, one can compile a long list of concessions, preferences, institutions and other policy measures that have been undertaken during the past three decades to protect, encourage and promote the small-scale sector in India.

The basic policy assumption is that small-scale units cannot enjoy the small economies of scale as are possible for gaint units. Thus policies need to be adopted that would compansate the units for their diseconomies.

Gandhian Scheme

Was this the original reasoning for the protection and promotion of the small-scale sector? We need to capture the environment and the mood of the 1940s to understand the justification for the demand to protect small-scale industries in India. It may be mentioned that the original idea was not scale of production, but it was related to mode, technique and location of production.

---

1. *The Daily*, May 19, 1981.

During the national struggle for freedom of the country, Gandhiji pleaded for rural industries, cottage industries and such industries which employed manpower *vis-à-vis* machine power. The justification for support to village industries and handicrafts was because the protection of these industries would directly help millions of the Indian rural poor.

The policy was directly related to the question of the employment and income of those who are now being identified as the ones below the poverty line.

The economists from India and abroad provided additional argument to support the contention of Gandhi. An international team of experts argued in the early 1950s: Firstly, that since all 'rural industries' were based on local raw materials, their promotion would help maximum utilisation of local resources and place additional demands on the organised sector. Secondly, because of the expertise and already existing high level of craftsmanship in the Indian villages, there would be no need for providing additional facilities for training to workers. And thirdly, since the production unit were small and located in rural areas and there was very little use of power and machinery, the capital scarce economy accompanied by labour surplus, this was an ideal proposal to encourage village and non-machine-based industries.

To sum up, the rationality for the policies, as visualised by economists, was in fact that Gandhi's suggestions were reasonable because these could be part of the strategy for heavy industry-oriented planned development of India. The Second Five Year Plan was indeed worked out on the assumption that most of the consumer goods would be produced outside the large and organised sector and the heavy industries would be the responsibility of the organised sector of the Indian economy.

The economists along with their contribution in providing economic justification to Gandhian strategy also contributed the new terminology for the industries which Gandhi pleaded for protection and promotion. Instead of defining the activities as rural non-mechanised and belonging to cottage units, the expression given was small-scale units.

The small-scale units were supposed to have all those features that Gandhiji talked about and it was more an expression which could accommodate production unit in the urban centre as also such activities which were talking advantage of modern techniques of production. Further, the new expression could allow easy adoption of the new organisational form of the corporation.

Official Betrayal

One wonders of the contribution of the economists, i.e., provision of a new terminology, was indeed as insignificant as it may appear to be. One fact, however, remains that we have never looked back. The Indian official policy only talks of scale. Scale, in turn, is related to the value of assets. How does one assess the value of assets employed by a production unit? There are a variety of built-in snags in the definition, what should be considered as 'asset' is a matter of convenience.

The criterion of small-scale sector in India is only in terms of the value of assets of the units. Where it is located? What is the source of raw material? What goods are being manufactured? How much of new employment is being generated? How rich are the owners? How much is the unit's turnover? Do they have foreign collaboration? These questions are of no significance.

There is, therefore, no wonder if Finlays, a monopoly house, has small-scale production units. It is also no wonder if the small sector is seeking to outdo the large-scale units in catering to the needs of foreign consumers. It is also no surprise that there are a few units in the small-scale sector that have a nationwide distribution network and their advertisement bill runs into millions of rupees. A family can have scores of small-scale companies, each enjoying fiscal and monetary concessions, without ever being questioned.

But is this the fault of those who are taking advantage of the loopholes in the policies or was there need for the government to modify their policies? We need to discuss these questions. However, the basic comment from friends may be: in which world are you living? Don't you know the realities and the importance of lobbies and vested interests?

30 Political Beliefs and Economic Reality[1]

In India, it is popularly believed that anti-monopoly legislation is a socialistic measure and the effective implementation of the Monopolies and Restrictive Trade Practices (MRTP) Act of 1969 would help reduce concentration of private economic power.

All Left parties appear to continue their faith in MRTP. The Young Turks in the Congress Party, who spearheaded the campaign for enactment of the MRTP Act in India, built their socialist image by seeking measures like nationalisation of private commercial banks and by exposing malpractices that were being resorted to by Indian big business houses. Even though it is late, we should start questioning popular political beliefs of this type and spread awareness about the objective character of various economic policies and programmes that have been taken up since political independence of India.

Enactment of the MRTP Act in 1969 was hailed as a socialistic measure. It formed a part of the progressive measures, but it has nothing to do with socialism. It is a measure that any person believing in 'free enterprise' would fight for. Since the emergence of monopolies in an economy poses a direct threat to free and fair competition, evolving of effective measures to curb emergence of private monopolies is an economic and political necessity for a rational and healthy operation of the free-market system. What is 'socialistic' in the MRTP Act that continues to be treated as a socialistic measure in the Indian political circles?

Two Objectives

The anti-monopoly legislation in India has two basic objectives. One, to ensure that business enterprises, which manufacture and control

1. *The Daily*, June 6, 1981.

a large part of the supplies of a commodity in the country, do not report to such practices that would restrict the normal functioning of a free and open market economy. For instance, if a manufacturer who controls a large part of the national supplies is proved to have indulged in holding back the supplies and deliberately creates an artificial market scarcity to raise prices, this would be a fit case for governmental action and anti-monopoly legislation. Similarly, any joint action by producers to take advantage of the helpnessness of the consumers and distributors would attract action by the government.

There is no need to discuss the technicalities of the legislation in India or elsewhere, as it would suffice to underline that one of the important components of the anti-monopoly legislation is to create conditions under which market system can operate without restrictions from any quarter.

The second part of anti-monopoly legislation in India is with reference to big business. This was claimed to be a special feature of Indian legislation. Under this part of legislation, it is expected that all enterprises which control large assets should obtain special permission of the MRTP Commission. It has to examine and make its recomendations to the government with regard to the new proposals from big business. The basic question to be answered is if the undertaking of the new activity by the applicant house or enterprise is likely to be in the 'public interest.'

No Check on Growth

The MRTP Commission cannot object to the expansion on the ground that the house was already very large or it was already enjoying a monopoly position. The Commission's only task is to give verdict with regard to public interest. There is no precise definition of public interest. Surely, to protect public interest would always be the responsibility of all states, irrespective of their being capitalist, liberal or of any other variety. In brief, anti-monopoly legislation in India or elsewhere has to be taken as a necessary part of the free enterprise-based political system.

For the operation of a free enterprise-oriented economy, it was not adequate to only adopt anti-monopoly legislation or ensure strict implementation of the spirit of the legislation. There are a host of other measures to be taken. For instance, it was of upmost importance that effective steps to be taken to protect consumer interest. Under this, adherence to quality control and standardisation is necessary. The consumers have to have the right to get satisfaction as promised by sellers at the time of the transaction. Full consumer satisfaction is also to be accompanied by stringent action against those who resort to unhealthy and unethical trade practices.

Consumer Rights

A variety of consumer rights are protected by law in the capitalist world. For instance, a buyer can obtain full refund for the goods bought if he was not satisfied, provided he returned the goods within a reasonable time and without breakage. There are, in some free world countries, special institutions and high officials are appointed to take quick action on consumer complaints regarding overpricing, poor quality or any other form of consumer exploitation.

One is not aware if these private industrialists had ever claimed their activities to be declared as socialist ones. Probably, if political parties in India at any time would press for consumer protection measures, these may be claimed to have socialism as an important component.

During the past 10 years, the growth of private big business has been phenomenal. The assets of the top business houses, the Tatas and Birlas, have reached more than ₹ 2,000 crore. By all measures, the degree of concerntration of economic power in private hands has got enhanced. Many are disturbed over these developments. It is alleged that the anti-monopoly legislation has not been effectively implemented.

The implied assumption in these assertions is that big business and private monopolies would not have emerged only if the government had earnestly adhered to the MRTP provisions. But is it not a fact that we have been calling a horse as a cow and then complaining that it does not give milk?! Do Americans claim that their anti-trust laws are expected to transform the US economy into a socialist one? Americans do not, but we Indians do.

31 Small Units being Swallowed Up[1]

The official list containing items reserverd for the small-scale sector has been ever enlarging. A few items have been added recently. At present, the number of items on this list stands at more than 800.

Apparently, this is sought to provide an exclusive market to the small-scale sector. In operational terms, the reservation of many items means the granting of monopoly premium to established large sector units belonging to big business and multinationals without serving the interests of existing small manufacturers or attracting the entry of new small-scale units.

To illustrate, soap is reserved for the small-scale units while Hindustan Lever, Tata Oil Mills and Godrej enjoy a very large share of the national market. Biscuits, bread and confectionary are included in the list and Britannia, a foreign-controlled company, has been in business for long and is reportedly doing well. In case of leather shoes, the domination of Batas is well known. Tooth paste, tooth brushes and tooth powder are supposed to have been reserved for the small-scale sector but who does not know of Colgate-Pamolive, Hindustan Lever, CIBA, Geoffrey Manners—all foreign-controlled companies—enjoying a dominant place in the Indian market. Who would deny knowledge of the place of WIMCO—a Swedish company—operating in the field of safety matches, another reserved item?

Large Units Dominate

Similarly, cycle tyres and tubes, fan belts, sewing machines, electric fans, door locks, steel furniture, nuts and bolts, safety pins, drums and containers, stencil papers, carbon papers and pressure cookers are found in the list but the market for each one of these is substantially under the

1. *The Daily*, July 29, 1981.

control of the Indian and foreign-controlled large sector. What purpose does the reservation policy in the case of these items then serve?

Once an item has been reserved for the small-scale sector, it is believed that no new large-scale unit would get established. In reality, such an impression would be incorrect. Large-scale units can be established provided the new units would undertake to be functioning exclusively for the foreign markets. In the leather shoe industry, a number of licences have recently been granted under this clause.

Supposing the unit once established is unable to find the requisite supply orders from abroad, will the unit be allowed to close down? Alternatively, what happens to the rejects and below standard production of the so-called export-based units? Will the products not be allowed to enter the national market? The fact is that, as in the past, the honeymoon with foreign buyers does not last very long. The one-time export-based units soon have to be accepted as legitimate children of the national market.

The second belief in the reservetion theory is that the large-scale units (existing at the time when the item being included in the list) would not be allowed to expand their output. This could ensure that the additional demand, arising out of the normal market expansion, would be wholly met by small-scale sector units. This belief is wholly a misplaced one. In the first place, many of the items reserved for the small-scale sector do not find a mention in the schedule to the Industries (Development and Regulation) Act (IDRA).

It is because of this that some of the monopoly establishments just do not bother about the national public policies on this issue. Additionally, under the present licensing system, five per cent per annum enhancement in capacity is automatic. And lastly, who bothers if any large-scale unit has been producing far in excess of the licensed capacity? What action can the government take?

What action has ever been taken against those who have openly refused to abide by the economic policies of the state? The bigger the unfit and more the seriousness of the economic violation, lesser would be the possibility of any punitive action. There is every possibility that the government may, without making any fuss, find a convenient excuse to approve the excess. This is precisely what was sought to be done by the Industrial Policy Statement of July 1980.

The large- and the small-scale sectors, therefore, have to live together and the small must compete with the big to prove its mettle. If this was to be so, why prohibit other large-scale units from entering? Is the reservation meant to protect the monopoly of the existing large-scale units or is it to protect and promote the small-scale sector? Because of the ban on entry of other big ones, the existing big ones receive a privileged position of domination in the national market. Was this the intention of the policy makers? To the best of our knowledge, the professed intentions were to the contrary.

Stiff Competition

In a situation where the large and the small have to cater to the same market, it is only natural that the small ones would find themselves at a disadvantage. To introduce a new product is difficult, consumer acceptability and preferences have already been built, combined with this is the capacity of the large sector to employ aggressive publicity campaigns. In India, unfortunately, there are no laws under which action could be taken against companies making false public claims. For instance, a multinational company has been advertising through the press, radio and television that the fans produced by them give cooler air.

How can a 'fan' make the air cool? A fan can only circulate air, it cannot cool. The limited point being made is that through the capacity to launch massive publicity campaigns, the large companies can and have made a mockery of the reservation policy.

The brand names go with large units and the small-scale units have to sell products under unknown brand names and without sophisticated packaging. The capacity of the small to compete with the large is indeed in the matter of price cuts. The small-scale products have to be sold cheaper. Since the raw material sources are the same and the large-scale units enjoy a varity of economies of scale, their cost of production is nearly the same. The sale prices of the same and similar products, however, are lower for the small and higher for the large.

Monopolies Grow

By implication, therefore, the large-scale units earn a monopoly premium on sale of their products. For instance, it is well known that most of the pharmaceutical units in the small-scale sector can only survive due to lower overheads and by offering much cheaper products. There is a genuine feeling that small-scale units do not adhere to quality controls as specified, and the small-scale manufacturers are indulging in a variety of unhealthy business practices. But can it be otherwise?

A number of items in the list are such which cannot be taken up for manufacture by many. For instance, electronic cigarette lighters, digital clocks, cooking ranges, GI bath tubs and video games are items which have a limited market of the elite and can be taken up by those who can manage to get not only the licence for import of capital machinery but also regular raw materials and 'assembly packs.' Thus, to reserve such items for the small-scale sector is nothing but granting official patronage to the few who otherwise happen to enjoy administrative patronage.

The spirit of reservations demands closing down of all large-scale units in the items reserved. Alternatively, there should be a plan requiring these units to reduce their output with each successive year. The present dependence on 'excise duty' margins does not make any sense. Will the government do it? Or, will the small-scale associations take up this task to point out the real implications of the reservation policies?

32 Self-Reliance and Foreign Capital[1]

The new Industrial and Foreign Investment Policy announced on May 31, 1990, proclaims to release Indian industry from "unnecessary bureaucratic shackles by reducing the number of clearances required from the government." As a part of this objective, it is proposed to allow foreign investment up to 40 per cent on an automatic basis subject to a 30 per cent restriction on import of capital goods. Similarly, larger freedom to Indian entrepreneurs in the matter of technology imports is in the offing. The policy explains that these and other proposals would be applicable to all manufacturing units in a 'specified list' to be announced later.

Predictably, the announcement generated a great deal of discussion at various fora. However, neither the policy statement nor the subsequent official clarifications throw light on the empirical basis for the decisions with regard to foreign investment and technology. Nor do they reveal any understanding of the nature of foreign private capital already existing in India. Significantly, the likely impact on the balance of payments, self-reliance, indigenous research & development (R&D), employment, India's stand on multinational corporations (MNCs) in the Third World fora and India's social and political spheres have not been spelt out clearly. Is it because the policy makers are not aware of the basic characteristics of MNCs and the long-term implications of the open-door policy for foreign private capital and technology? The answer might be in the affirmative for the political leaderships but could not be so for the high-profile economic advisors.

When it is decided to invite, permit or encourage large private corporations from outside the country to find a solution to Indian societal problems on the belief that MNCs would help solve India's

1. *Young Indian*, October 4 and 19, 1990.

major problems—may it be foreign exchange, inflation, unemployment, interpersonal inequities or regional imbalances—it is of importance to discuss direct and indirect implications of the new policy initiatives. First of all, one must recognise that MNCs are private corporations primarily guided by the philosophy of profit maximisation. MNCs are not in social service. There is a need to understand that societal problems cannot be the concern of private business. If one places faith on a wrong institution or instrument, one has only to wait for the day of disillusionment.

Secondly, we need to recognise that MNCs operate worldwide. Most of the largest MNCs originated from the USA, the UK and West Germany and have their headquarters located in one or the other part of the industrialised world with market orientation. In operational terms, however, no large MNC has one nationality. MNCs may not be country-specific but are economic system-specific. It would be difficult to say in India if Nestle (food specialties) should be treated as a Swiss Company or a Bahamas one. Similar would be the case with Pfizer whose foreign shareholder is registered in Panama, while the ultimate parent is located in the USA. Legal provisions differ from one country to another. It could be that a large MNC is treated as an Indian national company in India, but a foreign one in the UK, France or Japan. MNCs are not nationality-specific. Therefore, their top executives have no national hang-ups.

MNCs represent a network of private business enterprises having operations in large many geographic locations. For any network, the success or failure is not judged by the performance or profit of any single wing or business in a country. MNCs business perspective has to be global. It does not fall in the realm of objectivity to expect that MNCs would promote interests of any one nation. It is just not in their character. However, to the extent promotion of exports from a country served their objective of global profit maximisation, the MNCs would most certainly do so.

Thirdly, MNCs are in private business, and business means all activities that give a net advantage to them. Their choice of activity would depend on their understanding and assessment of market potential. MNCs would engage themselves in any activity that requires investment, market knowledge and experience, business connections, legal rights in tangible or non-tangible assets (ownership of patents, trademarks or monopoly rights) where from the corporation can extract economic return. MNCs, therefore, are not activity- or industry-specific either, Anything would do. If it was a tobacco company initially, it could take up hotel business or sale of vegetable oils later on. To shift the nature of business operations is normal as long as the new business offers higher return than the traditional industry. If the policy makers of the country develop a misplaced belief that MNCs would help India bridge technology gaps in hi-tech areas or any other industry, the fault does not lie with the MNCs. For lack of one's own understanding of business logic and reality, the business enterprises cannot be justifiably accused.

In the modern age, it is well accepted that the institution of the state has direct responsibility to lay down rules of the game even for private business. Public interventions are a pre-requisite for smooth functioning of even the market-oriented economies. In the Third World countries, however, the state has to play even a more important role. Many of the Third World countries have adopted regulatory mechanisms. From the view point of business promotion, MNCs are bound to take measures that would reduce the intensity of regulations for them. It would be considered a very legitimate action if an MNC decides to cultivate 'mutually profitable' relationships with those who control levers of political and administrative power. Investment in politics could be risky but also extremely remunerative. World history is full of instances when MNCs have not hesitated to sponsor coups against political leaderships who posed a threat to MNC business interests.

MNCs must aim at diversification in the long run though. Thus, to gain entry if the host country insists on the MNC manufacturing certain products, such conditions would be acceptable as long as the host country's regulations do not forbid diversification, new investments and expansion. If the host country on its own awards them Indian nationality and help build their business image, why should an MNC object? The policy makers in India have made the people believe that enactment of Foreign Exchange Regulation Act (FERA), imposing export obligations and insistence on diversification, is some sort of an unpleasant conditionality. Let anyone examine the record of large private corporations in India or abroad to find out how MNCs have been itching to engage themselves in export, of course, combined with rights to import. No MNC would like to invest in a country for the sake of dividends, technology payments or high salaries to the host country executives. MNCs being a part of international network of business activities cannot afford any one country unit (company or a branch) to live in isolation of the rest. Business autonomy is not a rule of the MNC institution.

MNCs can certainly be depended upon to promote exports as well as imports. Movement towards globalisation is their business philosophy. Can one place a faith in an international private business institution (the MNC) to earn net surplus of foreign exchange for India or any one country? To the extent exports are of raw materials and products that can only be produced in India, comparatively at cheaper prices, MNCs would export from India. The question, however, is not of sheer exports. An equally important issue is of export prices. If an MNC is buying from five countries, it is but natural that it would buy from the country that offers the lowest price. It has been widely recognised that the buying locations can shift as a business strategy to take advantage of the lowest price. To have a better appreciation of this aspect of international trade and capacity of MNCs, one needs to understand today's reality where in a number of commodities, MNCs enjoy near-monopsony status. In absence of producer-country alliances, buyers dictate the prices. MNCs can comfortably pitch one country suppliers against another.

MNCs are large international business networks with control over vast finances, massive framework of distribution and sales outlets in industrially advanced countries, advertising resources, press and communication systems; employing the best and the largest army of attorneys and lawyers, auditors and accountants, researchers and public relations men; and enjoying legal protection to monopoly rights on thousands of basic inventions, industrial processes, patents, trademarks and designs. The network of international information and the speed at which they operate cannot be matched by any one governmental system including the USA not to speak of India or any other Third World country. While formulating policies with regard to such powerful business institutions, policy makers cannot be casual and project their own illusions. The national costs can be high.

MNCs belong to a category of giants in relation to individual governments of many a country like India. If India wishes to harness and benefit from the powerful, we need to understand the natural aptitudes, the motivations, the capacity and other characteristics of MNCs. What we need to also appreciate is that MNCs are invariably aware of their own weakness and incapacity to fight against nationalism and ideologically committed national public systems. The only thing the MNCs yield to is public pressure. To them public means consumers and consumers cannot be easily brushed aside.

With fast changes in the global system of production, the MNCs would change their business strategies. For instance, instead of seeking to engage themselves directly in production (and make investments), MNCs may increasingly go in for marketing of goods manufactured by others. This could help avoid a direct conflict with labour. What the MNCs, however, insist upon would be the right to brand names. To strengthen this, MNCs would tend to emerge as the biggest patrons of mass media—TV, radio and the press. To remain dominant, it would be only expected that MNCs would insist on having legal and administrative support for patents and other forms of intellectual property rights. Trade and trading activity is a service industry. Expansion of specialised services is the new area, and it should surprise none if the USA and other advanced economies are asking for grant of entry of foreign private capital into insurance, construction, banking, consultancy and trade—external and internal. Given these likely trends, the pressure on the Third World countries would be mounted for lowering of regulations on national currencies. To meet the challenge of nationalism and related sensitivities, MNCs invariably try hard to wear related host country nationality caps and project their enterprises as promoters of local culture, music and traditions. It helps. Of late, MNCs have become more conscious that while avoiding direct political patronage in any host country, it is far more effective to find local partners who have high political clout and influence on national governments. This probably explains the recent growth of Birla-Yamaha, Tata-Unisys and Modi-Xerox type of joint ventures. No wonder, Indian big business which opposed British capital and took a nationalist stance with the Congress and Gandhiji is today finding it more profitable to be associates of MNCs. Can one be surprised if the Federation of Indian Chambers of Commerce and Industry (FICCI) and the Associated Chambers of Commerce and Industry of India (ASSOCHAM) have become the most vocal and loud supporters of MNC entry into India? Who controls FICCI or ASSOCHAM?

While these are some of the main characteristics of MNCs, we in India in general and policy makers in particular seem to have felt shy in recognising them. We do not attempt to debate and understand the multifaceted institution known as MNC. It is also possible that we prefer to ignore the reality and chose to follow hunches, beliefs and motivated suggestions. The state of affairs with regard to policy towards MNCs is best illustrated by the fact that Indian legislation does not recognise even the concept of a multinational corporation. While the government has not found it necessary to undertake an exercise on the identity of the institution of MNC, it is has not hesitated to take the 40 per cent foreign equity limit, fixed for the applicability of the FERA, 1973, to permit open entry. As a result, associates of a number of well-known multinationals are treated on par with wholly owned Indian companies. The beneficiaries include: Unilever, Philips, Kodak, BAT Industries, Swedish Match, Nestle, Hoechst, Ciba-Geigy, Alcan Aluminium, Pfizer, Singer, etc.

The fact also remains that control is being exercised by MNCs not only through the ownership of equity capital but also with the help of management rights which they bestowed upon themselves with the government's explicit consent and legal stamp of approval. In many cases, MNCs wield 100 per cent control while owning far less than 40 per cent foreign equity. Given such extensive control over the affairs of the company, it is obvious that foreign shareholders decide what to produce, where and to whom to sell and at what price, where to import from and at what price, which technologies to pursue and which products to promote. One needs to ask: would such a high degree of control in foreign hands be beneficial or inimical to self-reliant and independent development. If not, do we have the necessary instruments to make them work to the advantage of the country or, are we voluntarily surrendering national regulatory rights to intervene?

Coming back to the recent policy announcement, even if one accepts the official explanation that automatic entry of foreign investment up to 40 per cent is allowed only in specific areas, would such a policy continue to be applicable to the existing MNCs? In other words, would such 40 per cent foreign equity companies be restricted to product areas for which they apply to enter India initially or they would have the same freedom as enjoyed by non-FERA national companies? The scenario is not very difficult to imagine. Since the foreign equity would not exceed 40 per cent, new entrants would straight away qualify to be non-FERA national companies. It is quite a common knowledge how ex-FERA companies are now expanding into a variety of consumer goods both through direct manufacturing and through marketing of products manufactured by small-scale units in the former's brand names. There is no instrument with the government to restrict non-FERA companies (whether old or new entrants to India) to 'specified lists.' There is a long list of low technology/low priority consumer products manufactured or marketed by MNCs that are otherwise supposed to be engaged in hi-tech production processes.

Another anomaly which has not been given the due attention it deserves is with regard to the small-scale sector. The policy relaxations are in contradiction with the expectations, from the sector. Given the freedom to conclude foreign collaborations would the small scale or for that matter any entrepreneur insist on exports which the foreign collaborator is known to resist? Secondly, wouldn't the resultant excessive dependence on foreign technology alter the character of the small-scale sector to make it more capital-intensive and reduce its potential for employment generation? Thirdly, can we rule out the possibility of MNCs entering directly in the small-scale sector in the absence of any clear-cut guidelines with regard to foreign equity in the small-scale sector? Would an MNC-owned small-scale company satisfy the objective behind protecting and promoting small entrepreneurs?

One is not aware of any official study to assess whether the existing collaborations are borne out of genuine felt need for technology or were intended to blunt the edge acquired by the competitors through foreign brand names and trademarks. Such competition would without doubt lead to increased dependence on external sources for technology, machinery and raw materials.

33 Public Sector Enterprises

The Case for Restructuring[1]

Many of us, even today, continue to defend the Indian public sector as if it was a sacred cow. There are others who find the public sector a convenient whipping-horse to condemn the government. In this background, the proposal for the privatisation of public sector enterprises (PSEs) was received both with indignation and with a sense of relief. The primary reason, as put forth at various policy-making levels, was that the huge losses of the sector imposed a heavy burden on the national exchequer. Privatisation would not only help the government obtain large financial resources but would also put an end to the recurring liabilities. The argument calls for a critical examination.

It is true that a good number of the PSEs have been making losses. Most of them enjoy a monopoly or a near-monopoly status. Besides, the total monopoly in public utilities and infrastructure (power, transport, communications), the sector enjoys a dominant position in the production of fuel, basic and non-ferrous metals, fertilisers and defence production. It is necessary, therefore, to ask under what conditions would monopolistic establishments incur losses? In the normal course, a monopoly should not only be not making losses but must also earn monopoly rents. This proposition, however, would hold true when monopolies enjoy the freedom to determine prices as per the dictates of commercial principles. If the objective is to make profits only, then the only change required is to let the PSE managements have autonomy to fix prices as per the rules of the free-market structure.

---

1. This article appeared in the *Young Indian* on January 9, 1999.

The case for privatisation of PSEs on the plea for raising resources is probably the weakest. Sale of 'family silver' is never equated with income. To support revenue expenditure with proceeds from the sale of public property can never be a logical or sound economic policy alternative.

A hike in prices by PSEs will be resisted by the buyers of their products and services. It is a well-known fact that Indian consumers, individuals and corporates are accustomed to receiving many of the infrastructural services (power, water, local transport and the like) at ridiculously low and subsidised rates. Those who have always been votaries of low prices need to recognise that services and commodities that are cheap get grossly misused and wasted. Whatever may be the justification for low pricing of public utilities, one needs to keep in mind that at present the coverage of public utilities is confined only to a small section of the upper, educated and middle classes. Isn't it necessary, therefore, to ask: 'who benefits when public services are available at low prices or when power to agriculture is priced at zero rates? Obviously, the benefit is shared more by large agriculturists and no advantage flows to the landless and marginal farmers.

Supply of drinking water is an essential public service. Safe piped drinking water is available mostly in urban areas. Within the urban centres, these services, however, are mainly available to regularised municipal colonies inhabited by the comparatively well-to-do sections. Given this reality, is it not appropriate that the recipients of water supply should be obliged to pay full cost of the service? It is not uncommon for better-off families to buy bottled mineral water at a price of ₹ 10-12 per litre. This is tending to become a norm in metropolitan centres, particularly among the middle and upper strata of the population. Mineral water bottling plants have mushroomed in and around cities and major townships. One can safely predict that if municipal corporations were to raise water charges to cover the full cost and generate a marginal surplus to expand water supply networks, there would be stiff resistance. The educated, influential and vocal strata would quickly gang up to condemn such decisions.

It is not a matter of pricing of public utilities alone. There is, in fact, full justification in providing all basic and essential municipal services to the poorest strata of the population at zero pricing. The important issue is pricing of 'raw materials' and industrial inputs produced and supplied by the public system for conversion and manufacturing by the private sector. Prices in the public sector are administered by government departments. It is not easy to undertake upward revision of administered prices since this could fuel inflation. Prices of raw materials provided by public enterprises are deliberately kept low. There exists, however, no mechanism to regulate end prices charged by the private sector. The losses of public enterprises, in this manner, have a direct link to the profits of the private industry.

A reasonable case for privatisation of public enterprises would neither rest on loss argument nor on the argument that the government would have to raise resources to keep fiscal deficit within limit. One sees little justification in holding back the process of denationalisation for such enterprises which service a small elite and have little to offer to an overwhelming section of the Indian masses. For instance, airlines and the five-star hotels can have no claims on public subsidy. These should be run under pricing policies that result in profits. Why should the exchequer support luxury for the few, may they be high government officials or public men? Is it not true that Indian Airlines has come to stay as a club for Indian business, political, administrative and social elite? Nearly two-third of the internal air traffic, it is understood, is supported by less than 2 lakh clients. Air travel has become a normal mode of transport for most senior bureaucrats, parliamentarians and other elected representatives besides the business classes. Air services will never be for the general public in India; a common man in this country is priced out as even the subsidised rates are too high for him.

The labour force in Indian public enterprises is well organised. Since the ownership of public enterprises rests with the government, it has become natural for employees of public enterprises to demand equal status, remuneration and other facilities with their counterparts in government. Public sector enterprises, as a consequence, tend to become government organisations, ridden with all the ills like automatic promotion, low productivity, poor customer service and corruption that plague the government system. A government *babu* and a policeman are not known for their courteous behaviour. An average Indian has learnt to live with this. In the case of public enterprises, however, a client is not prepared to tolerate any misbehaviour or indifference of an accountant or a salesperson manning a commercial enterprise or a service counter. A customer demands attention and cordial service. Security of employment is taken as a licence for rude behaviour and poor performance. To change this attitude is a difficult task. It involves millions. And yet a start will have to be made. Will our trade union friends give this a thought?

Indian public sector suffers utter negligence on part of the government in the matter of appointing top managerial personnel. Many of the top executive positions often remain 'vacant' for a long time. Civil servants are nominated to look after multiple public enterprises as an additional charge. All bureaucrats do not have professional and management competence, nor do they have the time or inclination to get involved in production, marketing or management of commercial establishments. The system of proxy management has continued for many years. Such neglect helps breed inefficiency and lack of responsibility. The degree of reported corruption in public enterprises has reached high levels. Unscrupulous managers with close proximity to higher-ups are known to divert financial resources for personal advantage or to provide patronage. Trading margins on supplies to PSEs and government departments are only too well known.

The public sector needs to be restructured and reformed so that the sector can play an important role in the process of economic development and can help raise productivity of national assets. It is necessary to have a constructive look at the possibility of restructuring in individual cases instead of following a distorted policy of disinvestment for meeting the fiscal deficit. The proceeds of disinvestment should be utilised for reviving the units meeting specific public needs rather than for feeding the already bloated bureaucracy. The workers and their unions should be taken into confidence in this process.

34 Small-scale Sector

Traversing an Ambiguous Path[1]

The policies relating to the small-scale sector are increasingly subject to ambiguity, be it the reservation of products or fixing the investment limit for qualifying to be a small-scale unit. This is in addition to the significant element of confusion on the nature, justification and primary reasons for public support to the small-scale sector. Historically, the sector was related to the small man and small enterprise, operated predominantly with one's own and family resources of finance and labour. To protect the constituents of such a sector from the onslaught of large national and international monopolies appeared to be a socially desirable objective. Such a sentiment found wide support during the struggle against colonial rule that conspired against Indian industry, handicraft and rural industries.

Secondly, the sector was viewed as a manufacturing sector wholly dependent on local raw materials and local markets. The sector, therefore, had strong forward and backward linkages and was an organic part of local communities. For obvious reasons, the sector drew public support. Thirdly, it was generally understood that the sector promotes self-employment and did not use much machinery and power. It was an assumption that the small-scale sector has high employment potential *vis-à-vis* large and medium enterprises. Support to the sector was viewed as a step towards finding a solution to the unemployment problem of the country. This being particularly so for areas not well connected with national and urban markets. Fourthly, the small-scale sector was expected to be a decentralised system of production that mobilises small savings and gives the artisan and labour a sense of pride and an opportunity for full expression of his genius

1. *Young Indian*, February 6, 1999.

and personality. Fifthly, it was visualised that to help hold back movement of labour towards urban and already crowded industrial centres, the small-scale sector could help contain rural-urban migration and this has always found support from Indian planners and policy makers. Implied in the 'hold back' movement was also a realisation that the small-scale sector helps preserve a healthy family life and places limited demands on urban infrastructure. Sixthly, it was assumed that the small-scale sector would utilise indigenous technologies, machinery and equipments and hence not impose additional burden on scarce foreign exchange resources of the country. The sector was, in a sense, seen as the national sector of India the products of which would be most suitable to the taste and style of local populations. And seventhly, it was understood that the small-scale sector could be the best bet for educated and technically competent persons to innovate and put into practice new ideas. One could expand the list of such general assumptions that were associated with the small-scale sector.

The government has continued to emphasise on the need to provide support to the country's small-scale sector. Ever since India gained Independence and the Five Year Plans were launched, this fact has been repeatedly emphasised. However, the Gandhian model of industrialisation emphasised the importance of 'rural areas' and opposed machine-made products and this was modified as a result of the expert committee reports (that were, incidentally, funded by the Ford Foundation). In place of rural industries, the emphasis shifted to 'scale of production'. The sector was not to be locale specific. The scale of production was to be assessed in terms of the size of monetary investment. Ever since the 1950s the sole criterion for small-scale sector units has rested on the monetary value of investment. There have, however, been repeated changes with regard to what should constitute the 'investment' and what should be the upper limit to qualify for membership of the official small-scale sector. The entire discussion on the definition of a small-scale sector unit has been on the size of the fixed investment in plant and machinery. From ₹ 5 lakh as the upper limit in the mid-1950s, the size limit had been raised to ₹ 3 crore. It is now proposed to be brought down to ₹ 1 crore. The repeated hike in the investment limit provides an excellent example how objective reality gets ignored in the face of lobby pressure and hunches of an indifferent bureaucracy. Time and again, it has been proved that those units at the highest investment ranges form a negligible percentage of the constituents of this sector.

The small-scale sector of today includes enterprises engaged in production of many such goods which have a national market and which use imported raw materials. Many a unit in the small-scale sector imports and assembles CKDs (completely knocked down kits) or SKDs (semi-knocked down). The fixed capital requirements of such units are small and can conveniently be kept under the prescribed official monetary limits. The criteria for a small-scale unit are not related to any expectations with regard to employment obligations. Given a variety of modern technologies and their frequent upgradation combined with widening possibilities for use of electricity, the small-scale sector of today does not anyway have the looks of what was at one time contemplated. There is a tremendous growth in the service sector and information technology-related enterprises. There is a sea change in the environment. Yet, the official criterion of the small-scale unit continues to be viewed on the narrow base of capital alone.

There is an urgent need to revise the official criteria and bring in the nature of industry as an important factor determining the optimum size of investment. To have the size limit of investment as a cut-off point for all activities and all types of industries is illogical. Capital demands of different industries differ widely. The small-scale sector definition has to incorporate the self-employed character of the enterprise so that enterprises with proxy management can be kept out. Similarly, a distinction has to be made with regard to the nature of the technologies employed and the size and nature of the market that is addressed by the enterprise.

The small-scale sector is being assisted through preference in bank loans, provision of technical support, granting of preferential treatment in purchases and reservation of certain products for exclusive production in the small-scale sector. Each one of these measures helps to an extent. However, what is essentially being missed by the policy frame of the small-scale sector is the lack of appreciation of the 'market' to which these enterprises are catering. Today's market is being created by the frequency and the content of advertisements in the mass media. The 'market' of tomorrow will be determined by the information spread, credibility with regard to quality, convenience of availability and, above all, 'consumer acceptability.' Various factors contribute in the process of gaining consumer acceptance. The most important one being advertisement, packaging and public relations.

Small enterprises are not able to support financially or pay adequate attention to build and retain their markets. The new trend is in the separation of roles. Production is by small enterprises and 'market' creation and networking of sales distribution by larger corporations. In this manner, there can be complementarities between small and the big. The significance of this trend and its consequences over time are not being understood either by the policy makers or by the Indian industrialists. This is besides the question of relative bargaining power. Will the small man and his enterprise get their justifiable due? The experience of hand-made shoes marketed through national networks of leading companies and many more consumer items does not appear a happy one.

Large corporations enter into marketing arrangements with scores of decentralised units of the small-scale sector. The design, the packaging, the brand name and all critically important decisions are made by the large corporation. In this arrangement, the marketing corporations have little burden of establishing production units or hiring and managing labour or even bringing in new capital. The real power stays with the 'marketing corporation.' The suppliers remain at the mercy of the marketing system. The buyer can dictate terms to a small-scale sector unit by delaying payments for which legal remedy is inadequate. Reluctance of banks to provide working capital to small-scale sector has discouraged them from direct marketing. The supplier and buyer relationship is of perfect monopsony.

It is not recognised very often that in this mechanism the larger corporations [many of them being transnational corporations (TNCs)] reap all the advantages that the state provides to the small-scale sector. Indirectly, the public system supports big business through the small-scale sector route. Probably, this is a stage through which many such relationships are being established. If this type of relationship suits the small-scale sector in the short run, the larger marketing corporations have a long-term advantage. It was observed that this mechanism also came handy to violate the spirit of reservations for the small sector. There is every possibility that once a corporation comes to command market domination, it would find it more profitable to establish its own production with latest machines and technologies. This system would enable the emergence of product monopolies at a later stage. Monopolies have their logical implications for consumers. One does not need to harbour more on this aspect.

In the case of small-scale sector, the emerging phenomenon of talented and qualified young men seeking self-employment has to be recognised. Those who wish to go on their own instead of looking for jobs are now, relatively and in absolute numbers, more. Such young men need to be given encouragement and support. Even earlier, it was not state patronage as such which was responsible for the growth of the small-scale sector but the confidence it inspired among the entrepreneurs.

35

Ownership and Control Structure of the Indian Press[1]

India's newspaper industry has a high degree of concentration, and what is more disquieting is that trends suggest its accentuation with each successive year. This study has attempted to determine the precise degree of domination and control by Indian big business of the press. It is observed that ownership and control of the press does not rest within the industry; the present managements have vested interests and strong connections outside the newspaper industry. The linkages are strong. The desirability of delinking of ownership of the Indian press from big business and monopoly capital has been emphasised repeatedly. It has also been suggested that newspaper industry should be able to play a positive role in socioeconomic processes to further national development. How do we achieve these and what are the alternatives?

To delink the press from big business, one obvious alternative could be public takeover of top eight newspaper establishments. The first reaction of many would be against such a proposal. They would argue that radio and television in India are already under state control and these have not remained independent of influence and pressure from the party in power and the governments. In a democratic and multiparty system, the entire mass media cannot be left under the control of the government. This would imply monopoly of the ruling party on entire mass media. This is an important and probably a valid argument. However, we do need to mention that the takeover of the eight newspaper establishments under the control of big business would not mean state monopoly over the entire Indian press. Secondly, if the present units are to be taken over, the existing organisational forms need not necessarily be altered; the boards of managements can be so constituted as to ensure operational

1. This work was undertaken for the Second Press Commission in February 1981.

independence. And further, a built-in system could be developed to provide for representation to different sections of society. Additionally, there could be certain minimum guarantees to journalists, political parties and individual readers in matters of obligation to publish their viewpoints. It is not an impossible task, though it would be undoubtedly difficult. Thirdly, one should keep in mind that unlike other industries, newspaper readers would continue to have the option to shift from one newspaper to another. If owned newspaper was not objective or was in favour of a particular political party, this would easily be reflected in the level of newspaper circulation. With a choice to tune into another radio station, the listeners do not stick to one radio service all the time. And lastly, can one objectively assert that press managements, with big business interests outside the newspaper industry, would be able to withstand government pressure, under any political system? Ironically, the truth is that the big business-controlled press in India has been successful in influencing governments to deviate from declared public policies. The role of press has to be the promotion of public interest. There have, however, been occasional exceptions, but these cannot be said to be the rule. In brief, we feel that nationalisation of top eight newspaper establishments would be a necessary measure to reduce the hold of big business interests over the press.

We may also underline a few facts which need to be further examined by the Second Press Commission while deciding on many a basic policy issue. Firstly, it is well known that the Indian press continues to depend overwhelmingly on the imported raw material, i.e., the newsprint. More than three-fourth of the newsprint is obtained from abroad (see Table 35.1). Imports imply expenditure in foreign exchange and must be used carefully. There is no place for wasteful use of newsprint in India.

We must inquire into the pattern of end use of newsprint in India. We should ask the following two questions: one, 'how is scarce newsprint being shared' by big and small newspaper establishments? And, two, 'to what use is the newsprint put by different categories of users?' With regard to the first question, it can be said that since the Indian newspaper industry is dominated by big business, it is obvious that the main beneficiaries of newsprint allocation would be big business. Our point, however, is not this. We would like to view the question in terms of the percentage share of big newspapers in national circulation and compare it with share in the newsprint allocated. Table 35.2 shows this comparison for the years 1976 and 1977. It is seen that the big newspapers, which are mostly controlled by Indian big business, obtain a disproportionately larger share in the allocation of newsprint as compared to their share in circulation. The share of small newspapers (overwhelming number of which consisted of individual of family-based regional language newspapers catering to local readers) in circulation was 23.1 per cent but these papers received only 5.9 per cent of newsprint in 1976. On the other hand, big newspapers accounting for about 50 per cent of circulation received 67.6 per cent of the overall newsprint. Thus, the big business-controlled press was not only the main beneficiary, but also received a more favourable treatment from government in matter of newsprint allocations.

Table 35.1

Showing the Availability of Newsprint in India (1970 to 1977-78)

(Quantity in '000 tonnes)

Sl.No.	*Newsprint Source*	*1970*	*1971*	*1972*	*1973*	*1974*	*1975-76*	*1976-77*	*1977-78*
1.	Imported	142 (76.34)	200 (81.33)	220 (83.33)	140 (77.75)	220 (83.02)	164.41 (76.23)	181.00 (76.69)	176.81 (73.12)
2.	Indigenous	44 (23.66)	44 (18.03)	44 (16.67)	40 (22.22)	45 (23.77)	51.27 (23.21)	55.00 (26.88)	65.00 (26.88)
3.	Total	186 (100.00)	244 (100.00)	264 (100.00)	180 (100.00)	265 (100.00)	215.68 (100.00)	236.00 (100.00)	241.81 (100.00)

Note: Figures in parentheses indicate percentages.

Source: Based on data available from (i) *Report of the Fact Finding Committee on Newspaper Economic*, 1975, and (ii) *Press in India*, 1977 and 1978.

Table 35.2

Showing Group-wise Allocation of Newsprint and Circulation (1976-77)

Sl. No.	*Classification of Newspapers*	*Allocation ('000 tonnes)*		*Circulation ('000)*		*Percentage Shares*			
						Allocation		*Circulation*	
		1976	*1977*	*1976*	*1977*	*1976*	*1977*	*1976*	*1977*
	1	*2*	*3*	*4*	*5*	*6*	*7*	*8*	*9*
1.	Big	116.79	147.70	4745	5996	67.62	67.87	50.16	55.46
2.	Medium	45.70	54.40	2531	2646	26.46	25.02	26.75	24.47
3.	Small	10.23	15.48	2185	2172	5.92	7.11	23.09	20.09
4.	Total	172.73	217.52	9461	10814	100.00	100.00	100.00	100.00

Note: The classification of big, medium and small newspapers is based on circulation data.

Source: *Press in India*, 1977 and 1978.

It may be argued that big newspapers carry a larger news coverage and provide other features to the readers, and therefore, while their relative share in circulation was lower, their requirements of newsprint were bound to be larger. To have an objective scrutiny of this argument, one would need to go into, we would also need to inquire into, the precise nature of the materials published. Many an article and feature may in fact be aimed to promote markets for advertisers. However, it may be rewarding to have an estimate of the extent of advertisements carried by big and small newspapers. Do small newspapers carry as much advertisement as the big newspapers? Table 35.3 shows that out of six newspapers that were using more than 60 per cent of the newspaper space for advertisements, three belonged to the monopoly houses, one each to a political party, a family and a trust. This, however, is not a realistic basis to understand the extent of non-news use of the newsprint by the newspapers. If one takes the six newspapers, each utilising more than 60 per cent of the space for advertisement, one finds that out the total newsprint utilised by the six, the share of the monopoly house press was 88.3 per cent. Though one out of the six newspapers, in the high advertisement/news ratio category, was a political paper, its share in the newsprint utilised was only 4.2 per cent. A similar exercise for newspapers using 25-40 per cent of newspapers space for advertisement shows that here too, the big business press has the highest share (see Table 35.4). Their actual share in utilization of newsprint for advertisement would be still higher if one were to account for the number of pages also.

Allocation of larger space to advertisements implies wasteful use of foreign exchange and scarce newsprint. In a paper-scarce economy, society must choose between alternative uses of newsprint. Nearly 40-50 per cent of the newsprint in India is now being used for low priority consumption. Can this be justified when prices of school text books are skyrocketing? There are many other questions which need to be advertising. Where is the advertising? For what purpose and to whom are these advertisements addressed? What type of life style is being promoted? These questions have far-reaching economic, social and political implications. We hope the Second Press Commission would be able to examine them in a broader socioeconomic framework.

Table 35.3

Showing Category-wise and Advertisement Space-wise Distribution of Newspapers, 1976

	Percentage of Advertisement Space	*National Monopoly House*	*Local Industry and Business*	*Political Parties*	*Educational, Cultural, Religious Bodies*	*Families and Individuals*	*Individual*	*Others*	*Total*
	1	2	3	4	5	6	7	8	
1.	60% & above	3	-	1	1	1	-	6	
2.	50% & below 60%	7	1	-	-	5	12	25	
3.	40% & below 50%	13	12	3	2	19	28	77	
4.	25% & below 40%	16	17	4	6	29	113	185	
	Total	39	30	8	9	54	153	293	

Source: Based on data available in *Press in India*, 1977.

Table 35.4

Showing Category-wise and Advertisement Space Range-wise Circulation, 1979

Sl. No.	Category	Newspaper Utilising 60 per cent and above Space for Advertisements	Newspaper Utilising 25-40 per cent Space for Advertisements
	1	2	3
1.	National Monopoly Houses	88.3	38.8
2.	Local Industry and Business		30.8
3.	Political Parties	4.2	1.8
4.	Educational, Cultural and Religious Bodies	2.8	6.8
5.	Families and Individuals	4.7	22.1
6.	Total	100.0	100.0

Source: Based on the information available in the *Press in India*, 1977.

Trends in the newspaper industry are disturbing. Some of these have been mentioned by us in this study. With regard to the trends in concentration, one needs to enquire into the reasons for the trends. One reason that we consider responsible for this phenomenon is that newspapers with bigger circulation are cheaper than the smaller ones. Table 35.5 shows return per paisa to a newspaper buyer, in terms of page area. While a buyer of small newspaper gets 390.60 sq cm per paisa, a buyer of big newspaper get 657.09 sq cm for the same amount. The return is nearly 73 per cent higher in case of big newspaper which becomes possible for two reason: one, availability of larger share of newsprint and two, the capacity of carrying higher revenue-yielding advertisement. Big newspapers are able to operate better than the smaller ones—the economies of scale are understandable—but the advantages of patronage and built in preferences and subsidy can hardly be justified. The whole question of the economics of newspapers needs to be examined more carefully. The Press Commission may also like to consider how the allocation of advertisements by private corporate sector can be rationalised and how the high degree of patronage and discretion can be eliminated. For tax purposes, advertisements are treated as costs, and therefore, a good part of the cost of advertisements is met at the expense of the public exchequer. The need for regulation of advertisements is only too obvious. It is also observed that advertisements are now being systematically used, particularly by big business, to advocate their political ideology and beliefs and to denigrate those with whom they disagree. Academics who may happen to undertake studies are attacked by name through advertisements. The capacity of advertisements to influence and distort political processes should be a matter of serious concern. There is an urgent need to place all corporate advertisement under a common agency, as is the case with government advertisements. Further, it is equally important to relate the content of advertisements with national priorities.

Table 35.5

Showing Category-wise Returns per Paisa to a Newspaper Buyer, 1976-77

Sl. No.	*Category*	*Sq. Centimeters per Paisa*	
		1976	*1977*
	1	*2*	*3*
1.	Big	675.09	696.57
2.	Medium	590.39	551.70
3.	Small	390.60	370.64
4.	Total	452.57	349.07

Source: Based on data available in *Press in India*, 1977 and 1978.

If delinking of press, through takeover by autonomous boards of managements so constituted as to ensure independent operation, is not possible at this state, we do hope that improved regulation and correction of obvious anomalies would help reduce some of the present day problems. While exploring alternatives to the present press structure, it may also be of help to encourage political and educational newspapers in the country.